THE EMERGENCE
OF THE
COTTON KINGDOM
IN THE
OLD SOUTHWEST

D1564043

Counties of Mississippi, 1860

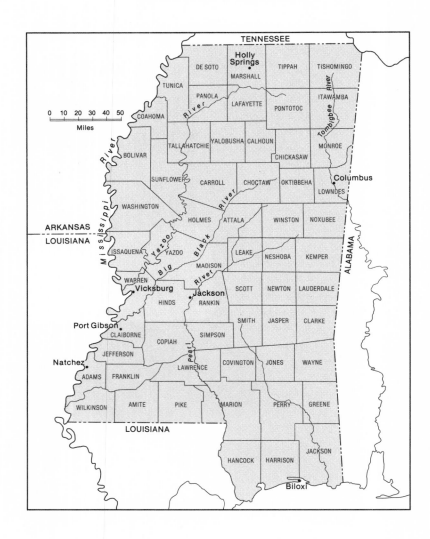

Based on Colton's 1855 map of Mississippi

The Emergence
of the
Cotton Kingdom
in the
Old Southwest

Mississippi, 1770–1860

John Hebron Moore

Louisiana State University Press

Baton Rouge and London

Designer: Sylvia M. Loftin
Typeface: Plantin
Typesetter: G & S Typesetters, Inc.
Printer: Thomson-Shore, Inc.
Binder: John H. Dekker & Sons

10   9   8   7   6   5   4   3   2   1

Library of Congress Cataloging-in-Publication Data

Moore, John Hebron.
   The emergence of the Cotton Kingdom in the Old Southwest.

   Bibliography: p.
   Includes index.
   1. Mississippi—Economic conditions.   2. Cotton
trade—Mississippi—History.   3. Plantation life—
Mississippi—History.   4. Slavery—Mississippi—
History.   I. Title.
HC107.M7M66   1987   330.9762   87-2803
ISBN 0-8071-1382-4
ISBN 0-8071-1404-9 (pbk.)

Portions of Chapter 7 were originally published, in slightly different form, as "Railroads
in Antebellum Mississippi," in *Journal of Mississippi History*, XLI (February, 1979),
53–81; the author acknowledges the Mississippi Department of Archives and History and
the Mississippi Historical Society.

To James Z. Rabun

Contents

Figures

Tables

Preface

From its inception in the 1790s until the Civil War, the history of the Cotton Kingdom in the Old Southwest exhibited accelerating economic and social change brought about by the great Industrial Revolution of the nineteenth century, which profoundly altered all of Western civilization. During the course of a single lifetime, millions of acres of virgin lands in half a dozen states were claimed from the forest and were converted into cotton farms and plantations. At the outset, agricultural methods were those of the preindustrial age, not greatly changed from those employed on medieval manors, but by the time the Civil War had brought the age of slavery to an end, agriculture in the Old Southwest had achieved a level of modernity that was not to be surpassed until the advent of gasoline tractors after World War I. During the intervening years, southwestern agriculturists had developed the type of upland cotton cultivated throughout the modern world and had devised all of the agricultural implements in use in the South as late as 1920. Meanwhile the efficiency of farm labor had increased tenfold. Workers who could cultivate and harvest a single acre of cotton in 1800 were in the 1850s working and gathering twelve acres of cotton plus corn and other lesser crops produced for home consumption.

At the birth of the southwestern Cotton Kingdom, people and commodities were transported no faster than a flatboat could drift with the river current or a horse could carry its rider. Overland movement of crops was restricted to the speed with which plodding oxen could draw wagons, and there were no roads as good as those used in the ancient Mediterranean world before the birth of Christ. Forty years later, steamboats brought cargoes of cotton from Vicksburg, Natchez, and Baton Rouge downriver to New Orleans at ten miles per hour and carried passengers from the port city northward against the current at half that speed. Within another ten years, steam locomotives hurried passenger and freight cars overland at five times the pace of stagecoaches, and by 1860 steam locomotives on a smooth stretch of track had attained the legendary "mile a minute." Equally astounding to the people of the time, the electric telegraph and cable had placed New Orleans, Memphis, Vicksburg, Natchez, and Columbus in direct, instantaneous communication with New York, London, and Paris.

In 1800 everything used by the inhabitants of the lower Mississippi was the product of handicrafts, with the occasional exception of lumber, which had been sawn by water-powered sawmills. By 1860, clothing, tools, machinery, and virtually all consumer products that reached farms and plantations had been fabricated by machinery in factories and shipped to the region over great distances by steamboats or by rail. From complete isolation the people of the southwestern Cotton Kingdom had emerged to become in all respects citizens of the modern Western industrialized civilization.

In writing this book I sought to trace the changes that took place during the building of the western portion of the Cotton South. To do so I examined the emergence of an agricultural society in the states of the lower Mississippi Valley that was created specifically to supply raw material to the textile factories of Great Britain, to western Europe, and to the American Northeast. I traced the evolution of agricultural technology and the corresponding changes in the institution of agricultural slavery, together with such supporting elements of the economy as the commercial towns, factories, railroads, and steam water navigation.

Although the southwestern Cotton Kingdom incorporated Alabama, Tennessee, Missouri, Arkansas, and Louisiana, Mississippi was the keystone of the arch. The Cotton Kingdom of the Old Southwest was born in the region stretching along the Mississippi River from Vicksburg to the boundary of Louisiana and looking to Natchez as its urban center. In the years that followed its birth, river planters introduced most of the agricultural innovations, and their new agricultural technology spread outward to eastern Mississippi and to the neighboring states. The qualitative leadership exhibited by Mississippi cotton growers during the first forty years in the history of the Cotton South was matched during the last two decades before the Civil War by quantitative superiority as well. In the 1850s, Mississippi was by far the largest producer of cotton among the southern states, and the state's planters were some of the most prosperous agriculturists in the Western world. I have therefore concentrated upon Mississippi, with special emphasis upon the agricultural region bordering the Mississippi and Yazoo rivers.

I thank the American Council of Learned Societies and the American Association for State and Local History for assistance with the research for this project. I owe special appreciation to my wife, Margaret DesChamps Moore, a historian in her own right, who unselfishly assisted me in the research and writing of this book.

1 Early Years, 1770–1839

The economic development of the state of Mississippi began in earnest with the founding of permanent settlements in the Natchez region by the British during the early 1700s. To be sure, the British were by no means the earliest Europeans to appear on the scene. First, during the sixteenth century, a Spanish exploring expedition commanded by Hernando de Soto had marched across the northern part of the state and had then floated down the Mississippi River. Later, in the eighteenth century, the French had established several temporary settlements within the state's boundaries. Permanent occupation of the state by Europeans, however, did not occur until Great Britain gained possession of the region at the conclusion of the French and Indian War.

While passing through the lower Mississippi Valley, de Soto's troops made one lasting, if involuntary, contribution to the development of modern Mississippi. The Spanish soldiers seeded the woods with European hogs, which escaped from droves accompanying the expedition as rations on the hoof. Lacking natural enemies apart from the Indians, the Spanish swine reverted to the wild and flourished in their new environment. In time their descendants lost the characteristics of domesticated hogs and retrogressed to an ancestral type of wild pig that later became famous as the Arkansas razorback. Consequently, when English settlers came to Mississippi, they found a bountiful supply of free pork awaiting them in the forests. Taking advantage of this natural abundance, the English soon replaced their traditional beef with pork as the principal source of protein in their diet.[1]

Shortly before the turn of the eighteenth century, the French established a fort and a small colony on the shores of the Bay of Biloxi to guard the southern river approach to Canada. A quarter century later the Louisiana authorities transferred the Biloxi settlers to the present site of New Orleans, the first solid ground upriver from the mouth of the Mississippi. For the remainder of the French period in the lower Mississippi Valley, Biloxi was merely a small fishing village of no significance.[2]

1. Lewis C. Gray, *History of Agriculture in the Southern United States to 1860* (1933; rpr. Gloucester, Mass., 1958), I, 8.

2. Edwin A. Davis, *Louisiana: A Narrative History* (3rd ed.; Baton Rouge, 1971), 37–56; Richard A. McLemore (ed.), *A History of Mississippi* (Hattiesburg, Miss., 1973), I, 117–27.

Although the authorities of colonial Louisiana concentrated their attention upon the region between New Orleans and Baton Rouge, they did perceive that the bluffs beside the river where Natchez is now situated possessed exceptional potential for agriculture. In 1716 they erected Fort Rosalie there and settled a few French families on already cleared lands obtained from the Natchez Indians who inhabited the area. Driven to desperation by mistreatment at the hands of the soldiers, the Natchez tribesmen revolted against the Europeans in 1729, massacring the white soldiers and settlers. With assistance from tribes hostile to the Natchez, the French army in Louisiana quickly crushed the revolt, almost exterminating the Natchez tribe in the process. Although this campaign eliminated all danger from the Indians in the vicinity of Fort Rosalie, no Europeans reoccupied the abandoned farms during the remainder of the period of French occupancy of Louisiana. Because the Biloxi colony was moved to New Orleans and the settlement near Fort Rosalie was abandoned, very few persons of French nationality were still residing within the boundaries of the present state of Mississippi when the French ceded Louisiana east of the Mississippi River (with the exception of the Isle of Orleans) to the British in 1763.[3]

During the six decades when the French ruled the lower valley of the Mississippi River, they contributed to the economic development of the Old Southwest by establishing a cypress lumber industry in Louisiana and by introducing slave-worked plantations modeled after their agricultural establishments on their Caribbean islands. The French also brought in cattle, fruits and vegetables, tobacco, rice, indigo, and a particularly valuable variety of upland cotton obtained originally from Siam. Nevertheless, French influence upon the later growth of neighboring Mississippi was largely indirect.[4]

The task of peopling the region north of Baton Rouge that became the nucleus of the southwestern Cotton Kingdom was eventually assumed by Great Britain, the only colonial power with a surplus population. The region east of the Mississippi River passed into Great Britain's possession as part of the spoils of the French and Indian War. In the process of demobilizing the swollen wartime military establishment, the British government rewarded deserving veterans of the army and navy with grants of

3. D. Clayton James, *Antebellum Natchez* (Baton Rouge, 1968), 5–11.
4. Gray, *Agriculture*, I, 60–84; John H. Moore, *Andrew Brown and Cypress Lumbering in the Old Southwest* (Baton Rouge, 1967), 4–9.

land in the region, which was to become known as the Natchez District of the Province of West Florida. Settlers began to arrive there in significant numbers in about 1770, and the newcomers quickly established a small town named Natchez and a permanent agricultural colony upon the bluffs overlooking the Mississippi River in the vicinity of Fort Rosalie.[5]

After France ceded Louisiana west of the Mississippi River and the Isle of Orleans to Spain in 1763, the Spanish government adopted a policy of denying the British colonists access to the port of New Orleans, thus blocking their commerce from the best water route to the sea. The agriculturists of the Natchez District found themselves with no better access than a tenuous route through small rivers and creeks that only small boats could navigate as far as Mobile. As a result, the settlers were restricted to primitive subsistence farming for the next two decades. Nevertheless, by developing a flourishing through illicit commerce with Spanish Louisiana, the British succeeded in securing their foothold on the east bank of the Mississippi River.[6]

During the final years of the American Revolution, with which the inhabitants of British Mississippi did not sympathize, the situation of the English in West Florida improved dramatically. Paradoxically, prosperity and economic growth arrived in the baggage train of a conquering Spanish army. Spain, during a long and unequal contest with Great Britain that began in the sixteenth century, had gained very few decisive victories; the conquest of West Florida in 1783 by a small force commanded by Governor Bernardo de Galvez of Louisiana was a rare exception. Leading French-speaking volunteers whose loyalty he had won by favorable economic treatment, Galvez reduced all resistance in Natchez, Baton Rouge, Mobile, and Pensacola and as quickly took steps to win the allegiance of the unwilling new subjects of His Most Catholic Majesty. Englishmen were appointed to administrative posts, residents of the Natchez District were exempted from taxation and military service, and Protestants were permitted to retain and practice their religion. Soon afterward the Spanish crown, acting on Galvez's advice, undertook to improve the economy of the Natchez District by purchasing all tobacco grown by the

5. Robert V. Haynes, *The Natchez District and the American Revolution* (Jackson, Miss., 1976), 3–26; James, *Antebellum Natchez*, 13–20.

6. Margaret F. Dalrymple (ed.), *The Merchant of Manchac: The Letterbooks of John Fitzpatric, 1768–1790* (Baton Rouge, 1978), 6–7, 11–13; Gray, *Agriculture*, I, 82–83; James, *Antebellum Natchez*, 14–21.

settlers at prices substantially above the market level. Under this benign Spanish rule, the British-speaking colonists imported black slaves and opened many new tobacco plantations, recklessly piling debt upon debt in the process. The system of agricultural price supports and the willingness of the Spanish authorities to grant lands to newcomers virtually for the asking lured immigrants from Great Britain and the United States into the Natchez District. As a result, the English-speaking white population increased rapidly, black slaves multiplied at an even faster rate, and the plantation emerged as the basic economic unit in the Spanish colony on the east bank of the Mississippi River.[7]

The French Revolution, however, menaced the security of the declining Spanish monarchy and forced the government at Madrid to make many adjustments in foreign and domestic policy. Motivated by a need for financial retrenchment as well as by a desire to win the friendship of western Americans for Spain, Manuel de Godoy, the prime minister, withdrew his tobacco subsidy from the residents of the Natchez District in 1790 and admitted American produce of many kinds into the New Orleans market. Unable to withstand this new competition from upriver, the tobacco planters of Natchez were forced out of business.[8]

The English-speaking colonists, trying to stave off impending ruin, experimented desperately with indigo only to be defeated by a plague of crop-destroying insects. Then, as a last resort, they planted upland cotton of the Siamese black seed variety, a plant that they had previously cultivated on a small scale for home consumption. At this point, fickle Dame Fortune chose to bestow her favors upon the Englishmen at Natchez once again. Saint-Domingue, Europe's principal source of cotton fiber and sugar, fell into racial conflict after the slaves were freed by French Revolutionaries and abruptly ceased to supply former customers of this once rich Caribbean island. With the plantations of Saint-Domingue inoperative, European demand for cotton pushed the price of that fiber to unprecedented heights at the very time when Natchez planters were entering the trade. By another fortunate coincidence, Eli Whitney's recently invented cotton gin became available to the new cotton growers of the lower Mississippi Valley, permitting them to take full advantage from the booming cotton market. Between 1795 and 1800 all of the former

---

7. John H. Moore, *Agriculture in Antebellum Mississippi* (New York, 1958), 17–18.

8. James, *Antebellum Natchez*, 48–50; Moore, *Agriculture*, 18–19.

slave-worked tobacco plantations of the Natchez District were successfully converted to the production of cotton, and New Orleans became
one of the world's leading cotton-exporting cities. When the Treaty of
San Lorenzo transferred the area to the possession of the United States,
the Natchez District, which had been a burdensome economic liability to
Spain, became a valuable economic asset to the new owner.[9]

After the French crushed the Natchez Indians in 1730, other tribes of
the Old Southwest seldom offered resistance to the advance of the white
man. Only the Creek Nation, which inhabited southern Georgia, Alabama, and eastern Mississippi, resorted to warfare in order to hold its
lands, and the Indians were crushed in 1814 by an army of frontiersmen
under Andrew Jackson. The peaceable Choctaws and Chickasaws who
occupied the northern two-thirds of the state of Mississippi depended
upon treaties with the American government rather than arms to protect
their territories against land-hungry white Mississippians. When Andrew Jackson, the famous Indian fighter, became president of the United
States in 1828, however, the principal chiefs of the southern tribes perceived that the federal government could no longer be relied upon to preserve their territories. Reluctantly, the Choctaws and Chickasaws of Mississippi, like the Creeks and Cherokees of Alabama and Georgia, signed
new treaties exchanging their old lands for new reservations west of the
Mississippi River. In this manner, the whites of the Old Southwest won a
bloodless but final victory over the red men. After the tribes emigrated to
the West in the early 1830s, their former holdings in northern Mississippi
were opened to settlement by white newcomers.[10]

In vivid contrast to the many immigrants who came to the southeastern English colonies during the seventeenth and eighteenth centuries
seeking political or religious refuge, virtually all whites who migrated to
Mississippi during the era before the Civil War did so solely to improve
their fortunes. By the time most of them had made the journey, the older
states from which they came had recognized religious and political freedom as basic rights for all Americans of Caucasian racial stock. With rare
exceptions white newcomers to the lower Mississippi Valley were agriculturists lured away from worn-out farms or plantations in the south At-

9. Moore, *Agriculture*, 19–26.
10. Arthur H. DeRosier, Jr., *The Removal of the Choctaw Indians* (Knoxville,
Tenn., 1970); Mary Elizabeth Young, *Redskins, Ruffleshirts, and Rednecks: Indian
Allotments in Alabama and Mississippi, 1830–1860* (Norman, 1961).

lantic states by the attraction of easily obtained fertile virgin lands. Thus knowledge of the economic development of Mississippi is of fundamental importance for understanding the social, political, and cultural history of the people of the state.

Mississippi possessed important natural economic advantages over the older southeastern states. Blessed with more fertile soils and a vastly superior system of inland water transportation, Mississippi, together with Louisiana, had surpassed South Carolina and Georgia as cotton producers by the third decade of the nineteenth century. In the case of Mississippi, the advantage of superior water transportation was crucial in promoting rapid settlement of the state. In comparison with shipping by water, hauling bulky commodities overland was so slow and expensive that merchants preferred to dispatch cargoes hundreds of miles by streams rather than haul their goods a few dozen miles over the unimproved dirt roads of the Lower South. Hence for all practical purposes, the most economical distance between two points was measured along water routes. From the standpoint of transportation, Mississippi River ports such as Natchez and Vicksburg were closer to European cotton markets than cotton shipping points in the piedmonts of Georgia and South Carolina.

Although navigable rivers radiated like spokes of a wheel from the interior to the ocean all along the southern coasts, the streams emptying into the Atlantic Ocean were tiny in comparison with the gigantic Mississippi River and even suffered beside many of its lesser tributaries. Furthermore, from the foothills of the Appalachian Mountains the land descended to the ocean in a relatively steep slope that fixed the head of navigation of southeastern rivers near their mouths. In the Old Southwest, in contrast, the Mississippi River system appears to have been designed by nature to meet the special requirements of cotton growers. Most of the land area in the western two-thirds of Mississippi that was suitable for cotton lay within practical hauling distance of landings on navigable streams emptying into the Mississippi. In the east and south, the Pearl and Tombigbee rivers served farmers almost as well. The marked superiority of facilities for water transportation in the Old Southwest over those of older portions of the Cotton Kingdom is reflected in the rapid growth of New Orleans and Mobile during the Steamboat Age (1820–1860), a period when Charleston and Savannah were declining in importance.

In addition to a vastly better system of waterways, the lower Mississippi Valley possessed much richer soils than the piedmonts of the Carolinas or Georgia. The best of the potential farmlands of the Old Southwest had been literally created by the Mississippi River. For uncounted centuries that river had overflowed its banks almost annually, depositing silt in much the same fashion as the Nile River in Egypt. By the time that Europeans arrived on the scene, successive deposits of river alluvium had built up a vast and almost level plain crisscrossed by a multitude of watercourses of all sizes. Inasmuch as the whole of the alluvian plain was still subject to flooding, farmers were unable to take full advantage of the soil until a system of levees had been constructed. In the case of the Yazoo-Mississippi delta, settlement was restricted to high ground along the riverbanks until after the Civil War. Many of the potentially productive lands, therefore, lay beyond the reach of antebellum cotton growers.

Rolling hills bordering the Mississippi River plain below the Yazoo-Mississippi delta also boasted fertile soils, and these were more accessible to settlers. Topsoil in the form of airborne dust carried from the Great Plains over many eons of time had been dropped among the trees of the Mississippi Valley. Because the tree-covered hills loomed above the plain like a screen, they received more of the wind-blown dust than the level country to the west or the rows of hills farther away to the east. Accumulations of this dust added to humus produced by rotting leaves of hardwood trees formed a deep rich loess covering a long, narrow strip of territory that ran along the Mississippi River between Woodville in the south and Vicksburg in the north.

To the east of the Yazoo-Mississippi delta, a dense hardwood forest covered the rolling hills of northern Mississippi. Leaf mold from these trees, lying undisturbed through the centuries, had mantled the clay hills with a thin, highly fertile layer of black soil, which was well suited for the culture of cotton until it was dissipated by erosion and overcropping.

A belt of pine barrens reaching northward from the Gulf coast for a distance of some 200 miles was generally unsuitable for agriculture. The pine forests grew upon extremely sterile, sandy soil that had once formed the bottom of a larger Gulf of Mexico, and pine leaves did not produce an enriching leaf mold equivalent to that of the hardwoods in the northern half of the state. Only in the valleys of rivers and creeks lay lands that could produce cotton profitably. For this reason, the pine barrens of the South really lay beyond the Cotton Kingdom proper.

With the exception of the Yazoo-Mississippi delta, the fertile soils of Mississippi rested upon a clay foundation of particularly soluble character. When exposed to water, this clay dissolved almost as readily as sugar, leaving behind a residue of sand. Consequently in a region of heavy rainfall, planting of row crops caused the land to become furrowed by gullies. Once-clear streams ran red, and the fertile topsoil gradually joined other sediment in the brown waters of the Mississippi River. For this reason the advantage of better soils that Mississippians enjoyed in the antebellum period was temporary everywhere in the state except in the Yazoo-Mississippi delta, where erosion was not a serious problem. Nevertheless, Mississippians were able to profit from their rich soils for the span of two generations—the age of the antebellum Cotton Kingdom.

Equipped with slaves, plantations, and the superior Siamese variety of cotton, the cotton producers of the lower Mississippi Valley amassed wealth at an astonishing rate during the first quarter century of the life of the antebellum Cotton Kingdom. Although cotton prices fluctuated wildly during this period, influenced by international events associated with the Napoleonic Wars, they were usually exceptionally high by the standards of the 1850s. At the same time the costs of land and slaves were comparatively low.[11]

In 1792 New Orleans merchants paid planters of the Natchez District four cents per pound for seed cotton and twenty-five cents for cleaned cotton. The price held steady through 1800. In the following year the price of cotton rose to thirty-two cents only to tumble to sixteen cents in 1802 when the news of the signing of the Peace of Amiens reached New York. By 1806 the price had risen to twenty cents. The next year, however, Jefferson's embargo badly injured the cotton export trade, severely deflating prices. In 1809, the year the embargo ended, William Dunbar recorded that the best cotton was bringing no more than fourteen cents in New Orleans. The outbreak of war with Great Britain in 1812 dropped the New York price below twelve cents. With the conclusion of hostilities in 1815, however, cotton prices bounded upward to thirty cents per pound. From that level, prices declined to twenty-eight cents in 1818 and to twenty-five cents in 1819, the beginning of the postwar depression.[12]

11. Gray, *Agriculture*, II, 682; Ulrich B. Phillips, *American Negro Slavery: A Survey of the Supply, Employment, and Control of Negro Labor as Determined by the Plantation Regime* (1918; rpr. Gloucester, Mass., 1959), 370.

12. John F. H. Claiborne, *Mississippi, as a Province, Territory and State, with Biographical Notices of Eminent Citizens* (Jackson, Miss., 1880) 140; Abijah Hunt to Robert W. Gray, November 11, 1800, and Wilkins and Linton to David Hunt, December 12, 1818, and February 26, 1819, all in Abijah and David Hunt Papers, Mississippi Department of Archives and History; Eron Rowland (ed.), *Life, Letters, and Papers of William Dunbar of Elgin, Morayshire, Scotland, and*

At the turn of the century, able-bodied adult slaves were selling for less than $400, and skilled slave craftsmen were obtainable for less than $1,000. At that time planters estimated that field hands earned their own-ers from $100 to $200 annually, minus the cost of their maintenance, which was not very great. Unimproved land suitable for cotton culture in 1799 was readily available in the vicinity of Natchez for $0.50 per acre, and cleared lands under cultivation were selling at from $2 to $10 an acre.[13]

On fertile valley lands, cotton produced about 1,500 pounds of seed cotton per acre and on upland lands about 1,000 pounds. During the early years of the nineteenth century, field hands could pick from 50 to 60 pounds of the Siamese cotton in a day. An extract from the cotton book of G. W. Lovelace dated October 1817, published in *De Bow's Review,* for example, listed the daily picking of nine slaves for one week on his plan-tation located on Sicily Island in Catahoula Parish, Louisiana. The nine slaves averaged 45 pounds of seed cotton per day. The largest amount picked by a single slave in a day was 78 pounds, and that slave's weekly average was 67 pounds. Over the course of a harvesting season, slaves gathered the equivalent of one and one-quarter to two 400-pound bales. Inasmuch as field hands could cultivate twice as many acres as they could gather during the harvesting season, in that period their picking capacity determined the acreages in cotton to be planted. In the early era, corn yielded much more per acre than the average in the 1840s and 1850s be-cause of the fertility of the loess soil that the pioneer cotton planters were working. On fresh lands in the old Natchez District, seventy to eighty bushels to the acre was the norm. This corn weighed about 70 pounds to the bushel.[14]

Natchez, Mississippi: Pioneer Scientist of the Southern United States (Jackson, Miss., 1930), 115, 344, 372; Gray, *Agriculture,* II, 682; David Holmes to White Turpin, October 21, 1815, in Benjamin L. C. Wailes Papers, Mississippi Depart-ment of Archives and History.

13. Christian Schultz, *Travels on an Inland Voyage Through the . . . Territories of Indiana, Louisiana, Mississippi and New Orleans; Performed in the Years 1807 and 1808* (New York, 1810), II, 139; F. Cumings, *Sketches of a Tour to the Western Country . . . Commenced at Philadelphia in the Winter of 1807, and Concluded in 1809* (Pittsburgh, 1810), 356–57.

14. Cumings, *Tour of the Western Country,* 323; James Hall, *A Brief History of the Mississippi Territory To Which is Prefixed a Summary View of the Country Be-tween the Settlements on the Cumberland River and the Territory* (Salisbury, N.C., 1801), reprinted in Mississippi Historical Society *Publications,* IX (1906), 555; Benjamin L. C. Wailes, *Report on the Agriculture and Geology of Mississippi, Em-*

Some of the profits of these early cotton planters were invested in fine houses, carriages, and thoroughbred horses, but most went into the purchase of additional land and slaves. The remainder was used to purchase cotton gins, cotton presses, sawmills, and other plantation equipment and machinery. In order to supply the requirements of the plantations, several local mechanics entered into the manufacture of plantation machinery. Eleazer Carver significantly improved upon the original Whitney saw gin built on Daniel Clark's Sligo plantation so that the fibers were less damaged by the saws, and others, including William Dunbar, introduced devices to clean dirt and foreign matter from the cotton after the seeds had been removed. As a result of these changes, cotton from Natchez sold at a premium until other portions of the cotton belt had adopted these improvements.[15]

Besides making improvements in the Mississippi version of Whitney's saw gin, Dunbar acquired the dubious distinction of being the first planter of the region to lose his ginhouse through fire, a disaster that a host of unfortunates would experience in the future. On a dry, frosty night in November 1806, seed cotton stored in the ginhouse on Dunbar's home plantation ignited, apparently by spontaneous combustion. In the resulting conflagration, Dunbar lost his gin, two cotton presses (one of them a famous iron screw press made in Philadelphia), a light carriage called a chaise, a large store of corn, and seed cotton from which the planter had expected to obtain 70,000 pounds of clean cotton. Dunbar and his slaves managed to save his residence, The Forest, only by enormous exertions. The old Scot estimated his losses at $20,000, a very large sum at that time. Dunbar was not able to put a replacement gin into operation until March 8, 1808. From this episode Mississippians learned to locate cotton gins at considerable distances from their residences, storehouses, and outbuildings.[16]

Mechanics of the Natchez area also invented and improved upon several kinds of cotton presses at about the turn of the century. Even in the

bracing a Sketch of the Social and Natural History of the State (Philadelphia, 1854), 132–34; De Bow's Review, XII (1852), 632–33; E. McKenzie, An Historical, Topographical, and Descriptive View of the United States of America and Lower Canada (2nd ed.; New Castle upon Tyne, 1819), 290.

15. Moore, Agriculture, 22–23; Wailes, Report, 167n, 168; Gray, Agriculture, II, 704; Rowland (ed.), Dunbar, 119–20, 328.

16. Rowland (ed.), Dunbar, 349–50, 356, 359–60.

early stages of their development, these machines added significantly to the incomes of Natchez planters, who used them to reduce the cost of transporting cotton to market. Cargoes of cotton packed loosely in bags filled the holds of ships without taxing their carrying capacities in terms of weight. Shippers therefore levied charges based on volume rather than on weight, a custom that made the cost of transportation dependent upon the number of packages in a shipment. The Natchez presses were able to compress 300 to 400 pounds of cotton fiber into bales no larger than the old 150-to-250-pound bags, the freightage was accordingly reduced. In a decade when American cotton bags delivered to Liverpool averaged 247 pounds in weight, for example, Dunbar sent a shipment of fifteen bales that averaged 309 pounds to New Orleans during November 1802. Five years later, a cargo of 166 bales shipped to Liverpool by Dunbar averaged 338 pounds. In the Southeast, less prosperous cotton growers were slow to adopt the expensive new machinery; some, in fact, continued to ship their crop in bags until the Civil War.[17]

Expansion of the cotton industry in the old Natchez District continued unhampered until 1811 except when the Republicans imposed embargoes, as they did periodically. In that year of the great earthquake, however, a fungus disease made its appearance in the Mississippi Valley, attacking the bolls of cotton plants with dire effect. The rot, as the disease was called, reduced yields of Siamese black seed cotton as much as 50 percent, thereby threatening to obliterate the crop in the Mississippi Valley even as indigo had previously been eliminated by insects. In subsequent seasons the rot attacked crops of Georgia green seed cotton imported in hope that the eastern variety would remain healthy. Only a few small crops of a variety brought in from Mexico and planted experimentally near Natchez were resistant to the epidemic.[18]

Throughout the Natchez District, planters laid down crops of the Mexican cotton as soon as they were able to obtain seed for planting. Be-

17. Claiborne, *Mississippi*, 144; Gray, *Agriculture*, II, 705; Wailes, *Report*, 173–76; Francis Bailey, *Journal of a Tour in the Unsettled Parts of North America in 1796 and 1797* (London, 1856), 292; Grand Gulf *Advertiser*, July 28, 1836; Rowland (ed.), *Dunbar*, 118–19, 356; James C. Bonner, *A History of Georgia Agriculture, 1732–1860* (Athens, Ga., 1964), 192.

18. *Southern Planter*, I (January and February, 1842), 17–18; Wailes, *Report*, 114–45; Claiborne, *Mississippi*, 114n; *Farmers' Register*, I (1834–35), 575; Arthur Singleton, *Letters from the South and West* (Boston, 1824), 113–14; *American Farmer*, II (1820), 116.

cause Mexican seed continued to be in short supply for several years, fields of Siamese black seed and Georgia green seed were planted alongside plots of the new cotton. Cross-pollination by wind and insects then took place between the three varieties, producing new cottons of widely differing characteristics. At this point in time several planters near Rodney employed a primitive form of plant breeding and succeeded almost by accident in developing a distinct and valuable strain from the mixed-breed cotton. Following the lead of Dr. Rush Nutt, a world traveler and amateur scientist, the neophyte plant breeders adopted the practice of selecting for planting cottonseeds that had the distinctive appearance of the Mexican variety. The breeders chose seeds that were covered with woolly white linters, rejecting the smooth black seeds typical of the Siamese cotton as well as the small green fuzzy seeds of the Georgia variety. In so doing, the planters believed that they were obtaining pure Mexican cotton. Actually they were getting a cotton of mixed parentage that had predominantly Mexican traits.[19]

The variety of cotton developed by the Rodney planters in this fashion happily combined the best characteristics of each of its ancestors. The plant was hardy and adaptable to different soils and temperatures like Georgia cotton. The quality of its fiber and its long staple was only slightly below that of the Siamese cotton. Like the Mexican cotton, the Rodney plant produced large bolls in profusion and, best of all, was completely immune to the rot. Although this immunity alone would have sufficed to guarantee its adoption by southern cotton growers generally, it soon proved to have still more valuable properties. Cotton pickers, who had been able to gather no more than 75 pounds of seed cotton from small-bolled Siamese or Georgia green seed, were able to pick 200 to 300 pounds of the Rodney cotton in a day. Writing in the early 1850s, Benjamin L. C. Wailes commented: "Fifty years since, fifty pounds a day was accounted fair work. Now the children double this; and two hundred pounds is not infrequently the average of the whole gang of hands, to say nothing of those who pick their four or five hundred pounds of cotton." The record day's picking in Mississippi exceeded 1,000 pounds. Inas-

---

19. *De Bow's Review*, X (1851), 668–69; Claiborne, *Mississippi*, 142–43; Horace S. Fulkerson, *Random Recollections of Early Days in Mississippi*, ed. Percy L. Rainwater (Baton Rouge, 1937), 12–14; John H. Moore, "Cotton Breeding in the Old South," *Agricultural History*, XXX (1956), 97–98; Wailes, *Report*, 143–44.

much as picking was the critical operation on a cotton plantation, a given number of farm workers could produce and harvest much larger crops from Rodney cotton than was possible with the older strains. Eventually it was discovered that Rodney cotton could be tailored to specifications by selective breeding; this development, however, came two decades later. With the Rodney cotton, planters of the Old Southwest were able to expand their production greatly without exceeding the ability of their slaves to harvest the crop. Looking back over a quarter century of cotton planting in Hinds County, Daniel O. Williams concluded that the most valuable improvement that he had adopted in this period was the replacement in 1829 of his old green seed and black seed cottons with the Petit Gulf, or Mexican, cotton.[20]

As reports of the Rodney cotton's immunity to rot spread throughout the Cotton Kingdom during the early 1820s, a demand for planting seed of this variety developed all across the Lower South. Commission merchants in New Orleans reacted by purchasing from Mississippi growers seed that they bagged and sold as Petit Gulf Cotton Seed, a name that referred to a geographic feature of the Mississippi River near Rodney. Their customers after trying the new product discovered that Petit Gulf did indeed live up to its billing—for a short time. Unless the Rodney selective breeding process was applied when choosing planting seed, the Petit Gulf cotton reverted to a close approximation of the Georgia green seed within three years. The tendency to degenerate was worth much to the growers of Mississippi; in order to preserve the quality of their crops, planters not knowing the secret had to buy fresh supplies of planting seed every other year.[21]

After experimenting in 1834 with Petit Gulf seed purchased in Augusta, Georgia, for example, "A Practical Planter" of Edgefield District, South Carolina, wrote in the *Southern Agriculturist:* "I . . . advise every planter of cotton, to procure this seed from New Orleans, let it cost what it will . . . , and to adopt the same plan every second or third year at farthest, for after that period it will become degenerated by mixture." In similar spirit "W. W. P." of Bertie County, North Carolina, wrote on June 20, 1834: "I am desirous of bringing to the notice of cotton farmers

20. Wailes, *Report*, 154; Vicksburg *Whig*, January 15, 1853; Gray, *Agriculture*, II, 689–90; Moore, *Agriculture*, 33–36; *Southern Cultivator*, XI (1853), 70.
21. *Southern Cultivator*, VI (1848), 19, and XI (1853), 70.

the advantages to be derived from planting 'petty gulf' seed. These are brought from the south, and take their name from a cotton growing district near the Mississippi, which produces them. . . . planters of the Red river are in the habit of receiving annual supplies to plant their crops." [22]

Hence local merchants in South Carolina, Georgia, and the other cotton-producing states of the Southeast began to stock planting seed obtained from New Orleans. As a result Mississippi cotton growers found a steady and lucrative market for their surplus Petit Gulf seed. Overall the trade in planting seed contributed substantially to the comparative prosperity of cotton growers of the Old Southwest, further increasing their advantages over their southeastern competitors. [23]

If the southeastern readers of the *Southern Cultivator* had heeded the advice of Daniel O. Williams of Hinds County, a friend of the leading cotton breeders of Hinds and Warren counties, they could have broken their dependence upon the cottonseed salesmen of the lower Mississippi Valley. In February 1853 Williams wrote that Mexican cotton deteriorated if planted on thin land but that on rich fresh ground it actually improved. Cottonseed from the best plants, Williams suggested, should be saved for planting. By ignoring Williams, planters of South Carolina, Alabama, and Georgia spent hundreds of thousands of dollars needlessly, by importing their seed from New Orleans. [24]

From the beginning of the nineteenth century until 1839, the cotton textile industry of Great Britain and the northern United States experienced dramatic growth. To the states of the Lower South, this phase of the Industrial Revolution represented virtually unlimited demand for their cotton fiber during all but a few exceptional years of war or depression. In this period the overriding problem of the agricultural population was how to increase production of the staple in order to satisfy the demand; overproduction of cotton was not destined to become a permanent condition until after the Civil War. In the process of increasing production, the planters of the Old Southwest enlarged their acreages under cultivation in cotton, improved their techniques of cultivating their market

22. *Farmers' Register*, II (1835–36), 122–23, 548–49.

23. Columbus (Ga.) *Enquirer*, March 1, 1838; Columbus (Ga.) *Southern Sentinel*, April 11, 1850; *Farmers' Register*, II (1835–36), 122–23; Macon (Ga.) *Messenger*, December 17, 1846; Montgomery (Ala.) *Journal*, December 20, 1849, and December 23, 1854; Moore, *Agriculture*, 34.

24. *Southern Cultivator*, XI (1853), 70.

crop, minimized their crops of foodstuffs, and bought additional slaves as rapidly as possible. A planter who came to Hinds County in 1830, for example, wrote in 1841: "Planters crowded every spot of their fields with cotton plants, and sent their ox teams to the Mississippi River for every grain of corn consumed upon their plantations. You might have travelled all day without seeing a corn field of any importance." The same could have been said of all the settled cotton-producing counties.[25]

In a lengthy set of resolutions adopted by a group of Hinds County planters meeting at Raymond in June 1839, the writers included an explanation for the general concentration upon cotton growing to the exclusion of everything else. They stated: "At a time when cotton commanded prices from 15 to 20 cents per lb., and corn could be purchased at 37½ or 50 cts. per bushel, pork at 3 or 4 cents per lb. and other necessaries at a rate proportionate, the planter, living convenient to market where the trouble of wagoning is not too great, was pursueing a true economy to devote exclusive attention to cotton and purchase those articles with the proceeds of its sale, which thus cost him less labor than would have been necessary to their domestic production."[26]

During the boom years preceding the panic of 1837, cotton growers overoptimistically expected to make "ten bales to the hand and fifty dollars for the bale," according to C. S. Tarpley of Willow Grove plantation in Hinds County, a reforming planter and advocate of building railroads. Although planters actually "made upon an average half the quantity, and sold it for little more than half that price, [and] received our pay in worthless Bank paper of the country, and paid it out and found ourselves in debt for the corn, pork and other necessary supplies that should have been raised upon our own farms." Attracted by the scent of easy money, planters, as well as would-be planters and farmers, deserted the states of the Atlantic seaboard in numbers large enough to affect adversely the economics of the Southeast. By far the greater number of these emigrants chose Mississippi as their new home, with the result that vast acreages along the Yazoo and Tombigbee river systems in northern Mississippi were brought under cultivation within a relatively short time.[27]

25. Raymond *Times*, May 7, 1841; [Joseph H. Ingraham], *The South-West, by a Yankee* (1835; rpr. New York, 1968), II, 89.

26. Raymond *Times*, August 2, 1839.

27. *Southwestern Farmer*, I (April 29, 1842), 89; *De Bow's Review*, VII (1849), 38–44.

Fortunately for the newcomers, if not for the original inhabitants, the Indian titles to the northern half of the state were extinguished during the early 1830s, and the land was opened up for settlement by the federal government at a time when most of the desirable land in the old Natchez District was already taken up. Stimulated by skyrocketing prices during the boom of 1833–1837, the immigrants swarmed into the hills of northern Mississippi, creating scenes similar to those of the California gold rush of 1849. With the aid of hordes of slaves brought in from the tobacco states and from the eastern cotton states, the new citizens of Mississippi placed the former domains of the Choctaws and the Chickasaws under cultivation in less than half a decade, enormously increasing the state's exports of the staple. Indeed, near the close of the decade of the 1830s, Mississippi emerged as the Old South's leading producer of the white gold, completely eclipsing South Carolina and outdistancing even Georgia, the former champion of the Cotton Kingdom.

In large measure, the great land rush into northern Mississippi was due to success attained by the cotton planters of the old Natchez District during the preceding decade. The fabulous wealth that many of them actually accumulated became part of the folklore of the period in a vastly exaggerated form, of course, in much the same fashion as the riches of the gold miners of 1849 and the Texas oilmen of the 1920s. In 1830, for example, it was reported that planters were clearing no less than $50,000 from a single crop of cotton. Because of this word-of-mouth advertising, Mississippi became for a time the Mecca of American fortune hunters, some of whom were to realize their fondest dreams. Capital was available on incredibly easy terms because moneylenders had also subscribed to the myth of the Natchez District. Indeed, many of the successful planters of the river counties funneled their spare cash into the area to buy land for themselves or to be lent to newcomers to the state.[28]

When the cotton boom came to an abrupt end in the autumn of 1839, Mississippi's antebellum Cotton Kingdom was established in approximately its permanent dimensions. Most of the land in the state suitable for cotton culture and adequately serviced by water transportation had already been claimed from the virgin wilderness. What remained for

28. Joseph G. Baldwin, *The Flush Times of Alabama and Mississippi: A Series of Sketches* (New York, 1854), 82–84; Edwin A. Miles, *Jacksonian Democracy in Mississippi* (Chapel Hill, 1960), 119–20; Morton Rothstein, "The Agricultural South as a Dual Economy: A Tentative Hypothesis," *Agricultural History*, XLI (1967), 375–82; McLemore (ed.), *History of Mississippi*, I, 343–50.

latecomers to occupy were tracts in the Black Belt situated in the interior between navigable streams too far removed from boat landings for economical operation and potentially rich Yazoo-Mississippi delta lands subject to annual overflow. The former could be used profitably only when railroads brought them within the range of access to a river port. The latter remained unavailable to agriculture until levees were constructed by the federal government in the postwar years.

By 1840 the state had received most of its white population and a very large part of its slaves. The land rush of the 1830s tapered off as a consequence of the financial panic of 1837, which ended the era of easy credit and virtually ceased two years later when the cotton price structure collapsed. Indeed, in all likelihood the number of persons moving into the state during the gloomy years of the early 1840s was exceeded by the number of bankrupted planters and farmers on their way to Texas.[29]

By 1839 the Mississippi slave-worked cotton plantation had demonstrated its superiority as a unit for producing the great southern staple. To be sure, thousands of farmers were raising cotton in Mississippi as their principal cash crop on a small scale and were doing so profitably. These small cotton growers patterned their methods of cultivation upon those of their planter neighbors, and many depended upon their neighbors for ginning and baling their crops. Whenever the circumstances permitted, farmers purchased slaves in order to enlarge the scope of their farming operations. By this period it had become transparently clear to most observers that the cost of growing cotton diminished as the size of the farming unit was increased until an optimum condition had been attained. A plantation ranging in size from 1,000 to 1,500 acres and worked by a crew numbering from 75 to 100 able-bodied field hands was generally regarded as ideal. Such a plantation could afford the desirable farm machinery, implements, and livestock and was the proper size for efficient management. Typical cotton plantations changed very little in their essential elements between 1840 and the close of the antebellum period. By means of mechanization, crop diversification, soil conservation, and refined methods of managing slaves, plantations evolved further to a peak of effectiveness just prior to the Civil War.[30]

29. McLemore (ed.), *History of Mississippi*, I, 292–94, 311–15; Moore, *Agriculture*, 59–73.
30. Vicksburg *Whig*, August 18, 1855; Gray, *Agriculture*, I, 529–39; Moore, *Agriculture*, 64–67; McLemore (ed.), *History of Mississippi*, I, 333–37; Herbert Weaver, *Mississippi Farmers, 1850–1860* (Nashville, 1945), 83–84.

2 The Agricultural Revolution, 1839–1849

During the late 1830s and early 1840s, the slave-plantation system of producing cotton, which had been extraordinarily profitable during the first three decades of the history of the Cotton Kingdom, was confronted by ten years of prices for the new southern staple that were disastrously low. To many contemporaries it appeared during the early 1840s that slave-worked cotton plantations had become as uneconomical as tobacco plantations had been in the old Natchez District of West Florida during the early 1790s, just before culture of the crop was entirely abandoned. To these observers cotton growers' only options were to replace cotton with other crops or to dismantle the slave-plantation system altogether. Mississippians, however, managed to avoid either of these alternatives by radically altering their agricultural methods. As a result, the period of abnormal cotton prices ultimately strengthened rather than destroyed the southwestern cotton plantation.

In Mississippi, the first pressure came upon the slave-plantation system just before the onset of the panic of 1837, when many newcomers to the state were placed in financial jeopardy by the specie circular issued on July 11, 1836, by Secretary of the Treasury Levi Woodbury on instructions from President Andrew Jackson. The presidential directive required that all payments for lands purchased from the federal government be tendered in gold and silver coin rather than in bank notes, the ordinary circulating medium of the United States, which the Treasury had been accepting heretofore. For debtors in the Old Southwest, Jackson's abrupt change to a deflationary monetary policy was disastrous because the supply of coin available in the region was not sufficient to permit them to make their annual payment to the U.S. Land Office. From 1833 through 1836, the federal land offices had sold 8,331,581 acres in Mississippi and 4,516,876 acres in Alabama, and most of this land had undoubtedly not yet been paid for. At the time when the specie circular was issued, all of the banks in the United States had between them only $45 million dollars in specie in their vaults.[1]

1. Robert V. Remini, *Andrew Jackson and the Bank War: A Study in the Growth of Presidential Power* (New York, 1968), 173; Young, *Redskins, Ruffleshirts, and Rednecks,* 175–78; Arthur M. Schlesinger, Jr., *Age of Jackson* (Boston, 1950), 127–28.

During the ensuing financial crisis, land speculators proved to be as vulnerable as farmers and planters. Many land companies and individuals were in debt for tens of thousands of acres of choice virgin lands in the Old Southwest that they were holding for resale at higher prices to prospective agriculturists. In a single district in northern Mississippi, for example, sixty-two speculators had obtained possession of nearly 1.5 million acres. One syndicate of investors from New York and Boston, the American Land Company, had acquired 200,000 acres in Mississippi. Another, the New York and Mississippi Land Company, had obtained title to 206,000 acres. From the latter firm, the Pontotoc and Holly Springs Land Company, made up of local speculators, purchased 49,440 acres. Fifty-two speculators in Choctaw and Chickasaw land allotments acquired over a million acres in northern Mississippi, whereas members of a smaller class of investors bought about 2.5 million acres in lots ranging from 2,000 to 10,000 acres. Unable to obtain the necessary specie, most of these speculators, together with a large number of their customers, were forced to default. Banks and commission houses that had lent purchasers of land large sums of money based on unrealistic evaluations of land and slaves also went under during the panic.[2]

With the demise of the state banks and the bankruptcy of many large New Orleans commission merchants, would-be purchasers of farms and plantations lost their principal sources of credit. Consequently, relatively few people were able to take advantage of the reduction in land prices that occurred after the fall of the great land speculators. The lack of credit was reflected in a sharp decline in public land sales in northern Mississippi. From a peak of 3,267,299 acres in 1836, sales dropped to 430,096 acres in 1837 and to 327,807 acres in 1838. In 1843, the nadir of the depression of the 1840s, only 73,392 acres were sold by land offices in the state.[3]

Farmers and planters who had managed to pay for their lands and slaves prior to 1837 were comparatively well situated during the panic. A great many others who were burdened with outstanding debts, however, found themselves in danger of bankruptcy. Looking back to his arrival in

2. Paul W. Gates, *The Farmer's Age: Agriculture, 1815–1860* (New York, 1960), 81–82; George R. Taylor, *The Transportation Revolution, 1815–1860* (New York, 1957), 342–43.
3. Young, *Redskins, Ruffleshirts, and Rednecks*, 177–78.

Mississippi during the boom years of the 1830s, M. J. Blackwell, a Methodist minister from Clarendon County, South Carolina, wrote during 1848 from his new home in Marshall County: "The land speculators had thousands completely in their power in the first settlement of the country, and used it to the temporal ruin of many, but their reign is over. . . . They came near breaking me up root and branch." Blackwell managed to weather the panic of 1837 and the ensuing depression of the early 1840s by selling off his best lands while retaining the least valuable acreage.[4]

Luckily for all classes of agriculturists, cotton prices did not collapse during the panic of 1837, as they were to do in 1839, but rather held reasonably firm for two more seasons. During the panic, cotton prices on the New York City market declined from about sixteen cents a pound in 1836 to ten cents in 1838 but rose from that low point to fourteen cents during 1839. The major break in the cotton market did not come until the winter of 1839–1840.[5]

The brief respite between the panic of 1837 and the severe depression of the 1840s that so closely followed almost certainly saved many Mississippians from total financial disaster when the depression struck. In retrospect, it is obvious that the panic of 1837, painful though it was for the population of the Old Southwest, nevertheless performed a socially beneficial service by ridding the region of the plague of speculators. On the debit side of the ledger, many newcomers to Mississippi who were not as fortunate or as resourceful as Blackwell were wiped out during the financial panic and subsequently emigrated farther west to recoup their fortunes.

Unlike the panic of 1837, which had been caused by domestic forces, the economic upheaval of the 1840s was international in scope. The severe decline in demand for southern cotton that occurred during the 1840–1845 period, in particular, was a consequence of overproduction within the British textile industry, which closed many mills during 1840 and kept the industry as a whole operating below capacity for the remainder of the decade. The resulting weak demand tumbled cotton prices from fourteen cents in the winter of 1839 to three cents for low grades of cotton in 1843. Prices did not reach ten cents again until 1850.[6]

4. M. J. Blackwell to Edmund B. Blackwell, November 30, 1848, in Edmund B. Blackwell Papers, William R. Perkins Library, Duke University.

5. Gray, *Agriculture*, II, 697; Phillips, *American Negro Slavery*, 370.

6. Douglas C. North, *The Economic Growth of the United States, 1790–1860* (1961; rpr. New York, 1966), 201–203.

Under the depressed conditions, cotton growers were obliged to start raising their staple crop much more cheaply in order to survive. Unfortunately, however, many of them were unable to adjust their farming methods soon enough to avoid seizure of their property by creditors. Consequently the civil courts of Mississippi became clogged with lawsuits during 1840, and local newspapers took on the aspect of courthouse bulletins, containing little except announcements of forced sales of property. In that troubled year not a few insolvent Mississippians tried to salvage something illegally from the wreck of their business affairs by fleeing with their mortgaged slaves and livestock across the border into the Republic of Texas. A much larger number, however, managed to hang onto their property in Mississippi until they could adapt to a more frigid economic climate.[7]

In the spring of 1840, most of the planters and farmers of the state were unable to obtain the usual credit against forthcoming crops of cotton from their commission merchants. Albert T. McNeal of Coffeeville, Mississippi, wrote James K. Polk in January of 1840, "Money is extremely scarce, and I have never in my life witnessed 'such screwing and twisting' to get it." Martin W. Phillips, Mississippi's foremost agricultural authority of the 1840s and 1850s, was only one of the thousands of farmers and planters who lost their property in the crash. "Fortunately," he recorded in his diary, "A friend was able to advance the money and give my wife time and opportunity to redeem [pay off the property]." Few other unfortunates in like circumstances were lucky enough to save their property with a last-minute loan. After traveling through Holmes, Yazoo, and Madison counties, James A. Orr wrote movingly of the devastation of plantations produced by the collapse of the cotton market and added, "When the storm broke over the banks the suits were so numerous in the courts that some of the lawyers had their declarations *in assumpsit* printed by the quire."[8]

Innovations in farming methods adopted during the depression by agriculturists throughout the southern Cotton Kingdom were so extensive as to constitute an agricultural revolution. More precisely, two concur-

7. Moore, *Agriculture*, 73, 109–22; Port Gibson *Herald*, April 3, 1845; Raymond *Times*, May 7, 1841.

8. John S. Bassett (ed.), *The Southern Plantation Overseer as Revealed in His Letters* (Northampton, Mass., 1925), 136; James A. Orr, "A Trip from Houston to Jackson, Miss., in 1845," Mississippi Historical Society *Publications*, IX (1906), 175; Franklin L. Riley (ed.), "Diary of a Mississippi Planter, January 1, 1840, to April, 1863," *ibid.*, X (1909), 336.

rent agricultural revolutions were under way in the Lower South during the 1840s, one in the Southeast and another in the Southwest. In the less fertile Southeast, cotton producers turned away from cotton as the sole staple crop, preferring grains, fruit, livestock, and even manufacturing. In the Southwest, in contrast, reforming farmers and planters did not seek diversification of crops on principle as their counterparts in the Southwest had done but rather aimed at reducing the cost of producing cotton fiber.[9]

For the first time in their experience, Mississippi planters during 1840 had to provide food for their families, slaves, and animals, as well as clothing for the slaves, drawing on such resources as their plantations possessed. Earlier, during the boom years, it will be recalled, most large cotton growers had concentrated all of their available labor upon the staple crop because work expended upon cotton was returning a greater revenue than work expended on corn or other foodstuffs. As a rule, the growers had cultivated their subsistence crops only at times when workers could conveniently be spared from the cotton fields. Consequently corn production in the plantation regions of the lower Mississippi Valley ordinarily fell far short of normal consumption during the 1830s, with the deficit being filled by imports from the Old Northwest. In 1839 this arrangement became unworkable. Planters and farmers therefore tried to seed sufficient additional acres in corn to satisfy their requirements and when necessary even reduced the size of their cotton crops. Colin S. Tarpley of Hinds County observed, "We were driven from necessity to break our intolerable bondage to the grain growing states, and raise within ourselves what was necessary for our own consumption." An editor of the New Orleans *Bulletin* concurred with Tarpley when he wrote that "the recent derangements of the currency have taught Mississippi planters . . . to husband their resources by 'raising all within themselves.'" Besides increasing their acreages planted in corn, planters expanded their output of sweet potatoes, cowpeas, garden vegetables, fruits, and other foodstuffs.[10]

9. Bonner, *Georgia Agriculture*, 73–203; Cornelius O. Cathey, *Agricultural Developments in North Carolina, 1783–1860* (Chapel Hill, 1956), 101, 106–11; Alfred G. Smith, Jr., *Economic Readjustment of an Old Cotton State: South Carolina, 1820–1860* (Columbia, S.C., 1958), 53–111; *Southern Cultivator*, XIV (1856), 111.

10. Moore, *Agriculture*, 72, 109–22; *Mississippi Free Trader and Natchez Gazette*, May 16 and 30, 1839; Raymond *Times*, June 21, 1839; *Southwestern Farmer*, I (April 29, 1842), 59.

After corn, the purchase of salt pork had been the largest item on the list of regular outlays for agriculturists of the lower Mississippi Valley during the 1830s. Although in that decade most of Mississippi's farmers and planters were raising herds of half-wild native hogs and cattle in a haphazard manner, very few men had bothered to salt down enough pork or beef to feed the inhabitants of their farms or plantations. Instead, Mississippi planters in particular had preferred to purchase their entire season's supply of salt meat through the commission merchants. William S. Archer, who had moved to Holmes County from Virginia in 1835 with about eighty slaves, for example, had to buy twenty-one barrels of pork for $399 in 1836 and twenty barrels for $410 in 1837, his largest single expenditures for both years. In 1843, however, fifty-two hogs were killed on Archer's Killona plantation, producing 7,837 pounds of pork. Under the harsh new conditions of the 1840s, many cotton growers of the Old Southwest, like Archer, developed a hitherto unaccustomed interest in the breeding of livestock, especially improved varieties of hogs.[11]

The pork shortage in Mississippi in 1840 presented small farmers with a welcome new opportunity. Ferdinand L. Steel and his brother, Edward, for example, were cultivating about twenty acres in Carroll County, raising cotton and corn. In 1839 they killed six hogs, which made about 420 pounds of salt pork, sufficient to feed the two men, their mother, and their younger sister for the coming year. The next year, however, the Steels rounded up enough wild hogs to make 2,227 pounds of meat when slaughtered and salted down. Most of the surplus they sold in the neighborhood.[12]

Native pigs, today called Arkansas razorbacks but then known as alligators or land pikes, were hardy beasts capable of foraging for themselves on the open range and entirely able to cope with predators of the wild, but these small animals produced inferior meat even when penned and fattened. A correspondent of the *Southwestern Farmer* wrote in 1842 that his neighbor maintained a herd of land pikes numbering from 300 to 425 head to supply his annual requirements of salt pork. He had to slaughter from 50 to 100 of these small animals, which required from 200 to 500 bushels of corn to fatten when penned. The land pikes generally became large enough to kill in twenty-six months. In contrast, Berkshire

11. Killona Plantation Journal (Mississippi Department of Archives and History); Moore, *Agriculture*, 93–101.
12. Ferdinand L. Steel Diary, January 17, 1839, and December 30, 1840 (MS in possession of Edward M. Steel, Jr., Morgantown, West Virginia).

hogs fed the same amount of corn would reach 200 pounds in twelve months.[13]

Because of the alligators' poor meat-producing characteristics, they were generally abandoned by planters, though not by farmers, during the early 1840s. In their stead, planters began to raise thoroughbred swine despite the necessity of feeding these more delicate animals at all seasons of the year. By the middle 1840s, Berkshires, Irish Graziers, and Woburn hogs had become commonplace throughout the plantation regions of Mississippi, along with crosses between these thoroughbreds and the old native swine. From Wilkinson County a correspondent of the *Southern Planter* wrote in 1842: "We of the South-West are fast getting into the inclination and condition to raise our own pork. The long snouts, slab-sides, and porcupine backs of our land pike and alligator breeds are fast being superseded by the neat, full and elegant contour and filling up of the Berkshires, the Woburns and the Graziers." During this period planters boasted in their local newspapers of remarkable weights attained by their favorite varieties of hog, and they bickered amiably over recipes for curing hams. G. S. Munson of Monroe County reported in the Aberdeen *Independent* during January 1853, for example, that he had "killed year before last, an eighteen months old hog weighing 452 lbs. neat; last year, one weighing 380 lbs; and this year, I slaughtered a three year old weighing 675 lbs, gross or 600 neat." A better candidate for the porcine championship of Mississippi, however, was a beast raised in Noxubee County. It weighed 1,400 pounds and was exhibited in Vicksburg during March 1851.[14]

In that period the smokehouse emerged as a vital element of the cotton plantation, an honor it was not to lose even when prosperity returned during the last half of the 1850s. Although the commercial traffic in salt pork was never entirely eliminated, planters of the state did materially reduce their reliance upon the packing houses of St. Louis and Cincinnati. On a Lowndes County plantation managed by E. Sanderson, for example, during the three-year period from 1854 to 1856, the plantation produced eleven tons of salted pork annually, sufficient to supply 143 slaves with the usual weekly ration of three pounds of meat.[15]

13. *Southwestern Farmer*, I (September 23, 1842), 19.
14. Quoted *ibid.*, I (April 29, 1842), 10–11; Aberdeen *Independent*, January 15, 1853; Vicksburg *Sentinel*, March 15, 1851.
15. Moore, *Agriculture*, 93–101; *American Cotton Planter and Soil of the South*, I (1857), 102.

Nevertheless, by the mid 1850s a good many planters who had been enthusiastic about the breeding of pure-blooded hogs during the preceding decade became convinced that the production of pork on their plantations was uneconomical. Although they could feed these animals well on corn, cowpeas, cottonseed, sweet potatoes, and peanuts, they were unable to prevent their slaves from killing and eating the young pigs. Charles Whitmore of Amite County finally decided in 1860, to cite one example, that he would buy his pork from Cincinnati because he could no longer stomach the frequent whippings that he had to administer to his slaves as punishment for stealing pigs. Daniel O. Williams originally expected his son to raise enough hogs to feed the slaves on their Deer Creek plantation in Issaquena County as he himself had been doing for years on his home plantation near Clinton. He soon, however, suffered disillusionment. On December 18, 1853, he wrote Sampson Williams: "I think it would be proper to hand cuff Merce, Brit, Joe, Bill & George every night after they have done work. . . . You will then be able to raise hogs enough. If you lose any after cuffing them, then hand cuff every man on the place." Whether Sampson followed his father's harsh instructions is unknown. It is certain, however, that he could not check the stealing of pigs, and he had to make annual purchases of pork from his commission merchant in New Orleans.[16]

Factory-made clothing and bedding purchased for the slaves had been another considerable item of annual expense for cotton planters during the 1830s. In their drive for economy in the 1840s, Mississippians installed spinning and weaving equipment on their plantations and assigned some women to weaving fabrics of cotton and wool on rainy days when they could not work in the fields. Other women prepared shirts, dresses, trousers, blankets, and cotton quilts from these homespun goods.

Of course abundant supplies of cotton were always readily available at no cost, but wool was not ordinarily produced on the plantations of Mississippi before the depression. To be sure, sheep were raised in small numbers during the 1820s and 1830s but only to supply lamb and mutton as delicacies for the table on special occasions. Of these animals, the editor of the Natchez *Free Trader* wrote in April 1842: "While the whole

16. Mack Swearingen, "Thirty Years of a Mississippi Plantation: Charles Whitmore of 'Montpelier,'" *Journal of Southern History*, I (1935), 210; Daniel O. Williams to Sampson Williams, December 18, 1853, in Daniel O. and Sampson Williams Papers, in possession of the writer.

world is agog after Berkshires and Durhams, nobody thinks of the long-legged, slab-sided, naked-bellied native sheep of Mississippi, a hardy, thrifty, light-fleeced, nimble-footed tribe that subsist on the little end of nothing and furnish the most racy, juicy and highly-flavored mutton in the world." Not being bred for wool, Mississippi sheep produced almost worthless fleece. Many planters therefore hurriedly imported thorough-bred animals during the 1840s and began, like Elias Jenkins of Choctaw County, to build up flocks capable of supplying their wool requirements. Jenkins wrote from his plantation, the Horse Pens, in 1857: "I have for the last eight or ten years kept on my plantation from 75 to 100 head [of sheep], which have cost me nothing except salting them once a week and keeping up my fences. . . . they have yielded me a profit by their wool of 50 per cent, independent of a fat lamb or sheep when I wanted it." [17]

Because protecting flocks of sheep from marauding packs of half-wild dogs, buzzards, and other natural enemies was not easy, many planters were less successful then Jenkins in producing wool. One who had had his troubles wrote in the *Hinds County Gazette* in 1857: "It is utterly futile to talk about raising sheep to any considerable extent in this State until we disencumber ourselves of these swarms of vile curs (the natural enemy of the sheep) which infest the land." Because of such difficulties wool continued to be imported into Mississippi for the use of plantations and local textile mills.[18]

As a by-product of the newly developed interest in livestock breeding, many farmers and planters introduced Durhams, Ayrshires, and other pure-blooded cattle into their herds of native Spanish stock in an attempt to obtain beef of edible quality. Usually the imported breeds did not thrive in the warm climate of Mississippi because natural grasslands were lacking. By the close of the 1840s, Mississippians generally had learned to be content with crosses between Durhams and the hardy native cattle, which could survive untended on the open range. Phillips reported to the U.S. commissioner of patents in 1848 that hogs were increasing in number in Mississippi, but the "more expensive cattle . . . [were] becoming less numerous." Seven years later Russell was told that plantations in the Natchez area were raising only enough cattle to "replace the draught oxen

17. Natchez *Free Trader*, April 21, 1842; *Southern Cultivator*, XV (1857), 11–12.
18. Raymond *Hinds County Gazette*, March 25, 1857; Moore, *Agriculture*, 106–107; Weaver, *Mississippi Farmers*, 97.

that are required." Beef production in the state continued to be negligible during the 1840s and 1850s, and cattle were raised then mainly for hides and to serve as draft oxen. A few Brahman cattle introduced experimentally from India showed promise of adapting to the climate and range and might have become the basis of a cattle industry had not the Civil War ended all attempts at large-scale cattle breeding.[19]

Despite the planters' efforts to spend as little money abroad as possible, during the 1840s and 1850s they remained dependent upon the upper Mississippi Valley for iron, copper, hempen rope and bagging, tools, and many kinds of machinery. Hence the ideal of plantation self-sufficiency was often approached during the late depression years but was never fully realized. Nevertheless, a general policy of stressing economic operation did significantly enhance the efficiency of cotton plantations in the Old Southwest.

In order to offset falling cotton prices, Mississippi plantation owners strove to increase their output of fiber to the maximum that their slaves could harvest and to improve the grade of their product. While pursuing the first of these objectives, they generally resorted (as will be discussed in the next chapter) to a primitive form of mechanization, using implements drawn by horses or mules so that farm workers could cultivate more acres than had been possible during the 1820s and 1830s, when hoes and turning plows were the principal instruments of husbandry. To achieve their second goal, planters usually adopted improved strains of Mexican cotton, which produced fibers of longer staple and gave larger yields per acre. In this period the cotton growers also improved the cleaning and packing of their product for market.

In addition to increasing their acreages under cultivation by mechanizing their farming operations, many planters throughout Mississippi improved their incomes during and after the depression by cultivating cotton of higher quality during the 1840s. Henry W. Vick developed the most popular of these improved strains of cotton on a Deer Creek plantation in Issaquena County. Vick was a large slaveowner who owned plantations in Warren County and in the newly opened Yazoo-Mississippi delta.

19. *Patent Office Report, 1850: Agriculture*, 509; Robert Russell, *North America, Its Agriculture and Climate: Containing Observations on . . . Cuba* (Edinburgh, 1857), 265–66; Charles E. Cauthen (ed.), *Family Letters of the Three Wade Hamptons, 1782–1901* (Columbia, S.C., 1953), 59; *Southern Cultivator*, IX (1851), 23–24; Vicksburg *Whig*, March 17, 1858.

Cotton Crops of Mississippi, 1837–1860

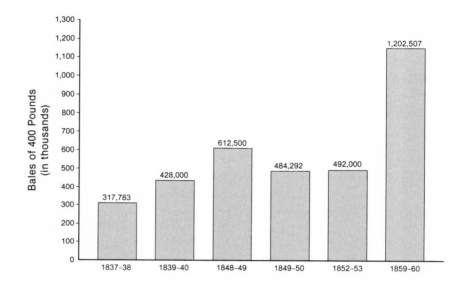

Sources: *Sixth Census, 1840,* pp. 226–29, *Seventh*
Census, 1850, p. 458; *Eighth Census; 1860:*
Agriculture, 85, Appendix B

Like his contemporaries, Vick knew virtually nothing of the young science of botany, and his important contribution to commercial plant breeding resulted from untutored curiosity and keen observation. He became interested in the breeding of fine cottons quite by chance. While visiting his Delta plantation, Nitta Yuma, on the banks of Deer Creek, a tributary of the Yazoo River, during the autumn of 1843, the planter noticed that there were many variations among individual plants in his fields of Petit Gulf cotton. Some plants were much larger than others; some bore many bolls, whereas others had few; and some were producing longer or finer fibers than the rest. His curiosity aroused, Vick began collecting samples of cotton from exceptionally prolific plants, which he examined in detail under a magnifying glass. One sample containing exactly 100 seeds caught his fancy because of its exceptionally long staple, and he preserved the seeds for future experimentation. When planted in a garden plot the following year, the sample produced a remarkably uniform crop of very high-quality cotton. Vick selected planting seed from the best of these plants and repeated his experiment for several seasons.[20]

Having become convinced that he had developed a new cotton of decidedly superior quality, Vick distributed seed to many of his friends during 1846. They, too, were delighted with his prolific long-staple Hundred Seed cotton and spread the news of Vick's achievement widely. Within a very short time, a heavy demand for planting seed of the new variety developed throughout the Lower South, and sales of the seed under imaginative brand names brought rich rewards to growers.[21]

Throughout the cotton-producing sections of Mississippi, profit-conscious cotton growers generally planted Vick's cotton under one brand name or another during the last decade of the antebellum period. Charles Allen, for example, planted Vick's Hundred Seed and Boyd's Prolific on his Warren County plantation in 1860. A few planters also supplemented their crops of Vick's improved Mexican cotton with smaller acreages of a totally different variety that Richard Abbey of Yazoo County had introduced from Lower California. Abbey's long-staple cotton, which he advertised vigorously under the trade name Mastodon Cotton, retained lint in the bolls through the winter, a property that made it possible to delay picking the Mastodon crop until the principal crop had been harvested.

20. Moore, *Agriculture*, 151–52; Vicksburg *Sentinel*, July 7, 1847.
21. Moore, *Agriculture*, 154–60; and "Cotton Breeding," 100–102.

A. W. Washburn, a planter and farm implement inventor of Yazoo County, was representative when he wrote in 1855: "My other variety is Mastodon, of which I plant a small portion of my crop every year for the late picking, and [I] do not pick a lock of it till I have picked every boll of the other kinds [of improved Petit Gulf cotton]. I then, generally in January, gather it without pains, getting good weights; pass it through a very common gin, and sell it in New Orleans for twenty five to fifty percent more than any other cotton." By supplementing his crop of Petit Gulf cotton with Mastodon, Washburn for several consecutive years was able to harvest a 400-pound bale to the acre and 10 bales to the hand on land that had been under cultivation without manure for twenty-five years.[22]

Most of the slaveowners of the state rejected Mastodon cotton, however, on the practical grounds that picking during January and February endangered the health of their slaves. They contended in letters to editors of local newspapers that working slaves in the fields during the cold rainy months was inhumane and that such practices should be condemned by public opinion. These writers and the majority of cotton growers were content to limit the size of their harvest to the crop that could be gathered before Christmas, the great agricultural harvest festival of antebellum Mississippi.

Some of the labor saved by mechanization of farming operations on plantations during the 1840s and 1850s was devoted to applying newly devised techniques of soil conservation. In earlier decades cotton growers had assumed that land would lose its fertility after ten to twenty years of cultivation in row crops. As they saw it, cotton growing was a continuous process of clearing woodlands, cultivating the fields for a limited period, and then abandoning exhausted tracts to pastures or rangelands. Writing in the *American Agriculturist* in 1846, Martin W. Phillips described the destructiveness of the system of farming then in vogue in Mississippi, as follows: Employing the "common careless mode of planting [cotton and corn], . . . [a planter] will make for five years good crops; the next five he will make ordinary [crops]; the next five still smaller [crops], until within less than twenty or twenty-five years he is forced to extraordinary exertions in working his land or to emigrate."[23]

22. Charles Allen Plantation Book, April 5, 11, and 17, 1860 (Mississippi Department of Archives and History); *Southern Cultivator*, XIII (1855), 340.
23. Quoted in *Southern Cultivator*, IV (1846), 134.

John L. Tindall of Monroe County was one of those who understood that destruction of the soil was caused by overcropping and erosion. In 1842 he wrote in the *Southern Planter:* "Our general mode of tillage is radically defective in two particulars. In the first place . . . our land is cultivated [only] in corn and cotton every year and soon exhausted. In the second place, most of us plow too shallow . . . the land is scratched about two inches deep, which makes about as much loose earth as the first heavy rain will wash off from all the rolling land."[24]

From the beginning of cotton culture in Mississippi, eroson of soil was recognized as a serious problem. At the turn of the nineteenth century James Hall noted that "the greatest inconvenience which attends the soil [in the vicinity of Natchez] is its loose, loamy nature which exposes it much to washing away, where the land is hilly or rolling." Thirty-five years later, Joseph Holt Ingraham wrote: "The rich loam which forms the upland soil of this state is of very slight depth—and after a few years is worn away by constant culture and the actions of winds and rain. . . . Every plough furrow becomes the bed of a rivulet after heavy rains . . . [and] the impalpable soil dissolves like ice under a summer's sun." In the old Natchez District, Ingraham saw thousands of acres of former cotton lands presenting "a wild scene of frightful precipices and yawning chasms which are increasing in depth and destructively enlarged after every rain." If the process was not checked, Ingraham warned, "the south-west portion of this state must become a waste, barren and wild." The same problem, differing only in degree, confronted planters and farmers in all parts of the state whenever they cultivated fields that were not level.[25]

According to Benjamin L. C. Wailes, a contemporary historian who interviewed a great many early settlers of the Natchez area, William Dunbar was the first Mississippian to begin the unending battle against erosion. Corresponding with President Thomas Jefferson, Dunbar learned that French peasants of the mountains laid out rows horizontally to minimize washing of the soil. After Jefferson suggested to Dunbar that the same system might be used advantageously in the vicinity of Natchez, the latter scientist and planter began to experiment with horizontal culture, or circling the rows, as the process came to be called, in the early years of the nineteenth century. At first Dunbar was ridiculed by neighbors who

24. *Southern Planter,* I (May and June 1842), 11–12.
25. Hall, *Mississippi Territory,* 555; [Ingraham], *South-West,* II, 86–88.

preferred the old system of plowing up and down the hillsides, but gradually all of the planters of the region were converted to Dunbar's system
of horizontal rows for cotton and corn. By the time of his death in 1811,
Dunbar was widely acclaimed for having introduced a valuable agricultural improvement into the region.[26]

Dunbar's system of horizontalizing was obviously useful to cotton
farmers and planters in two ways: it reduced loss of valuable topsoil by
erosion, and it made plowing of hillsides less strenuous for teams of
horses and mules. As a conservation measure, however, horizontalizing
on the Dunbar model was only partly effective. During the first three
decades of the nineteenth century, planters laid out their rows inexactly
by eye alone, as Dunbar had done. As a result, water would accumulate
in low places in an uneven row, eventually spilling over the top and beginning a gully. Even when rows were approximately level, the furrows
would eventually fill to overflowing, and the spillover opened gullies that
carried off valuable top soil.

During the 1830s and 1840s, changes made in Dunbar's system of
horizontalizing greatly improved the effectiveness of horizontal rows.
One of the most useful of these innovations was the development of
simple instruments employing plumb bobs or spirit levels, which permitted planters to lay out their guide rows quite accurately. More advanced
types of levels even allowed planters to lay out hillside rows with pre-
determined rates of incline. Such gently sloping furrows carried off rainwater very slowly and reduced the loss of topsoil to a minimum.[27]

An entry in the diary of Ferdinand L. Steel, the small farmer of Carroll County, suggests that horizontalizing with the aid of plumb bob–
equipped rafter levels was not confined entirely to the planter class. On
December 2, 1839, Steel wrote: "To prevent our wheat ground from
washing I made a rafter level . . . to ascertain the level of the land. The
plan I see recommended in a book written by a North Carolina farmer. I
laid out the lands from 6 to 8 feet apart, between every one of which I
made a deep furrow."[28]

Another important improvement made in the 1840s to Dunbar's original system of horizontalizing was the addition of drainage ditches to take

26. Wailes, *Report*, 153–54; Russell, *North America*, 268.
27. *Southern Cultivator*, VI (1848), 86, and VIII (1850), 66; *American Cotton
Planter and Soil of the South*, III (1859), 113.
28. Steel Diary.

off water from horizontal furrows and thus to prevent them from over-flowing. When planters first began to construct large ditches at the ends of rows, they learned that these ditches drained so rapidly as to be converted into very large gullies even more destructive of the field than the many small gullies common to unditched fields. During the 1840s and 1850s, Mississippi planters remedied this defect in the drainage system by several methods. In one, they laid out their drainage ditches with gentle inclines, cutting diagonally across hillsides instead of running vertically down the side of a plowed field. When laid out properly with accurate instruments, such as a rafter level with a plumb bob that T. C. Clark of Warren County described in the *Southern Cultivator*, or a "triangular spirit-level resting on a tripod for more convenient adjustment," which Benjamin L. C. Wailes mentioned in his *Report on the Agriculture and Geology of Mississippi*, drainage ditches carried off the water from the furrows without growing into crevasses. In another, planters lined drainage ditches running straight down hillsides with boards or timbers to prevent the rushing water from washing the sides and bottoms of the ditches. In yet a third method, they buried pipes constructed of lumber or bored-out logs at the end of rows to serve as underground drains. This latter drainage system was the most effective of the three, though by far the most expensive.[29]

R. D. Powell, a large planter of Lowndes county, was an advocate of hillside ditching. Before moving to the vicinity of Columbus in 1852, he had employed such a drainage system in Brunswick County, Virginia, for fifteen years. He had learned to eliminate gullies on his Virginia plantation, and he applied these lessons to his lands in Mississippi with similar results. Some of his friends adopted his system and were also enjoying some success in checking erosion. "Hillside ditches well run," Powell wrote in the *American Cotton Planter and Soil of the South* in November 1857, "will in a measure stop the spirit of emigration. The sunny South can be saved by them I know."[30]

Joseph Gray of Hinds County was widely credited with bringing the drainage system to the highest state of effectiveness achieved in Mississippi during the antebellum period. After years of experimenting on his plantation near Raymond, Gray concluded that horizontal rows combined with graded drainage ditches offered the best possible solution for

29. *Southern Cultivator*, X (1852), 229; Wailes, *Report*, 153–54.
30. *American Cotton Planter and Soil of the South*, I (1857), 325.

the problem of erosion. Determining that none of the common rafter levels in use in Hinds County at the time was accurate enough to lay out his ditches with the requisite precision, Gray developed an instrument of his own that had the fine adjustments of a surveyor's transit but lacked the telescope. In 1857 Gray applied for a patent for his "grade and horizontal level," and it was granted the following year. In July 1858 Gray gave a public demonstration at Raymond. Before an audience of prominent planters he laid out a row 180 yards long with a fall of three inches to twelve feet. To the surprise of the onlookers, the slope was found to be almost exact when checked with a transit. Convinced of the value of the instrument by this and other demonstrations, planters purchased a great many of the levels from Gray. After visiting Gray's plantation, G. D. Harmon wrote in the *Southern Cultivator* that Gray's system of horizontal culture could "save the South." "His place is quite rolling," Harmon wrote in amazement, "—been long under the plow, and not a wash did I see!"[31]

Throughout the life of the Cotton Kingdom, farmers and planters of Mississippi also continued a practice of the aboriginal agriculturists that was extremely useful in helping to preserve the fertility of the soil. This was the custom of the Indians of planting several varieties of cowpeas, plus pumpkins, squash, yams, and gourds, among their corn plants. The Indians had grown these vegetables in their fields of corn as a means of enlarging their food supply. Europeans, however, preferred to grow their vegetables, with the exception of cowpeas, in separate plots. Cowpeas they planted between the corn rows after the plants had matured, allowing the cowpea vines to cover the middles and climb the cornstalks. The whites gathered some of the ripe peas for food and for planting but left most of them in the field for hogs to eat. In the late fall and winter, cows, horses, and mules were turned into the fields to feed on the pea vines and cornstalks. In the early spring, farmers turned under the residue of the pea vines and cornstalks in preparation for spring planting. Because cowpeas were nitrogen-fixing legumes, they added fertility to the soil. Of equal importance, the cowpea vines covering the surface of the fields served to minimize the erosive effects of the heavy rains of later summer, fall, and winter.

Southwesterners, like agriculturists in the Southeast, observed at an early date that cotton yielded better when planted where corn and cow-

31. *Ibid.*, III (1859), 17–18; Raymond *Hinds County Gazette*, September 23, 1857; *Southern Cultivator*, XV (1857), 335, and XVI (1858), 321.

peas had grown the year before, and they accordingly developed a simple system of rotation under which two or three crops of cotton were followed by one of corn and cowpeas to take advantage of this effect. At first they incorrectly attributed the increase in fertility they obtained to corn, but by the 1840s and 1850s they realized that the cowpeas were responsible. By that time cowpeas were lauded in the agricultural periodicals as "the clover of the South," a title coined by Edmund Ruffin.[32]

Although Landon Carter of Virginia had advanced the theory before the American Revolution that cowpeas enhanced the fertility of soil by adding elements that plants had extracted from the air, Mississippians were generally unaware of this property of the cowpea before 1850. Even Martin W. Phillips did not know that cowpeas drew nitrogen from the atmosphere when he wrote about the virtues of cowpeas in the Jackson *Mississippian* in April 1849. "Pomona" of Lowndes County revealed a similar lack of knowledge when he wrote in the *Southern Cultivator* in June 1856: "It is the generally conceived opinion that pea crops gather from other sources, or have within themselves, the power of adding to their land . . . , but this doctrine is unsound." By 1860, however, virtually everyone acknowledged that cowpeas somehow improved farmland. Thomas Affleck, for example, reported to the commissioner of patents on November 15, 1849, that in Mississippi "the cow-pea is most commonly planted between the hills of corn after the second hoeing. . . . It is . . . as a fodder-crop and as an improver of the land that the plant is of greatest value to the South." A. G. Ailsworth of Madison County expressed the view of the majority of agriculturists when he wrote in the *Southwestern Farmer* on June 14, 1842: "I would here take occasion to say that every farmer ought to plant plenty of peas all over his cornfields; for aside from their value for stock, they are amply worth cultivating for their renovating qualities to the soil." Affleck estimated that cowpeas planted in cornfields yielded between ten and twenty bushels per acre when picked.[33]

Encouraged by their success in protecting their cornfields from erosion with crops of cowpeas, some farmers and planters began to extend similar protection to their cotton fields by sowing crops of winter ryegrass or Egyptian oats. In the *American Agriculturist*, for example, Phillips advised farmers in 1846 to prevent winter washing by sowing "in October,

32. *Southern Cultivator*, XIII (1855), 286, and XIV (1856), 183.
33. Gray, *Agriculture*, I, 199; Jackson *Mississippian*, April 20, 1849; *Southern Cultivator*, XIV (1856), 237; *Patent Office Report, 1849: Agriculture*, 158–59; *Southwestern Farmer*, I (July 1, 1842), 132.

Egyptian oats or rye on corn and cotton land, to be left on the ground until planting time." A great majority, however, depended upon horizontalizing alone to protect their cotton fields from washing.[34]

In addition to protecting their soils with drainage systems, Mississippians of the late antebellum period made systematic use of natural fertilizers. Beginning in the 1820s and 1830s, agriculturists throughout the state increased their yields of corn by burying surplus cottonseed alongside the corn plants and in the 1850s were using cottonseed to fertilize other crops as well. They also learned to plow under corn and cotton stalks instead of burning them, as had been the practice in the early period. In farming large acreages to the worker, as both planters and farmers did, virtually all of them rejected advice from eastern and northern agricultural experts to spread barnyard manures upon their fields. Martin W. Phillips explained the reasons in the *Southern Cultivator*. "We need not look to guano, lime, plaster, stable manures, peat, &c.," Phillips wrote, "[for] these are too costly." Another Mississippian commented that northerners "farm on a small scale and are forever dinning in our ears about the importance of barnyard and manure pens. But there is a vast difference between enriching a garden spot and a cotton plantation. Our want is the cheapest system of enriching and preserving large plantations—for it is outrageous humbuggery to talk of hauling manure over them." Planters, like Eli J. Capell, who experimented with guano, noted that this imported seabird manure increased yields of cotton and corn, but all concluded that the increases did not justify the cost of the fertilizer. Although chemical fertilizers became available in the late 1850s, Mississippians did not use them in significant amounts until after the Civil War.[35]

During the period between 1845 and 1860, many planters were so encouraged by the outcome of their soil conservation programs that they began to build permanent structures of brick to replace log or frame residences, slave quarters, ginhouses, and other plantation buildings. Wherever such developments took place, the occupants had given up the intention of emigrating further to the West and were planning to reside for the remainder of their lives on their present landholdings.

34. *Southern Cultivator*, IV (1846), 134.
35. *Ibid.*, II (1844), 45–46, VI (1848), 3–4, 117–18, XII (1854), 28; Herbert A. Kellar (ed.), *Solon Robinson: Pioneer and Agriculturist* (Indianapolis, 1936), I, 463; Moore, *Agriculture*, 59, 176; *American Cotton Planter*, II (1854), 367; New Orleans *Commercial Times*, June 20, 1846.

3   Horse-Drawn Implements

The development of a family of horse-drawn implements designed specifically for the cultivation of cotton and corn was a notable achievement that Mississippians shared with other antebellum southern agriculturists. In 1835, Thomas Spalding of Sapelo Island, Georgia, recalled that "the moment the cultivation of [short-staple upland] cotton moved into the interior country . . . the hand-hoe was exchanged for the plough," whereas long-staple Sea Island cotton continued to be exclusively cultivated by the hoe. From the beginning of commercial cultivation of cotton on the piedmont of Georgia and South Carolina as well as on the banks of the Mississippi River, land-rich labor-short farmers and planters tried to substitute "mule power for man power," as the phrase of the time expressed it.[1]

In both the Southeast and the Southwest, pioneer cotton growers planted cotton at the close of the eighteenth century, as they had formerly planted tobacco, on beds thrown up by crude turning plows. These plows, which were equipped with wrought iron points and wooden moldboards, were not far removed from the plow of the Middle Ages. Drawn laboriously by teams of horses or oxen, they penetrated the soil to depths of only two or three inches. Thus turn-of-the-century cotton producers were unable to break up the ground deeply enough to provide cotton plants with adequate room for growth unless the soil was heaped in beds. Unlike modern farmers, these agriculturists did not break up entire fields in preparation for planting. Instead they plowed up only enough ground to make their beds, leaving four- to six-foot spaces between the beds untouched by the plow.[2]

Horse-drawn rakes called harrows (triangular or rectangular frames of poles or timbers with teeth of wood or iron) prepared the soil for the seed-planting gangs by breaking up clods of earth and leveling the tops of beds. Originally field hands broadcast cottonseed over the loose earth on top of the beds and then covered them over lightly with hoes, but soon afterward it became the custom to sow the seed more sparingly in shallow trenches opened up with a small plow that lacked a moldboard. The

1. *Farmers' Register*, II (1835–1836), 361.
2. *Southern Planter*, I (January and February 1842), 10–11; *Southern Cultivator*, VI (1848), 130–31.

seeds in these trenches were covered by hoes or by wooden blocks dragged over the tops of the rows.[3]

When the young cotton plants reached a height of one or two inches, plow gangs used turning plows to open shallow drainage ditches at the base of the beds, throwing the dirt away from the rows. Agriculturists called this process "barring off" because the work was done originally with a bar-share turning plow. A week or two later, the plow gangs ran their turning plows through the ditches in reverse order, throwing the loose earth upon the sides of the beds. This procedure, called "molding," was intended to give the plants more earth to grow in while at the same time smothering young grass and weeds on the sides of the cotton rows.[4]

As the cotton plants grew larger, hoe gangs thinned the cotton once or twice with their heavy iron hoes, eventually leaving plants growing at intervals of about two to three feet. While this was being done, plowmen and plowwomen ran turning plows between the beds to loosen the soil and destroy grass, weeds, and vines. Planters, however, soon found that turning plows tended to cut the roots of plants if they were run close to the beds because they broke up the ground too deeply. To solve this problem, planters devised primitive implements to pulverize the surface of the earth without harming the plants. Triangular plow points (hammered from sheet iron by plantation blacksmiths) were fitted to light plow stocks at angles almost parallel to the beams so that the plowshares would barely penetrate the surface of the earth. These crude shovel plows opened the way for a new system of shallow culture of cotton that soon proved to be much more effective than the original relatively deep cultivation with turning plows.[5]

Martin W. Phillips of Hinds County, Mississippi, the Old South's ungrammatical authority on improved farm implements, wrote in 1842: "There is entirely too much reliance on the 'turning plough'; they will not do for a series of years as well as the shovel. . . . The shovel plough is

3. *Southern Planter*, I (January and February 1842), 14; *De Bow's Review*, II (1846), 132; John W. Monette, "The Cotton Crop," in [Ingraham], *South-West*, II, 281–83; *Patent Office Report (1849): Agriculture*, 313–16; Wailes, *Report*, 171.

4. Wailes, *Report*, 151; *Southern Cultivator*, VI (1848), 130–31.

5. Jackson *Southron*, February 20, 1841; Percy W. Bidwell and John I. Falconer, *History of Agriculture in the Northern United States, 1620–1860* (1925; rpr. New York, 1941), 303.

the cheapest, will perform well . . . [and] by making half shovels, twisted [shovels], [and shovels of] different sizes, a bed can be thrown up, you can bar off, etc." With regard to the latter implement, James M. Townes of Yalobusha County wrote: "When I first came to the state in 1836 . . . [the turning shovel] was more in use than any other turning plow."[6]

In the 1830s the shovels, half-shovels, and twisted shovels (used for molding cotton rows) were gradually superseded by plantation-made wrought iron sweeps. Sweeps were lightly constructed plows equipped with very small iron points to which sharpened strips of wrought iron were welded, forming a triangle when viewed from above. As time passed, the "wings" of the sweeps were lengthened until the plows would cut swaths three to four feet wide and thus could clean most of the space between the beds, or rows, at a single pass. In the 1850s, sweeps were further improved. In May 1852, for example, the ginmaker M. Donovan of Vicksburg was manufacturing "steel sweeps, that cannot be beat in the South." Whether made of wrought iron or steel, these "buzzard wing" plows were so cheap, so easily manufactured, and so effective that they continued in use in the lower South until he mid-twentieth century.[7]

A description of an Eagle sweep designed by Dr. William H. Eggleston during the mid-1830s is included in a journal of the Killona plantation. The wings of the plow point were made of wrought iron strips three inches wide, and they were twenty-one inches in length. The implement cut a strip two feet wide and could clean a middle between rows of cotton in two passes.[8]

During the 1830s and early 1840s, two other basic types of horse-drawn shallow-running implements were devised to work the space between rows of cotton and corn, one derived from the older shovel plow, the other from the harrow. The double-shovel plow was made by attaching a second plowpoint on an outrigger to a shovel plow so that the staggered plowshares covered twice as much ground as did those on the narrow single-shovel plow. This plow had been used in the East since 1820

6. Jackson *Southron*, March 10, 1842; *Southern Cultivator*, V (1847), 123; Daniel O. Williams to Sampson Williams, February 7, 1853, in Williams Papers.

7. *Southern Cultivator*, V (1847), 90; VII (1849), 118; XIV (1856), 53; and XVIII (1860), 9; Gray, *Agriculture*, II, 797; Swearingen, "Thirty Years," 202; Wailes, *Report*, 162; Vicksburg *Whig*, May 8, 1852; Jackson *Southron*, January 13 and April 7, 1842.

8. Killona Plantation Journal.

but was not introduced into Mississippi until the late 1830s. By adjusting the angle of the plowpoints with reference to the beam of the plow, double-shovels could be set to work at any desired depth, and the implements broke up strips of ground two to three feet wide. When run between rows of cotton and corn, double-shovel plows cultivated most of the furrow, leaving only the tops and sides of the rows to be chopped clean of grass and weeds by hoe gangs. These plows were widely used in Mississippi during the 1840s and 1850s and continued to be part of the equipment of farms until tractors replaced mules after World War II.[9]

Side harrows and cultivators composed a second family of implements that performed the same function as double-shovels with equal efficiency. Both were improved versions of the older harrow. These early harrows were dragged between the rows by teams of horses or mules. Lacking any provision for steering, such harrows often damaged cotton plants while breaking up clods in the furrows. Side harrows were refined, lighter versions of the older harrow to which plow handles had been attached for sake of control. In construction, a side harrow consisted of an ordinary plow stock to which a wooden crosspiece had been fastened at an angle of forty-five degrees. Iron teeth were driven through the crosspiece in the same plane as the beam of the plow and were bent so as to enter the ground at an angle. The implement resembled nothing as much as a horse-drawn garden rake. Being light and highly maneuverable, it was well designed for loosening the earth between the rows of growing crops. Because side harrows were cheap, easy to construct, and effective in operation, they became very popular in Mississippi.[10]

A cultivator was a slightly more sophisticated refinement of the original harrow. In the simplest form, cultivators were triangular wooden frameworks to which were fastened multiple small shallow-running plowpoints with wide shares. Plow handles attached to the framework permitted plowmen to steer these improved harrows as precisely as turning plows or double-shovels. In 1846, Martin W. Phillips commented that "with good cultivators or sweeps a hand can clean a 4 foot row in 2 or 3,

9. Bidwell and Falconer, *Agriculture in the Northern United States*, 304; Moore, *Agriculture*, 171–72; *Southern Cultivator*, V (1847), 90; Jackson *Southron*, February 20, 1841, January 13, 1842.

10. *Southern Cultivator*, IX (1851), 36, XVIII (1860), 98; Jackson *Southron*, January 13, 1842; *Southern Planter*, I (May and June 1842), 14; Moore, *Agriculture*, 171.

at the utmost, furrows." In improved later models of the cultivator, the frame was hinged at the apex of the triangle so that the implement could be adjusted to cover middles of varying widths. Adjustable cultivators of this sort could clean the entire space between rows of cotton or corn, leaving only the tops and sides of the rows to be chopped clean with hoes. These implements too continued to be used in single- or double-row versions until after World War II.[11]

In the two decades preceding the Civil War, farmers and planters universally adopted the scraper for removing grass, weeds, and vines from the sloping sides of rows of cotton or corn. The scraper, which apparently originated in Mississippi, was given extensive publicity by Martin W. Phillips. Because of his enthusiastically favorable reports of experiments conducted with the new implement, cotton growers from the Carolinas to Texas tried the tool, and most of them added it to their stock of farm implements. The device was so simple in design that a blacksmith using materials to be found in any shop could easily fabricate one from published descriptions. To make it, a blacksmith bolted a trapezoidal sheet of wrought iron or steel sharpened on two sides to an ordinary plow stock. When a horse or mule drew the scraper along the base of a row, the angled blade shaved grass and weeds from the sloping side of the row while also cutting grass and weeds in part of the middle, just as a razor removes whiskers from the face of a man. Cheap, simple, and effective, the scraper eliminated much laborious work previously done with a hoe. Testifying to the implement's efficiency, Daniel O. Williams wrote: "Scrapers lessen the hoe labor $\frac{1}{3}$." Francis T. Leak, who cultivated about 400 acres of cotton in Marshall County, wrote in 1845 after trying scrapers for a year: "Another season I must have 15 first rate scrapers made long enough and broad enough to shave the side of the ridge, and cover the middles." Because everyone who tried it found that the scraper lived up to its publicity, the implement became immensely popular with cotton growers throughout the South.[12]

11. *Southern Cultivator*, I (1843), 47, V (1847), 45, 90, 127, IX (1853), 166, XIV (1856), 53; *Southwestern Farmer*, I (April 15, 1842), 42; *De Bow's Review*, VI (1848), 131–34; Jackson *Mississippian*, August 23, 1859.

12. Daniel O. Williams to Sampson Williams, March [n.d.] 1853, in Williams Papers; Francis Terry Leak Diary (Typescript in the Southern Historical Collection, University of North Carolina, Chapel Hill), 57; *Southern Cultivator*, VII (1849), 53, VIII (1850), 98, IX (1851), 36; *American Cotton Planter*, III (1855), 244–45.

In similar fashion, the planting of corn and cotton was mechanized on advanced plantations with horse-drawn seed planters adapted from similar devices used in northern corn and wheat fields. One of the earliest of these devices was invented in 1842 by V. N. T. Moon of Madison County, Mississipppi, who wrote that his planter, drawn by one horse or mule, would open the ridge, drop the seed, and cover it at the same time. "Corn or peas, beans, &c.," he stated, "can be planted [with it] at any depth from one to six inches, and any distance apart from one to three feet." This machine, and others that performed the same functions, could plant cotton or corn much more swiftly and accurately than the three-man planting gangs of the 1830s.[13]

W. Seal of Marshall County, Mississippi, described his experience with one type of the new mechanical cotton seed planters in these words:

> I have in my possession some machines invented by James A. Steward, of Michelville, Tennessee, that performs its [sic] work admirably well. It opens the drill, drops the seed, and covers it more nearly and more regularly than it possibly can be done by hand. . . . I planted my entire crop with them last spring, also several of my neighbors. . . . It is truly a labor saving machine; it, with one mule and one hand, performs the labor of two mules and four or five hands, planting in the ordinary way.[14]

As might be expected, Martin W. Phillips tested and reported on all of the new planting machines that came to his attention. In April 1858, for example, he informed the readers of the *Southern Cultivator* that he had been "testing fully Randall['s] and Stewart's Cotton Planters, and can certainly, with a harrow to clean off [the] bed, and either of the Planters plant 8 to 12 acres per day." The price of the Randall machine, which was made in Georgia, was twelve to fifteen dollars, according to Phillips, and that of the Stewart planter, twenty-five dollars. "Another Planter," he wrote in 1859, "invented . . . by Dr. John Redhead of Mississippi, and shown at the Mississippi State Fair of 1858, is likely to take precedence, as it can be used for corn or cotton." In the fall of 1859, Phillips arranged for a public demonstration of the Empire Planter, which had been patented on August 31, 1859, by T. J. Bottoms, of Thomasville, Georgia.[15]

13. *Southwestern Farmer*, I (December 16, 1842), 116; *American Cotton Planter and Soil of the South*, II (1858), 115; III (1859), 56; *Scientific American*, I (1859), 56; *Southern Cultivator*, VIII (1850), 18, XIV (1856), 181, 298, XVI (1858), 226, XVIII (1860), 85.
14. *American Cotton Planter and Soil of the South*, II (1858), 115.
15. *Southern Cultivator*, XVI (1858), 187, XVIII (1860), 85; *American Cotton Planter and Soil of the South*, III (1859), 56.

Two other mechanical cottonseed planters invented by Mississippians received patents in 1856. One was invented by D. J. Beecher of Greenville, Mississippi, and the other by A. W. Washburn of Yazoo City. Beecher's machine may never have been offered for sale, but Washburn's was manufactured in Yazoo City and was highly advertised throughout the Cotton South. Based upon three rotating drums, Washburn's planter opened seed furrows to any desired depth, dropped the seed at any interval selected by the operator, and covered over the seed. Washburn offered to deliver his machines to any place in the southern states for the price of fifty dollars.[16]

The late antebellum seed-planting machines, both those with rotating drums and those with pyramidal hoppers and seed agitators, incorporated all of the principles upon which late nineteenth-century and early twentieth-century planters were based. Working quite effectively, mechanical seed planters would have been more widely adopted by Mississippians than they were, had planting been done at a time when plantation labor was in demand for other assignments. As there was little else to do of urgent nature during the spring, however, planters and farmers were generally content with their old planting gangs.

In line with the growing interest in farm mechanization during the 1850s, several Mississippi inventors brought out horse-drawn implements that performed more than one function at a time. The most successful of these devices was a combined cotton scraper and turning plow patented by George W. N. Yost, an overseer from Jefferson County. Another successful invention was the "hiller and scraper" patented by Dr. A. W. Washburn of Yazoo County, the inventor of the cotton planter. This precursor of postwar twin-row implements was a large, cumbersome machine mounted on four wheels and designed to be drawn by two horses or mules. A cotton scraper and a turning plow were mounted on each side of the body of the implement. As the hiller and scraper was drawn along with its wheels straddling a row, the scrapers simultaneously scraped both sides of the row, and the turning plows threw dirt on the sides of the row where the grass had just been removed. Similar double scrapers with minor modifications were devised by J. G. Winger, Patrick Sharkey, and a slave blacksmith belonging to Oscar J. E. Stuart of Holmesville, Mississippi. Planters particularly liked the implement invented by the slave,

16. Jackson *Mississippian*, April 16, 1856, and September 22, 1858; *Southern Cultivator*, XIV (1856), 181, 298.

and Stuart's plans to erect a factory for its manufacture were thwarted only by the Civil War. Former governor Albert G. Brown wrote Stuart that his slave's "double plow and scraper" went "a long way ahead" of both the common scraper and Yost's then-famous plow and scraper.[17]

Throughout the lifetime of the antebellum Cotton Kingdom, Mississippi agriculturists lagged far behind their northern counterparts in breaking up their land in preparation for planting, as northern visitors never tired of pointing out. On February 12, 1845, for example, Solon Robinson while on his first agricultural tour of the South saw in a single field in Yalobusha County "20 one horse, or one mule plows, skinning the surface of this light, loose, fine, sandy soil, and sending it on a voyage of discovery to the gulf of Mexico." A decade later, Edward R. Wells, a northern schoolteacher living in Vicksburg, echoed Robinson after visiting some Warren County plantations during March 1855. "In some lots," Wells wrote in his diary, "twenty Negroes with their roguish looking mules and *old time* ploughs were scratching the surface of the earth. The sight is ludicrous to one accustomed to the subsoiling of Seneca county [New York]."[18]

Mississippi cotton growers seldom denied that these northern critics of Mississippi plowing were right. Instead, virtually all of the agricultural reformers in the state urged farmers and planters to obtain plows that could break up the soil more deeply than those in common use. From Rankin County, for example, "Agriculture" wrote in the Jackson *Southron* on March 24, 1842: "Deep ploughing, then, is the only innovation I recommend in cultivation [of cotton]." Thomas Affleck wrote in the New Orleans *Commercial Times* from Adams County: "Important improvements have been annually made by our Northern neighbors by which time, labor and money are saved; yet we plod on with the same inefficient and expensive tools that were in use twenty years ago." John C. Jenkins scolded in the *Southern Planter:* "One of the most prominent faults in the

17. Moore, *Agriculture*, 184–89; *American Cotton Planter*, III (1855), 244–45; Raymond *Hinds County Gazette*, April 23, 1856; *Southern Cultivator*, XIV (1856), 298, XVI (1858), 226, XVII (1859), 199; Vicksburg *Whig*, October 14, 1856, March 10 and April 14, 1858; "Stuart Double Plow and Double Scraper," in the Broadside Collection, Mississippi Department of Archives and History; *Mississippi Planter and Mechanic*, I (1857), 305; Oscar J. E. Stuart to John A. Quitman, August 29, 1857, in John A. Quitman Papers, Mississippi Department of Archives and History.

18. Kellar (ed.), *Solon Robinson*, I, 449; Edward R. Wells Diary (Mississippi Department of Archives and History).

farming of our State is the shallow and superficial ploughing we are in the habit of giving our lands. A little loose earth is stirred on the surface about three or four inches deep . . . , leaving the tough clay subsoil entirely untouched." An editor of the *Southwestern Farmer* wrote: "To change our shallow and superficial manner of ploughing, and adopt a system of breaking up all our grounds, either annually or biennially . . . to at least double the depth we now run our plows, we consider the most important step toward improving our agriculture." [19]

There were reasons, of course, why agriculturists of the Old Southwest were slow in adopting northern plows. For one, northern factory-made plows were much more expensive than those fabricated in the local blacksmith shops. For another, soils in Mississippi were unlike northern soils, and plows designed for northern farms did not perform well in the cotton fields. Finally, as "Hebron" wrote in 1854 from Amite County: "Negroes are very careless, and it is extremely difficult to enforce the old adage, 'keep the tools in their proper place.' . . . [Besides] too many implements is an unnecessary outlay of capital." [20]

Despite these adverse influences, there was unmistakable progress in plowing throughout the agricultural regions of Mississippi. The greatest improvements were made during the 1850s. As a general rule, prosperous planters were more inclined to buy the expensive improved plows than their less wealthy fellow cotton growers. During the 1820s and 1830s, the original primitive turning plows with wrought iron points and wooden moldboards were gradually replaced with light and more efficient plows having both points and moldboards of wrought iron. Using good locally made wrought iron turning plows in 1842, for example, "I. of H." of Amite County was able to break up his land to a depth of "six inches, measured and no guesswork." "The loveliest sight to me," he wrote enthusiastically, "is a well-stocked plow running *in* the earth . . . like a water fowl sailing in the placid lake. . . . Why the plow does not command more love, I know not!" [21]

19. Jackson *Southron,* March 24, 1842; *Southern Cultivator,* IV (1846), 39; *Southwestern Farmer,* I (April 29, 1842), 28.

20. Kellar (ed.), *Solon Robinson,* II, 127; *Southern Cultivator,* XII (1854), 337–38.

21. *Mississippi Free Trader and Natchez Gazette,* January 24 and February 2, 1837; *Natchez,* February 20, 1830, and January 22, 1831; Raymond *Times,* January 12, 1838, and May 8, 1840; Vicksburg *Advocate and Register,* February 9, 1832; Vicksburg *Register,* January 4, 1838; Jackson *Southron,* April 7, 1842.

The shift to wrought iron farming implements is demonstrated by Francis T. Leak. While making plans for the coming year, Leak wrote in his diary during 1845: "We should have a full set of scrapers, a full set [of] bull tongues or scooters, a full set [of] turning ploughs, & a full set [of] large shovels [plows] & perhaps some iron tooth harrows and some Eagles [sweeps]." He had not yet adopted cultivators or double-shovels.[22]

In the 1840s the locally made wrought iron turning and breaking plows were challenged by cast iron plows fabricated in northern factories. These plows were sharpened at the factory and were case hardened so that they were very resistant to wear. Whereas wrought iron breaking and turning plows required frequent sharpening by blacksmiths, the case-hardened cast iron shares were never sharpened. When the point of such a plow became dull or was broken, a new point was merely bolted in its place. These plows were customarily sold with a supply of replacement plow points. Martin W. Phillips endorsed these cast iron plows and maintained that their higher cost was offset by the savings in lessened work for the blacksmith.[23]

In May 1856, Daniel O. Williams informed his son that he had belatedly made "a great discovery in plows. . . . It is a cast plow made in Louisville, [Kentucky], and [it] does not cost as much as the iron that it takes to make a [wrought iron] plow, and there is never any smiths work to do on it. I have abandoned all together the old Deer Creek & Hinds county plow, finding the Avery cast plow better."[24]

The transition first from wrought iron to cast iron and then to steel plows was described in 1848 by James M. Townes of Yalobusha County. Townes praised a wrought iron turning plow manufactured by local blacksmiths, who gave special care to the shaping of the moldboard. "They . . . turn our loose, black soil . . . perfectly and always keep bright . . . [but] It is best to have them laid with steel. . . . I think it best to have a set of cast [iron] plows to prepare the land for a crop, and a set of these to cultivate it." Townes was obviously correct in his analysis, for in 1856 the firm of William McCutchen & Co. of Vicksburg was carrying in stock sixty factory-made Hall & Speers cast plows that were "all

22. Leak Diary, II, 33.
23. Vicksburg *Sentinel*, January 4, 1845, and April 26, 1848; *Patent Office Report, 1848*, p. 509; *Southern Cultivator*, V (1847), 90, 153.
24. Daniel O. Williams to Sampson Williams, May 17, 1856, in Williams Papers.

wrought Iron laid with Steel," with a supply of extra points to fit them. Martin W. Phillips reported in 1848 that he was using both the Nourse, Ruggles & Mason turning plows and the Prouty & Mears turning plows, with cast iron chilled shares and "steel point self-sharpeners." [25]

Before the cast iron plows had won a secure place for themselves in Mississippi agriculture, vastly superior cast steel plows were introduced to cotton growers with much fanfare. As early as 1850, Bruner, Printz & Bruner of Vicksburg announced that they had received "100 of those celebrated *STEEL* Ploughs manufactured by Deere, Tate & Gould." Six years later Smith & Tharp of the same city began selling "Binkley's [*sic*] celebrated cast-steel plows." Phillips, of course, was not silent on the subject of steel plows. In 1855 he wrote to the editor of the *Southern Cultivator* that he had tested approximately fifty makes of plows, including the original steel Peacock plow and copies of that design manufactured by Prouty & Mears; Norse, Ruggles & Mason; and Hall. Although he had successfully employed two-horse Peacock plows on his plantation for fourteen years, he had concluded that a new steel plow manufactured by Thomas E. C. Brinley of Sampsonville, Kentucky, was superior to all other plows that he had tried because the Brinley plow's polished steel moldboard scoured clean in all types of soil. He advised the readers of the *Cultivator* that Brinley plows were well worth the eight dollars charged for a one-horse plow and twelve dollars for the two-horse model. [26]

Two years later, Phillips explained that there was a soil in Mississippi "black as coal when moist, much has grit in it, yet so adhesive that it sticks to iron, whether cast or wrought." The Brinley steel plow was "suited to this land," according to the sage of Log Hall. Furthermore, a Brinley plow that he had used for three years had been sharpened successfully by "a common negro [black]smith." [27]

During February 1858, F. A. Metcalf began to experiment with steel turning plows on Newstead plantation, located on Deer Creek in Washington County. On the eighteenth he recorded in his plantation journal: "Tried my steel plows this afternoon. They worked well." On March 3,

25. *Southern Cultivator*, V (1847), 43, VI (1848), 51, 85; Vicksburg *Whig*, February 27, 1856; Bidwell and Falconer, *Agriculture in the Northern United States*, 282.
26. Vicksburg *Whig*, December 14, 1850, and January 26, 1856; *Southern Cultivator*, XIV (1856), 53.
27. *Southern Cultivator*, XV (1857), 183.

Metcalf wrote: "Broke one of my new steel plows. It is quite a loss as it cannot be repaired very easily." The following day he added: "Broke another of my steel plows. Everything seems to break on my land!" Despite these accidents Metcalf remained committed to the improved plows. On June 11, he "borrowed six or eight steel mould board plows from Courtney—they do admirable work." At the time he was "running five sweeps in lieu of scrapers in the Boyd cotton. . . . they do excellent work." [28]

On March 31, 1859, planters living in the vicinity of Crystal Springs, Mississippi, conducted tests of several factory-made turning and breaking plows available for sale in Natchez and Vicksburg. J. W. Felt, a nurseryman on whose land the demonstrations took place, reported that the plows tested were two Brinley steel plows, one Calhoun & Atkinson No. 1, an iron plow with a steel point, and a Hall & Spere plow made entirely of iron. "The plows," he wrote, "were in good order, having been sufficiently used to polish their mould-boards." The steel Brinley breaking plow cut a furrow nine inches deep and ten inches wide; the Calhoun plow, one six inches deep by nine inches wide; and the Hall & Spere plow, one seven inches deep by seven and one-half inches wide. According to Felt, the Brinley breaking plow performed "almost double the work of the [iron] Hall & Spere [plow] does, and with nearly one-half the draft." [29]

The reactions of planters to the steel Brinley turning plow were so positive that Phillips obtained the rights to manufacture the implement and in 1859 erected a steam-powered factory in Jackson for production. In order to ensure that the plows made in Jackson were equal in quality to those manufactured in Kentucky, Phillips employed Thomas E. C. Brinley, the inventor, to superintend the manufacturing establishment. The products of the Phillips' Southern Implement Factory sold well in Mississippi, and the enterprise prospered until 1863, when its building was put to the torch by a Federal army under the command of General U. S. Grant. [30]

In a period when planting and cultivating of cotton and corn crops were successfully mechanized with horse-drawn implements, it is not

28. Newstead Plantation Records (Southern Historical Collection, University of North Carolina, Chapel Hill).

29. Natchez *Courier*, April 2, 1857; *Southern Cultivator*, XVII (1859), 166–67.

30. *Southern Cultivator*, XVII (1859), 39, 170–71, XVIII (1860), 134, 259; Jackson *Mississippian*, July 27, 1858; *American Cotton Planter and Soil of the South*, III (1859), 270.

surprising that attempts were made to invent machines with which to harvest the principal crop. In Mississippi at least one inventor devised a machine for the purpose. According to the editor of the Panola *Picayune,* A. H. Burdine, a planter of that county, constructed a device "that will relieve human fingers from the employment of picking cotton from the stalk." Apparently Burdine's device was a manually operated stripper, somewhat like the cradle used for harvesting grain, that combed cotton fiber and bolls when it was passed through a plant. As nothing further was heard of the Burdine cotton stripper, it may be assumed that it was not very effective in harvesting cotton. Quite possibly it was impractical because it gathered too much trash with the cotton.[31]

In any event an Alabama planter invented a horse-powered stationary machine called the "cotton leaf cleaner and boll picker," which was designed to clean trashy cotton before it went to the gin. According to the Nashville *Farmer's Banner,* "cotton bolls . . . [could] be gathered with as little care as you would corn, and taken to the machine [set up] either in the field or under cover. . . . Then the machine and the mules take out the bolls, leaf, dirt and everything, and the cotton comes through the gin as middling to good middling in quantity." Like the stripper, the cleaner did not prove successful, and no effective machines were developed for harvesting cotton until very late in the century.[32]

During the 1840s and 1850s, farmers without slaves as well as farmers owning three to five families of slaves followed the lead of planters in mechanizing their farm operations insofar as their financial resources would permit. "A Sunburnt Farmer" of Pontotoc County spoke for many of his less literate fellows when he wrote that he employed horse-drawn turning plows, sweeps, and harrows in cultivating his land. "I make it a rule," he wrote, "never to use the hoe when I can get around it—my word is plow, plow!" Ferdinand L. Steel and his brother, who were cultivating a small farm in Pontotoc County between 1838 and 1845 with only their own labor, did not own a cotton gin, but they utilized horse-drawn turning plows, shovel plows, and harrows to minimize their labor with hoes. They also made a horse-drawn rake to help them in gathering small grain after it had been cut.[33]

31. Vicksburg *Whig,* June 16, 1853; Raymond *Hinds County Gazette,* April 13, 1853; Panola *Picayune,* May 2, 1853.
32. Quoted in *De Bow's Review,* XIX (1855), 116.
33. Steel Diary.

Another Mississippi small farmer wrote in the *Southern Cultivator* during 1856: "I raise my own meat, wool, mules, flour, and, in short everything for the use of my small farm, and generally sell enough to pay expenses of the same, without taking any of the proceeds of the cotton crop. My land is all rolling, well circled, and with hillside ditches when necessary." He broke up his fields first with two-horse turning plows and then followed them with subsoil plows, a practice followed only by more progressive planters. Because of his deep plowing, rotation of crops, and land conservation methods his farm was improving rather than wearing out. As a result of his mechanization, he was able to cultivate "from 9 to 10 acres of cotton, and from 7 to 10 acres of corn to the hand as well as crops of wheat, rye and oats." In 1855 he harvested 1,500 pounds of seed cotton and six barrels of corn to the hand, a record of which any planter would have been proud.[34]

Agricultural workers of both races undoubtedly welcomed the advent of the steel hoe in the late 1840s as enthusiastically as they did horse-drawn farm implements, for it was much lighter than the old wrought iron hoe and held its edge much longer. When R. L. Allen, the northern implement manufacturer, visited Martin W. Phillips in 1847 during a tour of the South, that advocate of improved farm implements suggested to Allen that he manufacture a steel hoe for the South on a pattern that Phillips had devised. In 1856 Phillips commented: "*Of Hoes*, the Scovel Hoe [made on the Allen plan], on sale by Geo. W. Sizer, New Orleans, and Agricultural Warehouses generally, I have used since the first was brought out, and some of them now in use. . . . They are not as large as the Carolina hoe. Nine inches is large enough; eight inches [is] generally preferable." Daniel O. Williams suggested in 1858 that his son "order 2 or 4 dozen *half polished* cotton hoes from Bruff Brothers & Seaver, New York. No. 1 woman's hoe; No. 2 light man's hoe, $5.00 per dozen."[35]

Obviously farmers who used the hoe in their fields of cotton and corn were even more appreciative of the virtues of mechanization than planters who did not work in the fields themselves. It was not without significance that a mule or horse was used to every twenty to thirty acres under cultivation in counties dominated by small farmers as well as in counties where plantations were the most common agricultural units.[36]

34. *Southern Cultivator*, XIV (1856), 111–12.
35. Kellar (ed.), *Solon Robinson*, II, 127n; *Southern Cultivator*, XIV (1856), 52–53; Daniel O. Williams to Sampson Williams [n.d.], in Williams Papers.
36. *Eighth Census, 1860: Agriculture*, 84–87.

Table 1. Draft Animals in Mississippi, 1850–1860

Item	1850	1860
Horses	115,460	117,571
Mules and asses	54,547	110,723
Oxen	83,485	105,603
Acres under cultivation	3,444,358	5,065,755
Cultivated acres per horse or mule	20	22
Cultivated acres per team of oxen	82	94

SOURCES: *Seventh Census, 1850*, p. 456; *Eighth Census, 1860: Agriculture*, 84.

As Table 1 indicates, in Mississippi during the 1840s and 1850s there was a trend toward the use of greater numbers of mules, especially in areas where large plantations predominated. In 1841, Martin W. Phillips wrote in the Jackson *Southron:* "I . . . have used geldings, mares, mules and oxen for ploughing and waggoning; to the two latter I give a decided preference where their management is left to horse-lots and negroes." Many other planters had also come to consider mules superior to horses for several of the following reasons. The working life of mules was eighteen years as compared with twelve for horses. In the warm climate of Mississippi, mules were hardier and more resistant to disease than were horses, and they could be fed coarser fare than could horses. On the debit side of the ledger, mules cost more than plow horses. In 1849, for example, Mississippi-raised plow horses cost about $50 each; plow horses brought from Tennessee and Kentucky in droves cost $100; mules cost from $120 to $150. Saddle horses were sold for $200 to $275.[37]

During this period planters also came to prefer the largest size of mules despite the greater initial cost. In 1857, for example, Daniel O. Williams praised his son's recent purchase of several mules for use on their Issaquena County plantation. "Although you got your mules on reasonable terms (except the small one)," he wrote, "and they are of the average size of the old ones, I think it would have been better economy to have paid $200 a piece for the largest size mules, as they could pull so

37. Jackson *Southron*, February 20, 1841; Gray, *Agriculture*, II, 852; *Patent Office Report, 1849: Agriculture*, 141, 160–61; *Southern Cultivator*, V (1847), 61, VII (1849), 50.

much larger plows." When estimating the yearly expenses for his Deer Creek plantation, the elder Williams allowed for the purchase of two mules.[38]

Unlike other planters, Williams chose teams of oxen rather than mules for breaking up land in the spring in preparation for planting. As a subscriber to the agricultural periodicals and an advocate of improved agricultural implements, Williams used deep-running subsoil plows that placed a heavy strain on teams to break up his land. In 1854, he wrote from his home plantation near Clinton in Hinds County to his son who was managing their plantation on Deer Creek in Issaquena County: "I am now plowing oxen. I find they will do as much plowing as mules, & it saves the mule team for cultivating. . . . You might start 3 or 4 ox plows to advantage. You ought to keep at least 20 oxen."[39]

Farmers and less affluent small planters generally preferred to use plow horses rather than mules because of the lesser initial cost, and they probably made more extensive use of oxen than planters did. The well-known agricultural writer Thomas Affleck reported in 1849 to the U.S. commissioner of patents that agriculturists were breeding horses of Spanish origin common to southern Mississippi, called "pine tackeys," to strong, well-bred mares to produce serviceable plow horses that were almost as durable as mules. Pine tackeys of twelve to fourteen hands in height cost from $20 to $50, horses from $50 to $100. Because workhorses were cheaper than mules, farmers could afford to maintain larger herds of them, and in several counties where farmers greatly outnumbered planters they obviously did so. In Tishomingo, a county in the northeastern corner of the state with few slaves, for example, there was a horse for every seventeen acres in cultivation, an exceptionally high proportion of draft animals to cultivated acreage.[40]

Teams of oxen were used on both farms and plantations throughout the antebellum period to perform labor considered too heavy for horses and mules. John C. Jenkins of Adams County wrote in *De Bow's Review* in 1854: "The ox . . . over the entire extent of the planting States is universally used for draught in all the hauling done upon our plantations in

38. Daniel O. Williams to Sampson Williams, July 18, 1856, and May 16, 1857, in Williams Papers.

39. *Ibid.*, April 6, 1854, in Williams Papers.

40. *Patent Office Report, 1849: Agriculture*, 160–61; *Eighth Census, 1860: Agriculture*, 84.

taking our crops to ports for shipment, and in bringing from the boggy swamps the millions . . . of cords of wood annually sold to our river steamers." According to Affleck, "a large number are annually consumed in the teams [for cotton wagons] from the [poor] state of the roads during the hauling season, the carelessness of planters and overseers, and the cruelty and rascality of negroes who often drive the beasts for days with scarcely any feed, reserving what was given them for use on the road to sell for their own benefit." Most of these steers were "large brick-colored or brown oxen with . . . singularly twisted ram-like horns." Three-year-old unbroken steers sold at prices ranging from six dollars to fifteen, and well-trained teams brought from thirty-five to sixty dollars. The principal tasks assigned to oxen were the pulling of large wagons and log carts. On one occasion during February 1858, the road was so muddy that F. A. Metcalf had to employ eight yoke of oxen and three drivers to drag a cotton wagon loaded with only four bales of cotton from his plantation on Deer Creek in Washington County to a river landing. When the roads were dry, four yoke of oxen could pull a wagon loaded with eight bales of cotton. These draft oxen were fed corn, shucks, crabgrass hay, and sometimes peavine hay while working. At other times they grazed like other cattle in the woods.[41]

The increased usage of draft animals characteristic of Mississippi agriculture during the last thirty years of the antebellum period was not without cost to farmers and planters. In addition to the capital they invested in mules, horses, and oxen, they also had to make heavy expenditures of valuable labor to provide animal feed. They had to plant larger acreages of corn than would have been necessary for the human population of farms and plantations alone, of course, and they had to put up enormous quantities of corn fodder to be used both during the working season and in the winter, when stock could not find enough food in the fields to sustain them.

When the ears had formed on the nearly mature corn plants, workers went into the cornfield to pull leaves for fodder. This work was regarded as especially unpleasant, as it was performed in periods of high temperatures and humidity, and slaveowners believed that fodder pulling imper-

41. *De Bow's Review*, XVII (1854), 627–28; *Patent Office Report, 1849: Agriculture*, 161, and *Patent Office Report, 1850: Agriculture*, 187–88; Newstead Plantation Records, I, February 19, 1858.

iled the health of slaves more than any other regular summer labor. During a day's work, a field hand gathered from 300 to 400 pounds of corn blades, as the leaves were called. These leaves were tied in bundles weighing 7 or 8 pounds and were left in the sun to dry. Afterward the bundles were either stacked in cocks or placed under some kind of shelter to be preserved until winter. On many plantations all of the leaves of the corn plants were harvested before the ears were gathered.[42]

When the ears of corn were harvested, the shucks were saved and dried for stock feed. Many agriculturists of the period believed that dry shucks were even more nutritious for horses, mules, and oxen than fodder. Because the dry shucks were very coarse, animals ate them reluctantly, and many planters used some kind of horse-powered machine to shred the shucks before feeding them to draft animals. Most commonly, working stock was fed a mixture of fodder or shucks and grain, usually dried corn, three times each day, but oats were frequently substituted for the corn.[43]

Cowpeas of several varieties originally obtained from the Indians were universally planted in the cornfields to provide food for all kinds of livestock. Only small quantities of the peas were harvested for replanting and for human consumption, but the luxuriant vines were a source of livestock food second in importance only to corn. Some of the vines were cut with the hoe and dried in the sun before being stacked in the field or placed in storage buildings. This hay was regarded as superior to fodder for winter stock feed, but comparatively little was harvested because of the heavy labor involved at a time when all hands were needed for picking cotton. Most of the peavines raised in Mississippi were therefore used by turning horses, mules, cattle, hogs, and sheep into the peafields during the late fall and early winter. The residue of the vines not consumed by the animals was turned under when the land was broken up for planting.[44]

---

42. Gray, *Agriculture*, II, 814–15; *Patent Office Report, 1849: Agriculture*, 142, 149–52, 154, and *Patent Office Report, 1850: Agriculture*, 187–88; *Southern Cultivator*, IV (1846), 71, XVIII (1860), 98.

43. Gray, *Agriculture*, II, 814–15.

44. *American Cotton Planter and Soil of the South*, III (1859), 88; *Patent Office Report, 1849: Agriculture*, 149–51, 158–59, and *Patent Office Report, 1850: Agriculture*, 257–64; *Southern Cultivator*, IV (1846), 78–79, V (1847), 90, 142, VI (1848), 35–36, 150, IX (1851), 116; *Southwestern Farmer*, I (June 10, 1842), 109, (July 1, 1842), 132, (September 2, 1842), 205, (December 16, 1842), 116; Wailes, *Report*, 194–96.

Increasingly during the 1840s and 1850s, large fields of oats were raised on farms and plantations for stock feed. No excessive amount of labor was required in planting, cultivation, and harvesting, and the oat crop usually produced well. Both the dried seed and stalks were harvested for winter feed, and animals were also turned into unharvested oat fields to graze. Oats, however, were believed to be much less nutritious for horses and mules than corn, the preferred grain.[45]

Thus it is obvious that the farms and plantations of antebellum Mississippi produced significant quantities of stock feed for home consumption that were not taken into account by the federal censuses. In addition to the grain that was harvested and reported, the cornfields of the state yielded uncounted thousands of tons of leaves and shucks that were far from insignificant in value. These same fields produced vast quantities of unharvested pea vines that were consumed by livestock. Thus the thirty-five bushels of corn that the average acre produced in the late prewar period was only a part of its useful production. Martin W. Phillips maintained with some bitterness that Mississippians never received credit for the enormous crops of animal feed that they laid aside each year, and the surviving evidence suggests that he was correct.

Strangely enough, the growing preference of planters for mules as draft animals did not extend to breeding. "We are indebted to Kentucky and the other more northern States for our supplies of horses and mules. Great droves are brought down and sold among us every year," D. C. Graham from Franklin County informed the U.S. Patent Office in December 1850. From Noxubee County "thousands and tens of thousands of dollars are annually paid to Tennessee, Kentucky, Ohio, Missouri, Indiana and other States for horses, mules, bacon, pork, &c," a correspondent of the Macon *Mississippi Patriot* complained in 1854. Similarly, "Franco" asked in the Panola *Lynx:* "Is not Mississippi as suited to the raising of horses, mules, sheep and hogs . . . as Tennessee? And yet these things we buy of Tennessee. We pour into her lap and that of other states at least one half the profits of our productive energies."[46]

45. Frederick L. Olmsted, *A Journey in the Back Country* (New York, 1860), 176; *Patent Office Report, 1849: Agriculture,* 153; *Southern Cultivator,* IV (1846), 39, XIII (1855), 276; *Southwestern Farmer,* I (April 29, 1842), 58; Wailes, *Report,* 187; Vicksburg *Whig,* March 31, 1859.

46. *Patent Office Report, 1850: Agriculture,* 187–88; Jackson *Mississippian,* April 28, 1854; Panola *Lynx,* January 18, 1845.

Beginning in the 1830s, many writers urged Mississippians to raise mules instead of importing them at high prices. "Joseph," of Egypt farm on the Big Black River in Hinds County commented in 1839: "Mules are of such value that planters will take every care to get them. . . . [They] will certainly find that to raise them is preferable to buying." At that time, Joseph's neighbor Martin W. Phillips was exhibiting a three-year-old jack imported from Malta that stood fifteen hands high. A few other jacks were entered in county fairs during the 1840s, but their numbers remained very small. In 1841, Phillips knew of only five in Mississippi. The number increased slowly during the next two decades, but the total was never large. In 1855, C. G. S. Clifton wrote from Greene County: "The animals affording most profit to the stock raiser in this vicinity are horses and mules, other animals being less profitable than cotton. They can be raised to three years old at an expense of $35, and will sell from $75 to $100 each." In 1856, R. Cordill of Hinds County was one of the few breeders of asses and mules in the cotton-producing section of the state. In March of that year he offered for sale at auction "eight Jennetts from two to six years old, four fullbred Maltese and Black Hawk [asses], and a few half Maltese and Black Hawk." In October 1859, J. J. Williams of the state agricultural bureau attended a fair at Summit in Pike County and reported: "The display of stock, especially horses, was highly creditable. . . . [There were] enough young mules and horses, with jacks and stallions to convince us that in a few years Pike would be independent of Tennessee and Kentucky for horse and mule power." Elsewhere a small number of farmers were also raising a few mules for their own use. The vast majority of Mississippi agriculturists, however, never showed interest in breeding either plow horses or mules.[47]

Despite their inexplicable failure to raise their own mules, Mississippi planters succeeded in mechanizing the process of planting and cultivating their crops of cotton and corn during the 1840s and 1850s to a point as high as any they reached during the nineteenth century. The next significant advance in mechanization, the replacement of horses and mules with gasoline-powered tractors, was not to be achieved until the interval between the two world wars.

47. Raymond *Times*, August 9, 1839; Jackson *Southron*, February 20, 1841, and May 31, 1843; Natchez *Free Trader*, June 14, 1843; *Patent Office Report, 1855: Agriculture*, 40; Vicksburg *Whig*, March 19, 1856; Jackson *Mississippian*, October 18, 1859; *Southern Cultivator*, XIV (1856), 111–12.

4 Late Antebellum Machinery

Even as planters of the Old Southwest were moving beyond their counterparts in the older cotton-producing states of the Southeast in mechanization of their farming operations during the 1840s and 1850s, so were they ahead in adopting improved machinery. Richard Abbey of Yazoo County, who had become famous for introducing Mastodon cotton, wrote in 1849 after making his first visit to Georgia and South Carolina: "I was *perfectly astonished* to see the poor little trifling gins—the little, worthless gin-houses, and the worse than 'no account' [cotton] presses in common use." In Mississippi, cotton gins and cotton presses had been steadily improved since the turn of the century. In about 1830, John W. Monette, the historian of the Mississippi Valley, wrote of gins in the old Natchez District, for example: "A good gin-stand, with sixty to sixty-five saws, running from daybreak in the morning until eight or nine o'clock [at night], will gin out as much [lint] as will make three or four bales." Although the basic principles of the gins and presses remained the same from 1800 to 1860, these mechanical devices increased in size and speed of operation as manufacturers employed better materials and improved metalworking machinery in their construction.[1]

By the mid-nineteenth century the gins commonly employed in Mississippi ranged in size from forty to eighty saws, with sixty-saw gins being the most common. Benjamin L. C. Wailes wrote that typical gin stands of the period were about six feet wide. In order to reduce friction, their two rotating horizontal cylinders turned on iron axles mounted in composition metal boxes. Their gin saws were made of two pieces of cast steel and were fastened to the cylinders at intervals of one inch. These gins produced from one and one-half bales to twelve bales of cleaned cotton per day, depending upon size, make, and speed of operation. Prices of the gins varied according to the number of saws, with three to four dollars per saw being a common charge by manufacturers.[2]

During the 1850s, planters were increasingly tending to install gin stands of the largest size in their ginhouses. Sampson Williams, for ex-

1. *Southern Cultivator*, VII (1849), 169; Monette, "The Cotton Crop," in [Ingraham], *South-West*, 289.
2. Wailes, *Report*, 171.

ample, used two eighty-saw gins manufactured in Bridgewater, Massachusetts, to clean his annual cotton crop of about 300 bales, produced on his Deer Creek plantation in Issaquena County. One was the Bates, Hyde & Company Eagle gin stand; the other was a E. Carver & Co. "improved" cotton gin. Daniel O. Williams, his father, wrote to Sampson in 1857: "I like Carvers *Improved Stand* (his last make) better than any gin I ever saw. If you get one be certain to get an 80 saw gin."[3]

G. D. Harmon, the famous overseer, writing from Madison Parish, Louisiana, during 1860 commented that the steam-powered ginhouse on Compromise Place contained four eighty-saw gins. Two were Eagle gins manufactured by Bates, Hyde & Company of Bridgewater, Massachusetts; the other two were Gullett gins, invented by Benjamin D. Gullett of Aberdeen, Mississippi, and manufactured by Gunnison, Chapman & Company of New Orleans, the only gin manufacturer located in the Crescent City. Gullett, Gladney & Company of Aberdeen, Mississippi, also manufactured the Gullett gin in a small factory located in that town.[4]

In August 1860, Charles Allen of Warren County ordered a gin stand from E. Carver of Bridgewater, Massachusetts, through the mercantile firm of Cobb, Manlon & Company of Vicksburg. Allen's specifications for this gin were: "75 saws, 9½ inch cylinder [of] wood, with saws added, 13 inches [in overall diameter]—saws 1¾ in. wide [distance between saws]—11 teeth to [the] inch." This gin was for Nanechehaw plantation, where Allen cultivated 794 acres with sixty field hands, producing a cotton crop of 375 bales of cotton and 6,400 bushels of corn.[5]

During the late antebellum period, cotton gins used in Mississippi were either constructed to special order by local gin makers or purchased from cotton gin factories through dealers in Vicksburg, Natchez, Memphis, Columbus, Mobile, or New Orleans. The two factories in Bridgewater, Massachusetts, mentioned above were perhaps the largest cotton gin factories in the United States. According to W. K. Orr of Orrville, Alabama, they each built approximately 1,000 gins annually and employed work forces of about sixty mechanics. These establishments, however, were rivaled by Daniel Pratt's factory at Prattville, Alabama, by

3. Daniel O. Williams to Sampson Williams, May 16, 1857, in Williams Papers.
4. *Southern Cultivator*, XVIII (1860), 343; New Orleans *Delta*, May 9, 1860.
5. Charles Allen Plantation Book.

Samuel Griswold's factory at Griswoldville, Georgia, and for a time by E. T. Taylor & Company's factory at Columbus, Georgia.[6]

Daniel Pratt's gin factory, located fourteen miles from Montgomery, Alabama, on Autauga Creek, was founded in 1833. Pratt greatly enlarged his successful gin-making operations in 1854 by erecting a new three-story building of brick equipped to manufacture a thousand gins a year. The factory in 1858 was producing "between eight and nine hundred gins that will average fifty-five saws to the stand. It supplies principally Mississippi, Louisiana and Texas with Gins." In January 1859, Pratt stated that he had sold approximately 13,000 stands during his twenty-eight-year career. He maintained an agency in New Orleans through which his gins were sold to customers in the lower Mississippi Valley and in the Southwest. In Vicksburg, L. C. Moore & Company was agent for Pratt gins. Samuel Griswold's Cotton Gin Factory near Macon, Georgia, which had been partly owned by Pratt at one time, was also a large southern manufacturing establishment. Powered with steam, Griswold's factory turned out nearly 900 gins yearly, most of which were sold to cotton growers of the Southeast. At its peak of production in 1854, the factory of E. T. Taylor & Company of Columbus, Georgia, a third large southern gin-manufacturing establishment, produced 1,000 gins while possessing the theoretical capacity of making 1,500 gins. At that time Taylor's work force numbered fifty persons. Unlike the other two factories, however, the Taylor factory did not survive the panic of 1857. At the close of the antebellum period, Pratt was clearly the most successful gin manufacturer in the South. His enterprise survived the Civil War and grew into the Continental Gin Company, the nation's largest postwar manufacturer of machinery for cleaning cotton.[7]

Many local craftsmen working in small machine shops competed successfully with both the large northern and the southern cotton gin manufacturers during the 1840s and 1850s. In 1850 the editor of the Vicksburg *Whig* commented that "there are gin-makers in almost half the towns of the State, many of whom furnish excellent stands carefully and strongly

6. *American Cotton Planter and Soil of the South*, I (1857), 105.
7. Montgomery (Ala.) *Advertiser*, December 22, 1858; *American Cotton Planter and Soil of the South*, I (1857), 156–57; Prattville (Ala.) *Southern Statesman*, August 27, 1859; Vicksburg *Whig*, December 28, 1859, and September 11, 1860; George White, *Historical Collections of Georgia* (New York, 1854), 505, 570.

made one at a time—not machine work, furnished in a showy style, flimsily put together, like many of those from the Yankee firms." At the time the editor of the Vicksburg newspaper was engaged in a controversy with Martin W. Phillips, who had described the gin manufactured by Carver, Washburn & Company of Bridgewater, Massachusetts, as the best available. The editor wrote: "We have the authority of many . . . planters who have tried both for saying that the stands of Messrs. A[twood of Mississippi]. are superior to the Carver, or any other now in use." To clinch his case, the journalist concluded: "We know one planter who, this year, sold his cotton at 13 cents, and he attributed the high price entirely to the superior Atwood stand. He could never get more than his neighbors while using the Carver [gin]." "Hinds" of Cayuga, Mississippi, also gave the Atwood gin a strong endorsement. In April 1860, he wrote: "I bought a Carver's Stand in 1845, and used it until last year when I purchased one of Messrs. Atwood, and am satisfied that I should have profited if I had set the Carver aside after the first year, and purchased one of Messrs. Atwood. They gin decidedly faster, the draft is much lighter, and [they] make better cotton."[8] In 1856, however, Phillips acknowledged himself that the Carver gin had become obsolete. In a letter to Noah B. Cloud, editor of the *American Cotton Planter and Soil of the South,* Phillips reported that a fifty-five-saw Carver stand would produce no more than 3 bales per day when worked at maximum speed. Under ordinary usage it turned out only 2 bales per day. Phillips calculated that it would take him fifty-five days to gin 100 bales using the Carver stand.[9]

After a few more years of testing gins, Phillips gave high praise to the products of Jacob Hewes of Clinton and Benjamin D. Gullett of Aberdeen. "Jacob Hewes," he wrote in the *Southern Cultivator* in 1860, "living in Clinton, Miss., makes a Gin Stand which has been, quality and quantity, second only to the Gullett Stand, and many prefer it on the score of [its] being less complex and lasting longer [than the Gullett gin]." Phillips was able consistently to gin six bales per day with a sixty-five-saw Hewes gin stand.[10]

Upon reading that one of Daniel Pratt's fifty-saw gin stands had ginned five bales weighing 2,462 pounds in twelve and one-half hours, S. M.

8. Vicksburg *Whig,* April 13 and 16, 1860; *Southern Cultivator,* VIII (1850), 56–57, 85.
9. *American Cotton Planter and Soil of the South,* I (1857), 40.
10. *Southern Cultivator,* XVIII (1860), 366–67.

Wells of Hinds County wrote to the editor of the Jackson *Mississippian* that gins "equal in point of workmanship and superior in point of speed" were being manufactured in Clinton by J. & J. Hewes. Wells's sixty-five-saw gin of this make was turning out eight bales of cotton daily.[11]

In 1859, Phillips acquired a gin from Gullett, Gladney & Company of Aberdeen, Mississippi, that he promptly tested against his Hewes gin. He then dispatched samples of cotton ginned by both machines from the same supply of seed cotton to his commission merchant in New Orleans and received a report that both were good but that the sample ginned by the Gullett gin was the better of the two. When he had somewhat more experience with the new gin behind him, Phillips pronounced the "Gullett the best Stand in the south." In like spirit, G. D. Harmon wrote from Madison Parish, Louisiana: "I was completely convinced last fall, at the State Fair, at Jackson, Miss., that the Gullett Gin Stand was the best machine in the country, and now that I have two of them in operation by the side of two 'Eagle Stands,' I am confirmed in that opinion by *actual demonstration*." With steam power, the Gullett eighty-saw gin stands produced twelve bales each per day, while the Eagle stands produced only eight. Harmon concluded that the Gullett gins "not only gin faster than any other stand, but they make a better sample."[12]

In September 1860, Phillips reported that he had worn out his Gullett gin made by Gullett, Gladney & Company of Aberdeen, Mississippi, and was then operating a replacement Gullett made by Gunnison, Chapman & Company of New Orleans. "My gin Stand," he wrote, "can turn out ten bales per day, our plantation way; that is, as most of us do, gin from daylight until hands are done unloading [the cotton] wagon at night, when all quit work together." Although the Gladney gins had cost twice as much as some gins, the quality of the product justified the difference, Phillips maintained.[13]

Although Phillips usually reported favorably upon the various gins that he tested, he roundly condemned one machine produced by the Columbus Cotton Gin Factory belonging to the E. T. Taylor & Co. of Columbus, Georgia. In 1859 he informed his readers through the pages of the *Southern Cultivator* that he had bought a Taylor gin several years previously. "I was afraid it would burn up my gin house," he fulminated,

11. Jackson *Mississippian*, February 3, 1854.
12. *Southern Cultivator*, XVII (1859), 238, and XVIII (1860), 343.
13. *Ibid.*, XVIII (1860), 339.

"[it was] such a rattling thing, such [a] cotton, rat-gnawing looking thing. . . . Never before or since did I see such a rattling affair nor a worse sample [of cotton produced by a gin]. . . . I have been glad . . . of the chance to take a broad sweep at that Taylor stand, some $200 worse than thrown away." Phillips's complaints to the manufacturer had gone unanswered, probably because the firm was in such dire financial straits that Dr. E. T. Taylor, the senior partner, had attempted suicide.[14]

Late in the decade of the 1850s, a different type of cotton gin appeared in Mississippi. Instead of steel saws, the "roller" or "cylinder" gin used a vast number of spring steel wires to separate cotton fiber from seed. In principle this gin was closely related to the wire combs, or cards, that had been used to clean wool and cotton since the eighteenth century. The new machine was, in fact, an improved version of Eli Whitney's original cotton gin, which had utilized iron wire fingers to pull fiber through narrow slits in the box, leaving the seed behind on the other side. Whitney had patented both the systems of saws mounted on a rotating cylinder and wires fastened to a similar cylinder, although the saw gins, and not the wire ones, had won universal adoption. With much improved design and vastly superior materials, the wire gin of the 1850s presented a serious challenge to conventional saw gins.[15]

During 1851, Thomas Affleck of Adams County described a new gin that had recently been installed on a neighboring plantation. "It is," he wrote, "the invention of a gentleman named Parkhurst. Instead of saws, cards are used for removing the lint from the seed; it is then blown strongly against a close wire cylinder which revolves, and from which the lint is taken by vibrating or revolving rods." In August 1859, a lowland planter of Panola County wrote that he had used "for my last crop, the Roller Gin" and had found the new machine to be "infinitely superior to any gin I have ever tried." His roller gin had been manufactured in New York and had been distributed by David McCombs of Memphis. Because the steel wires of the roller gin were flexible rather than rigid like the cast steel teeth of a saw gin, the machine was not harmed if hard objects got into the hopper. In June of that same year Phillips wrote that he had a new ginstand constructed "on the cylinder principle. . . . I am free to

14. *Ibid.*, XVII (1859), 238; Columbus (Ga.) *Enquirer*, November 11, 1856.
15. *American Cotton Planter and Soil of the South*, I (1857), 104; *De Bow's Review*, XXVI (1859), 238; *Southern Cultivator*, IX (1851), 23–24.

say the day is not far distant when the Cylinder stands must drive all others out of use." [16]

Without exception all of the gins used in Mississippi during the antebellum period wore out rapidly, rarely lasting more than two or three seasons. Before petroleum products became available, there was no satisfactory lubricant for moving metal parts of machinery. Beef tallow and lard made from pork were most commonly used to grease the iron machine parts of the time, although from time to time cottonseed oil was tried because of its availability. W. K. Orr of Orrville, Alabama, an expert on cotton gins, gave this authoritative advice in 1857: "Tallow should never be used on a gin. I have seen boxes worn out when the oil cup on the binder was full of tallow. . . . I would recommend lard oil." As cottonseed oil, beef tallow, and pork lard were none of them very effective in reducing friction, bearing points of machinery wore rapidly and tended to overheat unless they received careful attention from the operator. Orr also strongly recommended that the belting used to propel cotton gin stands be improved. "All planters using a leather band," he wrote, "ought to cut them up into back-bands and hame-strings [for mule harness], and purchase a seven or eight inch India rubber belt, which will not cost more than a leather one." [17]

During the 1840s and 1850s, a power-driven accessory for cotton gins came into common usage in Mississippi. This machine, called a feeder, conveyed seed cotton into the gin stand after extracting dirt and trash from the seed cotton by means of mechanical beaters. Of this device G. D. Harmon wrote in 1859: "Another southern invention that should be patronized is [Jedediah P.] Prescott's Gin Feeders. They are manufactured in Memphis, Tenn., and sold at $1 per saw of the gin-stand. . . . One hand can attend to four gins [with the feeder], with a small boy to supply the hopper with cotton." Phillips said of the Prescott Eclipse Cotton Gin Feeder, which was patented October 13, 1857: "It is so constructed as to deliver the cotton from the hopper into the box for saws, whether there be two bales ginned or if there be six or eight and with more regularity than 2 or 3 men can feed the gin." Another, similar device patented October 9, 1855, by H. H. Fultz of Holmes County increased the speed of a gin by "from 20 to 50 per cent, the bolls [being]

16. *Southern Cultivator*, IX (1851), 23–24, and XVII (1859), 288, 359.
17. *American Cotton Planter and Soil of the South*, I (1857), 105.

often discharged uncut, thus preventing the gumming of the saws." These and other feeders used in the 1850s kept "the ginner from standing constantly over the gin stand in the dust and downy lint, which everyone knows is very detrimental to his health."[18]

Machinery for pressing cleaned cotton into bales was improved as much as cotton gins during the 1840s and 1850s. During the 1820s and 1830s, two types of screw presses were in common use in Mississippi. One, invented by David Greenleaf, employed two vertical wooden screws to drive a follower (or piston) into a box opening onto the second floor of a ginhouse. Two workmen turned the screws by hand, compressing the cotton within the box as far as they could with short wooden levers. Then a horse was used to turn the screws by means of a long lever to complete the final compressing of a bale. According to Monette, "the requisite number of hands will put up and bale with a common press about ten or twelve bales a day, by pushing." The other press was cheaper and simpler than the Greenleaf press. This machine, popular in Georgia, South Carolina, and north and east Mississippi, used a single screw to operate the follower in an overhead box. A horse or horses turned the screw by means of levers thirty to forty feet long that were attached to the top of the screw. This crude press was filled with cotton by workmen who climbed a ladder carrying baskets of lint that they dumped into the box. Much labor was expended in transporting lint from the ginhouse to these presses, which were usually situated some distance away. The worst feature of the A presses, however, was that they could not produce bales heavier than 400 pounds without undue effort. "Agricola" also pointed out that the "common single screw" press could not be used in rainy weather and that the wind blew "off from the baskets much cotton as it is taken from the press room to the box."[19]

On better-run plantations the Greenleaf press was superseded during the 1840s and 1850s by several more efficient machines. One of these, the Newell press, popular on large plantations in the later period, was a vertical press built into the ginhouse, which featured a single cast iron screw designed to apply great force to the bale. Because ninety revolutions of

18. Carrollton *Mississippi Democrat*, August 27, 1845; Wailes, *Report*, 172–73; *Southern Cultivator*, XVIII (1860), 54, 336–37, 339; *American Cotton Planter and Soil of the South*, I (1857), 104; *De Bow's Review*, XVIII (1855), 739–40; Vicksburg *Whig*, August 27 and September 18, 1856.
19. Wailes, *Report*, 173–75; Monette, "The Cotton Crop," 290; *Southwestern Farmer*, I (May 13, 1842), 77–78.

the screw were required to extend the follower into the cotton box, baling with this machine was slow when horses or mules supplied the motive power. When driven by a steam engine, however, the powerful press very swiftly produced bales weighing as much as 600 pounds. Phillips described the Newell press as "one of the best single Iron screw presses." Writing in the *Southwestern Farmer* in 1842, "Agricola" commented that "all of these objections [to double-screw and A presses] are remedied by use of the Newell press."[20]

The McCombs press, which competed with the Newell press, used two hinged levers to compress the bale rather than a screw. These levers stood beneath the cotton box like an inverted V. When the legs of the V mounted on rollers were drawn together by cables or chains, these beamlike levers drove the followers into the cotton box with great force. According to Benjamin L. C. Wailes, fifteen revolutions of a windlass working the cable were required to make a bale. Affleck, however, maintained that "one horse easily brings a 450 pound bale down to shipping size in eight revolutions." Phillips wrote in 1857, "I see in my notebook, September 19, 1855: 'I pressed today, with six hands, fifteen bales averaging 480 lbs. by 10½ o'clock [in the morning].' . . . My press is constructed by [David] McCombs . . . in Memphis, Tennessee."[21]

Lewis Lewis's revolving-lever cotton press, patented in March 1852, was an improvement on the McCombs press, as only three and one-half revolutions were required to make a bale. The levers of this press were operated by "two racks or segments, revolving around a stationary pinion. . . . That portion of the lint-room floor cut by the circle is attached to, and revolves with the press. All the working and wearing part of it is of cast iron." The press was manufactured in Vicksburg by the foundry of VanLoon, Paxton & Company until that establishment was destroyed by fire.[22]

Stephen Duncan, one of the largest planters in the Old Southwest, acquired a Lewis press and gave the inventor the following testimonial, dated October 4, 1853: "I think it the best 'single bale' press ever in-

20. Wailes, *Report*, 175; *Southern Cultivator*, VIII (1850), 102; *Southwestern Farmer*, I (May 13, 1842), 77–78.

21. *Southern Cultivator*, VIII (1850), 102, and IX (1851), 24; Wailes, *Report*, 175–76; *American Cotton Planter and Soil of the South*, I (1857), 103.

22. *Southern Cultivator*, XII (1854), 119; *American Cotton Planter*, II (1854), 117–18; broadside advertisement of the Lewis press issued by the manufacturers, VanLoon, Paxton & Co., Vicksburg, in possession of John Hebron Moore; Vicksburg *Whig*, April 26, 1855.

vented. I think five hands could press 60 bales in 12 hours, averaging 450 lbs. The task for my hands is 40 bales, which they complete before 5 o'clock, P.M., when they work with ordinary spirit." William Ryan, manager of Duncan's Oakley plantation, stated, "I can make 50 bales Cotton on . . . [the Lewis press] with 5 hands, averaging 460 lbs., from sun-up to sun down." Samuel Nelson of Issaquena County observed these presses at work on the plantations of Wirt Adams and Colonel John W. Bowie and wrote: "The Press requires not more than one horse-power for ordinary bales—say 500 lbs." William McCray of Holly Grove plantation in Yazoo County reported that the first bale he pressed with the Lewis machine, using two small mules for power, was reduced to twenty-one inches thick, "at least 5 inches smaller than any bale I have ever made on any other press." [23]

As the cotton presses improved in efficiency, it became apparent that rope binds were not able to hold the bales to their smaller dimensions. Planters and press manufacturers, therefore, began to try to devise non-stretching bindings strong enough to withstand the pressure of the compressed cotton. David McCombs, for example, in 1850 developed hoops of wood fastened by iron rings, which he provided in sets to make a bale for twelve and one-half cents per set. Phillips endorsed the McComb hoops, commenting that he had "ordered a burner [to make notches in the hoops] and rings for my entire crop." Wailes described iron straps painted to prevent rust from staining the cotton, which were coming into use on large plantations. These straps were fastened with rivets fitting into "holes previously punched at the proper distances." In 1857 the editor of the Natchez *Courier* reported that the large planter William Minor of Adams County had received a patent for a new method of securing iron straps. "It consists in cutting short parallel slits in both ends of the iron hoop, and then through them making an oval aperture, so as to receive an iron plug. The hoop is so fixed as to be ready to be adjusted to a compressed bale." Throughout the 1850s, however, conservative cotton buyers continued to be skeptical of the value of wood or metal fasteners for cotton bales and showed a preference for bales bound with ropes in the old fashion. [24]

Of the machinery in common use on plantations in Mississippi during

23. VanLoon, Paxton & Co. broadside; *American Cotton Planter*, II (1854), 118.

24. *Southern Cultivator*, VIII (1850), 102, and IX (1851), 24; Wailes, *Report*, 177; Jackson *Mississippian*, December 2, 1857.

the 1840s and 1850s, gristmills ranked third in importance, after cotton gins and cotton presses. A. de Puy Van Buren, a northern schoolmaster who taught in Yazoo County, Mississippi, wrote: "Connected with the cotton-gin, the planter has a corn-mill, where he grinds all his corn into meal. Here, on his own premises, is the fountain, from which so much Southern wealth flows—from which all the 'corn-dodgers' and 'hoe-cakes' spring." Phillips repeatedly recommended a corn mill invented by Willis P. Coleman, who had planted in Hinds and Rankin counties before he moved to New Orleans to establish a factory to produce his mill. According to Phillips, Coleman's machine had taken a premium at the Crystal Palace in New York City, where it had ground a bushel of meal in five minutes. In 1857 the experimenter of Log Hall commented: "I have also succeeded with Coleman's Corn Mill (of New Orleans) by doing more work with a fourteen inch stone and light work for mules than with Straub's Mill, with twenty-two inches and hard work for mules." In 1860, Phillips insisted that "Coleman's mill, inch for inch of size, will grind a tenth more corn into good meal, and cool it at that" than any other mill with which he was acquainted. Dr. J. Redhead of Amite County, a locally prominent inventor, operated a corn mill invented by an engineer on the Woodville railroad that ground fifty bushels of corn a day with two horses. Of this machine Eli J. Capell wrote: "It is a first-rate piece of workmanship, and one of the most simple things I ever saw." Whether made by local mechanics or by factories in North or South, gristmills were essential equipment for plantations.[25]

Corn-shelling machines, which became available in Mississippi during the 1830s, gradually won acceptance by planters during the last two decades of the antebellum era, although on many farms and plantations the tedious and laborious process of removing the grains from the cobs continued to be done by hand. In 1842, Daniel O. Williams expressed regret that "few . . . of these useful, simple and cheap machines . . . [were] to be found in the country." For a year he had used one that had been manufactured by R. Van Allen, New York, and sold by a New Orleans dealer in agricultural implements and machinery for twenty-two dollars. Williams wrote: "The wheels are made of cast iron, and the machine runs very

25. A. de Puy Van Buren, *Jottings of a Year's Sojourn in the South; or First Impressions of the Country and Its People; with a Glimpse of School-teaching in That Southern Land, and Reminiscences of Distinguished Men* . . . (Battle Creek, Mich., 1859), 154; *Southern Cultivator*, VI (1848), 86–87, and XIV (1856), 68; *American Cotton Planter and Soil of the South*, I (1857), 40, and IV (1860), 167–68.

light, [with] only one hand [being] required to turn it. It will shell . . . half a bushel of corn to the minute, or thirty bushels an hour." Characteristically, Williams added: "A merciful man is merciful to his slave; this machine will exempt them from much unpleasant labor, that of shelling corn by hand, which has generally to be done after night[fall], when the labor of the day is closed, and occupies them from one to three hours one night in every week." The price of the machines declined during the depression, so that Dr. Walter Wade of Ross Wood Plantation in Jefferson County near Rodney was able to buy a sheller in 1846 for only thirteen dollars. By 1850, agricultural implement dealers in New Orleans were regularly carrying corn shellers in stock.[26]

In the antebellum period, planters fed their horses, mules, and milk cattle upon dried corn leaves (called fodder), crushed cornstalks, and a ground-up mixture of corn grains and cobs. Grinding machines like the Excelsior corn and cob crusher described in 1857 by G. D. Harmon pulverized dried ears of corn so that stock could eat and digest the mixture. Manufactured by Elmers & Forkner of Cincinnati, the mill cost twenty-five dollars. With one mule for power, Harmon, using the number one size mill, ground "$\frac{1}{2}$ bushel of meal as fine as 'little hominy,' or what we used to call in Georgia grits. I grind with ease . . . 12 to 15 bushels per hour. Ears of corn can be ground so fine as for one-fourth of it to be fine meal."[27] G. D. Mitchell of Cedar Grove plantation in Warren County strongly recommended a slightly different type of machine, a straw and corn shuck cutter. This mill, invented by I. F. Brown, a member of the firm E. T. Taylor & Company of Columbus, Georgia, Mitchell wrote in 1852, "will cut straw, shucks, hay, fodder, potatoes, &c. with unparalleled rapidity. . . . it will cut fifteen bundles of usual sized oats in twenty-two seconds." The cutter was sold by Taylor for thirty dollars. A similar machine, John and Thomas A. Bones's "patent self-sharpening straw and shuck cutter," was advertised in the *Southern Cultivator* during 1856.[28]

From Hinds County, Mississippi, Solon Robinson wrote in 1848 that William Montgomery of Aurora Hill plantation in that county had tried unsuccessfully to dam a stream so he could drive a sawmill. Robinson

26. *Mississippi Free Trader and Natchez Gazette*, November 5, 1836; *Southwestern Farmer*, I (September 16, 1842), 13; Walter Wade Plantation Diary (Typescript in Mississippi Department of Archives and History), II, 143; *De Bow's Review*, VI (1848), 133; Vicksburg *Whig*, March 19, 1856.

27. *De Bow's Review*, XV (1857), 227, 307.

28. *Southern Cultivator*, X (1852), 202, and XIV (1856), 68.

advised Montgomery to purchase one of Page's patent circular sawmills, made in Baltimore, Maryland, saying "that these sawmills are just the thing wanted in a country where they cannot have water mills, and where all kinds of sawed lumber, as is here, very scarce and dear. Upon every plantation there is already a horse power to which the sawmill might be attached at the gin house." Although Robinson did not encounter many of them, not a few plantations were operating sash sawmills with horse-power. Dr. J. Redhead of Amite County in that same year, for example, put up a sash sawmill of his own invention, for which he had applied for a patent. According to Eli J. Capell, Redhead's sawmill was attached to the inventor's ginhouse and was driven by the horsepower that was ordinarily used for his gin stand. When three teams of mules were used, the sawmill would produce 800 feet of boards per day. On some large plantations sawmills were driven by the same steam engines that powered the gin-houses. In 1845, Robinson visited Joseph Dunbar of Jefferson County on home plantation and learned that this owner of several plantations oper-ated a steam sawmill. Dunbar assured Robinson that "he had saved more than the cost of it, in getting lumber for his own buildings."[29]

On large plantations where four eighty- or ninety-saw gin stands were required to gin the cotton crop, planters were faced with the choice either of putting up two separate ginhouses, each with its own horsepower, or a single large structure powered by a steam engine. Francis T. Leak chose the former route. He built two ginhouses, each of which he equipped with two fifty-saw gins costing $250 for the pair. Wade Hampton III, who owned several plantations in Issaquena and Washington counties, elected to power his large ginhouses with steam engines. Joseph Dunbar of Jef-ferson County, George Messenger, who planted on Big Black River, and Joseph Davis of Warren County were some of the many large planters of the western counties of Mississippi who used steam power during the late antebellum period.[30]

The editor of the Vicksburg *Whig* in 1854 described a plantation steam engine that had been manufactured by the Vicksburg Foundry for Haller Nutt of Natchez. "This engine," the journalist wrote, "has a twelve inch

29. Kellar (ed.), *Solon Robinson*, I, 487, and II, 130; *Southern Cultivator*, VI (1848), 86; Vicksburg *Whig*, August 3, 1858.

30. Leak Diary, II, 96, 281; Wade Hampton III to Mary Fisher Hampton, June 3, 1866, in Cauthen (ed.), *Family Letters of the Three Wade Hamptons*, 122; Janet S. Hermann, *The Pursuit of a Dream* (New York, 1983), 11; Kellar (ed.), *Solon Robinson*, I, 487; Vicksburg *Whig*, August 3, 1858.

cylinder with three feet stroke, cast iron bed plate under the cylinder, circular steam chest, improved globe throttle, wrought iron pitman, slides upon turned columns, plummer block and shafts planed—all turned and fitted up in the best style—combining strength, weight of metal, and the most approved pattern." Two similar engines were being made for "Judge Perkins of Louisiana . . . and Judge Montgomery of Mississippi."[31]

In 1856 the editor of the Vicksburg *Whig* remarked that he had seen a steam engine and boiler hauled through the streets of the city en route to the plantation of George Messenger on Big Black River. The engine, manufactured by A. B. Reading, was "of a size to run four Gin stands, a corn mill and a saw mill." Reading's steam engines, according to the journalist, were "made heavier than those of the same power usually made in the North." Two years later he examined a steam engine in Reading's machine shop "of some forty-five or fifty horse power" that was being manufactured for a Louisiana planter. At the time several other, similar engines were in various stages of completion. In the late 1850s, plantation engines were being manufactured in Vicksburg by A. M. Paxton's foundry and machine shop as well as by Reading's Vicksburg Foundry.[32]

Wailes wrote: "The great majority of gins are propelled by horsepower. Steam, however, is coming very much into use on the large river plantations. . . . In Washington County there has recently been erected a very spacious and complete gin house containing four eighty-saw stands, in which a very complete steam-engine supplies the power by which the seed cotton is elevated, ginned, and pressed, and the bales lowered [to the ground level of the ginhouse]." Robert Russell, an English traveler, recorded that "Whitney's saw gin . . . is often driven by a small steam engine, but more frequently by mules." A. de Puy Van Buren, the northern schoolmaster, also encountered a sawmill and cotton gin propelled by steam on a plantation located on the Yazoo River. Since Dr. Rush Nutt had first demonstrated the practicality of powering cotton gins with steam engines on his plantation near Rodney around 1830, this type of motive power had become increasingly popular with large planters.[33]

31. Vicksburg *Whig*, September 6, 1854.
32. *Ibid.*, August 3, 1858, May 26 and 30, 1860; Natchez *Courier*, September 28, 1858.
33. Wailes, *Report*, 179; Russell, *North America*, 267; Van Buren, *Sojourn in the South*, 126; Claiborne, *Mississippi*, 141.

By the late 1850s, advice given in 1849 by Daniel Lee, editor of the *Southern Cultivator*, had proven to be sound. When a correspondent asked about the desirability of using a steam engine to drive a cotton gin, Lee had replied: "If a planter had to purchase mules or horses to drive cotton gins, doubtless steam would be cheaper for that purpose. But ones having mules [enough] had probably better gin with them than to buy an engine . . . [as] the latter will cost from five to six hundred dollars, with boilers, &c. attached." Six to eight mules costing from $150 to $200 each would indeed have been more expensive for the planter than a small steam engine. The engine, however, was more costly to fuel with cord-wood or coal than mules fed with corn and fodder raised on the planta-tion. The real advantage of steam engines over horsepower was that the engine could operate several gin stands and a cotton press simultane-ously, whereas mule teams could not drive more than two gins at once. Thus large rather than medium or small planters were more apt to pur-chase steam engines.[34]

On large plantations where steam power was employed, factorylike structures with towering chimneys of brick or sheet iron dominated the skyline. These buildings each housed several gin stands, a cotton press, a grist and flour mill, a sawmill, and probably lathes, circular saws, and other woodworking machinery, all of which were propelled by means of belting and shafting by a steam engine located in an adjacent building. Steam machinery of this kind represented such a substantial investment of capital and was of such local economic importance that it was logical during the Civil War for invading Federal troops to single out such gin-houses for destruction.

On plantations using horsepower and teams of horses to propel ma-chinery, much less capital was invested in the ginhouses, and these struc-tures were much less imposing in appearance. Dr. J. Redhead's ginhouse on his plantation in Amite County was fairly typical. This building was forty feet wide and fifty-nine feet long, with the gearing and horse path located on the ground level beneath the floor where the gin stands were mounted. Wailes described the gearing of such ginhouses as follows:

> The running gear consists of a large central wheel, twelve to fifteen feet in di-
> ameter . . . [mounted on] a massive upright shaft which rests on an iron
> gudgeon, and turns in a metallic [s]ink in a large wooden block sunk in the

34. *Southern Cultivator*, VII (1849), 24.

ground. . . . Cogs . . . bolted to the rim of the wheel . . . play into a vertical spur-wheel on one end of a horizontal shaft, to the opposite end of which the band wheel or drum is attached. A leather band about a foot in width connects this with the trundle-head of the gin stand, and puts the machinery in motion.

The large wheel was made of wood with either hardwood or cast iron cogs. The central shaft was rotated by two large beams fastened to it, to which teams of horses or mules were hitched.[35]

Francis T. Leak described the contents of a typical ginhouse of this variety in his journal in these words: "Nov. 4, 1854. Yesterday morning about 9 or 10 o'clock, one of my Gin houses caught fire and burnt up destroying about 25 bales of cotton, 2 Gin stands, a mill, Cotton Feeder, Thresher, Fan, 100 to 200 bushels of oats, some tools, and a large quantity of cotton seed. Total loss about $1800 or $2,000."[36]

Phillips in 1860 criticized the common ginhouses of Mississippi because they were not "constructed [so] as to economize labor." Instead, he said, "They are [built] on the principle of finding work for negroes. . . . At the North there is a constant desire for barns constructed to save labor; why not here in Gin Houses?" He closed with an appeal for mechanics to design machinery to lift the seed cotton to the ginning floor and to move the lint into the presses. Much that he asked for, however, was already in operation in the steam-powered ginhouses of the river counties.[37]

35. [Ingraham], *South-West*, II, 289; *Southern Cultivator*, VI (1848), 86; Wailes, *Report*, 178.
36. Leak Diary, III, 345.
37. *Southern Cultivator*, XVIII (1860), 367.

5 Agricultural Slavery

The history of the institution of slavery in Mississippi, like that of agriculture, dates from the beginning of permanent British settlement of the Natchez District of the Province of West Florida. By that comparatively late period, a century and a half after the founding of Jamestown, both the plantation as an economic unit and slavery as a system of forced labor were firmly established in the mainland south Atlantic colonies as well as in the British insular possessions. As a matter of course both discharged officers of the British army and navy and influential civilians who received land grants in West Florida from the Crown intended to develop slave-worked plantations in the new colony. Therefore, British immigrants of the 1760s brought slaves with them into the Natchez District and imported additional blacks as rapidly as circumstances permitted. Yet, all of the new planters experienced serious difficulties in finding markets for the products of their plantations because the best water route to the sea, the lower Mississippi River, was controlled by an unfriendly Spain. Thus under the circumstances it can be inferred that the early British settlers brought slaves into Mississippi as much for reasons of social status as because of economic considerations, although the two motivations were closely connected.

Apparently early British immigrants into the Natchez District arrived expecting to produce tobacco, the staple crop of the south Atlantic colonies, for they modeled their system of slavery after that of the mainland tobacco colonies rather than that of the sugar colonies of the West Indies. This development was fortunate for the slaves of Mississippi inasmuch as tobacco plantation slavery was less harsh than sugar plantation slavery.

North American tobacco culture demanded constant though not physically taxing labor from farm workers. To be sure, each tobacco plant required much individual attention, and the soil between the hills upon which the plants were growing had to be chopped frequently with hoes to keep it free from grass and weeds. Preparation of the ground for planting, however, was the only aspect of tobacco cultivation demanding greater strength than women or teenaged children possessed. Indeed, women were generally as useful in the tobacco fields as men. For this reason, American tobacco growers customarily bought equal numbers of men and women, in sharp contrast to the sugar planters of the West Indies, who purchased many more male than female slaves. Planning to grow tobacco after their plantations were established, British slaveowners in the Natchez District maintained work forces from the outset that were equally divided between the sexes. William Dunbar, for example, worked seven men and seven women on his plantation near the present site of Baton Rouge in 1776. When he increased the number of his plantation slaves several years later, he bought three men and three women.[1]

Although it was undeniably harsh by mid-nineteenth century standards, the kind of agricultural slavery that emerged in British West Florida during the 1770s was much less rigorous than slavery in Jamaica or Saint-Domingue at that time. Because of the very heavy labor required to cultivate and process sugarcane in the tropics, it was extremely difficult for the small minority of whites and slaveowning mulattoes living in the islands to maintain discipline among the slaves on Caribbean sugar plantations. In constant terror of slave revolts, the whites and mulattoes resorted routinely to extreme measures in suppressing the first signs of rebellion. Nevertheless, despite atrocious disciplinary measures, slave revolts were frequent in the sugar-producing colonies.[2]

In contrast to the situation in tropical colonies, slave insurrections rarely occurred in temperate North American because living and working conditions there were less unpleasant for slaves than elsewhere. Furthermore, the presence of large numbers of women and children in the North American slave population made revolts unlikely. Obviously men with women and children had more to lose in an uprising than despairing single men who gambled nothing but their lives. Finally, there can be no doubt that slaves were less discontented with their lot in situations where there were equal numbers of males and females, especially if the slaves were permitted to enjoy a measure of family life.[3]

1. Rowland (ed.), *Dunbar*, 23; Clement Eaton, *A History of the Old South: The Emergence of a Reluctant Nation* (3rd ed.; New York, 1975), 214–15.
2. Harry P. Owens (ed.), *Perspectives in American Slavery* (Jackson, Miss., 1976), 43; Thomas O. Ott, *The Haitian Revolution, 1789–1804* (Knoxville, Tenn., 1973), 13–18; Richard B. Sheridan, *Sugar and Slavery: An Economic History of the British West Indies, 1623–1775* (Baltimore, 1973), 221, 254–56; Pierre de Vaissière, *Saint-Domingue: La Société et la vie Créoles sous l'Ancien Régime, 1629–1789* (2nd ed.; Paris, 1909), 165–69, 180–94.
3. John B. Boles, *Black Southerners, 1619–1869* (Lexington, Ky., 1983), 174–75; Carl Degler, *Neither Black nor White: Slavery and Race Relations in Brazil and the United States* (New York, 1971), 64.

Judging from a unique journal of his plantation operations kept by William Dunbar, plantation slaves in Mississippi during the 1770s were faring about as well as slaves on newly established plantations in the British south Atlantic colonies. In the latter half of that decade, Dunbar grew small quantities of indigo as a market crop on his plantation near Baton Rouge while producing corn, upland rice, peas, pumpkins, and sweet potatoes to feed his family, slaves, and livestock. The planter also maintained a plantation garden, as well as a fruit orchard, to supply fresh vegetables in season. For meat, Dunbar raised hogs to provide pork, which he cured, salted, and stored in his smokehouse. The former British army officer kept several teams of oxen for pulling plows and lumber carts and for transporting logs from the swamp and forest, but he did not raise cattle for beef. Dunbar housed his slaves in frame cabins built with squared timbers and covered over with rough cypress boards rather than in log cabins typical of the nineteenth-century agricultural frontier. The interior walls of Dunbar's slave cabins were covered with plaster to make them warmer in winter. Every year, Dunbar issued a jacket, a pair of trousers, and a pair of shoes to the men and a jacket, a "petty Coat," and a pair of shoes to the women.[4]

Although Dunbar considered himself to be an indulgent master, he punished his slaves more severely than was usual in Mississippi during the next generation. In 1776, for example, he sentenced a woman runaway to be imprisoned in irons for four days and then given 25 lashes with a cowhide whip. Two years later, he ordered that two male runaways be given five separate beatings of 100 lashes each. Luckily for the slaves, the planter underwent a change of heart before the two men were whipped to death. Dunbar ordered, however, that each man upon returning to work in the fields have a small log chained to his ankle so that he could not run away again. On still another occasion Dunbar imprisoned an intoxicated male slave in the plantation "Bastile" and threatened him with 500 lashes unless he confessed where he had obtained the rum. After the frightened slave admitted that he had stolen a key to Dunbar's storeroom and had taken a bottle from his master's supply, Dunbar remitted the flogging but forced the black to work for several days with a heavy chain fastened to his leg. Dunbar's severe punishments of delinquent slaves had

4. Rowland (ed.), *Dunbar*, 23–67.

predictable results. More than once slaves ran away when threatened with a flogging.[5]

Dunbar's plantation, like those of his fellow colonists, was primarily a lumbering operation throughout the British era but produced enough food crops to feed the people living on the plantation. Dunbar's slaves felled red oak and white oak trees on high ground for making barrel headings and staves and cypress trees in the swamps for squared timbers and lumber. Women labored in the sawpits like the men but were not employed in the dangerous work of logging. In the agricultural operations of the plantation, men, women, and older children cultivated indigo, corn, rice, and vegetables with hoes. The very heavy labor of breaking land for spring planting, however, was reserved for men, using crude plows drawn by teams of oxen.[6]

While the Spanish were governing southern Mississippi between 1779 and 1798, the population grew much more rapidly than in the preceding British period, with the increase in the number of slaves paralleling the growth in the white populace. A census taken in 1784 revealed that 1,121 whites and 498 slaves were living in the Natchez District. Eight years later, the total climbed to 4,364, and in 1798, the year in which the Dons departed from the city of Natchez, the population was estimated to be 6,000, of whom 2,400 were slaves.[7]

When the Spanish authorities began to encourage the production of tobacco on a large scale after the conquest of West Florida in 1779, existing subsistence plantations such as Dunbar's were quickly converted to the cultivation of the staple crop, and many new tobacco plantations were established in the Natchez District during the next few years. With tobacco yielding 1,500 to 2,000 pounds per acre in the rich loess of the Natchez region (more than twice the output of the eastern tobacco states), and a bounty from the Spanish government of ten silver dollars per hundredweight, the local planters became extremely prosperous, and the tobacco slave plantation became a vigorous economic institution. Agricultural methods and the type of plantation slavery employed in the old Natchez District came to resemble the Virginia model more closely with each passing year until the tobacco subsidy was finally withdrawn in 1790. In this period the shift from lumbering to tobacco culture was

5. *Ibid.*, 29–30, 46–47, 55.
6. *Ibid.*, 23–74.
7. McLemore (ed.), *History of Mississippi*, I, 168–69.

clearly beneficial to the plantation slaves, inasmuch as the labor involved in the latter activity was much less arduous than in the former.[8]

After experimenting disastrously with indigo for several years following the loss of the tobacco subsidy, planters along the Mississippi River found a promising new market crop in cotton between 1793 and 1795. With their slave organizations already adapted to the cultivation of tobacco, the plantations of the old Natchez District were readily changed over to cotton, a plant that was considerably easier than tobacco to grow in quantity as a row crop. To begin with, it was not necessary to sprout young cotton plants in hotbeds before transferring them to the field, as was done with tobacco. Then, too, during the growing stage, cotton, unlike tobacco, was not pruned of tops and lower leaves. Finally, the cotton fiber did not have to go through a complicated curing process before being packed for shipment to market. The transition from tobacco to cotton was easy because cultivation of the two row crops was the same, with the work being done with identical farm implements. The space between the rows of growing plants in both crops was broken up regularly with hoes, plows, and crude harrows to keep the soil loose and free from grass and weeds. Another point of similarity was that the acreage to be planted in either cotton or tobacco was determined by the number of acres that a single worker could harvest, for in both cases a worker could raise more to maturity than he could gather. Because the growing cotton plants required less care than tobacco, and because it was simpler to harvest cotton, a given number of workers could produce and harvest more cotton than tobacco. For these reasons, cotton was found around Natchez at the turn of the nineteenth century to be even more suitable than tobacco for large-scale production with relatively unskilled, and relatively unwilling, slave labor.[9]

During the lifetime of the antebellum Cotton Kingdom, most of the slaves of Mississippi were employed on cotton plantations and for the first four decades of the nineteenth century lived and worked under conditions dictated by the centuries-old gang system according to which slave

8. Jack D. L. Holmes, *Gayoso: The Life of a Spanish Governor in the Mississippi Valley, 1789–1799* (1965; rpr. Gloucester, Mass., 1968), 90–93.

9. Clement Eaton, *The Growth of Southern Civilization, 1790–1860* (New York, 1961), 27–29; Gates, *Farmer's Age*, 102–103, 136–37; Phillips, *American Negro Slavery*, 207–11, and *Life and Labor in the Old South* (Boston, 1929), 112–15.

labor was organized. Under this system slaves labored in groups under the direction of a slave who performed no physical labor himself and was called variously a driver, a slave driver, or a Negro driver. Depending upon the season of the year, many kinds of work gangs were employed on cotton plantations. There were plow gangs, hoe gangs, cotton-picking gangs, corn-pulling gangs, fence-building gangs, land-clearing gangs, ginning gangs, cotton-pressing gangs, and still other gangs. As a rule, men and women worked interchangeably in these gangs, except when they were felling trees, rolling logs, digging ditches, or performing other heavy or dangerous physical labor. In such cases, women were excluded from the gangs, in accordance with the custom started in the 1760s. The gang system placed heavy emphasis upon disciplined group activity while discouraging individual initiative on the part of agricultural workers other than the drivers, specialists, and skilled plantation craftsmen. Essentially, field hands were worked under the gang system like teams of oxen, as the title of driver implied. As in the case of teams of draft animals, members of slave gangs labored less for rewards when work was well done than to escape punishment for inadequate performance.[10]

From the viewpoint of a slaveowner, the chief defect of the gang system was that the pace of the gangs ultimately diminished to that of the slowest workers despite the best efforts of drivers and overseers. Clearly workers in the gangs commonly conspired among themselves to reduce the pace by means of slowdowns, and plantation slaves throughout the South in the nineteenth century were experts at determining just how fast they must work in order to avoid punishmment.

In 1857, for example, the slaves on Hopewell plantation in Lowndes County, where the gang system was still in effect, carried out a successful campaign of passive resistance during the growing season. Plowmen and women performed their work haphazardly, skipping large portions of the field and not plowing up the roots of grass and weeds in areas where they did pretend to work. For their part, members of the hoe gang slowed their pace and skillfully covered over grass with loose earth while leaving the roots intact. Unable to persuade the field hands to do their jobs properly, and suspecting that the driver was himself involved in the conspiracy,

10. Gray, *Agriculture*, I, 548–49; Eugene D. Genovese, *Roll, Jordan, Roll: The World the Slaves Made* (1974; rpr. New York, 1976), 318–19; Phillips, *American Negro Slavery*, 264; Charles S. Sydnor, *Slavery in Mississippi* (1933; rpr. Gloucester, Mass., 1965), 9.

Slave Population of Mississippi, 1860

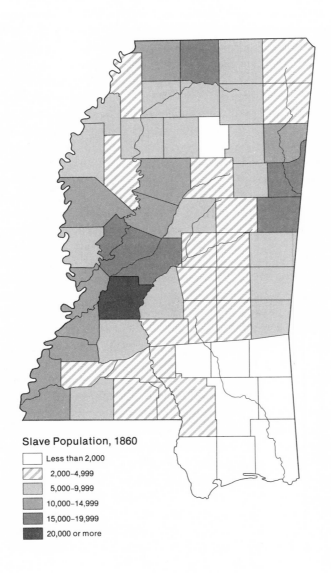

Slave Population, 1860

☐	Less than 2,000
⧄	2,000–4,999
▨	5,000–9,999
▨	10,000–14,999
▨	15,000–19,999
■	20,000 or more

Source: *Eighth Census, 1860: Population*, 270

the overseer in desperation took personal charge of the hoe gang. He reassigned the pace setter and ordered the no doubt infuriated and humiliated driver to take a place in line. Having tied himself down by taking over the hoe gang, the unfortunate overseer lost all semblance of control over the secretly gleeful plow hands, who plowed even less effectively than before. The overseer, faced with the probable loss of the whole cotton crop, sought help from his immediate superior, Richard D. Powell, who was agent in Alabama and Mississippi for the owner, John Hartwell Cocke of Virginia. Powell went to Hopewell to investigate the situation and was apparently briefed by the driver on the extent of the resistance movement and its objectives. Knowing that punishment, no matter how severe, could not force the slaves to save the crop, Powell sensibly negotiated. He offered the field hands a "good barbecue & one or two days rest" when the crop was properly laid by. To preserve some of his dignity, Powell threatened the slaves with punishment at the end of the season if they did not return to working properly. Having gotten what they wanted—humiliation of the overseer and a holiday celebration—the slaves returned cheerfully to their duties. The driver, back in his accustomed position of authority, surely enjoyed the discomfiture of the overseer, who had received a memorable tongue lashing from his superior. This by no means isolated incident revealed that the old system of management was dangerously vulnerable to organized passive resistance by the slaves.[11]

Indeed, within plantation slave gangs, the pacesetters had nothing to gain by moving briskly but rather much to lose, inasmuch as they would have to live with their resentful fellows after returning to the quarters. Furthermore, the driver's whip was not a satisfactory antidote for the disease of passive resistance; the cowhide, when applied vigorously, incapacitated the recipient for several days. The slaveowner was then deprived of a slave's valuable service for a time, to his financial loss. The detrimental effect of severely whipping a slave is illustrated by an entry in the plantation account book kept by Joseph M. Jayne, a planter of Rankin County who owned forty-eight slaves in 1860. Big George, one of his workers, ran away on January 2, 1854, and did not return to the plantation until January 16. The angry slaveowner had the runaway whipped that day so brutally that Big George was bedridden until January 27.

11. Richard D. Powell to John Hartwell Cocke, August 14, 1857, in Willie Lee Rose (ed.), *A Documentary History of Slavery in North America* (New York, 1976), 254–55.

Jayne thus deprived himself of the labor of an important worker for eleven days in addition to the fourteen days lost while Big George was away from the plantation. Big George, however, did not absent himself again during the remainder of the antebellum period.[12]

Similarly, imprisonment was hardly a punishment to be feared by lazy field hands, who would rather lie about indoors than chop cotton under a hot Mississippi sun, unless the confinement were made so uncomfortable as to endanger their health, a result slaveowners obviously wished to avoid. For these reasons, plantation slaves working under the gang system were able generally to avoid overtaxing themselves while working in the fields, regardless of the wishes of their owners. Indeed, northern visitors to Mississippi often commented upon the leisurely pace of plantation gangs, which they considered to be much slower than the work rate of northern farm laborers.[13]

On large cotton plantations the daily activities of the various gangs were supervised by head drivers, trusted and experienced slaves who wielded considerable authority and enjoyed many special privileges. A cowhide whip, carried as a British army officer of World War I did his swagger stick, and often a horse provided by the plantation owner so that the head driver could make his daily rounds, were the badges of office. The head driver was feared and respected, if not loved, by the agricultural slaves under his authority mainly because he assigned the individual slaves to work gangs. Thus the head driver had the power to make a particular field hand's lot in life either easier or more unpleasant. Furthermore, head drivers on some plantations were authorized to mete out punishments to delinquent workers, even including floggings.

Head drivers were responsible to the whites in charge of their plantations. Sometimes the person in authority was the plantation owner or his son, but it was commonly a white employee of the planter, called an overseer. On many plantations, however, the owner required that his head driver report directly to him periodically upon such matters as the state of the crops, the health and morale of the slaves, and the relations existing between the field hands and the overseer. At such times, adverse reports from the head drivers about their conduct always meant trouble for

12. Joseph M. Jayne Plantation Account Book (William R. Perkins Library, Duke University). See entries for January 2 to 26, 1854.

13. Eaton, *History of the Old South*, 240; Genovese, *Roll, Jordan, Roll*, 298–305; Kellar (ed.), *Solon Robinson*, II, 276–78.

the overseers and not infrequently resulted in dismissals. Thus, agricultural slaves sometimes had a potent advocate in their head driver as well as a stern taskmaster, for he could protect them somewhat from mistreatment by an overseer.[14]

The following comments by former slaves afford a glimpse of the attitude of the slaves toward the drivers. Allen Manning had been a slave on a small plantation in Clarke County near Quitman. He said: "Ole Master didn't have any overseer hired, but him and his boys looked after the place and had a Negro we called the driver. We-all shore hated that old black man." Ephraim Robertson, who had belonged to Allen Morrison of Hinds County, said that "the drivers would whip you harder than the Marster because the Marster knew if he hurt you or killed you, it was his loss." Robert Young, who had lived on a plantation about twelve miles east of Crystal Springs, recalled that his father had been the driver on the plantation belonging to Gus Watkins, on which there were twenty slave cabins and about 100 slaves. Watkins's son Henry acted as overseer. Young said: "My pappy was a big strong nigger, an' hepped Marse Henry control de udder darkies. Marse Henry would git him to throw 'em while he whupped 'em wid a bull whip."[15]

Inasmuch as the gang system of agricultural slavery required close supervision and maximum regulation of the lives of the slaves, blacks were housed under barrackslike conditions in cabins clustered closely together in small villages. These agricultural villages were called slave quarters, or merely the quarters. When not on an assignment elsewhere, each slave was required to be in the quarters under direct control of the overseer or head driver. Like regular soldiers of eighteenth-century European armies, cotton plantation slaves living under the gang system arose together at daybreak six days in the week, marched in units to the field to do their work and then marched back to the quarters at the end of

14. Leslie H. Owens, *This Species of Property: Slave Life and Culture in the Old South* (1976; rpr. New York, 1978), 112–35; Kenneth M. Stampp, *The Peculiar Institution: Slavery in the Ante-Bellum South* (New York, 1956), 37, 41, 151; James H. Stone, "Black Leadership in the Old South: The Slave Drivers of the Rice Kingdom" (Ph.D. dissertation, Florida State University, 1976); William L. Van Deburg, *The Slave Drivers: Black Agricultural Labor Supervisors in the Antebellum South* (Westport, Conn., 1979).

15. George P. Rawick (ed.), *The American Slave: A Composite Biography* Ser. 1, 2, and Supplement (Westport, Conn., 1977), Ser. 1, *Oklahoma and Mississippi*, Vol. VII, p. 216; *Mississippi*, Vol. IX, Pt. 4, p. 1852, and Vol. X, Pt. 5, p. 2409.

the day, ate their evening meal in a common mess hall, and then retired to their cabins, where they were required to remain until summoned to duty in the morning by the plantation bell or the head driver's horn.

Keeping the slaves in their quarters at night was a responsibility of the luckless overseer, and few overseers were able to discharge this obligation successfully. Young slaves were quite adept at slipping away from their cabins under cover of darkness to frolic at some secluded rendezvous, often returning to the quarters only in time to answer the horn of the driver. The pace of gangs was of course even slower than usual on the day after such frolics. Even on Sundays, when field hands were required to perform no labor, they were supposed to remain in the vicinity of the quarters unless they had received special permission to go elsewhere on the plantation. In practice, however, slaves were allowed to leave the quarters to go for walks, to fish in the streams, or to attend supposedly secret religious services held in brush arbors deep in the woods. Although slaves were required to remain on the plantation, they did not find it difficult to evade detection by the whites while visiting neighboring farms or plantations. If they were caught away from the plantation without a written pass, slaves were liable to arrest, confinement in the county jail, and a whipping under Mississippi law. Few, however, were ever caught, and most considered the fun worth the risk.[16]

Under the gang system prevailing in Mississippi from the 1760s until the 1840s, agricultural slaves were seldom able to live together as families in houses of their own. The principal exceptions to the rule were privileged head drivers, skilled craftsmen, and sometimes the assistant drivers, who were permitted wives and cabins of their own. Although the building and repairing of slave cabins were integral parts of the annual routine on developing plantations, the construction of housing tended to lag behind growth of the plantation population. Inasmuch as cultivating and gathering the crops of cotton and corn took precedence over all other activities, house building was generally relegated to the winter months. As a result, slaves on new plantations were crowded into crude log cabins lacking floors and windows and having barely enough space for them to

16. Genovese, *Roll, Jordan, Roll*, 617–19; Anderson Hutchinson (comp.), *Code of Mississippi, 1798–1848* (Jackson, Miss., 1848), 513–14; William K. Scarborough, *The Overseer: Plantation Management in the Old South* (Baton Rouge, 1966), 67–68; Sydnor, *Slavery in Mississippi*, 77–79.

spread their cotton pallets. Under these circumstances, individual privacy was inconceivable and family life all but impossible.[17]

Making the situation in such overcrowded slave cabins somewhat less unpleasant than it might otherwise have been, planters customarily allowed their slaves to choose which cabins they would occupy, a privilege that permitted something like normal relationships to develop between men and women. Certainly, rural slaveowners did not attempt to segregate their slaves by sexes in the quarters, as Victorian tenets might have suggested, because they had an all-important stake in a high slave birthrate. As a rule, planters did not interfere with the sexual proclivities of their slaves in any way. Instead, they rewarded slave women for bearing children, without concern for the paternity of the children, and took particular pains to ensure that infants and small children were well cared for physically. Unfortunately, however, they provided no instruction for young children before they were old enough to go to the fields. As soon as infants were weaned or even sooner, they were placed in a plantation nursery, where, under the supervision of the planter's wife (or under that of the overseer if the planter did not live on the premises), older slave women cared for them while the mothers were at work in the fields. The older boys and girls not yet of working age were fed separately in the plantation kitchen and were allowed to play around the quarters under the general charge of older slaves. In this era planters did not require slave mothers to assume many responsibilities for raising their offspring, and indeed these women had little time to spend with their small children. The planter and his wife bore the primary responsibility for the welfare of slave children.[18]

Nevertheless, despite the handicaps of communal housing and child rearing, and indifference toward slave family relationships on the part of the white ruling class, strong ties did develop between men, women, and their children in thousands of cases. In time, Mississippi slaveowners even came to realize that family bonds among their slaves were valuable assets to their plantations and that such bonds should be actively encouraged.

17. Genovese, *Roll, Jordan, Roll*, 525–26; Stampp, *Peculiar Institution*, 292–95; Sydnor, *Slavery in Mississippi*, 40–44.
18. Genovese, *Roll, Jordan, Roll*, 458–75; Owens, *This Species of Property*, 182–213; Stampp, *Peculiar Institution*, 312–14; Sydnor, *Slavery in Mississippi*, 62–63.

Several developments occurring early in the nineteenth century tended to mitigate the dehumanizing effects of the gang system of agricultural slavery in Mississippi as elsewhere in the Lower South. One such development, the expansion of the Cotton Kingdom, generated an ever-increasing demand for slaves, which in turn caused an upward trend in prices for slaves between 1800 and 1860. A second was the closing of the overseas slave trade in 1808, which intensified the shortage of slaves caused by the shift from tobacco to cotton. A third development, occurring during the 1820s, was the adoption of Mexican cotton as the standard variety in Mississippi, which increased the value of slaves as agricultural workers by increasing their ability to pick cotton.

Mexican cotton, it will be recalled, produced more abundant yields than its predecessors and could also be harvested more easily. Ordinary field hands were able to pick about sixty pounds of seed cotton a day in fields of Siamese or Georgia green seed cotton; in fields of Mexican cotton, they could gather 250 pounds with no more exertion. The fourfold increase in picking capacity of slaves heightened the profitability of cotton plantations because no corresponding jump in cost was involved. As a result, the value of a slave to a cotton planter rose accordingly. By making slaves scarce, costly, and indispensable as agricultural workers, these developments impelled cotton planters from self-interest to provide tolerable living conditions for their plantation slaves. In fact, it soon became a truism that the success or failure of a cotton plantation depended as much upon the birthrate and general health of the slaves as it did upon the size and quality of the cotton crops.

A fourth, unrelated noneconomic development, the spread of evangelical Protestantism throughout the Old Southwest, occurred by coincidence at about the same time as the emergence of the Cotton Kingdom. The upsurge in religious fervor also tended to improve the treatment of plantation slaves generally. During the first two decades of the nineteenth century, a tidal wave of religious fervor engulfed the lower Mississippi Valley. Beginning in Logan County, Kentucky, during 1800, a burst of revivalism brought tens of thousands of converts into the Baptist, Methodist, and Presbyterian churches. These were conservative, evangelical denominations that valued the souls of slaves on a par with the souls of their owners. Originally, all three denominations were opposed in principle to slavery, but each was forced eventually to modify its views in order to appeal to southwestern cotton growers, a class of men on the make who were determined to own slave-worked plantations. Even while they were being compelled to compromise their beliefs by accepting slavery as not un-Christian, the three churches continued to insist with considerable effect that slaveowners were responsible to God for both the material and the spiritual welfare of their human charges. Furthermore, the major Protestant denominations in the Old Southwest tried and punished slaveowners among their congregations for misusing slaves, and churchmen marshaled public opinion against slaveowners not of their congregations who were reputed to treat their slaves badly.[19]

Throughout the entire antebellum period, the living conditions of agricultural slaves were also affected by the current stages of development of the plantations on which they were living. Most antebellum cotton plantations passed through three of these stages in the plantation life cycle. In the first, or pioneer, phase, a new plantation was carved out of the forest or canebrakes and was brought gradually into cultivation over a period of several years. In the second, mature phase, a plantation attained full production, with enough new ground being brought under cultivation annually to replace fields rendered unproductive by loss of soil fertility. In the final, declining stage, all woodlands on the plantation from which new fields could be created by clearing had been exhausted, and the fields still being cultivated were of marginal fertility.

Until the 1850s ushered in effective methods of soil conservation, the fertility of corn and cotton fields on rolling terrain diminished inevitably from year to year because of soil erosion. Planters throughout the Lower South consequently expected to be able to cultivate land in row crops for only about ten years before the fields became uneconomical. When tracts finally lost enough fertility to be unprofitable to cultivate, planters either converted those lands into pastures or abandoned them altogether to grow up in weeds and bushes. Wise cotton growers anticipated the destruction of land by acquiring tracts larger than they planned to cultivate at the time when they were setting up plantations, so that they would have a reserve of virgin soil to exploit in the future. When the land reserves were nearing exhaustion, or when a successful planter was enlarg-

19. John W. Blassingame, *The Slave Community: Plantation Life in the Antebellum South* (New York, 1972), 169–71; Margaret DesChamps Moore, "Religion in Mississippi in 1860," *Journal of Mississippi History*, XXII (1960), 223–38; Walter B. Posey, *Frontier Mission: A History of Religion West of the Southern Appalachians to 1861* (Lexington, Ky., 1966).

ing the scope of his agricultural operations, he purchased fresh land for a new plantation, usually located in another county or state. Then he gradually shifted his slaves from the old plantation to the new over a period of several years. Thus, while slaves were engaged in opening a new plantation, whether in the 1820s or the 1850s, they inevitably lived for a year or two under comparatively primitive conditions.[20]

American cotton planters moving into new cotton plantations at any time between 1800 and 1860 almost always erected log cabins for themselves and their slaves. Over the next few years, they gradually improved these rude habitations by adding floors and chimneys and sometimes by boarding over the interior walls. Francis T. Leak, for example, recorded in his diary in 1850 that "the inch plank with other old inch plank & a few refuse have been used in flooring negro houses."[21]

When a plantation had been brought into full production after five to ten years, the original log cabins were often replaced by small frame houses boasting brick chimneys and shuttered windows, which were usually raised on foundations several feet above the ground for the sake of sanitation and coolness in summer. Robert Russell described housing of this sort on a plantation near Washington, Mississippi, which he visited in 1856. "Their cabins," he wrote, "made of sawn wood were twenty feet in length by eighteen in breadth, white-washed without and within, and the floors laid with wood raised a few feet above the ground. The interior had a naked appearance, as there was no furniture except the beds and a few chairs." During the late 1850s the northern schoolmaster A. de Puy Van Buren saw similar housing in Yazoo County. On one plantation, he wrote, "the field hands have their quarters near by the house some thirty rods to the right. These consist of little frame cabins, boarded with cypress, and white washed." Elsewhere, he added, "they are often log cabins." Like many other planters in the Mississippi Delta, F. A. Metcalf of Washington County replaced his log cabins during the later years of the 1850s. Although he had his own steam-powered sawmill, Metcalf complained after finishing all of his new frame cabins that "I could have built the quarters quicker and cheaper of brick."[22]

The arrangements described in *De Bow's Review* during 1851 by a

20. Moore, *Agriculture*, 37–41.
21. Leak Diary.
22. Russell, *North America*, 264; Van Buren, *Sojourn in the South*, 207–208; Newstead Plantation Records, February 2, 1858.

large slaveowner whose plantation was located on Big Black River were not unusual. In a well-drained area shaded by trees, the planter had constructed twenty-four frame houses for his 150 slaves. These houses were sixteen by eighteen feet, whitewashed inside and out, and were equipped with brick chimneys. The houses were arranged in two rows and were spaced fifty feet apart. Four cisterns provided water for the inhabitants of the little village.[23]

Dugal C. McCall, who operated a small plantation, a brickyard, and a sawmill in Jefferson County near Rodney, provided somewhat differently for his slaves. In 1850 he constructed several frame buildings, each containing four one-room apartments, for his slave families. Each room was provided with a brick chimney and hearth. As these houses were completed, McCall demolished the older cabins that they replaced.[24]

On a few large home plantations of wealthy planters during the 1820s and 1830s, and on many established plantations of all sizes during the 1850s, frame slave cabins gave way to neat brick cottages when the owner erected a permanent residence of brick for himself.[25]

In the pioneer stage of the cotton plantation life cycle, the diets of slaves and whites alike were generally restricted to the basic foodstuffs, dried corn and salt pork supplemented by fish, game, berries, and wild fruits taken from nearby woods and streams. As the plantation became more developed, fresh corn, sweet potatoes, beans, and peas as well as various garden vegetables were added to the diet. On fully developed plantations of the 1840s and 1850s, poultry, eggs, mutton, beef, milk, butter, fruits, and vegetables became staple items on the plantation menu. It should be stressed, however, that, in all periods between 1800 and 1860, plantation slaves received ample quantities of the basic ration (a peck of cornmeal and three to five pounds of salt pork per week for each adult), even though the diet at times may have been seriously deficient in important food elements.[26]

Robert Russell, who visited the Natchez area during the 1850s, was told that "the common allowance for an able-bodied negro is half a pound

23. *De Bow's Review*, X (1851), 623.

24. Dugal McCall Plantation Journal (Southern Historical Collection, University of North Carolina, Chapel Hill). See entries for February 1850 through February 1851.

25. Sydnor, *Slavery in Mississippi*, 41–42.

26. Sam B. Hilliard, *Hog Meat and Hoecake: Food Supply in the Old South* (Carbondale, Ill., 1972).

of bacon a day, with Indian corn, molasses and vegetables of different kinds in their season." The practice of issuing weekly rations that the slaves prepared for themselves had recently been abandoned in that region. "However liberal the allowance might be, it rarely served until the day of distribution again came around," Russell wrote. "The food of the negroes is, therefore commonly cooked in one kitchen, and divided at every meal."[27]

During the decades of the 1830s and 1840s most of the slaves of Mississippi, like their owners, were housed in the crudest sort of log cabins having dirt floors and chimneys made of sticks and mud. Between 1833 and 1837 an enormous land rush into northern Mississippi brought more than 100,000 slaves into the region recently vacated by removal of the Choctaw and Chickasaw Indians, and these black newcomers were set to work hacking farms and plantations out of the virgin forests. At the same time, many other slaves were transferred from worn-out plantations in southwestern Mississippi onto the alluvial lands along the Yazoo-Tallahatchie river system. In both areas, inhabitants of the new plantations and farms lived for periods of from five to ten years under primitive conditions. Consequently, the lucky slaves left behind on the old home plantations located between Woodville and Vicksburg were much more comfortably situated than were the host of involuntary pioneers in the northern part of the state.[28]

During the agricultural revolution of the 1840s, agricultural slavery in Mississippi—which had never been a static institution—changed profoundly for the better. Of the many developments affecting the lives of slaves during this period, the most far-reaching was a basic alteration in the way cotton planters regarded land. They had traditionally looked upon the soil as a commodity to be used and consumed; in the new economic climate they came to value their lands as permanent assets. With cotton prices falling to historic lows during the first half of the decade, it became uneconomical—and for many financially impossible—to continue the custom of opening new plantations to replace older ones worn out by farming methods that made the soil infertile. Realizing that they must prolong the productive lives of existing plantations, cotton growers began to protect the soils of their hilly lands against erosion with elaborate drainage systems while adopting such techniques of soil conservation

27. Russell, *North America*, 266.
28. Gray, *Agriculture*, II, 899–900; Moore, *Agriculture*, 68–69.

as systematic rotation of crops and fertilization with surplus cottonseeds and legumes. For the agricultural slaves, the trend away from the habit of opening new plantations periodically meant that decreasing numbers of them would be compelled to live under primitive conditions. Whereas a majority of slaves in Mississippi were engaged in opening new plantations in the northern half of the state in the 1830s, a great many during the 1850s were living more comfortably on fully developed plantations that provided them with improved housing, a more varied and nutritious diet, and much less strenuous work.[29]

When interviewed by Works Progress Administration (WPA) workers during the 1930s, virtually all of the former Mississippi slaves retained vivid memories of the cabins they had inhabited on farms or plantations just before the Civil War. A few, mainly from the river counties, had lived in brick cabins. Benjamin Whitley Smith, for example, had been a slave on Saulsbury plantation, located near Woodville in Wilkinson County. His owner, F. H. Hooks, "lived in a big white house with round columns. . . . De slave quarters wuz brick and the slaves wuz well cared for." The testimony of Ruben Fox, who had lived in Washington County on a plantation belonging to Junius Ward, was similar. He said, "All of the houses in the quarter where we lived was made of brick. Some says the brick was made right there on the place." Dora Franks, who had belonged to George Brewer of Choctaw County, related: "We was livin' on de Troup place den, near ole Hamilton, in one of de brick houses back of de house whar dey uster keep de slaves."[30]

A vast majority of these former slaves who survived to be interviewed, however, had lived in crude log cabins equipped with chimneys made of clay, such as those described by Arron Jones of Marshall County. He said, "We lived at the quarters. They were good log houses, with dirt and stick chimneys." Lucy Donald of Rankin County said, "Our cabins wuz little one room huts built ob logs wid mud an' straw chimneys." Rena Crawford of Marshall County said that her quarters had been "chinked log cabins with stick and mud chimneys." Belle Caruthers, also of Marshall County, said, "Their houses were log cabins, with stick chimneys, daubed with mud. We cooked, ate and slept in one room, no matter how big the family." Vinnie Busby's quarters in Rankin County were composed of

29. Moore, *Agriculture*, 174–78.
30. *Slave Narratives*, Ser. 1, *Mississippi*, Vol. VII, Pt. 2, pp. 769, 783, Vol. X, Pt. 5, p. 1977.

somewhat better cabins. She related that "de cabins we lived in wuz built of logs split open an' pegged together. . . . Dese chimneys was made ob sticks, dirt and straw."[31]

The furnishings of the log cabins described in the *Slave Narratives* consisted of beds and a chair or two. The beds were like those described by Ed Crum of Copiah County: "Beds was made by poles bored into de walls at head an' foot part on lil' sticks to hole hit up." In Marshall County such beds were called one-legged or two-legged "aggies," according to the number of supporting upright sticks. On a plantation near Osyka, Nelson Dickinson had slept on a bed "that had ropes tied all through it; dey wus wrapped and platted an' made the bed lie soft." More commonly canvas or strong cotton cloth was stretched over the frame of poles to support a mattress. According to Arron Jones, of Marshall County, the mattresses were made of "ticks stuffed with shucks and rye. . . . They was pretty comfortable." Cotton, corn shucks, and hay were the usual mattress stuffings. The chairs were homemade, with bottoms made of cowhides, canvas, vines, or wood. Adults occupied the bunks; children slept on pallets spread on the floor. In warm weather, the children preferred to sleep outdoors. The adults then spread their mattresses on the porches of the cabins. When the mosquitoes were bad, the family moved indoors and built a smoky fire in the hearth to drive the insects away.[32]

The mechanization of cotton plantations, as described earlier, benefited plantation slaves in many different ways. By increasing a field hand's productivity, for instance, the new horse-drawn implements enhanced the value of his services to his owner, resulting within a few years in something resembling the free worker's raise in wages. Newly developed seed planters, cultivators, scrapers, and double-shovels, although not greatly enlarging the cotton crop, did significantly increase production of corn, peas, beans, sweet potatoes, fruits, and garden vegetables. The improved supply of foodstuffs greatly enhanced the quality and variety of the diets of whites and blacks on the plantation while permitting the planter at the same time to build herds of beef and dairy cattle, hogs, and sheep. Because icehouses were introduced into the plantations at this

31. *Ibid.*, Vol. VI, Pt. 1, p. 308, Vol. VII, Pt. 2, pp. 365, 534, 637, Vol. VIII, Pt. 3, pp. 1185–86.

32. *Ibid.*, Vol. VII, Pt. 2, pp. 525, 534, 537, 602–603, Vol. VIII, Pt. 3, pp. 1185–86.

time, it became possible to provide agricultural slaves with much more butter and milk than heretofore.

The circular icehouse Francis T. Leak constructed on his plantation in Marshall County during January 1856 was probably typical. It measured fifteen feet in diameter and was twelve feet deep. Leak filled it with twenty-six and one-half wagon loads of ice two and one-half inches thick that had been cut locally. Callie Gray, who had been a slave on a plantation belonging to James Fant of Marshall County, described a similar ice-house. She told the WPA interviewer: "We had ice all right, but we never thought of setting food on it, and couldn't have ef we had wanted to 'cause the ice house was too onconvenient. It was built of two layers of brick with charcoal between, and the only opening was at the top. They would collect ice offen the lake and the ponds in winter and dump it in there and cover it with cotton seed. Den in the summer they would make ice cream with it and sometime them would pound it up and put it on a sick person's head." [33]

A vast majority of the former Mississippi slaves who were interviewed by WPA interrogators agreed that they had been well fed during the 1850s. Sally Dixon, for example, who had lived on a new plantation that Crawford White was opening on the Bogue in the Yazoo-Mississippi delta, related: "There was always plenty to eat; meat, molasses, peas, bread, taters and greens. The big old smokehouse was always filled with meat. We raised the hogs and cured the meat. My Pa brought home all the game we wanted for hisself and children. Bout the only thing Master had to buy for us was shoes, and he sure did get good ones." Aron Carter, who had belonged to William Gwin of Lincoln County, said: "De eats wuz good; better dan ah' gets now by a long shot. Dere wuz greens, bacon, peas, rice, milk, butter, loads of fish, possum, rabbits, birds—jes' eberythin'." Simon Durr, who had belonged to Michael Durr of Copiah County, testified: "Mos everything was growed and made right deir on de plantation. De cows from de green pastures furnished all de milk and butter, de drove of hogs furnished all de meat and lard. De vegetables, taters an' meal come from de fiels. De lassis wuz made from de cane, de barn yard wuz full of chickens, turkeys and ducks which gib us all de fresh eggs and fowl meat we could use.

33. Leak Diary, January 4, 5, and 9, 1856; *Slave Narratives*, Ser. 1, *Mississippi*, Vol. VIII, Pt. 3, p. 863.

De candles, soap, cheese, cloth, and most everything wuz made right deir." [34]

Charles Davenport had lived on Aventine plantation, which belonged to Gabriel Shields, an in-law of the famous Surgets of the Natchez District. Born about 1845, Davenport had a happy boyhood on this large old plantation. His pleasanter memories included some of the meals he had enjoyed. He described them as follows:

> Us slaves was fed good plain grub. 'Fore us went to the fiel', us had a big breakfas' o' hot bread, 'lasses, fried salt meat dipped in corn meal, an' fried [sweet] taters. Sometimes us had fish an' rabbit meat. When us was in the fiel' two women 'ud come at dinner time wid baskets filled wid hot pone, baked taters, corn roasted in de shucks, onions, fried squash, and biled pork. Sometimes dey brought buckets o' cold buttermilk. It sho' was good to a hongry man. At suppertime us had hoecake an' cold vittles. Sometimes dey was sweet milk an' collards. Mos' every plantation kep' a man busy huntin' an fishin' all de time. If dey shot a big buck us had deer meat roasted on a spit. On Sundays us always had meat pie or fish or fresh game an' roasted taters an coffee. On Christmas de Marster 'ud give us chickens an' barrels o' apples an' oranges. [35]

Harriet Miller, who had lived on a plantation west of Magnolia belonging to Mike Cook, was one of the few who had unpleasant memories of the food the slaves had eaten. She said: "Dey neber hed much ter eat. De white folks got de good grub en de slaves got common grub. No slave ever got a biskit [of wheat flour], en dey never got eny cakes or pies. Sumtimes dey would mix meal en 'lasses up en baked it fur a cake." She added: "When dey wurk in de field dey got meat in deir greens, en dey had meat in de quarters ebery Sunday, and ebery Sunday dey got some butter from de big house." She also said: "All de slaves had patches round deir houses, corn en tater patches, en had deir own gardens, but wuz not 'lowed ter have chickens, ner hogs, ner cows." [36]

As the profitability of the plantation improved with cost reductions attributable to mechanization, planters doubtless were able to clothe their slaves more adequately. Women who could now be spared from the field more often made dresses, shirts, trousers, overcoats, and quilted comforters padded with cotton that were even warmer than the traditional woolen blankets. [37]

34. *Slave Narratives*, Ser. 1, *Mississippi*, Vol. VII, Pt. 2, pp. 359, 626–27, 654–55.
35. *Ibid.*, p. 570.
36. *Ibid.*, Vol. IX, Pt. 4, p. 1501.
37. Moore, *Agriculture*, 73, 106, 144.

Most of the former slaves said that their clothing had been manufactured on their plantations. Aron Carter, for example, said: "Mos everything we wears is made right on de plantation. All our clothes, en everything. At killin' time de leather o' de animals wuz dried an' cured, an' soaked to get it brown, and when it wuz ready we cut it an' make our shoes. We even make homemade tacks." Sally Dixon recalled that "the women on the place wove the cloth our clothes was made of. Every night my Ma had to spin six cuts of cotton before she went to bed. Some of the cloth was dyed in colored stripes. It sure was beautiful, but most of it was left white. We wore the same clothes in the winter that we wore in the summer sept more of them in winter." Ruben Fox said: "All our clothes was made and given to us. They even made the cloth they used with one of them spinning wheels. Our socks was knitted out of wool, and they sure did keep us good and warm. Our shoes was bought. I felt like I was the finest thing in the land when I got a pair of them boots with brass tips on the toes." Polly Turner remembered that "we had warm clothes in de winter an' cotton clothes in de summer. We raised our own wool an' cotton an' de slaves made hit into cloth." Ed Crum related that "now on rainy days mammy an' all de womens would weave an' spin in de loom house makin' clof—lowell, you know, fo us clothes. When we wo' shoes dey was russetts, an' one of the mens on de place made 'em." Robert Young had a recollection similar to Crum's. He said: "Us all woe lowells whut de darkies made fo' us out'n clof dey made on de loom. Overseer, he seen to hit dey wove at night. Dey wuked till 'bout nine an' had taller can'els to see by." [38]

Daniel O. Williams, like most planters, issued his slaves sets of summer and winter clothing. As a rule he purchased the cloth for his women to manufacture into dresses for the women and trousers and shirts for the men. On March 8, 1853, he instructed his son Sampson: "Remember never give out linsey clothing before the 1st December. If you do, most of the negroes will wear them out in the warm months of September, October & November." In 1858, the elder Williams purchased a Wilson and Wheeler sewing machine for making slave clothing. It could do as much work in a day as twelve seamstresses. His wife enjoyed the machine so

38. *Slave Narratives*, Ser. 1, *Mississippi*, Vol. VII, Pt. 2, pp. 343, 354–55, 537, 626–27, 771, Vol. X, Pt. 5, p. 2407.

much that she herself assumed the task of making all of the garments for the slaves.[39]

Perhaps the most important improvement in the lives of the plantation slaves during the last two decades of the antebellum period wrought by the mechanization of the cotton plantations was the emergence of a new system of managing slave labor. Because horse-drawn implements required skilled farm workers in order to be effective, they made obsolete the gang system designed to direct the labor of unskilled and unwilling workers. At this time a revised version of the task system long used on rice plantations in Georgia and South Carolina gradually replaced the gang system.

Although the old hoe gang continued to be used in modified form throughout the last two decades of the antebellum period, cultivation of the crops with horse-drawn scrapers, cultivators, and double-shovels was performed increasingly under the task system. The varying gaits of horses and mules meant that plowmen and plowwomen simply covered too much ground and became too scattered to permit close supervision by a driver. Therefore it became necessary to give each plow hand his or her own daily work assignment for which he or she would be held accountable at the end of the day. The allotment of individual tasks also demanded, if the new system was to be profitable to the owner, that plow hands have positive, rather than negative, incentives to do their utmost. Even under the ancient gang system, slaves could "break, waste, destroy, idle away time, feign sickness, run away, and do all manner of things to vex and torment . . . [their owners]." Equipped with expensive implements and most costly mules, agricultural slaves had far greater opportunities for undetectable sabotage than ever before. To cite only a few examples, they could cut roots of cotton or corn by guiding their implements too close to the plants, or they could damage a lightly constructed planter, scraper, cultivator, or double-shovel by running the implement into an obstruction, or, even worse for the planter, they could injure a valuable mule in a dozen different ways.[40]

Francis T. Leak, a large slaveowner operating several plantations in northern Mississippi, provided an illustration of the manner in which the

39. Daniel O. Williams to Sampson Williams, March 8, 1853, and [n.d.], 1858, in Williams Papers.
40. Kellar (ed.), *Solon Robinson,* II, 278.

shift from the gang to the task system occurred. In the spring of 1846 he was tasking plow hands on his home plantation near Holly Springs while continuing to work his hoe hands in gangs. A scientific agriculturist who subscribed to the *Southern Cultivator* and performed agricultural experiments, Leak tasked his plowmen and plowwomen very precisely. On May 21, 1846, for example, he required that workers using horse-drawn harrows cover 17,000 yards before leaving the field every day. On May 27 he assigned plowmen and women "running around the cotton" forty-five rows 440 yards long. While chopping through his cotton fields for the first round of the growing season, Leak became aware that his gang of twenty-four workers was deliberately slowing its pace. At the beginning, the gang "chopped through about 40 acres a day." By May 23 the slaves had gradually slowed the pace until they were hoeing only 24 acres. Within a few more days they were clearing only 15 acres between sunup and sundown. During the first week of hoeing, the gang worked 175 acres, the second 140 acres, and the final week of the first round, 105 acres. Instead of resorting to the driver's whip to increase the slaves' productivity as most slaveowners would have done, Leak decided to convert his hoe gang to the task system. On the first day of the second round of hoeing, he assigned the men fifteen rows to be completed before returning to the quarters and the women thirteen. The following day he increased the men's task to eighteen rows while leaving the women's task at thirteen rows. Noting that "the hoe hands with a few exceptions did their tasks," he continued tasking at that rate. Satisfied with his new system, he commented, "We were too long in going the first round because the hands were not tasked."[41]

While ordinary field hands gained new means of striking at their owners as a result of plantation mechanization during the 1840s and 1850s, skilled workmen handling power-driven machinery undoubtedly acquired still greater bargaining power. By apparent carelessness for which no one would punish him, a busy ginner could fail to lubricate the bearings of a gin stand sufficiently to prevent the soft iron from wearing quickly. By a little more carelessness, that same skilled workman could permit the ginning machinery to overheat to the point where cotton caught fire. With still less risk, gin workers could store away damp cotton that would eventually ignite by spontaneous combustion, almost cer-

41. Leak Diary, entries for May 6 through 27, 1846.

tainly burning down the ginhouse. Running no risk of retribution at all, any slave working around a gin stand could damage the gin saws by dropping into the hopper a few rocks, some scrap iron, or pieces of wood mixed in with the loose seed cotton. Similarly, pressmen could easily damage the machinery of the cotton press or sawyers ruin an expensive sawmill. These opportunities for mischief were as nothing beside the opportunities of steam engine crews on large plantations. Without exerting themselves, skilled slaves, by allowing the boilers to explode, could blow the engine house and its contents to smithereens, drenching the ginhouse and its inhabitants with scalding water and superheated steam and probably destroying the nearby ginhouse with all of its expensive machinery.

When the possibilities for retaliation against owners or overseers, in addition to the long-standing threat of arson, are taken into account, it is not surprising that planters, who were not stupid as a class, eventually learned to dangle a carrot before their slaves as well as threaten them with the traditional stick.

Solon Robinson, after making a second trip through the Lower South to observe agricultural practices there, reported in 1849 upon the conclusions of hundreds of planters who had experimented with the new methods of managing slaves. "Upon a plantation where they are universally well treated," he wrote, "they [the slaves] can, by a promise of rewards, be induced to quicken their speed in a busy time; but under a system of bad treatment and attempted force, they will at such a time slacken their speed and perform their work in a more careless and slovenly manner." [42]

Merely avoiding sabotage by his slaves was not enough, of course, to ensure that a planter would produce and harvest a large crop of cotton. He first had to train his field hands to use horse-drawn implements with precision, and then he had to motivate them to use their recently acquired skills to the best of their ability. Consider, for example, the demands made on plowmen on plantations where rows of cotton and corn were given a measured slope of five degrees off the horizontal so as to promote drainage while minimizing erosion. In order to plow as precisely as necessary, plowmen had to be artists in handling mules and turning plows. Above all, they had to take great pride in their work. In any event, their performances were extraordinary, for a modern farm worker with the latest machinery would not find it easy to plow across hillsides to the

42. Kellar (ed.), *Solon Robinson*, II, 277.

requisite degree of accuracy. Obtaining willing cooperation from the field hands was most imperative during the harvesting of the cotton crop; a lack of enthusiasm could mean that 150 pounds rather than 300 were picked by a worker during the day.

John Gilmer of Lowndes County encouraged his cotton pickers to work diligently by offering them rewards. "I have never known anyone," he wrote, "to succeed in getting hands to pick well who drove by the lash. This should be the last alternative." He divided the workers into classes and offered prizes to the best pickers in each category. He gave calico dresses to female winners, shoes to the men, and pocket knives to the boys. A booby prize for "a lazy fellow holding back too much" was an uncomfortable ride on a rail. How well his system worked was indicated by the weights picked by twelve of his best hands. Chany picked 387 pounds, Evelen 333, Mary Ann 330, Miles 273, Calif 300, Edward 258, Jack 246, Anny 243, Tempa 244, Ned 236, and Maria 231. On five successive days Chany, the best picker, brought in 335, 358, 382, 387, and 386 pounds. When his pickers all worked well for a week, Gilmer gave them a holiday, apparently the following Saturday.[43]

Having learned the important lesson that contented slaves were more productive workers than unhappy slaves, planters began actively to encourage family life among the agricultural slaves as they long had done with their house servants. In addition to improving their slaves' food and clothing, large planters generally provided separate cabins for slave families during the 1840s and 1850s. Permanent arrangements between men and women were now perceived as promoting tranquillity within black plantation society. Of almost equal importance, newly acquired responsibility for wives and children made running away almost impossible for adult male slaves. Thus, quite by accident, cotton planters hit upon a very potent method of reducing absenteeism among their workers.[44]

In a lengthy series of articles on the care of slaves published in *American Cotton Planter and Soil of the South*, Dr. John Stainback Wilson of Columbus, Georgia, strongly recommended that planters should foster family life among their slaves. "There is certainly nothing more inti-

43. *Southwestern Farmer*, I (October 7, 1842), 35.
44. Erskine Clarke, *Wrestlin' Jacob: A Portrait of Religion in the Old South* (Atlanta, 1979), 70–71; Genovese, *Roll, Jordan, Roll*, 454–58; Herbert C. Gutman, *The Black Family in Slavery and Freedom* (New York, 1976), 79–80; Stampp, *Peculiar Institution*, 340–49; Sydnor, *Slavery in Mississippi*, 29, 39.

mately connected with the health and usefulness of the negro than properly regulated matrimonial connections," he wrote in one article. In another, he said: "To foster the home and family feeling as much as possible, negroes should be divided into families, and each family, should, if practicable, have a separate house; and to each house should be attached a small garden plot." Wilson explained that it was in planters' self-interest to promote the formation of slave families. "Such an arrangement," he argued, ". . . will . . . bind the servant to the master with more than triple cords—will be better and more effectual than handcuffs and chains." The evidence suggests that in the 1850s most slaveowners in Mississippi shared Wilson's views.[45]

William Ethelbert Erwin of Lowndes County, for example, not only required his slaves to live in families, but also spelled out the obligations of husbands and wives. Rule 2 in his list of "Rules to be Observed on my Place from & after the first of January 1847" specified: "Each Family to live in their own house. The husband to provide fire wood and see that they are provided for. . . . The wife to cook & wash for the husband and her children and attend to the mending of clothes. Failure on either part when proven shall and must be corrected by words first, but if not reformed to be corrected by the whip."[46]

As an additional inducement for male and female slaves to marry, planters permitted slave families to maintain their own vegetable gardens, poultry yards, and hog pens, and some slaves were allowed to keep milk cows. The slaves were almost always permitted to sell their surplus vegetables, eggs, chickens, ducks, pigs, milk, and butter either to their owners or to slave entrepreneurs from neighboring villages, who retailed this produce from door to door to urban white housewives or sold it through village markets. Indeed, during the 1840s and 1850s, most towns and villages of Mississippi were supplied mainly with fresh vegetables, eggs, chickens, and fish by plantation slaves of the vicinity.[47]

In an unusual entry in his plantation book dated May 23, 1855, William E. Erwin inventoried the chickens in possession of his slaves on his

45. *American Cotton Planter and Soil of the South*, IV (1860), 415, 463–64.
46. William Ethelbert Erwin Plantation Book (Southern Historical Collection, University of North Carolina, Chapel Hill).
47. Genovese, *Roll, Jordan, Roll*, 535–40; Hilliard, *Hog Meat and Hoecake*, 182–84; Owens, *This Species of Property*, 53–54; Van Buren, *Sojourn in the South*, 41, 208.

plantation in Lowndes County. According to Erwin's list, fifteen families or individual slaves were raising fowl. As typical examples, Harry and his wife, Hannah, owned seven hens, two roosters, and nineteen chicks, and Caesar and Norah owned four hens, one rooster, and thirteen chicks.[48]

Like most planters, Daniel O. Williams was determined that his slaves be adequately fed. He always planted enough acreage in corn to provide an abundance for his animals and slaves, and he regularly sowed all of his cornfields in peas and pumpkins. He raised large crops of sweet potatoes and Irish potatoes and considered the latter to be "the cheapest food that you can save for the negroes." He counseled his son Sampson not to substitute molasses for part of the meat ration as some slaveowners were doing and stressed that "fat meat, beans & peas is the only strong negro diet."[49]

Williams not only permitted his slaves to have gardens of their own but virtually forced them to do so whether they wanted to raise vegetables for themselves or not. He regularly instructed Sampson to provide the slaves on the Deer Creek plantation with garden seed because he was "very anxious that they should have a fair chance to raise their vegetables." In January 1858, he wrote to Sampson, "You should not regard a few dollars expense in getting garden seed for the negroes. A great deal less meat will do them when they are well suplied [sic] with vegetables." On another occasion he wrote, "I think that 3 lbs of meat pr week is a good allowance with vegetables, equal to 5 lbs. without." Williams also provided each of his slave families with a sow and encouraged them to raise pigs for themselves. In May 1854, he wrote: "They will raise plenty for themselves if you will only start them right. Mine have every one raised an abundant supply. Let each one in good faith have his own. My negroes keep their hogs gentle, generally slop[p]ing [them] at the door of their Cabbins, and they are very attentive to their piggs." Williams, however, advised against allowing slaves to have their own milk cows. Instead, he recommended that his sons keep the milk cows under their own charge and personally see that the milk was distributed equitably among the slaves. He also urged his sons to supply the slaves regularly with wheat flour.[50]

48. Erwin Plantation Book.

49. Daniel O. Williams to Sampson Williams, January 13, and February 9, 1858, in Williams Papers.

50. Daniel O. Williams to Sampson Williams, May 13, 1854, January 15, May 16, October 19, 1857, January [n.d.], February 22, March 29, 1858, all *ibid.*

Williams' attitude toward his slaves was a mixture of humanitarianism and exasperation. On one occasion he instructed his son "always to treat your young negroes with kindness and humanity. I would feel better satisfied to make 5 bales to the hand with such treatment than to make 10 bales to the hand under the driving cruel system." On another, he wrote to Sampson: "I hope that you will never be led astray by reflections of your own, or by the force of bad example to treat your negroes unkindly. They are very ignorant, treacherous, and agravating [*sic*], thieving & lieing, but they take all the hard work off of you, and deserve kind & humane treatment."[51]

The unnamed Mississippi planter who published an article about management of slaves in *De Bow's Review* in 1851 was an exception to the general rule. He permitted his slaves to raise poultry and cultivate gardens of their own but forbade them to sell any of their produce off the plantation. Instead, he gave each of them five dollars at Christmas to spend in the nearby town.[52]

During and after the agricultural revolution in Mississippi, cotton planters commonly allotted to slave families small tracts of land from one to ten acres in size, upon which they could raise cotton or corn as a cash crop of their own. President James K. Polk was one of the many slaveowners who followed this plan. He permitted his slaves to raise cotton upon plots assigned to them, and his overseers sold the slaves' cotton for them. In 1849, they raised about 8,400 pounds of seed cotton, or about five bales. On June 17, 1855, overseer John A. Mairs wrote to Mrs. Polk: "You wanted to know hough much you had to pay your negroes. You in ginerly pay them about 200 hundred dollars at a time." On Brookdale Farm, to cite another typical example, the slaves were allowed to cultivate such crops as the slaveowner designated. An entry of February 23, 1856, in the plantation journal revealed what these slaves were earning: "Harry . . . hauled home Frank's corn and fodder, and Joe's fodder." Frank was paid $23.57 for fifty and one-half barrels of corn and 150 bundles of fodder, and Joe $1.25 for 180 bundles of fodder.[53]

When interviewed by WPA researchers during the 1930s, many for-

51. Daniel O. Williams to Sampson Williams, April 17 and May 13, 1854, *ibid.*
52. *De Bow's Review,* X (1851), 624.
53. Bassett (ed.), *Southern Plantation Overseer,* 187, 210; Brookdale Farm Journal (Mississippi Department of Archives and History).

mer slaves (most of whom, of course, were young children during the 1850s) recalled that their parents worked plots of land assigned to them. One of these was William Flannagan, who had been a slave on the plantation of a Captain Ashley in Attala County near the town of Kosciusko. Ashley allowed his slaves to raise small crops of cotton or corn, which he sold for them. He allowed his slaves to spend their earnings as they wished. Another was Henry Gibbs, who had belonged to David Cottrell, whose plantation was located three miles east of West Point. Gibbs told the interviewer: "Dere was a rule dat de niggers must have half of every Saturday. Den, all nearly, would go fishin, unless dey worked in dere own patches. Sometimes dey raise things and old Marster would buy em, and de niggers would have dere own spending money for things they wanted to buy. Dis was given to de waggoner, and he'd go to town and buy what dey want." Another was Anda Woods of Hinds County, who related: "Marse had one good p'int us all laked. He would give us a acre or two o' land to tend for ourselves. He'd buy what us raised on hit, and in dat way us could have a little spending money or some to shoot craps wid." Wright Stapleton was yet another. He had belonged to a slaveowner named Pierce who lived in Rankin County near Puckett. Stapleton recalled that his father often worked in his plot at night by the light of pine torches and that his owner gave him the proceeds from sale of his produce.[54]

The slaves had other means of obtaining money besides working garden patches and small crops of cotton and corn. Polly Turner had lived during the 1850s on a plantation located on Woodson's Ridge in Lafayette County near Abbeville. She related that her owner, William Turner, had allowed his slaves to raise chickens for sale to a tavern in Abbeville. A white handled the actual sales so that the tavern keeper would know that the chickens had not been stolen. The planter also allowed slaves to earn money by picking cotton at night by moonlight. Polly Turner recalled also that "Old Marster used to let us gather chestnuts an' hazelnuts on Sundays, and den when the wagons was goin' to Memphis we could put out sacks on dem, and dey wud sell dem for us an' let us have de money; we would generally spen' hit fur lockets an' finger rings; I spec dey wuz brass, but us wuz jus' as proud of dem as dey wuz puor gol'." Callie Gray, who had been owned by James Fant of Marshall County, had a similar story to relate. She said: "Uv course sometimes the women wanted some

54. *Slave Narratives*, Ser. 1, *Mississippi*, Vol. VII, Pt. 2, p. 733, Vol. VIII, Pt. 3, p. 823, Vol. X, Pt. 5, pp. 2021–22, 2391.

fancy folderols they couldn't git on the plantation. Ef it was summertime they would pick blackberries, or wild grapes, or persimmons and sell 'em in town on Sadd'day afternoon."[55]

To be sure, a few highly vocal planters forbade their slaves to grow cotton, believing that the slaves would be tempted to steal from the owner's cotton houses, but a surprisingly large number of slaveowners actively encouraged their slaves to raise the staple crop. In such cases, the planters ginned and marketed the slaves' cotton for them, paying the slaves in goods or cash money.[56]

With mule-drawn implements coming into wider use on cotton plantations, planters were increasingly able to afford to allow their slaves leisure time during the growing season and still raise abundant crops of cotton and corn. Thus it became a common practice during the 1840s and 1850s to observe frequent holidays on the plantations and to release most of the slaves from their duties on Saturday afternoon. Sundays, of course, had long ago become holidays for agricultural slaves. Furthermore, the spreading of the task system throughout the Black Belt contributed to the same result. When plowmen were given daily or weekly personal assignments, they could gain additional free time for themselves by working at a faster pace than the norm, for they were permitted to leave the field when their assignments were accomplished.[57]

Some planters rewarded their agricultural slaves for work well done by holding parties for them. Mary Jane Jones, who had been a slave in Jefferson County, recalled: "De white folks used to give balls fur us and we had them in the hospital on the place where they left the babies when they went to the fields in the daytime. The music we had was fiddles and drums and sometimes just singing and calling figures." Others allowed the slaves to join with slaves from other nearby plantations to hold a "frolic," like those described by Robert Weatherby:

> Now us had our frolics long wid church gwine. When a frolic wuz on we would have to git a pass from our masters to go lak we had to git it to go any whar off de plantation. We had merry times at dese gatherings. We danced to fiddle music and guitars. De dancing wuz de ole square dance, whar dey swung deir partners an' called the sets. Den different ones would cut fancy steps by deir

55. *Ibid.*, Vol. VII, Pt. 2, p. 343, Vol. VIII, Pt. 3, p. 865.
56. Genovese, *Roll, Jordan, Roll*, 535–40; Gray, *Agriculture*, I, 564–65; Sydnor, *Slavery in Mississippi*, 31, 97; Weaver, *Mississippi Farmers*, 53.
57. Bonner, *Georgia Agriculture*, 198; Charles C. Davis, *Cotton Kingdom in Alabama* (Montgomery, 1939), 58; Eaton, *Southern Civilization*, 101.

selves, an' de ones could cut de mos' steps wuz counted de bes' dancer. We'd
have play games lak cross questions and crooked answers, handkerchief an'
thimble, an de lak o' dat. If we had 'freshments it would alwas' be ginger
cakes, parched peanuts an lasses candy. Now we had regular candy pullings too
and dey wuz a heap o' fun. Den we had regular buck dances too. We went to de
woods for dese. We'd take planks to dance on." [58]

Wise planters made social events for their slaves from tasks that would
ordinarily have been drudgery. Jerry Eubanks, who had been a slave on a
plantation near Columbus, had belonged to such an owner. He related:
"We had corn shuckings. Sich and sich a man would have 500 bushes of
corn to shuck and invite de slaves from neighbor plantations to come.
Didn't need no pass den. We'd all go shuck and holler and whooping—
den dere would be a big supper. Dere would be gallons of whiskey. De
boss would go around wid de jug, so we could holler clear. Cut the phlem."
Eubanks also recalled cotton-picking events held at night. "Dis," he said,
"would be when dere wuz a moon shining bright. I went to many a one.
Dis would be a big to-do and plenty of whiskey and eats after ten or
eleven o'clock." [59]

On most farms and plantations, Christmas was the harvest festival. At
this time slaves were usually given a week or more of holiday. From Yazoo
County in 1855, A. de Puy Van Buren wrote: "Throughout the country,
on every plantation, there is a merry time—a joyous leisure from all
work; Merry Christmas is with them all. The negroes, whole troops of
them mounted on mules, male and female, laughing and singing go from
one plantation to another; thus gathering in jolly groups, they feast and
frolic and dance the time away." The slaves Van Buren saw appeared
prosperous. "They are all dressed in the best, many of them in broad-
cloth," he wrote. "They have their nice white dickies on, their boots are
blacked, and a white or silk handkerchief is sure to display itself from
some one of their pockets, or from their hand." [60]

Most of the time, the recreations enjoyed by the black people on farms
and plantations were those they created for themselves. "De pleasures de
slaves had wuz things lak fishing, hunting, an' frolicing," Sylvia Floyd, a
former Simpson County slave, said. "Dey usually had a picknic once or
twice a year." Tony Cox, of the same county, remarked: "Gib us a dog,

58. *Slave Narratives*, Ser. 1, *Mississippi*, Vol. VIII, Pt. 3, p. 1245, Vol. X, Pt.
5, pp. 2241–42.
59. *Ibid.*, Vol. VII, Pt. 2, p. 695.
60. Van Buren, *Sojourn in the South*, 117.

fishin' pole an' de woods, an' us found eber thing ter make a little nigger happy."[61]

While plantation workers were acquiring more time to themselves as a result of mechanization and the modified task system, the custom developed in Mississippi as elsewhere in the Cotton Kingdom of compensating field hands for work performed during their leisure hours. Planters preferred to pay slaves for work done at night or on weekends with other released time, but quite often they paid slaves for such services in cash money at the prevailing rate for white laborers.[62]

William E. Erwin's plantation book provides an illustration of the practice of paying slaves for labor performed at times when they were not ordinarily required to work. An entry dated December 1846, for example, revealed that he had paid twenty-five slaves for several days' labor performed during the Christmas holidays at the rate of fifty cents per day.[63]

F. A. Metcalf treated his slaves on Newstead plantation, located on Deer Creek in Washington County, much as did Erwin. On December 26, 1858, he recorded in his journal: "Paid up my negroes for their work." The next entry, written the following day, said: "Gave permission to nearly all the negroes paid to visit Greenville to do their trading."[64]

Slaveowners as a class were always uneasy at the prospect of the slaves' having money of their own to spend, yet most of them accepted the associated risks as unavoidable. Indeed, within the limits of the Black Code of the state, plantation slaves were permitted by their owners to spend their earnings much as they pleased. Most of the slaves' earnings were spent for Sunday finery and such luxuries as coffee, tea, sugar, and wheat flour, but some was used to purchase whiskey. Despite state laws, county ordinances, and stern prohibitions from their owners to the contrary, slaves were apparently able to obtain this illicit commodity without too much difficulty. There were always whites willing to sell whiskey to slaves whenever they had money to buy it. Parenthetically, some slaveowners issued whiskey to slaves when the weather was cold and wet, and it was not uncommon for slaves to manufacture it for themselves. Plantation

61. *Slave Narratives*, Ser. 1, *Mississippi*, Vol. VII, Pt. 2, pp. 523, 745.
62. Eaton, *Southern Civilization*, 110, 190; Phillips, *American Negro Slavery*, 305–306; Stampp, *Peculiar Institution*, 164, 166–67; Sydnor, *Slavery in Mississippi*, 21–22.
63. Erwin Plantation Book.
64. Newstead Plantation Records.

slaves, however, usually did not have to purchase tobacco, as this near necessity was supplied by their owners.[65]

That slaves were indeed able to improve their living conditions through their newfound ability to earn and spend money is suggested by the bitter complaint of an Alabaman published in the *American Cotton Planter and Soil of the South*. "The constantly increasing independence and impudence of the negroes cannot but be observed by all," he fulminated in 1860. This lack of the proper subordination among the slaves was due, he believed, largely to allowing the blacks to "ape fashions of their masters and mistresses in their dress. . . . Why, sir, go to a city or village, or even a country highway near any country church on a Sunday, and what do we see? The streets completely blocked by Hoops, umbrellas, fancy coats, vests, and cast-off finery generally—to say nothing of flashy jewelry of every description."[66]

From the beginning of agricultural slavery in Mississippi, there was some specialization of labor among plantation slaves. At the earliest time blacksmiths were needed to sharpen soft wrought iron hoes and plow-points, and they were even more essential to plantation operations when horse-drawn implements came into vogue. Similarly, carpenters were always needed in a society where virtually everything from houses to farm implements was made on the premises from wood. In the mature phase of plantations the need for brick increased and brickmakers and brick-layers began to be trained. From the time when plantations first acquired cotton gins and presses powered by horses or mules, trained specialists were needed to operate and take care of the machinery. Sawyers, for instance, were necessary to work sawmills, and millers, corn mills and gristmills. When large plantations acquired steam engines to propel the many machines found in elaborate ginhouses, specially trained slaves had charge of the engines while other skilled workmen had the responsible jobs of firing the furnaces and tending to the boilers. Skilled hostlers and several assistants cared for the herd of mules and teams of oxen, together with their harnesses and other equipment. Leather workers repaired shoes and harnesses. To this list can be added plantation boatmen, fishermen, and hunters. Among the women, some acted as nurses in the hospi-

65. *Slave Narratives*, Ser. 1, *Mississippi*, Vol. X, Pt. 5, pp. 1918, 2363–64; Gray, *Agriculture*, I, 564–65; Stampp, *Peculiar Institution*, 290; Sydnor, *Slavery in Mississippi*, 96–101.
66. *American Cotton Planter and Soil of the South*, V (1861), 26.

tal, some looked after the children, and some were spinners, weavers, and seamstresses. In the late 1850s, these makers of plantation clothing were provided with sewing machines on some large plantations.[67]

By the 1830s, slave carpenters and masons were being trained like their free white counterparts by being apprenticed as boys to white master craftsmen. It became common practice for planters to select intelligent boys around the age of ten for such training. They were then apprenticed under contract to master workmen, who worked them without wages paid to the owner until the apprentices were eighteen. By that time, the young slaves had become certified journeymen craftsmen qualified to work at their trades like white journeymen. After their training was completed, the young black journeymen returned to their plantations to work at their crafts. These slave journeymen were not sent into the fields except in dire emergencies. Instead of working in the fields when their services were not needed on the plantation, craftsmen were hired out at high wages to white master craftsmen in nearby towns or villages, who were usually anxious to obtain such help. By the 1850s a not insignificant portion of the skilled workers of Natchez, Vicksburg, and Columbus were hired skilled slave journeymen from nearby plantations.[68]

Together with the drivers, skilled specialists such as carpenters, sawyers, masons, and blacksmiths made up a privileged middle class among the agricultural slaves. Even before separate housing was provided for agricultural slave families, these specialists usually had their own cabins, wives, and special rations of food and clothing. The privilege they most prized, however, was the status symbol of exemption from unskilled manual labor. When working away from the plantation under hire to white mechanics of the towns, these journeyman slaves worked and lived much like white journeymen. When not actually on the job, they were able to come and go as they chose. They were, in fact, quasi-free blacks who enjoyed the life-style of the white lower middle class.[69]

On plantations where owners resided, house servants were the most fortunate subclass of agricultural slaves. They ate the same food as mem-

---

67. Genovese, *Roll, Jordan, Roll,* 388–89; Owens, *This Species of Property,* 176–81; Sydnor, *Slavery in Mississippi,* 6; Weaver, *Mississippi Farmers,* 52–53.

68. Eaton, *Southern Civilization,* 84–85; Sydnor, *Slavery in Mississippi,* 8; Weaver, *Mississippi Farmers,* 52–53.

69. Genovese, *Roll, Jordan, Roll,* 393–94; Stampp, *Peculiar Institution,* 58–59, 151, 167.

bers of the planters' families, wore their owners' hand-me-down clothing, and almost always enjoyed better living quarters than the field hands.
Planters, believing that the appearance of their domestic servants reflected their own prosperity, dressed their domestic servants well, especially for occasions when the blacks were to be in the public eye. Planters
used their house servants in the fields only in the direst of emergencies
and characteristically overstaffed their big houses. Consequently house
servants were more likely to be afflicted by boredom than by overwork.
Living in very close proximity to whites, domestics were better able to
absorb white culture than agricultural workers, and they were certainly
held in higher esteem by their owners than were the ordinary field hands.
Maids and valets assigned to their owner, his wife, and children traveled
with the family, and some of them learned to read and write. Offsetting
their obvious advantages over field hands to some degree, house servants
were under close supervision by whites almost all of the time, and their
owners did not usually permit them to participate in the social activities
of the agricultural slaves. Apparently, however, domestic servants were
able to accept isolation from most of the black population in exchange for
privileges and superior living conditions.[70]

The occupational division of the slave force on a large plantation is illustrated by a list of slaves on Charles Allen's Nanechehaw plantation in
Warren County, dated January 1, 1860, in the plantation book. On the
plantation there were 113 slaves, of whom 38 were children. Among the
77 slaves of working age, 55 were described as field hands and 5 as swamp
hands (loggers). Slaves having special assignments were a carpenter, a
carter, the overseer's cook, a nurse for the slave children, and 9 slaves who
made up the staff of Allen's big house. The planter's manservant, a cook,
a housekeeper, 2 house maids, and a male house servant with general duties worked within the residence. A gardener, a stable boy, and a girl who
milked cows and washed clothes were yard servants. In 1860, 793 acres
were under cultivation on Nanechehaw plantation. Of these, 200 acres
were planted in corn and 565 acres in cotton. That year the plantation
produced 375 bales of cotton (6.8 bales to the hand and 0.66 bales to the
acre) and 121 wagon loads of corn that shelled out at 6,400 bushels (189

70. Genovese, *Roll, Jordan, Roll,* 331–65; [Ingraham], *South-West,* 247–49;
Owens, *This Species of Property,* 106–20; Stampp, *Peculiar Institution,* 41–42,
59, 161, 280, 323–28, 337–39; Sydnor, *Slavery in Mississippi,* 3–5.

bushels to the hand and 32 bushels to the acre.) This was an exceptionally large production for Warren County.[71]

The lot of slaves belonging to white farmers was quite different from that of plantation workers. In contrast to plantation slaves, who rarely saw whites other than overseers or members of their owners' families, farm slaves lived in as close association with the families of their owners as domestic servants did on plantations. They worked beside whites in the fields at the same jobs as the white sons and daughters of the farmers. In cases where a farmer owned only one or two slaves, those slaves ate at the same table with the whites and often slept under the same roof. Both whites and blacks on farms wore similar coarse work clothing except when going to church or to town. Sharing the lives of the white farmers as farm slaves did, however, was not an undiluted blessing. Although blacks worked no harder than the members of their owner's family, those hard-driving farmers demanded much of themselves, their wives, their children, and their slaves. There can be little doubt that farm slaves toiled harder for longer hours than their counterparts on cotton plantations. Moreover, some farm slaves did not enjoy the benefit of labor-saving tools and horse-drawn equipment that were standard on plantations after the 1830s. Perhaps worst of all, farm slaves were under even stricter twenty-four-hour supervision by whites than were the plantation house servants. In brief, farm slaves shared more of the culture of their white owners than plantation slaves but paid for the somewhat dubious privilege with the same grueling labor that the white farmers all performed routinely.[72]

Rose Brown, who had belonged to a storekeeper in the village of Bankston in Webster County, probably expressed the prevailing slave's view of working on farms when she said: "My peoples was allus lucky, de white folks treated us right. We never was owned by farmers, so our wurk wasn't so hard." Riley Moore, who belonged to Bennett Moore, also of Webster County, a farmer who owned six families of slaves, was more emphatic. He said that the Moore farm had been "Hell-on-earth." According to Riley Moore, the "niggers lived in little shoddy log cabins an' slept

71. Charles Allen Plantation Book.
72. Gates, *Farmer's Age*, 139–40; Gray, *Agriculture*, I, 488–92; [Ingraham], *South-West*, II, 26; Frank L. Owsley, *Plain Folk of the Old South* (Baton Rouge, 1949), 10, 13, 14–16, 193–205; Sydnor, *Slavery in Mississippi*, 68–69; Weaver, *Mississippi Farmers*, 39.

on whatever he could get. . . . We had home-made shoes called 'Red Rippers,' half 'nuff lowells clothes to wear, an' half 'nuff to eat. Didn't know what Christmas Day was."[73]

Although progressive planters resorted to incentives during the later decades of the slavery era in an effort to obtain a maximum of labor from their slaves, very few indeed abandoned the use of the whip altogether. A planter from Mississippi who published his exceptionally humane instructions to his overseer in *De Bow's Review* during 1859 made this point unmistakably clear. He wrote: "You are not allowed to take hold of the negroes to whip them, nor to beat them with sticks or clubs, or in any other manner than the most usual with the assistance of the driver and the other negroes." Another Mississippi correspondent of the same publication advocated good living and working conditions for slaves: "I cultivate about ten acres of cotton and six of corn to the hand . . . and have as few sour looks and as little whipping as almost any other place of the same size." The northern agricultural expert Frederick Law Olmsted described an incident on a large plantation near Natchez in which a female slave was whipped in his presence because she had been slipping away from the hoe gang, and he believed that this was regarded as an ordinary occurrence. Even ministers continued to use the lash on their slaves. Hamilton McKnight, pastor of the Baptist church in Liberty and owner of a nearby plantation called Brookdale Farm, recorded in his plantation record book on April 12, 1856, that he had "caught Joe and Nis stealing rice and punished them at night, Nis 75 and Joe 35 straps." Only the severity of the beatings was exceptional.[74]

When former Mississippi slaves were queried by WPA interviewers, virtually all had vivid recollections of the whipping of slaves on their farms or plantations. The following testimonies are typical of a very large number. Jennie Webb had belonged to Fredman Dent of Rankin County, who owned about forty slaves and 400 acres of land. She related: "My Ole Marse wuz good to us an' wanted us cared for right, but sometimes our over-seers would git pretty rough. De slaves wuz whipped at times.

73. *Slave Narratives*, Ser. 1, *Mississippi*, Vol. VI, Pt. 1, p. 285, Vol. IX, Pt. 4, pp. 1569–71.

74. *De Bow's Review*, X (1851), 625, XXVI (1859), 579; Olmsted, *Journey in the Back Country*, 84–86; Lucille Griffin (ed.), "The Plantation Record Book of Brookdale Farm, Amite County, 1856–1857," *Journal of Mississippi History*, VII (1945), 30.

De men wuz mos' always tied to trees to be whipped an de women wuz made to lie down. Dey used bull whips." Arron Jones had belonged to Rufus Jones of Marshall County. He related that "the overseer . . . was pretty mean. . . . He punished the niggers for disobedience and for fighting mongst themselves by whipping them." Tom Wilson had belonged to James Wilson, a farmer of Copiah County. He said: "I sho' has seen m' mammy an' lots mo' git whuppins. Marse Jim, he had a strop er leather stuck in de slit end of a staff, an' he sho' did whup 'em layed across a barr'l." Mollie Williams belonged to George Newsome of Copiah County. She said: "I seen plenty of darkies whupped. Marse George buckled my mammy down an' whipped her 'cause she run off. Once when Marse George seen pappy stealin' a bucket of 'lasses an' toting it to a gal on 'nother place, he whupped him, but didn't stake him down. . . . So I 'member he looked jes like he was jumpin' rope an' hollering' 'Pray Marster' ever time he strop hit 'im. Ruben Fox, who had lived on Junius Ward's plantation in Washington County near Greenville, testified: "The biggest thing the slaves got punished 'bout was fighting amongst their selves. Boss tried to stop that and sometimes he would have to whip them 'bout it. He didn't always know when they fought so there was mighty little punishment. There was so much to do on that place as we didn't have time to get in much devilment." [75]

Many of the former slaves blamed overseers rather than their owners for the whippings they had witnessed. James Lucus, who had belonged to several owners, spoke for many when he said: "Hit wasn't de marsters what was so mean, hit was dey trashy po-white over-seers an' agents; dey was mean as bull-dogs." Mattie Logan at seventy-nine years of age still enjoyed the memory of the occasion when the slaves on an adjoining plantation drove away an unpopular overseer by placing a harmless king snake in his bed. The overseer had been wise enough to recognize a warning that the next one would be a rattlesnake, and he acted accordingly. [76]

Despite significant improvements in living and working conditions achieved during the later decades of the antebellum period, all of the slaves in Mississippi, whether urban or rural, continued until the Peculiar Institution was abolished to live with the ever-present threat that

75. *Slave Narratives*, Ser. 1, *Mississippi*, Vol. VII, Pt. 2, p. 722, Vol. VIII, Pt. 3, p. 1186, Vol. X, Pt. 5, pp. 2252, 2347, 2378.
76. *Slave Narratives*, Ser. 1, *Oklahoma and Mississippi*, VII, 190, *Mississippi*, Vol. VIII, Pt. 3, p. 1331.

their families would be separated. Churches, slaveowners, and the white public at large all regarded separation of husbands from wives and especially the separation of small children from their mothers as the greatest evil associated with slavery. Reflecting this sentiment, bills were regularly introduced into the Mississippi legislature during the 1850s to prevent breaking up of families, but all such acts failed to become law. Slaveowners, when writing their wills, often attempted to keep mothers and children together, and they went to considerable trouble to arrange for small children to stay with their mothers when they had to sell slaves.

Nevertheless, slave families continued to be separated, for property rights always took precedence over personal rights of free men or slaves. Reformers who sought to preserve the slave family were always defeated by this fundamental legal principle. As property in the eyes of the courts, slaves were subject to seizure and sale to satisfy debts of their owners. As property, slaves were divided among their owner's heirs upon his death, and sometimes children and their mothers went to different new owners. As a result of this overriding reverence for property rights, slaves could safely assume that they would undergo at least one change of ownership during their lifetimes, with the probability that their domestic relationships would be disrupted in the process. Worse than physical punishment and forced labor was the breakup of the families by change of ownership, the greatest catastrophe that endangered all slaves.[77]

The slave quarters on antebellum cotton plantations were more than prisons for their black inmates; they were small rural villages. The inhabitants of these villages, together with the slaves on neighboring plantations and farms, composed a black community with customs, aspirations, and beliefs different from those of the ruling white community. When the Cotton Kingdom came into existence just before the turn of the nineteenth century, the slaves of the Southeast had already developed what John Boles has described as an Afro-American culture derived from a mingling of African and British-American elements. This culture came to the Old Southwest with the slaves who migrated there from the states of the Atlantic seaboard.[78]

Unfortunately, we will probably never know very much about the cul-

77. Blassingame, *Slave Community*, 89; Carl Degler, *Neither Black nor White*, 26–39; Genovese, *Roll, Jordan, Roll*, 43–49; Hutchinson (comp.), *Code of Mississippi*, 510–42; Phillips, *American Negro Slavery*, 489–514; Stampp, *Peculiar Institution*, 192–236; Sydnor, *Slavery in Mississippi*, 253.
78. Boles, *Black Southerners*, 142.

ture of the slaves because most of the scanty sources of information that
have survived were accounts by whites who knew very little about that
culture. Realizing that whites wished to eradicate any traces of a distinctive black culture and impose their own upon the slaves, blacks understandably made a fetish of secrecy. They tried to keep the whites in ignorance of what they thought and did and told whites only what they
believed whites wanted to hear. Slaveowning whites generally deluded
themselves that they understood the minds of their childlike slaves in in-
timate detail, when in fact they hardly knew how the blacks thought at
all, not even their body servants. Indeed, blacks knew the whites far
better than the whites knew them. In their pride as masters, the white
slaveowners did not bother to dissemble in the presence of their slaves
and often forgot that blacks were overhearing their conversations. Consequently, what was said in the big house soon reached the quarters, while
little that transpired in the quarters ever became known in the owner's
"mansion."

From memoirs of slaves who made their way to freedom and from the
testimony of former slaves gathered in the 1930s by WPA interviewers,
we know with certainty that a folk religion was central to the black culture of Mississippi's slaves. The doctrinal content of this religion was derived from Protestant Christianity, whereas the religious services were
apparently those of the white camp meetings of the early nineteenth century, modified to conform to the tastes of the blacks. Deprived by slavery
of hope for significant improvement in their earthly lives, rural blacks
found solace in the Christian promise of a hereafter in which they would
be free of sorrow, pain, and labor and would be equals with their former
masters. For obvious reasons, the story of the escape of the Hebrews
from captivity in Egypt was particularly appealing to slaves. Virtually all,
however, rejected Paul's instructions to the runaway slave to return to his
master, a text that white preachers often used in their sermons when
preaching to slaves. Riley Moore, a former slave in Webster County, expressed the resentment of the blacks for what they recognized as self-
serving religious instruction by whites. He said: "When Sunday come
they would preach fo' de white folks at 11 o'clock an' to de niggers in de
evenin'. They would take a text tellin' us niggers—don't steal, be good to
Massa an' missus an' don't run away. Dey ought to have been hung fo'
preachin' false doctorin. They was no such thing in de Bible." [79]

79. *Ibid.*, 167; *Slave Narratives*, Ser. 1, *Mississippi*, Vol. IX, Pt. 4, p. 1570.

Although a large minority of the slaves in Mississippi attended white religious services or received religious instruction from white ministers, most of them found the decorous services of the Presbyterians, Methodists, and even the Baptists alien to their culture. They much preferred the emotional singing and preaching that had characterized the camp meetings of the early part of the century, and in their own clandestine meetings held in the woods at night or on Sundays, they duplicated the white camp meetings as closely as they were able. In the words of Minerva Grubbs, a former slave in Simpson County who had been owned by Louis Howell, "Us went to the white folks church, an' sit on back seats, but didn't jine in de worship. You see, de white folks don't git in de spirit. They don't shout, pray, hum, and sing all through services lak us do. Dey don't believe in a heap o' things us niggers knows 'bout." [80]

Like the early white Methodists and Baptists, the blacks chose their preachers for their zeal rather than for their religious education. Sometimes the black congregations held contests to determine which of several candidates would lead their services. In such contests, the one who was best able to arouse the emotions of the members of the congregation was the one selected to be the preacher. The process was described by Robert Weatherby, a former Rankin County slave, as follows:

> When we wanted to have our own services we collected up an' went to de woods an' built big brush arbors an' at night we'd build great big fires an' had sho' nuf services. We could sing an' shout, an' dat what we wanted to do. Dey would hum an' morn [moan] all through the services. De preachers didn't hab no book learning, but when a darkie wanted to be a preacher, he wuz given a try-out by gitting up an' trying to preach a time or two, an' if he suited de folks an' dey thought he could preach, dey would say for him to preach, an' if he didn't suit 'em, dey would say for him not to.

In common with many of the whites of the antebellum period, blacks believed that trances inspired by the singing, dancing, and preaching at their services signified salvation. [81]

From the testimony of the former slaves in Mississippi there can be no doubt that services held while working together in the field and in their secluded brush arbors were the most important recreation for the blacks. Clara C. Young, who had been a slave on a plantation near Aberdeen, said, "De mos' fun we had was at our meetin's." These communal activi-

80. *Slave Narratives*, Ser. 1, *Mississippi*, Vol. VIII, Pt. 3, pp. 892–93.
81. *Slave Narratives*, Ser. 1, *Mississippi*, Vol. X, Pt. 5, p. 2239; Donald G. Mathews, *Religion in the Old South* (Chicago, 1977), 190–93.

ties also obviously relieved some of the tensions imposed on the blacks by slavery and contributed to the preservation of their mental health. The importance of these underground churches to the slaves is evident as well from the fact that the blacks after Emancipation acted quickly to organize their own churches free from all white interference, and they made these institutions the core of black postbellum society, with their preachers acting as political, social, and religious leaders.[82]

As we have seen, the lives of agricultural slaves in Mississippi changed significantly between the beginning of the Cotton Kingdom and the close of the antebellum period. With the passing of the pioneering years during which farms and plantations had been hacked out of virgin forests, and with the adoption of animal-drawn farming equipment, agricultural labor became much less arduous, and living standards improved significantly for the workers. The monetary worth of slaves rose to new heights as they learned how to use the new farm equipment effectively, and the concern of their owners for their health and morale increased proportionately with the improvement in their output. Black families headed by males replaced the older matriarchial units, and these new families acquired something resembling property rights in their gardens and patches of cotton or corn. Slowly but surely the black population was being drawn into the money economy of the state, a development fraught with implications of additional social change. Although the laws of the state had drawn tighter bonds around the slaves, persistent, patient, passive resistance by the whole agricultural slave population had secured important new freedoms. If any further evidence is needed to demonstrate that the institution of slavery had failed utterly to crush the spirit of the Mississippi slaves, we may consider the testimony of a child of the 1850s: "De darkies use to pull pranks on de patrols by stretchin' grape vines across de road to throw de horses. At other times de slaves 'ud git a little riled up an' jump de traces a little by fighting back wid fire." With the slaves possessed of such a spirit, it is not surprising that they sought freedom in vast numbers by peacefully leaving the plantations during the Civil War when Federal troops approached.[83]

82. *Slave Narratives*, Ser. 1, *Mississippi*, Vol. VII, Pt. 2, p. 169; Boles, *Black Southerners*, 167.
83. *Slave Narratives*, Ser. 1, *Mississippi*, Vol. VII, Pt. 2, p. 742.

6 Rural Whites

Throughout the era of slavery, the population of Mississippi, like that of all other southern states, was overwhelmingly rural. Agricultural slaves outnumbered all other social classes in that state from the late 1830s until the Civil War; farmers made up the bulk of the rural whites. Planters, although far fewer in number than the farmers, were the most economically significant social class. They owned more than half of the rural slaves and produced most of the state's cash crop.

In addition to the three major social classes of agriculturists, there were several less well known minor rural classes whose members were not engaged in agriculture and who were seldom landowners. Woodsmen who earned their livelihoods by logging, rafting, sawmilling, extracting turpentine and naval stores, burning charcoal, and cutting firewood for the steamboats, railroads, and towns formed one such nonagricultural class. Herdsmen who grazed their cattle on public lands in the pine barrens of south Mississippi formed another. A third comprised commercial freshwater fishermen who sold their catches to the inhabitants of farms, plantations, and towns and professional hunters who earned their livings by selling hides and furs.

The poor whites described by travelers unfamiliar with the region were usually not poor whites at all. Instead, they were cattlemen, lumbermen, charcoal burners, turpentiners, hunters, and fishermen whose rough garb and rude habitations led outsiders to believe that they were mired in poverty and ignorance.

As elsewhere in the Lower South, the planter class stood at the apex of the social pyramid in Mississippi, with the relative rank of individuals determined by their wealth in land and slaves rather than by family background. The dividing line between slaveowning farmer and planter was never cleanly drawn during the antebellum period, but agriculturists who worked in the fields with their slaves were commonly considered farmers. By the same token, planters were expected to own enough slaves to require them to devote their full time to administration of their estates. As a rule, cotton growers who possessed the equivalent of twenty to twenty-five able-bodied adult slaves were considered to be planters. In such cases the total number of slaves they owned, counting children and elderly persons, would usually be much larger than twenty. Similarly, there was no commonly accepted minimum acreage for a plantation. Planters, however, usually owned more than 500 acres.[1]

Table 2 gives a breakdown of Mississippi's population between 1800 and 1860. Some of the planter families of the Natchez area at that time were among the richest people not only in the South but also in the nation as a whole. The foundations of their agricultural fortunes were laid during the 1790s when tobacco plantations of the old Natchez District were transformed into astonishingly profitable cotton plantations. Successful proprietors of these pioneer southwestern slave-worked cotton plantations often constructed elaborate homes for themselves and always purchased lands and slaves wholesale. In many cases their children and grandchildren not only preserved their inheritances but continued to acquire slaves and plantations. They purchased sugar plantations in Louisiana and cotton plantations in the river counties of northern Louisiana, Arkansas, and in the Yazoo-Mississippi valley of Mississippi. Possessing ample capital for experimentation, these very large planters—called cotton nabobs by the envious—led the Cotton South in mechanization of their plantations and in the development of improved farming methods as well as in the accumulation of wealth.[2]

In 1859 a resident of Vidalia, Louisiana, observed that both Levin R. Marshall and Stephen Duncan, each of whom produced more than 4,000 bales of cotton annually, lived in Natchez but derived much of their income from plantations located in neighboring states. Yet even these great slaveowners had not always been the largest producers of cotton in the area. The Louisianian added: "The great estates of the two princely planters of this region, the late Samuel Davis and Francis Surget, Esqs., always produced three to five thousand bales each until their deaths divided the estates among the heirs." To this list could be added the names of John Routh, A. V. Davis of Concordia Parish, Louisiana, Frederick Stanton of Natchez, and James Surget, brother of Francis Surget. Stanton, who had made his fortune as a commission merchant, for example, operated six plantations totaling 15,000 acres with a labor force of 444

1. Bruce Collins, *White Society in the Antebellum South* (New York, 1985), 5–23, 38–40, 64–65, 87–96, 98, 106, 139, 160–62, 174, 180; James Oakes, *The Ruling Race: A History of American Slaveholders* (New York, 1983).

2. Gates, *Farmer's Age*, 147–52; James, *Antebellum Natchez*, 131–61; Morton Rothstein, "The Agricultural South as a Dual Economy," 378–82; McLemore (ed.), *History of Mississippi*, I, 343–50.

Table 2. Population of Mississippi, 1800–1860

Year	Whites	Free blacks	Slaves	Total
1800	5,179	182	3,489	8,850
1810	23,024	240	17,088	40,352
1820	42,176	458	32,814	75,448
1830	70,443	519	65,659	136,621
1840	179,074	1,366	195,211	375,651
1850	295,718	930	309,878	606,526
1860	353,901	773	436,631	791,305

SOURCES: *Seventh Census, 1850*, p. 449; *Eighth Census, 1860: Population*, 269.

slaves. In 1859 he grossed $122,000 (about $2,400,000 in 1980 dollars) from the crop of 3,000 bales produced on his three cotton plantations.[3]

The number of superplanters, of course, was very small. In a painstaking search of the manuscript census schedules for 1850 and 1860, William K. Scarborough was able to identify only nineteen persons or business combinations who owned as many as 300 slaves in Mississippi. This number included Wade Hampton III of South Carolina and Philip St. George Cocke of Virginia, who were not residents of the state. Two other large slaveholdings in Warren County belonged to partnerships; one was Elgee and Chambers and the other Turner and Quitman.[4]

The number of planters in antebellum Mississippi has never been ascertained. When the federal census for 1850 was taken, 5,343 persons described themselves to the census takers as planters, but ten years later only 3,098 claimed to belong to that category. Demonstrating the absence in 1860 of generally accepted definitions for the terms planter and farmer, almost all of the slaveowners engaged in agriculture in Warren County listed themselves as farmers, whereas most of the persons owning as many as thirty slaves in Lowndes County that year identified themselves as planters. Even in Lowndes County, however, not a few substantial slaveowners—such as John Perkins with 44 slaves, Allen Brooks with 81, and William S. Cox with 114—described themselves modestly as farm-

3. *Southern Cultivator*, XVII (1859), 191; Gates, *Farmer's Age*, 147–50; Will of Frederick Stanton, July 13, 1855, in Will Book III, 125–29 (Office of the Clerk of Chancery Court of Adams County, Natchez, Mississippi).
4. McLemore (ed.), *History of Mississippi*, I, 343–47.

ers. A reasonably accurate count of planters in the state could be compiled from data in the manuscript census schedules for 1850 and 1860, but no one to date has attempted this monumental task.[5]

Herbert Weaver carried out the most extensive analysis of the manuscript census schedules for Mississippi yet undertaken. After studying the returns from twelve representative counties for 1850 and 1860, he estimated that the planter class comprised about 20 percent of the white agricultural population of that state and that planters owning as many as fifty slaves and 500 acres of improved land were less than 8 percent. In the western Delta-Loess region of twenty-three counties, where many large plantations were located and where the population was more than half slave, the proportion of larger planters was greatest. In his sample counties—Adams, Bolivar, Issaquena, Hinds, and Jefferson—18.97 percent of the heads of families engaged in agriculture in 1860 owned fifty or more slaves, and 22.74 percent owned as many as 500 acres of improved land. Small planters with slaveholdings numbering between twenty and forty-nine slaves made up 26.19 percent, and those with improved land-holdings from 200 to 499 acres, 25.74 percent. Weaver estimated that small planters in this fertile region made up 25 percent of the white agricultural population, and larger planters 20 percent. For the interior portion of the state's Cotton Kingdom situated north of Jackson between the Delta-Loess region and the Alabama border, Weaver found that the proportion of small planters to large planters was much larger than in the river counties. Overall the planter class in this region made up only 15 percent of white agriculturists. Small planters owning from 200 to 499 acres of improved land composed 10.50 percent of white agricultural households in Weaver's sample counties, and those with slaveholdings of twenty to forty-nine slaves were 8.14 percent. On the basis of landholding, the larger planters were 5.32 percent, and on the basis of slaveholding 3.22 percent. The southern portion of the state south of Jackson and east of River-Loess counties lay outside of the principal cotton-producing region. With cotton produced there mainly in river and creek bottoms, the number of planters was negligible.[6]

I compiled the count of planters in some prominent cotton-producing counties given in Table 3 for 1860 from Weaver's data and from the Manu-

5. Manuscript Census Returns, 1850 and 1860, Lowndes and Warren Counties, Schedule 1.
6. Weaver, *Mississippi Farmers*, 40–42.

Table 3. Number of Planters in Selected Mississippi Counties, 1860

County	White heads of families engaged in agriculture No.	Small planters[a] No.	Small planters[a] %	Medium planters[b] No.	Medium planters[b] %	Large planters[c] No.	Large planters[c] %	Total planters
Adams	234	59	44	53	40	22	16	134
Bolivar	392	90	63	34	24	18	13	142
Hinds	861	247	71	84	25	17	5	348
Issaquena	95	27	37	25	34	21	29	73
Jefferson	380	91	52	69	39	15	9	175
Lowndes	741	135	61	72	32	15	7	222
Marshall	1,476	201	76	53	20	9	3	263
Scott	777	116	98	2	2	—	—	118
Warren	462	119	63	52	28	17	9	188
Total	5,918	1,085	65.2	444	26.7	134	8.1	1,663

[a]Owners of twenty to forty-nine slaves.
[b]Owners of fifty to ninety-nine slaves.
[c]Owners of one hundred or more slaves.

SOURCE: Manuscript Census Returns, 1860.

script Census Returns, 1860, Schedule 1, Slaves. From this sample it appears that about 10 percent of the planters in the state owned 100 slaves or more at the close of the antebellum period, and 25 percent, 50 to 100 slaves.

The significance of planters in the valley of the Tombigbee River has not been sufficiently emphasized by Mississippi historians. Travelers, who provided so many descriptions of Natchez and Vicksburg, rarely visited Columbus, and less complete files of newspapers have survived from that town than from the Mississippi River ports. It is instructive to compare Lowndes County with Warren County for 1860. Table 4, compiled from the compendium of the 1860 census for that year, reveals that there were surprising similarities between these eastern and western counties.

Although the average output of cotton in Lowndes County in 1859 was slightly greater than 4.5 bales per hand, the larger planters produced significantly more than farmers and small planters. Thomas C. Billups, for example, worked 2,160 acres of improved land and owned 241 slaves. Eight of his slaves were children fourteen years old or younger, and only five were over sixty years of age, an exceptionally small proportion of young children and superannuated slaves. His work force of 156, aged from fifteen to fifty-nine years, cultivated an average of 13.85 acres to the hand and produced 7.88 bales of cotton, 115.38 bushels of corn, and 7.69 bushels of sweet potatoes to the hand. As such planters usually cultivated cotton and corn in a ratio of two acres of cotton to one of corn, it can be inferred that Billups' plantation was producing approximately a bale of cotton to the acre and thirty bushels of corn to the acre. In order to provide meat for his slaves, Billups maintained a herd of 700 hogs.[7]

Lacking direct contact with the corn and pork-producing states of the Old Northwest enjoyed by the counties bordering on the Mississippi River and its tributaries, the counties of the Tombigbee River Valley maintained a higher degree of self-sufficiency in foodstuffs than did other plantation regions of the state. From Table 5 it will be noted that the agriculturists of Monroe, Lowndes, Noxubee, Oktibbeha, and Chickasaw counties raised somewhat more than 100 bushels of corn to the hand, whereas such leading western cotton-producing counties as Wilkinson, Bolivar, Issaquena, and Yazoo averaged 55.99, 62.88, 86.51, and 72.91 bushels to the hand, respectively.[8]

7. Manuscript Census Returns, 1860, Lowndes County, Schedule 1.
8. *Eighth Census, 1860: Agriculture* and *Population.*

Table 4. Comparative Statistics for Lowndes and Warren Counties, 1860

Item	Lowndes	Warren	Colum-bus	Vicks-burg
			Urban center	
Planters	210	188	—	—
Slaves held				
20–29	57	58	—	—
30–49	65	61	—	—
50–74	44	34	—	—
75–99	28	18	—	—
100 or more	16	15	—	—
300 or more	0	2	—	—
Population				
Whites	6,895	6,896	1,714	3,138
Slaves	16,730	13,763	1,590	1,402
Free blacks	4	37	4	37
Total	—	—	3,308	4,590
Improved acreage	167,373	110,484	—	—
Cash value of farms	$7,726,695	$5,141,828	—	—
Rural population of working age	10,970	9,626	—	—
Cotton				
Bales produced	51,234	36,338	—	—
Bales per worker	4.67	3.77	—	—

SOURCES: *Eighth Census, 1860: Agriculture*, 84–87, and *Population*, 264–71.

Planters who ran the risks of disease and high water to establish plantations on the mosquito-infested Yazoo-Mississippi floodplain were reaping the richest rewards from the culture of cotton in Mississippi during the 1850s. Alluvial soils were incredibly fertile along the banks of the Mississippi and Yazoo rivers and such tributaries as Deer Creek, producing bumper harvests in years when high water was not a serious problem. In Issaquena County, located wholly on the floodplain, cotton growers in 1859 averaged a phenomenal 8 bales to the hand, a figure suggesting that some planters were harvesting more than 10 bales to the hand. The whole crop of the county averaged slightly more than a bale to the acre. Wade

Hampton II, for example, reported in November 1855 that the cotton lands on his 2,529-acre plantation, Walnut Ridge, in that county were producing more than 2 bales to the acre. His slaves were picking 15 bales each day. He added: "I have sent to N. Orleans for supplies, and have ordered presents for all my people. Besides these gifts they shall have a glorious Xmas, and I will do everything to keep them in good spirits." The following year Sampson Williams picked 321 bales of cotton with forty hands on Daniel O. Williams's plantation, located on Deer Creek near the present town of Anguilla.[9]

Similar conditions undoubtedly prevailed in neighboring Washington County, although no returns were received from the census takers in 1860. In 1849, however, a year in which the cotton crop was reduced by as much as a third by frosts in mid-April, Washington County agriculturists averaged 5.26 bales to the hand and 0.66 bales to the acre. In 1855, William R. Elly produced 499 bales of cotton on his plantation situated on Lake Washington in that county. Inasmuch as 55 of his 100 slaves were adult field hands, he averaged 7.5 bales to the hand. Samuel Worthington, Jr., son of an original settler in Washington County and one of the Delta's larger planters, recalled that "a bale of cotton to the acre was an average crop, though more was often made, and thirteen or fourteen to the hand was made, and in exceptionally good years as high as sixteen to the hand. . . . There were steam cotton gins with corn meal mills attached on every plantation."[10]

In Yazoo County, where a portion of the farmlands were on the floodplain and the remainder on the brown loess hills, the average yield of cotton in 1860 was 4.88 bales to the hand. How much more productive the alluvial lands were than the hill lands can be seen from a statement of A. W. Washburn of Yazoo City. In 1855 he wrote, "My average crop for a series of years has been a standard bale (400) to the acre, and ten bales to the hand." In Bolivar and Tunica counties in the northern half of the Delta, yields exceeded five bales to the hand. Even in recently and thinly

9. Wade Hampton II to Mary Fisher Hampton, November 17, 1855, in Cauthen (ed.), *Family Letters of the Three Wade Hamptons*, 40; Statement of Sampson Williams Account, July 15, 1857, Cleveland Brothers and Company, New Orleans, and Report of Sale of Sampson Williams' Cotton, June 14, 1856, George M. Pinchard and Company, New Orleans, in Williams Papers.

10. See Table 5; William R. Elly Plantation Book (Mississippi Department of Archives and History); William D. McCain and Charlotte Capers (eds.), *Memoirs of Henry Tillinghast Ireys: Papers of the Washington County Historical Society, 1910–1915* (Jackson, Miss., 1955), 355.

Table 5. Agricultural Production per Farm Worker, 1860

County	Percentage of slaves	Number of inhabitants aged 15–59	Acres of improved farmland[a]	Bales of cotton[a]	Bushels of corn[a]	Bushels of sweet potatoes[a]
		Yazoo-Mississippi Delta				
Bolivar	86.2	6,392	13.32	5.23	62.88	2.71
Coahoma	76.1	3,771	10.37	3.53	62.41	3.03
Issaquena	91.9	4,606	12.28	8.93	86.51	1.41
Sunflower			No returns			
Tunica	79.7	2,534	11.53	5.12	70.80	3.78
Washington			No returns			
Yazoo	75.8	13,114	13.67	4.88	72.91	12.16
		Mississippi River Counties of the Old Natchez District				
Adams	99.6	10,002	10.33	2.97	40.24	7.79
Claiborne	84.9	7,847	16.21	4.22	66.64	10.56
Jefferson	79.9	8,318	14.82	3.71	63.16	10.29
Warren	82.2	9,626	11.47	3.77	60.10	5.56
Wilkinson	83.0	8,825	12.76	4.46	55.59	10.67
		Brown Loam and Loess Hills				
Amite	64.3	6,247	15.84	2.79	65.67	25.26
Carroll	65.5	11,318	14.51	3.78	100.73	14.06
Copiah	53.1	7,858	13.51	2.85	71.37	12.64
DeSoto	58.8	12,397	14.11	3.23	67.28	7.22
Franklin	59.0	4,060	15.85	3.33	75.79	15.02
Hinds	70.0	17,216	11.04	3.17	59.73	10.36
Holmes	70.0	9,160	14.95	4.56	92.33	11.37
Madison	76.4	12,775	18.77	4.01	93.50	16.83

Rankin	51.4	6,839	13.17	2.65	72.81	14.83
Tallahatchie	64.1	4,449	12.34	3.57	83.87	11.11

Tombigbee River Basin

Lowndes	79.4	10,790	15.25	4.67	105.49	10.88
Monroe	59.7	11,319	13.57	4.09	101.20	17.36
Noxubee	74.1	10,888	9.54	4.60	118.11	13.53

Prairie Black Belt

Chickasaw	54.3	8,263	12.39	3.20	104.35	11.53
Oktibbeha	58.8	6,665	13.64	2.99	99.71	12.69
Pontotoc	33.3	11,038	13.18	2.19	91.71	10.63

North Central Hills

Attala	35.0	7,018	13.03	2.07	80.81	9.12
Calhoun	19.7	4,451	12.64	1.83	75.87	12.57
Choctaw	26.0	7,706	11.40	1.75	77.86	14.30
Clarke	47.0	5,329	8.82	1.72	55.89	14.65
Kemper	48.9	5,898	15.07	2.61	84.32	18.59
Lafayette	42.3	8,169	12.42	2.36	78.84	9.06
Lauderdale	38.8	6,671	12.22	1.90	71.69	18.75
Leake	32.7	4,561	12.34	2.24	67.79	12.61
Neshoba	25.3	3,988	13.73	1.42	67.49	15.63
Newton	36.8	4,538	10.75	1.80	76.34	12.12
Scott	35.7	4,055	9.48	1.76	73.01	15.99
Simpson	37.3	2,805	13.81	1.66	71.88	18.24
Smith	28.6	3,599	10.35	1.53	67.55	15.78
Tippah	27.3	11,255	12.61	1.80	72.73	7.24
Winston	39.0	4,750	14.44	2.04	76.00	14.30

Continued on next page

County	Percentage of slaves	Number of inhabitants aged 15–59	Acres of improved farmland[a]	Bales of cotton[a]	Bushels of corn[a]	Bushels of sweet potatoes[a]
		Tennessee River Hills				
Itawamba	19.3	8,718	10.99	1.40	71.99	11.49
Tishomingo	19.3	12,178	8.77	0.94	72.56	6.79
		Pine Hills				
Covington	34.6	2,051	12.35	1.45	75.77	25.33
Greene	30.9	1,059	6.29	0.13	45.37	24.02
Jones	11.9	1,563	9.29	0.40	52.17	20.30
Lawrence	40.2	4,515	11.81	1.52	62.28	11.57
Marion	45.6	2,130	11.36	1.11	57.38	16.42
Perry	25.9	1,237	7.78	0.24	59.75	32.21
Pike	30.8	7,607	7.66	1.12	41.29	8.97
Wayne	52.6	1,918	9.80	1.42	50.02	13.22
		Gulf Coast Meadows				
Hancock			No reports			
Harrison	23.9	2,530	3.18	0.11	19.08	7.27
Jackson	29.0	2,011	1.29	0.00	7.31	4.90
		Counties Not Reporting in 1860[b]				
Hancock	33.6	1,925	1.89	0.036	4.94	
Sunflower	69.6	676	8.83	2.81	49.39	
Washington	92.9	4,975	11.88	5.26	85.34	

[a] Per worker.
[b] Statistics are for 1850. In 1850 a late freeze reduced the cotton crop from one-third to one-half.

settled Coahoma and Sunflower counties, the yields were more than
3.5 bales to the hand.[11]

In 1855 a Vicksburg correspondent of the Washington (D.C.) *National Intelligencer* described an ideal plantation on the Yazoo-Mississippi
delta. The plantation should have about 1,600 acres, with a thousand
under cultivation. In order to work 750 acres in cotton and 250 acres
in such food crops as corn, peas, and sweet potatoes, there should be
seventy-five "effective" hands. These, with children and old people
who would not ordinarily work in the fields, would represent a slave
population of about 135 or 140. Fifty mules would be needed for draft
animals, along with twelve yokes of oxen. The normal complement
of livestock would be 100 cattle and 300 hogs. Equipped with the
necessary quarters, wagons, gins, press, corn mill, and blacksmith
and carpenter's tools, he estimated that the establishment would cost
$150,000 if there were no steam engine. Properly managed, he maintained, such an enterprise would produce eight bales to the hand and a
bale to the acre. Estimating that expenses of annual operation would be
about $100 per hand, he calculated that the net return would be about
$12,000.[12]

The explosive growth of the counties of the Yazoo-Mississippi delta
during the 1850s is revealed by the statistics in Tables 6–8. When these
figures are interpreted, however, it should be recalled that a late freeze
reduced the 1849–1850 cotton crop of Mississippi from one-third to one-half of normal. We can assume that the adverse weather affected all of the
river counties similarly, although the more northerly Yazoo-Mississippi
river counties would probably have been harder hit by cold and excessive
rain than the better drained hill counties. Nevertheless, a comparison between the Delta counties and the hill counties along the river reveals a
different pattern of economic growth. The 1859 crops of the older western counties of Adams, Warren, and Hinds were larger than the 1849
crops by factors of 1.70, 1.96, and 2.76, respectively. The eastern river
county of Lowndes produced a 1859 crop 3.39 times as large as the 1849
crop. In contrast, the 1859 crop of Tunica County was larger than the
1849 crop by the factor of 18.17; Bolivar County's crop 7.08 times as
great; and Issaquena was 4.87 times larger. Yazoo County, partly in the

11. *Southern Cultivator*, XIII (1855), 340; also see Table 5.
12. Vicksburg *Whig*, August 18, 1855.

Table 6. Land Values in the Yazoo-Mississippi Delta, 1850–1860

	Land values			
County	1850	1854	1857	1860
Bolivar	$ 739,211	$1,973,599	$6,465,838	$ 8,759,270
Coahoma	375,940	785,055	3,334,455	5,100,395
Issaquena	996,405	2,047,259	4,259,599	6,576,505
Sunflower	200,140	813,775	2,406,962	—
Tunica	267,770	934,876	1,987,101	4,217,575
Washington	3,296,875	5,083,194	7,416,162	—
Yazoo	1,831,839	3,255,474	5,571,555	10,287,227

SOURCES: *Seventh Census, 1850*, p. 456; *Eighth Census, 1860: Agriculture*, 84; Appendix A.

hills, showed the smallest increase of the Delta counties. Its crop of 1859 was only 2.90 times that of 1849.[13]

Planters in the counties occupying the uplands bordering the Mississippi River and the Yazoo-Mississippi floodplain from the borders of Louisiana to Tennessee generally obtained above-average crops of cotton. In Wilkinson and Claiborne counties in the old Natchez District, and in Madison and Holmes counties north of Jackson on the border of the Delta, yields exceeded four bales to the hand. In the remainder of the brown loess region, the average yield was greater than three bales to the hand with a few exceptions. Amite County, Rankin County, and Copiah County were located on the interior boundary of the brown loess belt. Yields there were about two and three-quarters bales to the hand.[14]

In the counties occupying the uplands between the brown loess region and the Tombigbee River Valley, soils on the hills were thin, and good farmlands were generally located in the valleys of small rivers and streams. Average yields in this region were the smallest of any part of the Mississippi Cotton Kingdom, ranging from one and one-half to two and one-half to the hand. The best of these lands were found on the prairie with

13. *Seventh Census, 1850*, pp. 456–60; *Eighth Census, 1860: Agriculture*, pp. 84–87; Value of Taxable Lands and the Number of Slaves in Each County, as Assessed in the Years 1854 and 1857, by Madison McAfee, Jackson, *Mississippian*, August 10, 1858.
14. Table 5.

Table 7. Slaves and Cultivated Acreage in the Yazoo-Mississippi Delta, 1850–1860

County	Cultivated Acreage		Slaves			
	1850	1860	1850	1854	1857	1860
Bolivar	16,973	85,188	2,180	3,069	5,847	9,078
Coahoma	11,478	39,139	1,391	1,926	3,653	5,083
Issaquena	27,631	56,596	4,105	4,991	6,201	7,244
Sunflower	5,966	—	754	1,513	1,993	3,917
Tunica	6,015	39,341	917	1,301	1,946	3,483
Washington	59,126	—	7,836	9,357	11,185	14,467
Yazoo	107,298	179,288	10,349	11,438	13,574	16,716

SOURCES: *Seventh Census, 1850*, pp. 447, 456; *Eighth Census, 1860: Population*, 270, and *Agriculture*, 84; Appendix A.

Table 8. Cotton Production in the Yazoo-Mississippi Delta, 1849–1859

County	Cotton Production (bales)	
	1849	1859
Bolivar	4,723	33,452
Coahoma	2,430	13,325
Issaquena	8,461	41,170
Sunflower	1,900	—
Tunica	717	13,025
Washington	26,179	—
Yazoo	22,052	64,075

SOURCES: *Seventh Census, 1850*, p. 458; *Eighth Census, 1860: Agriculture*, 85.

limestone-enriched soils in Oktibbeha, Chickasaw, and Pontotoc counties. Yields in the first two counties were about three bales to the acre. Pontotoc County, which had less prairie land within its boundaries, produced an average of only 2.19 bales to the hand.[15]

15. *Ibid.*

In the Tennessee River hill section in the northeastern corner of the state, and in the pine lands to the south and east of Jackson stretching down to the Gulf of Mexico, production of cotton was minimal. Limited to restricted locations of comparative fertility in generally infertile regions, farmers and planters were able to raise less than one and one-half bales to the hand.[16]

Although there were striking regional differences in the growing of cotton during the 1850s, other aspects of agriculture throughout the state were surprisingly uniform. The degree of farm mechanization, for instance, cannot be measured by the number of horses and mules in a given area. The Gulf coast and pine woods aside, farmers and planters generally employed a horse or a mule for every twenty acres. Noxubee County in the Tombigbee River Valley produced 4.60 bales of cotton and a record 118.11 bushels of corn to the hand. Yet planters and farmers used fewer horses and mules than in any other cotton-producing county. On average each animal there cultivated 33.65 acres. At the other extreme, the number of acres worked by a horse or mule averaged 17.1 in Scott County, where the yield was only 1.76 bales and 73 bushels of corn to the hand. In Issaquena, the foremost cotton-growing county, there was a mule for every 21.47 cultivated acres. In Madison County, where yields were high, a horse or mule was allotted for every 29.88 acres. The only difference of consequence between sections with regard to draft animals is that a greater proportion of mules was employed in plantation areas, whereas farmers used more less-expensive horses to pull their plows and cultivators.[17]

As in the case of draft animals, there were few distinct regional variations in the production of corn, the principal food crop grown by farm workers. Only the five-county hinterland of the city of Columbus showed a regional peculiarity. As already mentioned, the yields of corn there were a hundred bushels to the hand or more. Elsewhere yields ranged from an exceptionally low minimum of 40.29 bushels to the hand in Adams County to 100.73 bushels in Carroll County. In Pontotoc County the yield was 91.71; in Issaquena County 86.51. In most of the counties the rate of production ranged from 60 to 80 bushels for each inhabitant of working age. It appears, therefore, that farmers and planters alike produced roughly the same amount of corn for each agricultural worker. It

16. *Ibid.*
17. Calculated from *Eighth Census, 1860: Agriculture*, p. 84.

was not, as has often been assumed, that farmers produced more corn than planters but rather that they produced less cotton. This distinction is especially evident in Tishomingo and Itawamba counties, where slaves represented less than a fifth of the population of working age. There agriculturists produced about a bale of cotton per worker, a minimum figure, and 72 bushels of corn, an unexceptional yield in terms of the food crop.[18]

Although some of the Mississippi River planters of the 1840s and 1850s were members of families who had enjoyed wealth and high social position for several generations and could thus lay claim to being southern aristocrats, the great majority of planters in the state definitely could not. With very rare exceptions, large landowners and slaveowners of the Atlantic seaboard states did not emigrate to the Old Southwest, although a small number, such as Philip St. George Cocke and Wade Hampton III, did invest in absentee plantations in Mississippi. Aside from the western river counties, the Mississippi Cotton Kingdom was largely settled by small cotton farmers and planters from the piedmonts of Virginia, Georgia, and the Carolinas who had deserted eroded cotton and tobacco lands in the Southeast for fresh lands in the Old Southwest. These agriculturists naturally gravitated toward areas of fertile soils. In the uplands they preferred either the lime-rich prairie lands of the Columbus area or lands upon which hardwoods were growing. Some found limited tracts of fertile soils in valleys of rivers and creeks running through generally infertile lands. Even in Tishomingo County, located in the highlands of northeastern Mississippi, where the population was made up mostly of corn farmers who grew very little cotton, eighteen planters owned twenty-five slaves or more, and two, David W. Spence and Thomas Irons, owned more than ninety-five. A third, Thomas Burrus, owned seventy-seven.[19]

Most of the white immigrants who came to Mississippi from the East between 1800 and 1840 were members of southeastern rural middle and lower middle classes. In ethnic origin they were a mixture of English and Scots-Irish, with a sprinkling of Germans and Huguenot French. In the main their culture was that of the backcountry. Prior to the emergence of the Cotton Kingdom in the late 1790s, the ancestors of these new citizens

18. Table 5.
19. Manuscript Census Returns, 1860, Tishomingo County, Mississippi, Schedule 1.

of Mississippi had been impoverished subsistence farmers who raised tobacco and indigo to buy what they could not make on their farms, and comparatively few of them owned slaves. Because they possessed only a minimum of farm tools and implements, their methods of farming were necessarily crude.

Farmers of the piedmont upon beginning to cultivate cotton as a cash crop naturally applied the same rough culture to the new crop that they were accustomed to using on tobacco and corn. Unfortunately, this system of clean culture of row crops promoted erosion of the thin layer of topsoil that covered the uplands of the Southeast, ultimately ruining the lands for cultivation. When cotton brought unprecedented prosperity to the backcountry agriculturists, they imitated the lowland planters by buying slaves and eventually enlarging their farms into small cotton plantations. The possession of slaves permitted them to expand the size of their farming operations and to increase their profits, but if anything, slavery caused them to make their cultivated lands infertile more quickly than they could have by their own efforts. Within a generation these new cotton farmers and planters had skimmed the cream from their landholdings in their native states and were on the move into western Georgia, Alabama, and Mississippi. Once in the Southwest they continued to use the same primitive farming methods that had ruined their former cotton farms and plantations until they learned better techniques, as they gradually did.[20]

John Baxter Fraser, who farmed near the present-day town of Bishopville, South Carolina, was representative of the early eastern growers of upland cotton. Son of a Scottish immigrant who married the daughter of a Presbyterian minister, Fraser acquired land in the Sumter District at about the turn of the nineteenth century. With the aid of seventeen adult slaves, he cleared land and began to cultivate cotton, corn, and wheat. In some of the first cleared fields, he planted an orchard of apples and peaches, growing corn between the young trees. Fraser housed his wife and five children in log cabins. In 1805, he cultivated forty acres in green seed cotton and produced fifteen bags of ginned cotton, each weighing approximately 300 pounds. That year he sold his cotton for eighteen cents per pound, grossing about $800. In the fall he acquired a fourteen-

20. Bonner, *Georgia Agriculture*, 49–72; Gray, *Agriculture*, II, 683–90; Alfred G. Smith, Jr., *Economic Readjustment of an Old Cotton State: South Carolina, 1820–1860* (Columbia, S.C., 1958), 2–109.

saw gin, which ginned about 500 pounds of seed cotton a day, for $42. His other agricultural equipment consisted of three plows, hoes, axes, a pit saw, and a cart. In 1805, Fraser had about seventy acres in cultivation, or about four acres per hand. His crop of 4,500 pounds of cotton averaged a mere 0.66 of a 400-pound bale to the hand. At that period Fraser was planting peas in his cornfields and was fertilizing his corn with his surplus cottonseed. Despite his low level of productivity, Fraser prospered. By 1819 his plantation had grown to 1,060 acres and his force of slaves to forty-one.[21]

In the early 1840s one of John Baxter Fraser's sons with relatives and friends left South Carolina, seeking better soils in Mississippi. Columbus C. Campbell wrote in April 1842 from his new home near Hamburg in Franklin County: "You can repair your affairs in one year here as much as you can there in three." Campbell, who had experienced financial disaster in South Carolina, was particularly happy that there was no imprisonment for debt in Mississippi. He wrote: "Here no jail is polluted with honest debtors, so a man has no dread of being treated as a criminal because he is unfortunate." Campbell added that "already my five nephews give it [Mississippi] preference over So. Ca." John Barrett also settled in Franklin County not far from Campbell's farm. He wrote back to the Fraser family in April 1842, "I have just entered a quarter section of land that will yield a *400* weight bale of cotton to the acre and 40 bu. corn to do. I have just finished circleing 20 Acr. I calculate to plant 50 acr. in cotton next year and 35 to 40 in corn." John Fraser, John Baxter Fraser's son, emigrated to Yalobusha County, where he established a plantation "on the South Side of Yellow Busha River about two miles from a public place known as Gray's Post Office Port." He estimated that his lands would yield "1000 to 2000 pounds of cotten [*sic*] per acre." "I know," he said, "you can make as much here in one year as you can make in three years where you live [Sumter District, South Carolina]."[22]

New cotton growers from the East generally prospered in northern Mississippi during the 1830s. From the older cotton planters of the river counties they acquired superior Mexican cottonseed and a system of horizontal culture, and with the latter they benefited from more fertile

21. John Baxter Fraser Papers, 1804–19, in possession of Margaret Des-Champs Moore, Tallahassee, Florida.

22. Margaret B. DesChamps (ed.), "Some Mississippi Letters to Robert Fraser, 1841–1844," *Journal of Mississippi History*, XV (1953), 181–89.

soils, excellent water transportation, and, above all, favorable cotton prices. Small cotton planters throughout the cotton-growing regions of the state purchased more land and slaves to become medium-sized planters, and successful cotton farmers grew into small planters. Whatever their scope of operation, all categories of Mississippi cotton growers of this period had much in common. They were industrious men on the make who were determined to enlarge their holdings in land and slaves. Generally ill educated and grossly materialistic in outlook, the rising class of Mississippi planters appeared to some outsiders to exhibit the more objectionable traits of the nouveau riche. Yet these rough agriculturists treated one another with exaggerated courtesy—perhaps to avoid fatal quarrels—and were as hospitable to friends and strangers as lonely, isolated folk always are.

Solon Robinson, the northern agricultural writer, has provided a description of conditions in northern Mississippi during the mid-1840s, a part of the state where a majority of the state's planters were living during the last two decades of the antebellum period. In 1845, Robinson found most of the population living in log cabins. At that comparatively late date in the settlement of the Indian cessions, sawmills were still rare and sawn lumber expensive. Stopping for the night near Coffeeville in Yalobusha County not far from President James K. Polk's plantation, Robinson was entertained by Tom Hardiman, a planter who lived in a "low log cabin, built on the universal, never-varying pattern of two rooms with a broad hall between." Hardiman introduced the writer to John T. Leigh, one of the larger planters of the region who had moved to Mississippi from Virginia. Leigh invited Robinson to spend several days at his plantation residence.[23]

Leigh and his family resided in a cluster of log cabins on a plantation just emerging from the pioneer phase of development. The planter's residence proper was a common two-room log cabin with a hall, or dogtrot, between. Several other similar cabins located nearby provided accommodations for children and for guests. The family's meals were prepared in a log kitchen situated some distance from the lodging cabins, and the food was carried, often through the rain, to the planter's quarters by numerous house servants. A log storeroom completed Leigh's residential complex.[24]

23. Kellar (ed.), *Solon Robinson*, I, 451.
24. *Ibid.*, 458.

Leigh's slaves numbered about ninety and were housed in a village of similar log cabins, which also included the residence of the overseer, who at the time of Robinson's visit was Leigh's son. Of these slave quarters Robinson commented somewhat wryly that some of the cabins were "neatly furnished and provided with household matters and things, and others were exactly the reverse, and look just like some white folks' houses." Leigh's slaves lived together as families in separate cabins of their own. Leigh maintained a plantation nursery for the small children under the charge of an older woman who had no duties to perform other than feeding and caring for the children. Leigh allowed slave mothers a month to recuperate after bearing a child before returning them to the field. Until the child was weaned, the mother returned from the fields to the nursery several times a day to nurse the infant.[25]

In keeping with the modified task system, Leigh's slaves cooked their own meals for themselves in their cabins. They either carried their breakfasts and lunches with them to the field or had hot food brought to them from the quarters by older children. The final meal of the day was prepared and eaten in their cabins. Leigh provided a weekly ration for each family with an allotment of three and one-half pounds of salt pork and one and one-half pecks of cornmeal for each adult and a lesser amount for children. In all seasons of the year, the slaves could draw all the sweet potatoes from the storage cribs that they wanted, because the plantation produced more than could be eaten by the human population. In season, the weekly ration was supplemented by turnips, squashes, onions, fresh corn, and other garden vegetables in addition to melons and peaches. In the year before Robinson's visit to Mississippi, Leigh cured 16,000 pounds of pork. This was the first time in the ten-year history of the plantation that all of the year's supply of meat had been produced on the premises.[26]

In the period since Leigh and his brother had first opened the plantation in 1835, he had brought 640 acres of land in the valley of Perry Creek under cultivation, which he worked with a force of thirty-five field hands. Leigh cultivated about 300 acres of cotton, 200 acres of corn, and 60 to 70 acres of oats, with the remaining cleared land devoted to the slave quarters, attached gardens, and an orchard. Robinson did not record how many acres Leigh owned. The planter averaged 135 acres of cotton, somewhat less than half a bale to the acre and approximately four

25. *Ibid.*, 455.
26. *Ibid.*, 456–57.

bales to the hand. His upland plantation was therefore producing more than the average for the state but much less than the better plantations in the river counties. After a decade of hard work Leigh was still clearing woods to make new fields, although he was ahead of his neighbors in constructing a system of drainage ditches. Leigh used seventeen horses and mules to cultivate his crops and three yokes of oxen for plowing and the sort of heavy pulling that tractors would do today. His livestock included 50 cows, 70 sheep, and 200 hogs.[27]

After making a second visit to Leigh's plantation in 1849, Robinson published the following interview with that north Mississippi planter:

> The most of my negroes have families, and live as you see in very comfortable cabins, nearly as good as my own, with good fire places, good floors and doors, comfortable beds, plenty of cooking utensils and dishes, tables and chairs. But, I intend in the course of another year to build them a new set of cabins, of uniform size so as to correspond in appearance with the overseer's house. Those who do not have families of their own, mess together.
>
> I give each of them 3½ lbs. of bacon, clear of bone, per week, and of the same quality as I use myself, and which I make upon the place, and generally about a peck and a half of corn meal, not being particular about the measure of that, as I raise plenty of corn and grind it in my own mill, and [I] wish them to have all they can eat without wasting it. I also give them sweet potatoes, and plenty of vegetables in the season of them. Those who choose to do so can commute a part of the meat rations for an equivalent in molasses. I also give them a liberal supply of fresh meat from time to time during the year.
>
> They also, as you see, all have their own hen houses, and as "master's corn crib is always open," they raise an abundance of eggs and fat chickens to eat or exchange for any other luxuries they wish. Besides, my negroes raise a crop of cotton every year for their own use, and several of the most provident of them always have money, often to the amount of fifty to one hundred dollars.
>
> You will observe that the children are all taken care of and fed during the day at the nursery, upon corn bread and fat, and hominy and molasses.
>
> All the cotton clothing and part of the woolen is spun and wove by women kept employed at that business on the plantation. I give my negroes a feast and frolic every Christmas. I was born and bred among slaves. In buying and selling, good masters are always careful not to separate families. Two of my men have wives on President [James K.] Polk's plantation, which adjoins mine, and whom they are free to visit every Saturday night and remain with until Monday morning.

Although by no means all of the planters of Mississippi met Leigh's high standards, he was fairly representative of a large number of successful

----

27. Albany (N.Y.) *Cultivator*, X (1843), 161–62; Kellar (ed.), *Solon Robinson*, I, 455–58.

planters of the interior who resided on their own plantations and managed their own agricultural affairs.[28]

Although most of the planters of antebellum Mississippi lacked formal educations, they were not uninformed about events in the Western world. Most of them subscribed to several newspapers affiliated with their political parties. Ordinarily, the list would include a local weekly newspaper published in the county seat and a daily paper from one of the principal commercial towns, such as Natchez, Vicksburg, Columbus, or Memphis; another daily from Jackson, the state capital; and one or more dailies from the great cotton seaports of New Orleans or Mobile. Individuals who were particularly interested in politics also subscribed to a newspaper from Washington, D.C., and perhaps one from Richmond, Virginia, or from Charleston, South Carolina. Many planters also subscribed to religious and agricultural periodicals. After the telegraph system went into service during the 1840s, newspapers published in the larger towns began to carry national and international stories that were about as fresh as news in present-day journals. A surprisingly large number of them purchased books from booksellers in Natchez, Vicksburg, or Columbus, and their libraries contained works on religion, political history, and medicine as well as English classics. Elisha Worthington, who had plantations in Washington County, Mississippi, and in Chicot County, Arkansas, was an exceptional case. His library contained 5,000 volumes. Planters of all sizes were accustomed to exchanging views and information at formal meetings of political clubs and agricultural societies, at their churches, and at countless social gatherings.[29]

A former slave who had lived on a plantation three miles east of West Point related to a WPA interviewer that his master had been completely illiterate. Henry Gibbs said: "My Mars David [Cottrell] couldn't read or write, but Miss Elsie was an educated scholar. . . . He'd say, 'Elsie, come read me de news what de paper has,' [and] he would sit by her while she read." Cottrell had begun his career as an overseer "on the Martin place on Tombigbee River."[30]

At the opposite end of the pole from Cottrell was Francis Terry Leak.

28. *De Bow's Review*, VII (1849), 380–81; Kellar (ed.), *Solon Robinson*, II, 290–91.
29. McCain and Capers (eds.), *Memoirs of Henry Tillinghast Ireys*, 352.
30. *Slave Narratives*, Ser. 1, *Mississippi*, Vol. VIII, Pt. 3, p. 820.

In 1847 he listed a dozen publications to which he was subscribing. They included the Memphis *Appeal*, the Jackson *Mississippian, De Bow's Review*, the *Southern Cultivator*, Columbia (S.C.) *Illustrated Farmer's Friend*, the *Universalist Herald*, and the Charleston (S.C.) *Schoolfellow*. His wife was also subscribing to *Godey's Ladies' Book*.[31]

Unaccustomed to luxury before coming to Mississippi, most of the immigrant planters and would-be planters did not give a high priority to physical comfort. Instead, they were content to construct for themselves the crudest kind of double log cabins, usually without floors or windows, and similar single log cabins for their slaves. Their chimneys were commonly made of wood or of straw and clay. Like their slaves they ate dried corn and salt pork, supplemented by wild fruit, berries, and nuts, fish, and such game as deer, wild pigs, squirrels, rabbits, opossum, partridge, dove, ducks, and geese. They wore the same kind of coarse homemade everyday clothing as their slaves. When labor could be spared from clearing land and cultivating crops, these cotton growers gradually improved or replaced their original log buildings. When lumber became available, they laid floors and boarded over the logs. During the late 1840s, when the great depression was finally waning, a rural building boom developed in the Cotton Kingdom during which one- or two-story frame houses replaced the earlier log buildings. At that time the planters began to pay some attention to the grounds around their houses, planting ornamental trees and cultivating green lawns. Flower gardens became common around plantation residences during the 1840s and 1850s, as did fruit orchards and ornamental trees and shrubs.[32]

As a class, small and medium planters of Mississippi were very active in politics, and many of them held local, county, and state offices, seeking the prestige that such positions conveyed upon the occupants. Broadly speaking, medium and large planters tended to affiliate themselves with the Whig party, whereas small planters and farmers preferred the party of Andrew Jackson. Planters also chose their religious denominations along similar class lines. The great planters were Presbyterians, Episcopalians, and Catholics; the planters with fifty slaves or more were Meth-

31. Leak Diary, I, 116.
32. Oakes, *Ruling Race*, 81–87; McLemore (ed.), *History of Mississippi*, I, 410–12.

odists or Presbyterians; and the small planters and farmers generally belonged to one of the several varieties of Baptist churches.[33]

Planters of Mississippi apparently tried to model themselves after the
old established planter class of the Atlantic seaboard, sometimes with
amusing results. In so doing, however, they adopted the beneficial belief
that planters' children should be properly educated to take their places in
polite society. Consequently, like Americans of later eras, the new planters determinedly set about providing their children with the educational
advantages that they had not enjoyed themselves. They enrolled their
sons and daughters in local academies and female seminaries, and after
graduation many of the boys were sent to college. Prosperous planters
sent their sons to such northern institutions as Miami University in Ohio
or to Harvard, Princeton, or Yale. Less affluent planters sent their sons to
nearby, less expensive colleges such as the universities of Mississippi or
Alabama or to such denominational colleges as Mississippi College or
Oakland College. Practical fathers prepared their sons for future careers
in planting by having them study medicine so as to be better able to care
for their property in slaves.[34]

Regrettably, little is known today about the farmers of antebellum Mississippi. Unlike the planters, they left comparatively few written documents behind for the edification of modern historians. From observations
about them made by travelers, planters, and townsmen, and from such
records as wills, tax assessments, property deeds, and federal census
schedules, however, historians have been able to determine something
about the lives farmers led.[35]

Because land was readily available and comparatively cheap, most farm
families in the cotton-producing areas of Mississippi owned the lands
they cultivated. Even among small farmers who owned no slaves, land-

33. Eaton, *History of the Old South*, 313–14; Miles, *Jacksonian Democracy in
Mississippi*, 169; McLemore (ed.), *History of Mississippi*, I, 380–410, 444; Moore,
"Religion in Mississippi in 1860," 223–38; Posey, *Frontier Mission*, 339.

34. Eaton, *Southern Civilization*, 2, 113–19, and *History of the Old South*,
440–41; Charles S. Sydnor, *The Development of Southern Sectionalism, 1819–
1848* (Baton Rouge, 1948), 300–304.

35. Collins, *White Society*, 84–96; Eugene Genovese, "Yeoman Farmers in a
Slaveholder's Democracy," *Agricultural History*, XLIX (1975), 331–42; Daniel R.
Hundley, *Social Relations in Our Southern States*, ed. William J. Cooper (Baton
Rouge, 1979), 191–222; Owsley, *Plain Folk*.

ownership was common, as the following examples demonstrate. In 1860, 43 small farm families owned their land in Jefferson County, whereas 36 did not. In Hinds County the comparable figures were 68 and 29; in Lowndes County, 198 and 45; in Marshall County, 447 and 229. In Tishomingo County, the preeminent county of small farmers in the highlands of northeastern Mississippi, 1,155 farm families without slaves were landowners, and 816 did not yet hold titles to their farms. It may be taken for granted that larger slaveowning farmers were also landowners. In Jefferson, Marshall, and Lowndes counties, to cite three examples, all slaveowning agriculturists owned land.[36]

Like planters, farmers generally purchased more land than they were able to cultivate in order to allow for future expansion of their farming operations and for exhaustion of land under tillage. In areas of the Mississippi Cotton Kingdom where white farmers were more numerous than planters and slaves, farms averaged from two to four times as many uncultivated acres as cultivated acres for each agricultural worker. To cite a few examples for 1860, in Lawrence County there were 11.81 acres of cultivated land and 45.28 acres of uncultivated farmland to the agricultural worker. In Neshoba County the comparable averages were 13.73 cultivated acres and 37.06 uncultivated acres to the hand; in Winston County, 14.44 cultivated acres to 42.84 uncultivated acres to the hand; and in Tishomingo County, 8.77 cultivated acres to 26.66 uncultivated acres of farmland to the farm worker. These figures would lead one to expect a typical farmer with a wife and several children under fifteen years of age to cultivate about 20 acres and to own another 50 or 60 acres of woodland. This estimate bears out Weaver's conclusion that half of the farms in the northeastern hills had fewer than 100 acres in cultivation (see Table 9).

Within the boundaries of the Mississippi Cotton Kingdom, ownership of slaves was common among members of the farmer class. Although it is debatable whether agricultural slaveowners possessing twenty to thirty slaves of all ages should be classified as planters or farmers, agriculturists owning fewer than twenty slaves were certainly regarded as farmers. Judged from the census of 1860, this class of small slaveowner was large. In Hinds County, for example, 108 farmers owned no slaves, whereas 305 owned between one and nineteen slaves. Surprisingly, in the latter cate-

36. Manuscript Census Returns, 1860, Jefferson, Hinds, Lowndes, Marshall, and Tishomingo Counties, Schedule 1.

Table 9. Landholdings per Worker of Improved and Unimproved Farmland, 1860

County	Inhabitants of working age[a]	Improved farmland (acres)	Unimproved farmland (acres)	Improved farmland per worker (acres)	Unimproved farmland per worker (acres)
Counties with a Majority of Slaves					
Coahoma	3,771	39,139	120,070	10.37	32.11
Holmes	9,160	136,992	208,384	14.96	22.75
Issaquena	4,606	56,596	108,472	12.29	23.55
Tunica	2,543	29,341	91,085	11.53	35.80
Warren	9,626	110,480	186,089	11.47	19.33
Yazoo	13,114	179,288	411,121	13.67	31.35
Counties with a Majority of Whites					
Lawrence	4,515	53,352	204,428	11.81	45.28
Neshoba	3,988	45,787	147,780	13.73	37.06
Smith	3,599	37,283	118,947	10.35	33.05
Tishomingo	12,178	106,824	324,680	8.77	26.66
Winston	4,750	60,630	203,488	14.44	42.49

[a] Fifteen to fifty-nine years old.

SOURCE: Computed from *Eighth Census, 1860: Agriculture*, 84, and *Population*, 265–69.

gory 179—more than half of the slaveowning farmers—owned ten slaves or more. In Lowndes County a similar situation prevailed. Among 519 farmers, 243 were not slaveowners, whereas 276 possessed between one and twenty slaves. In Bolivar County, 148 farmers were nonslaveowners, and there were 101 owners of fewer than twenty slaves. Of 659 farmers in Scott County, 275 were slaveowners. In Marshall County 1,213 farmers were listed in the census schedules in 1860. Of this total, 533 were small slaveholders. Even in Tishomingo County, where planters numbered fewer than fifty, there were 467 owners of fewer than twenty slaves in addition to 1,963 farmers who had no slaves (see Table 10).

Smith Simmons, a former slave, described the establishment of one slaveowning farmer. He told a WPA interviewer:

Table 10. Slaveholdings of Farmers, 1860

County	0 Slaves	%[a]	1–4 Slaves	%[a]	5–9 Slaves	%[a]	10–19 Slaves	%[a]	Total of farm families
Adams	24	28	11	13	16	18	36	41	87
Bolivar	148	59	36	14	22	9	43	17	249
Harrison	68	70	15	15	11	11	6	6	100
Hinds	108	21	110	21	116	23	179	35	513
Issaquena	9	41	2	9	3	14	8	36	22
Jefferson	82	40	40	20	35	17	48	23	205
Jones	340	79	66	15	19	4	6	1	431
Lowndes	243	47	103	20	68	15	105	20	519
Marshall	680	56	181	15	165	14	187	15	1,213
Scott	384	58	140	21	84	13	51	8	659
Tishomingo	1,963	81	261	11	109	4	97	4	2,430
Wayne	188	78	21	9	24	10	8	3	241

[a] Percentage of total population.

SOURCE: Manuscript Census Returns, 1860.

I was born in Montgomery County about six miles from Winona. . . . The place we lived on was small. There was only three large families on it. Each family ate in their own house. There wasn't no quarters or eating kitchen like the big places had. Our beds was home made stead, with rope cords to hold the mattress. We was always fed mighty good, peas, greens, meat, lasses, and plenty of milk. . . . My master's name was Mr. Dick Blaylock. His wife's name was Miss Janie. They had seven children. . . . My white folks lived in a common box house. . . . They didn't have no overseer or driver. Master looked after everything himself. I don't believe there was more than one hundred acres in the place. Old Miss and Old Master couldn't so much as write their own name. The only person with any learning was one of my Master's daughters. She was the one that visited around. In that way she got her learning just catch as could. We didn't know nothing about religion. There wasn't no church to go to, and we never as much as heared about the Bible or Baptizing. Saturday at twelve o'clock we was let off from work. The women did their washing, and the men didn't do nothing. Saturday nights we most always had a dance. The banjo and the pat of the hands was the music we had. Sundays was rest and play day. No church to go to, no work.[37]

Farmers, like planters, usually tended to settle in woodlands upon coming to Mississippi. Consequently, they had to clear their lands of trees and underbrush before their fields could be brought into full production. It usually took them several years to remove enough of the stumps from new fields to permit them to use a plow effectively. Initially they planted their crops of cotton and corn haphazardly among the standing dead trees and stumps, and they worked their growing plants with hoes. Again like the planters, they erected double log cabins as habitations for themselves and their families and single cabins for their slaves if they possessed any. Characteristically, farmers cleared all grass and weeds from around their houses and used pigs in their yards to keep down the population of dangerous snakes.[38]

Farmer families cooperated with one another to perform tasks too difficult for a man and wife to accomplish alone. They gathered together to construct cabins, corncribs, smokehouses, and barns, to roll logs, to construct split-rail fences, and to shuck corn. In return for help from his neighbors, a farmer would lend them a hand in turn.[39]

Thomas Dabney, one of the few wealthy Virginians who actually took up residence on a Mississippi plantation, did not get along well with his

37. *Slave Narratives*, Ser. I, *Mississippi*, Vol. X, Pt. 5, pp. 1935–39.

38. Owsley, *Plain Folk*, 67–77.

39. *Ibid.*, 104–15; Edward M. Steel, "A Pioneer Farmer in the Choctaw Purchase," *Journal of Mississippi History*, XVI (1954), 237–38.

farmer neighbors after settling in Warren County in 1835 on a 4,000-acre plantation. His daughter recalled:

> It was the custom among the small farmers in his neighborhood to call on each other to assist when one of them built his house, usually a log structure. Accordingly, one day an invitation came to the newcomer to help a neighbor to "raise" his house. At the appointed time he went over with twenty of his men [slaves], and he did not leave till the last log was in place and the last board nailed on the roof, handing over the simple cabin quite completed to the owner. This action, which seemed so natural to him, was a serious offense to the recipient, and, to his regret, he was sent for to no more "house-raisings."

Somewhat later Dabney dispatched a crew of twenty slaves to assist a farmer clean his grassy fields. The farmer afterward "said that if Colonel Dabney had taken hold of a plough and worked by his side he would have been glad to have his help, but to see him sitting up on his horse with his gloves on directing his negroes how to work was not to his taste."[40]

Joseph H. Ingraham left an unflattering description of the farmers who brought their crops to market at Natchez during the 1830s. He wrote:

> There are many small farmers who drive their own oxen, often conveying their whole crop on one waggon. These small farmers form a peculiar class, and include the majority of the inhabitants in the east part of this state. . . . They are in general uneducated, and their apparel consists of a coarse linsey-woolsey, of a dingy yellow or blue, with broad-brimmed hats; though they usually follow their teams barefooted and bare headed, with their long locks hanging over their eyes and shoulders. Accost them as they pass you, one after another, in long lines, cracking their whips, which they use instead of the [ox] goad . . . often fifteen and twenty feet in length, including the staff—and their replies will generally be sullen or insulting. . . . At home they live in log-houses on partially cleared lands, labour hard in their fields, sometimes owning a few slaves, but more generally with but one or none. They are good hunters, and expert with the rifle, which is an important article of furniture in their houses. Whiskey is their favourite beverage. . . . They are uneducated, and destitute of the regular administration of the gospel.[41]

Farmers' social lives centered around their churches, Ingraham notwithstanding, more often Baptist churches than Methodist or Presbyterian churches. Because the population of farmers was widely dispersed, the rural churches rarely served congregations of more than fifty families. Their rude church buildings were also their social centers. The farm folk customarily attended church several times a week. There were services

---

40. Susan Dabney Smedes, *Memorials of a Southern Planter,* ed. Fletcher M. Green (4th ed.; New York, 1965), 67.
41. [Ingraham], *South-West,* II 170–72.

on Sunday, business meetings and perhaps church trials on Saturday, and prayer meetings and songfests on week nights. The farmers regarded their ministers with great respect and looked to them for leadership in political and social matters as well as matters of religion. During the 1830s, 1840s, and 1850s, farmers displayed a keen interest in politics, almost always voting for the candidates of the party of their hero Andrew Jackson. Not being wealthy enough to afford to hold virtually unpaid public offices, they rarely became candidates themselves. Instead, they supported planter or lawyer politicians who espoused their viewpoints. Representing a large majority of the voters of the state, they controlled politics indirectly from the time the Constitution of 1832 was adopted until the Civil War.[42]

Economically and politically independent, farmers were fiercely democratic in their outlook. They considered themselves inferior to no man, and they reacted to slights or insults with lethal violence. When planters came into contact with members of the farmer class, they prudently treated the farmers with the greatest courtesy, usually addressing them as "Captain" or "Major," depending upon their ages. For their part, farmers displayed none of the class hatred toward their planter neighbors that Karl Marx would have expected. Not only were farmers treated with respect by planters, but they were sometimes kinsmen of the planters themselves. Of even greater importance in forming their attitude toward planters and their slaves, the farmers to a man expected to become planters before they died. They were, in fact, one of the most optimistic agricultural working classes that the world has ever seen. With luck and good weather, farmers expected to make enough money each year to expand their operations, perhaps buying a slave from time to time until they were rich enough to leave the fields themselves. Because so many of them actually realized this goal of becoming planters, the remainder saw themselves as having a stake in the slave-worked plantation system. With such a frame of mind, farmers joined the Confederate army in large numbers and astonished the world by their courage, endurance, and loyalty to a cause that outsiders did not believe to be their own.

From the English period in West Florida until the 1850s, a thriving cattle industry flourished in the vast pine forests of southern Mississippi.

42. Owsley, *Plain Folk*, 96–104, 138–42; McLemore (ed.), *History of Mississippi*, I, 284–309, 420–46; John R. Skates, *Mississippi: A Bicentennial History* (New York, 1979), 79–104.

During the colonial era, merchants of Pensacola and Mobile enjoyed a large export trade in deer hides, which they shipped to English and European customers for the manufacture of shoes. These Gulf coast merchants provided the Indians with firearms and ammunition for hunting deer, and they swapped trade goods for deerskins. The Indians responded to these incentives by increasing their slaughter of these animals, eventually reducing the coastal herds to the vanishing point. When the flow of deerskins diminished, both whites and Indians turned to raising cattle to meet the demand for hides, grazing their herds on wire grass and cane in the pine forests that stretched from the seacoast inland for a distance of 200 miles. Competition for feeding grounds for their herds led to conflict between the white cattlemen and their Indian counterparts from Georgia through Mississippi. They stole or slaughtered each other's cattle and ambushed one another on frequent occasions. Eventually the defeat of the Creeks by Andrew Jackson in 1814 left the coastal forests of the Mississippi Territory in uncontested possession of the white herdsmen, who proceeded to increase their herds until the range cattle in the Lower South numbered in the millions. This expansion of the herds led to destruction of the range by overgrazing during the 1840s, which forced the cattle industry westward into Louisiana and Texas. As the cattlemen withdrew during the late 1840s and 1850s, woodsmen in increasing numbers moved into the forests in search of timber, naval stores, charcoal, and firewood.[43]

The Indian and white cattle industries can be glimpsed in federal documents relating to the Mississippi Territory during the years following the seizure of West Florida by the Americans. In a petition to Congress from Mobile and Baldwin counties, for example, twenty-seven residents describe themselves as "owners of considerable stocks of cattle in the said counties, which in a district so unsettled, naturally range during the winter season over an extensive tract of country." They complained that many of their cattle had been seized or killed by militiamen serving with General Andrew Jackson during the Creek War of 1813–1814. In January 1815, to cite another case, Return J. Meigs wrote of "a large

43. Gray, *Agriculture*, II, 887; Nollie Hickman, *Mississippi Harvest: Lumbering in the Longleaf Pine Belt, 1840–1915* (Oxford, Miss., 1962), 9–14; Forrest McDonald and Grady McWhiney, "The Antebellum Southern Herdsman: A Reinterpretation," *Journal of Southern History*, XLI (1975), 147–66; Owsley, *Plain Folk*, 23–77.

number of white men, Citizens of the United States, who have driven
great numbers of Horses and Cattle on the Indian lands lying within the
proper limits of the Mississippi Territory. . . . Some of them I am told
possess very considerable property: have large stocks of Horses and black
cattle—they destroy the only ranges which Indians have to support their
stocks in winter." In a third instance, the editor of the Washington (D.C.)
Intelligencer wrote about the waves of American frontiersmen who customarily rushed into territories recently acquired from Indians before
the lands were surveyed and placed on the market by the government.
Such seizure of lands was then occurring in the area acquired from Spain
in 1811, he maintained. He added that "the first intruders were composed of mere huntsmen and herdsmen, who were influenced by the
double consideration of game and range for their stock."[44]

During the 1820s, 1830s, and 1840s, a class of livestock owners in
south Mississippi pastured herds of cattle numbering into the thousands
on publicly owned forest lands. The "large brick-colored or brown oxen
with their singular twisted ram-like horns" subsisted upon the wire grass
that carpeted the parklike Piney Woods during the summer and fall and
upon the young cane that flourished beside ponds and watercourses during the winter and spring. Cattle owners identified their animals with
brands that were recorded in the county courthouses as legal evidence of
ownership. Although the cattlemen did not feed their cattle, they did provide the beasts with salt at cattle pens, or "stampedoes," scattered across
the range. Like cowboys of the Southwest of a later generation, they annually rounded up their cattle for branding and marketing. Cattle sold for
beef were herded in great droves to Mobile, New Orleans, and lesser port
towns along the Gulf coast. In the 1840s, for example, as many as 2,000
head could be seen at one time in the little coastal village of Pass Christian. Beef cattle were marketed when they were three or four years old
and during 1850 were fetching ten to twelve dollars a head in Mobile and
New Orleans. Most of the cattle, however, were raised for their hides
rather than for beef.[45]

44. Clarence E. Carter and John Bloom (eds.), *The Territorial Papers of the
United States* (Washington, D.C., 1934–), VI, 492, 642n, 750–51.

45. *Patent Office Report, 1849: Agriculture*, 155, and *Patent Office Report,
1850: Agriculture*, 260; John F. H. Claiborne, "A Trip Through the Piney Woods,"
Mississippi Historical Society *Publications*, IX (1906), 487–538; Canton *Independent Democrat*, December 2, 1843; Natchez *Free Trader*, May 29, 1844; *Southwestern Farmer*, I (September 9, 1842), 3.

Because Mississippi cattlemen followed their herds across the wooded range, their families lived most of the time in temporary log huts rather than in permanent habitations. Although pine lands in southern Mississippi were available at minimum government prices in almost unlimited quantity, the cattlemen rarely bothered to acquire title to much acreage because they did no farming and already had full use of the public lands for grazing without cost. They did, however, raise vegetable gardens on plots of land where cattle and horses had been penned. On these manured plots they grew corn, upland rice, and sweet potatoes, their principal foodstuffs. Sweet potatoes, in particular, grew abundantly in the sandy soil enriched with animal manure, producing from 300 to 500 bushels per acre. Not surprisingly, the herdsmen were reputed to eat sweet potatoes at every meal. Like all pastoral people of any place and age, the herdsmen of southern Mississippi enjoyed much more leisure than agriculturists, which they devoted to their favorite rural sports of hunting and fishing.

William H. Sparks has left us one of the few descriptions of the herdsmen of Mississippi. In his *Memories of Fifty Years,* he recalled that the southeastern part of Mississippi was occupied by immigrants from the less prosperous areas of Georgia and the Carolinas who settled in the pine forests where there was forage for their immense herds of cattle. The cattlemen raised small crops of foodstuffs in the relatively fertile soils of river and creek bottoms and paid for their few purchases with the proceeds from the sale of hides and live cattle. As a class, Sparks wrote, the herdsmen were "illiterate and careless of the comforts of a better reared, better educated . . . people."[46]

Henri Necaise Nicholson, who had belonged to a French-speaking cattleman in Harrison County, has given us a rare description of that industry from a slave's viewpoint. His owner, Ursan Ladiner, had owned four slaves. Ladiner's house was "'bout 60 feet long, built o' hewed logs, in two parts. De floors was made of clay. Dey didn't have lumber for floors den. Us lived right close to de Big House in a cabin." Nicholson added: "My Marster didn't raise no big crops, jus' corn and garden stuff. He had a heap of cattle. Dey could run out in de big woods den, and so

46. William H. Sparks, *The Memories of Fifty Years: Containing Biographical Notices . . . in the Southwest* (Philadelphia, 1870), 331–32.

could de sheeps. He sol' cattle to N'awlins an' Mobile where he could get the best price."[47]

The contemporary historian John F. H. Claiborne has left us the best description of antebellum Mississippi cattlemen at roundup time, the brief period in which they performed most of their year's hard labor. When the cattle were to be brought together for branding, he wrote: "Half a dozen of them assemble mounted on the low-built shaggy, but muscular and hardy horses of that region, and armed with raw hide whips of prodigious size, and sometimes with a catching rope or *lasso* of plaited horsehair, they scour the woods in gallant style, followed by a dozen fierce-looking dogs." After separating their animals from those belonging to others, "they gallop thirty or forty miles a day, and rendezvous at night at the *stamping ground*. Here they *bivouac* in the open air; a fire of lightwood logs is soon kindled. . . . a young steer or perhaps a fat buck that has been killed during the ride is speedily cut into stalks and set up on sticks before the fire to broil." The meal is washed down with branch water "just touched perhaps with a little 'old-corn.'" With their hobbled horses grazing nearby, the weary cowboys after a little banter "stretch themselves around the blazing pile on skins or blankets, contented, happy, and at peace with the world."[48]

Eugene Hilgard, the state geologist of Mississippi, attributed the demise of the cattle industry in southern Mississippi during the late 1840s and 1850s less to overgrazing than to the almost universal practice of burning the underbrush in the woods at times of the year when fire would kill the roots of the wild grasses. In 1860 he wrote that "the pasturage of that region is disappearing before the fires at a fearful rate. . . . The beautiful park-like slopes of the Pine Hills are being converted into a smoking desert of pine trunks on which blackened soil the cattle seek more vainly every year the few scattered, sickly blades of grass whose roots the fire has not killed." Whether by fire or by overgrazing, the range was destroyed and with it the way of life of the antebellum Mississippi cattlemen.[49]

When Claiborne traveled on horseback across the Piney Woods in 1841,

47. *Slave Narratives*, Ser. 1, *Mississippi*, Vol. IX, Pt. 4, pp. 119–20.
48. Claiborne, "Trip Through the Piney Woods," 521–22.
49. Eugene W. Hilgard, *Report on the Geology and Agriculture of the State of Mississippi* (Jackson, Miss., 1860), 361.

he saw the cattle industry at its peak but did not observe much evidence of the lumber industry that was to replace it within a few years. Nevertheless, he was perceptive enough to foresee that lumbering would eventually come. After commenting upon the luxuriant natural grass pasturages of the forests, the historian added: "But the great source of wealth in this country must ultimately be—for it is now scarcely thought of—the lumber trade. The whole east is thickly planted with an almost unvaried forest of yellow pine. Finer, straighter, loftier trees the world does not produce. . . . The . . . [pine] is particularly large, shooting up frequently a smooth and limbless stem sixty feet, and of proportionate circumference. The time must arrive when this vast forest will become a source of value. The smoke of the steam mill will rise from a thousand hills. Rafts and lumber boats will sweep down the Pearl, the Leaf and Chickasawhay."[50]

Claiborne's prediction that a major lumber industry would emerge in south Mississippi was fulfilled even sooner than he anticipated. In 1852, Benjamin L. C. Wailes, another historian, traveled through the interior of southern Mississippi and along the Gulf coast. He encountered many herds of cattle but fewer than Claiborne had seen. What especially impressed Wailes was new lumber and naval stores industries that had recently come to prominence in that area.[51]

Wailes observed numerous steam sawmills in operation along the shores of bays and at outlets of rivers along the Gulf coast. He found one at Gainesville, "about the head of tidewater on the Pearl River," two more at Pearlington eight miles above the mouth of Pearl River, and several others on Back Bay and at Mississippi City. According to Nollie Hickman, the authority on lumbering in southern Mississippi, only a few small water-powered sawmills were located along the coast and on the rivers of the interior of southern Mississipi before 1840, and the lumber industry did not grow significantly until the steam mills were constructed in the later part of the decade. In 1850, sixteen steam sawmills were located in Harrison County alone, and these mills consumed about 88,000 logs and produced 17 million board feet of lumber.[52]

50. Claiborne, "Trip Through the Piney Woods," 523.
51. John H. Moore (ed.), "A Visit to South Mississippi in 1852: Some Selections from the Journal of Benjamin L. C. Wailes," *Journal of Mississippi History*, XVIII (1956), 18–32.
52. *Ibid.*, 24–25; Hickman, *Mississippi Harvest* 17–30.

The mills along the lower reaches of the rivers that flowed through the Piney Woods to the Gulf coast were supplied with timber by loggers and raftsmen working in the interior. These woodsmen felled trees and cut them into logs and then hauled the logs to a watercourse with caralogs pulled by teams of oxen. Raftsmen formed the logs into rafts and floated those unwieldly craft downriver to the mills in times of high water. As a rule, professional logmen contracted with mill owners to provide logs at a stipulated price, and the mill owner advanced supplies to the logging contractor against delivery of the logs. Sometimes loggers contracted to harvest timber on lands belonging to the mill owners, but more often they took the logs from public lands without authorization. The state and federal governments made sporadic efforts to prevent thefts of timber from public lands, but such attempts to protect the public domain were almost always ineffective. In rare instances where timber thieves were brought to trial, sympathetic jurors who were probably timber thieves themselves found the defendants innocent of the charges brought against them. Consequently loggers believed that they had a right to exploit the public forest lands as they wished. Nevertheless, the possibility of prosecution made them suspicious of strangers and averse to publicity. Travelers who might have left us descriptions of this large forest industry were not welcomed in the logging camps. As a result the thousands of people employed in the pine forests were virtually unknown to the inhabitants of the Cotton Kingdom.[53]

Members of logging crews spent most of their lives in semisecret logging camps where they lived in crude huts. Axemen were expected to cut ten logs a day, and they were generally paid at the rate of ten cents a log. Rafting required somewhat greater skill than felling trees; raftsmen were therefore paid about $1.50 per day. Woods foremen drew regular wages of $35.00 to $40.00 per month. Timber operators were paid varying prices for their logs, depending upon the supply of timber at the mills and upon the demand for lumber. In 1847, for example, Alexander Scarborough sold 300 pine logs to mill owner Calvin Taylor for $3 per thousand board feet. The logger received $137.00 for his timber, or $0.47 per log. Twelve years later when business was better for the mills, Taylor paid Hiram Williams $0.735 per log. Inasmuch as the loggers were cutting timber on lands they did not own, they were out of pocket only for the labor of

53. Hickman, *Mississippi Harvest*, 101–14.

felling the timber and transporting the logs to the mill. Thus the logging operators and their employees were making respectable livings, even though their life-styles would not have appealed to inhabitants of the farms, plantations, or towns.[54]

Slaves were employed in all aspects of the lumber industry. Large lumber firms like that of Andrew Brown of Natchez used more black workers than whites in the mills, in rafting, and in logging. Smaller operators utilized a higher proportion of whites but bought or hired slaves whenever they were able to do so. The slave narratives compiled by WPA workers contained testimonies from three former slaves from the Piney Woods of southern Mississippi who had worked as loggers. Ben Richardson, who had been born near Poplarville, had belonged to a professional logger. Richardson said: "My marster lived in a log house too. It jes' looked passable. One story with six rooms an' a kitchen off the house. He only farmed 24 acres. Most of his slaves cut an' hewed timber, an' hauled it to the mills with oxen. Den he hired most of his slaves out to other plantations." J. W. Farley was also a logger. His owner hired him out to a white timberman who tasked him at the daily rate of ten logs per day at ten cents per log. Farley himself was paid ten cents a log for every one that he cut above ten. Being an outstanding axeman, Farley was usually able to cut twenty logs per day. He saved money while he was a slave and was able to go into business for himself after the Civil War, becoming one of the larger log men in the Black Creek area. In his later years, mill owners at Moss Point extended him credit of $20,000 on an open account. Tom Newell, who was born in Yazoo County, was taken by his owner to the Gulf coast, where he cut logs for a time and then worked in a steam foundry. After his owner died, he was taken to Kosciusko, where he was hired out to cut timber.[55]

In addition to the extensive logging and sawmilling industries along the Mississippi and Yazoo rivers and their tributaries in western Mississippi and in the Piney Woods of southern Mississippi, several other forest-related industries employed significant numbers of people. By far the largest of the lesser forest products industries was the cutting of cordwood for sale to steamboats and railroads and to the inhabitants of the

54. *Ibid.*, 38, 40–42, 102.
55. Moore, *Andrew Brown*; *Slave Narratives*, Ser. 1, *Mississippi*, Vol. VII, Pt. 2, pp. 710–11, Vol. IX, Pt. 4, pp. 1636, 1838–41.

towns, who used it as fuel. Many hundreds of woodchoppers were regularly employed beside all rivers and creeks navigated by steamboats. They cut cordwood, transported it to the riverbank, and stacked it to await the coming of the next steamboat. Ingraham wrote that much of the fuel for steamboats was supplied by "squatters" who lived on the riverbanks. "They sell wood to the steamboats for a means of subsistence," he wrote, "seldom cultivating what little cleared land there may be around them. There are exceptions to this, however. Many become eventually purchasers of the tracts on which they are settled, and lay foundations for fine estates and future independence." Tyrone Power encountered a somewhat different class of woodcutters from the squatters described by Ingraham. He wrote: "I commonly found the labouring woodcutters to be North-country men, or from the western part of Michigan. They informed me that they can clear fifty dollars a month for the seven months they can work in this region, and that four or five seasons are sufficient to enable a saving man to buy a farm in the West." In 1860 the census taker reported a party of woodchoppers in Warren County numbering eleven men aged from twenty-one to fifty-three. Two were from Ohio, one was from Missouri, one from Ireland, and seven were from Germany.[56]

The woodcutters were as hard hit by the depression of the early 1840s as the farmers and planters. John F. H. Claiborne wrote in 1842: "The wood business on the river is not so profitable as formerly, steamboats being able to purchase at $2 per cord and sometimes for $1.50." With the revival of the cotton industry and the building of railroads during the late 1840s and 1850s, the demand for cordwood to fire steam engines and locomotives greatly increased. Similarly, the expansion of the towns and an increase in the number of steam-powered factories further enlarged the fuel requirements of the state. At the height of prosperity at the close of the decade of the 1850s, the wages of woodchoppers employed in preparing firewood rose from a dollar a day to fifty dollars per month. In like manner, the demand for charcoal used in blacksmith's forges and in various kinds of metalworking shops also increased during the 1840–1860 period. Woodsmen reduced wood to charcoal by burning billets in crude ovenlike kilns in an oxygen-poor environment. Compared with the hosts

56. [Ingraham], *South-West*, I, 253; Tyrone Power, *Impressions of America* (Philadelphia, 1836), II, 118; Manuscript Census Returns, 1860, Warren County, Mississippi, Schedule 1, Free Inhabitants, entries 1027, 1046–50, 1055.

engaged in preparing firewood, however, charcoal burners were always few in number while exerting a significant economic effect.[57]

The southern naval stores industry gradually expanded southward from North Carolina during the early nineteenth century. After tapping the trees in the pine barrens along the Atlantic coasts of South Carolina and Georgia, the turpentiners slowly invaded the pine forests along the Gulf coast. In 1843, a North Carolinian engaged in the business conducted tests on the pines in the vicinity of Mississippi City. The results of these tests were encouraging, and increasing numbers of people began to tap the trees in earnest. A correspondent of the Jackson *Mississippian* reported in May 1849 that "the business of making turpentine is becoming better understood, and immigrants from North Carolina are already at this work in south-eastern Mississippi." In June 1849 another correspondent of that paper wrote: "The piney woods are filling up fast with immigrants from North Carolina and Georgia engaged in the turpentine business." Major F. Leech erected a turpentine distillery, apparently the first in the state, at Napoleon in the spring of 1849. In a test run of two weeks, he distilled 2,500 gallons of spirits of turpentine, 600 gallons of camphine (used for lamps), and 250 barrels of rosin. In 1852 Wailes passed through woods that had been turpentined and then accidentally burned. By 1860 the turpentine industry had become firmly established in southern Mississippi, and many whites and slaves were engaged in tapping the trees.[58]

In 1852 Wailes described a naval stores industry new to Mississippi, the extraction of tar from lightwood and pine knots. Woodsmen had prepared kilns similar to charcoal kilns near Gainesville by digging basinlike holes in the sides of hills. They then filled the cavities with resin-rich lightwood and covered the wood with layers of pine straw and earth so as to make an airtight oven. The wood was ignited, and as it burned slowly, liquid tar collected in a low part of the basin. The workmen drew off the liquid tar through a duct from which it poured into barrels. Four to five days were required to extract all of the tar from the contents of a kiln. A cord of lightwood produced two barrels of tar, and the kilns were built

57. *Southwestern Farmer*, I (September 9, 1842), 5; Eaton, *History of the Old South*, 285; *Southern Cultivator*, XVIII (1860), 99.

58. *Southwestern Farmer*, I (January 20, 1843), 155; Percival Perry, "The Naval Stores Industry in the Old South, 1790–1860," *Journal of Southern History*, XXXIV (1968), 523–24; Jackson *Mississippian*, May 18 and June 15, 1849.

with capacities ranging from 25 to 100 cords. Buyers paid from $1.50 to $2.00 per barrel for pine tar at the kilns and resold it in New Orleans for $2.50 to $3.00 per barrel. Like lumbermen, the turpentiners and tar burners paid nothing for land or for the pine timber that they harvested.[59]

Completing the list of white rural social classes in antebellum Mississippi was an obscure group of people who preferred leisure to the accumulation of material possessions. These were folk who squatted in the woods and forests. Some were hunters who killed deer, bear, and wild cattle for their hides. Others were commercial fishermen. Living by preference as the early pioneers had done, they raised their own foodstuffs on clearings in the woods and obtained their meat from fish and game. These woodsmen were reputed to make whiskey, which they sold to slaves on the plantations, and they were suspected of trafficking in stolen goods with the blacks and of stealing planters' cattle and hogs. Van Buren, for example, wrote: "The poorer people living in the backwoods, besides being lumbermen, are frequently 'cow-boys,' and steal the planters' cattle, which they kill and sell in market." Visitors who saw them on infrequent occasions considered them to be a debased class of whites deserving of both scorn and pity. They failed to recognize that these latter-day frontiersmen were enjoying a life-style of their own choice. Not for them was the heavy labor of the woodchopper or even the occasional hard work of the herdsman. Like their descendants of the present day, these otherwise-minded people probably pitied the folk who had to toil from dawn to dusk for a living.[60]

The poor white class that many historians of the Old South have described was apparently absent from antebellum Mississippi. To be sure, persons who were physically or mentally handicapped, some widows and orphans, and the impoverished elderly sometimes qualified for the label "poor white." The demand for labor, however, was always great in the rapidly developing prewar economy. Furthermore, land was so cheap, and the forests and streams so full of game and fish free for the taking, that any able-bodied person of sound mind could find employment. In that era, Mississippi was indeed a land of opportunity for whites of all classes, though not for blacks, whether slave or free.[61]

59. Moore (ed.), "South Mississippi in 1852," 23.
60. Van Buren, *Sojourn in the South*, 153.
61. Collins, *White Society*, 6, 180; J. Wayne Flynt, *Dixie's Forgotten People: The South's Poor Whites* (Bloomington, Ind., 1979).

7   Water and Rail Transportation

The establishment of a highly successful cotton economy in Mississippi during the antebellum era resulted in large part from the adaptation of the steam engine to water and overland transportation. First, beginning in 1812, steamboats provided superior transportation for the cotton-growing areas bordering on the Mississippi and Tombigbee rivers and their tributaries. Then, during the 1840s and 1850s, the construction of railroads brought satisfactory transportation facilities for the first time to vast acreages situated between the navigable waterways of central and northern Mississippi, thereby making these lands available to farmers and planters. In this fashion the Mississippi Cotton Kingdom was extended to its prewar geographic limits.

Inhabitants of the lower Mississippi Valley relied mainly upon flatboats and keelboats to carry their produce to market at New Orleans during the first two decades of the nineteenth century. As the name implies, flatboats were boxlike wooden vessels having neither bows nor sterns. Crudely roofed over for most of their length, flatboats were floating warehouses that drifted downstream with the current. They were navigated by crews ranging in number from six to twelve, depending upon the size of the vessel. Most of these simple craft were constructed along the Ohio and upper Mississippi rivers for transporting coal, bar iron, corn, salt pork, flour, lumber, and other products of the Old Northwest to customers in the lower Mississippi Valley. After the original cargoes were discharged, the flats were reloaded with cotton bales for delivery to New Orleans. At their final destination in the Crescent City, flatboats were taken apart by "breakers," who salvaged the lumber from which they were constructed. Having disposed of their boats, the flatboatmen returned home over the Natchez Trace on foot or horseback or, at a later date, as deck passengers on northbound steamboats.[1]

Although the northwestern flatboats provided relatively inexpensive means of transportation for Mississippi cotton growers, they were slow, and they arrived at the river landings at uncertain times. Flatboats also

1. John W. Monette, "Progress of Navigation and Commerce on the Waters of the Mississippi River and the Great Lakes, A.D. 1700 to 1846," Mississippi Historical Society *Publications*, VII (1903), 485–93; Natchez *Courier*, April 21, 1837, April 23, 1845; Moore, *Andrew Brown*, 73–97.

required disproportionately large crews in relation to the size of their cargoes, and, not being capable of traveling upstream, they could make only one trip to New Orleans. These limitations made flatboats unable to compete with steamboats when these new Mississippi river vessels became available in adequate numbers. After losing the cotton trade to the steamers during the 1820s, flatboats carried rapidly growing quantities of lumber to New Orleans from mills located along the Mississippi and Yazoo rivers.

Keelboats, which were also used to carry cotton during the early 1800s, were long, slender river craft having pointed bows and sterns like canal boats. They ranged in length from forty to seventy feet and were from six to nine feet in width. Unlike flatboats, the keelboats could travel both upstream and down. When drifting downstream, a couple of oarsmen and a steersman could keep a keel on course, but a much larger crew was required to move one against the current. In deep open water, keels bound upriver were rowed laboriously by many oarsmen. In shallow water where the current was not too swift, boatmen pushed them along with poles. When heavily laden or when in rapid currents, the keels were "cordeled." At such times crewmen in two skiffs rowed ahead of the cargo boat hauling long cables, which they fastened to stout trees growing along the shore. Then, using the cables alternately, the crew pulled the keelboat along with a capstan mounted at the bow. Aided by their narrow beams, keelboats could navigate streams too small for flatboats or steamboats.[2]

On the eve of the steamboat era, the Mississippi River traffic carried by flatboats, keelboats, and rafts was large. In 1809, approximately a thousand of the simple river craft arrived at New Orleans. Twelve years later the number of arrivals at the Crescent City had grown to more than 2,000, although steamboats were then engaged in carrying cotton from Natchez to the seaport.[3]

Although steamboats drove keelboats but not flatboats off the principal waterways during the 1820s, keelboats continued to supplement steam

2. Leland D. Baldwin, *The Keelboat Age on Western Waters* (Pittsburgh, 1941); Seymour Dunbar, *History of Travel in America* (2nd ed.; New York, 1937), 269, 281–82; Louis C. Hunter, *Steamboats on the Western Rivers: An Economic and Technological History* (Cambridge, Mass., 1949), 25, 52–59, 243–44; Monette, "Navigation," 481–82.

3. John G. Clark, *New Orleans, 1718–1812: An Economic History* (Baton Rouge, 1970), 313.

navigation on small streams until the Civil War. In Mississippi, keels were to be found during periods of high water on the lesser tributaries of the Yazoo, Tombigbee, and Pearl rivers and on such narrow streams emptying into the Mississippi as Bayou Pierre and Big Black River. During 1837, for example, some twenty of these craft were hauling cotton from plantations along the Big Black to Grand Gulf, where the bales were reloaded on steamboats for the final leg of the voyage to New Orleans. During a boating season of about five months, Big Black keelboats averaged eight round trips each, transporting about fifty tons of cargo each way. In this period, the keelboatmen charged a dollar per hundred pounds of freight on the upriver trip. Their downstream rates were about half as much.[4]

The steamboat era on the Mississippi was initiated by Robert Fulton. Fulton's vessel, the *New Orleans*, arrived at the Crescent City in January 1812. Subsequently this first Mississippi River steamboat steamed back and forth between Natchez and New Orleans until it was sunk by a snag in 1814. During the next few years Fulton and his associates added three other steamboats, the *Vesuvius*, the *Aetna*, and a second *New Orleans*, to their fleet.[5]

Five years after the *New Orleans* had entered the cotton-carrying trade between Natchez and New Orleans, 17 steam-powered craft were in operation on the Mississippi River. By the close of 1818, 31 steamboats were at work on the great river, and 30 more were under construction in the boatyards, according to a list compiled by an observer from Louisville and published in the New Orleans *Gazette*. Included in this list were 2 new vessels, the *Volcano* and the *Johnson*, which made their first appearance at Natchez during the winter cotton season of 1818–1819. In 1820 the Mississippi River fleet rose to 69, in 1836 to 381, and by 1850 to 740. Thus a giant freshwater merchant navy sprang into existence almost overnight to transport the enormous and rapidly increasing cotton crops of the lower Mississippi Valley to the seaport of New Orleans.[6]

The rapid increase in the steamboat traffic on the lower Mississippi

4. Vicksburg *Sentinel*, March 26, 1834, and November 23, 1847; Canton *Herald*, December 1, 1837.

5. Hunter, *Steamboats*, 12–26, 67, 72, 82, 114, 129, 135, 146, 169, 392, 552, 655; Monette, "Navigation," 497–99.

6. Hunter, *Steamboats*, 33; Natchez *Mississippi State Gazette*, November 7, 1818, and January 9, 1819.

River during the 1820s was reflected in the number of vessels calling at
the port of Natchez. During the week of December 10–17, 1828, for example, no fewer than twenty-six steamboats arrived and departed from
the wharves at Natchez-under-the-Hill. A majority of these vessels were
traveling between Louisville and New Orleans, but some, such as the
Natchez and the *Attakapas*, made regular round trips between Natchez
and New Orleans. The *Attakapas* was small, carrying from 500 to 600
bales of cotton.[7]

According to the contemporary historian John W. Monette, there were
728 arrivals and departures of steamboats at New Orleans during 1830.
At the height of the boom of the 1830s in 1836, the figure was 1,561. In
1840, when the severe depression of early 1840s was devastating the
Cotton Kingdom, the arrivals and departures of steamboats from New
Orleans nevertheless increased to 2,187. In 1844, the figure had risen to
2,570.[8]

A valuable description of Mississippi steamboats and their system of
operation during the 1830s was published by a correspondent of the
Natchez *Courier*, who based his account on information supplied to him
by clerks of steamboats. According to his informants, a medium-sized
Mississippi River vessel of about 350 tons' burden when completely
equipped cost about $40,000. A vessel of this size could carry a cargo of
1,500 bales of cotton, while the largest size could take twice as much.
The *Ellen Kirkman*, one of the largest steamboats of the period, departed
from Natchez in January 1838 with 3,300 bales of cotton on board. The
editor of the Natchez *Courier* commented that this was "the largest cargoe
of cotton by one thousand bales, that ever passed down the Mississippi."
At this date the charge for carrying a bale of cotton from Vicksburg to
New Orleans was $1.50; from Natchez the rate was fifty cents less. Steam-
boats plying regularly between Vicksburg and the Crescent City customarily made one round trip each week and could continue operations
throughout the year. Although the expenses of operating a steamboat of
this size, including wages of approximately $2,000 per month for officers
and crew, were considerable, the earnings were disproportionately large
during the boom of the 1830s. In many cases the owners of steamboats

7. Natchez *Southern Galaxy*, July 10, 24, 31, August 21, and December 18,
1828.
8. Monette, "Navigation," 517–18.

realized sufficient profit in the first year to pay for the cost of their craft. The average life of steamboats was less than five years, and even when they survived the hazards of the river that long they were retired from the trade. Sometimes the deposed river queens ended their careers as wharfs or grocery stores permanently moored at various river landings.[9]

During the 1840s and 1850s, Mississippi River steamers continued to grow in size. The second *Sultana*, for example, entered the trade in 1848 and became a favorite with Mississippians during the 1850s. Of Cincinnati construction, she was 306 feet long and 80 feet in beam and was propelled by two engines having cylinders thirty inches in diameter with a ten-foot piston stroke. In addition to the main engines, the *Sultana* boasted two auxiliary engines. One, called a doctor, pumped water to her six boilers. The other was used for hoisting freight. Rated at 1,800 tons, the *Sultana* could carry more than 3,500 bales of cotton at speeds of ten miles an hour. The *Magnolia*, which began her run between Vicksburg and New Orleans in December 1850, was a rival of the *Sultana*. Constructed at a cost of $70,000, the 1,800-ton vessel provided exceptionally luxurious accommodations for 120 first-class passengers. The *Magnolia* was one of the first of the Mississippi River steamboats to be lighted with gas and "when lit up at night . . . [presented] a magnificent appearance." Not to be outdone in elegance by the *Magnolia*, Captain Thomas P. Leathers installed a steam calliope in his *Natchez*, with which he gave hour-long concerts at his ports of call.[10]

During the 1850s, numerous large vessels like the *Natchez*, the *Princess*, the *Sultana*, the *Magnolia*, and the *Vicksburg* served many river ports between Memphis and New Orleans. Steamboats that made regularly scheduled runs were called packets; others coming and going as the vagaries of business dictated were known as tramps. Packets usually ran between Vicksburg and New Orleans during the cotton-carrying season and extended their itineraries to St. Louis at other times of the year. Even large steamboats were able to navigate the Mississippi throughout the year, and only rarely were such craft forced to lie idle because of insufficient water in the Mississippi River.[11]

9. Natchez *Courier*, June 16, 1837, and January 5, 1838; Hunter, *Steamboats*, 20–21, 64, 100–103, 112–13, 358, 384–89.
10. Vicksburg *Whig*, March 9, 1848, and December 3, 1850; Hunter, *Steamboats*, 23, 143, 185n, 473, 543, 607, 648; Natchez *Courier*, December 2, 1857.
11. Harnett T. Kane, *Natchez on the Mississippi* (New York, 1947), 299–311; Edward Quick and Herbert Quick, *Mississippi Steamboating: A History of Steam-*

The Mississippi River steamboats of the 1840s and 1850s carried very large cargoes of cotton. Monette, the distinguished contemporary historian of the Mississippi Valley, wrote, "In January, 1846, the splendid steamboat Maria, from St. Louis, arrived at New Orleans with the enormous load of 4058 bales of cotton." The *Maria* was not unique among the Mississippi packets of the era. The *Montgomery*, which went into service in 1848, was designed to carry 4,000 bales of cotton. In September 1859 the packet *Charmer* brought 3,928 bales of cotton from Vicksburg to New Orleans. In September 1860 the steamboat *Vicksburg* delivered 3,620 bales from the city for which she was named to the metropolis.[12]

Monette reported that ordinary steamboats during the 1840s, when fully laden, "made their trips at the rate of ten or twelve miles per hour, down the stream, and from six to eight miles per hour against the current, above Natchez. Some superior running boats traversed the river at the rate of ten or twelve miles an hour against the current below Natchez." He related that the steamboat *J. M. White* traveled the 285 miles between New Orleans and Natchez in twenty hours and thirty minutes during May 1844, an average speed of almost fourteen miles an hour. Speeds of steamboats had increased dramatically in two and a half decades. The steamboat *Tamerlane* established a record run between New Orleans and Natchez in March 1819. Her time of sixty-six hours shaved nine hours and forty-five minutes off the previous record, set by the *James Ross* a few months earlier. In 1819, the brag speed upriver for a steamboat was four miles per hour.[13]

A smaller class of steamboats transported to New Orleans cotton from Yazoo City on the Yazoo River. Under usual conditions these boats found enough water in the Yazoo to operate throughout the year, and at times of high water could go much further upstream. In 1834, for example, a dozen vessels were hauling cotton from Yazoo City. Altogether they brought out about 40,000 bales worth more than $2 million. The *Le Flore*, which had been constructed especially for the Yazoo River trade,

---

boating on the Mississippi and Its Tributaries (New York, 1926), 96–97, 219–30, 320–22; Hunter, *Steamboats*, 105, 321–22, 333, 542.

12. Monette, "Navigation," 508–509; Vicksburg *Sentinel*, September 29, 1849; Jackson *Mississippian*, September 16, 1859; Vicksburg *Whig*, September 12, 1860.

13. Monette, "Navigation," 504; Natchez *Mississippi State Gazette*, March 10, 1819.

could carry fifty tons of cotton when the water in the river was no more than three feet deep. The packet *John Wesley* was fairly typical of Yazoo boats during the 1830s and 1840s. She was 135 feet long and 26 feet wide and like big Mississippi River steamers had dual paddlewheels. The *J. M. Sharp* was one of the last vessels to join the Yazoo fleet before the Civil War. She was 136 feet long, 30 feet wide, and drew only twenty-six inches of water when empty. Her two engines had sixteen-inch cylinders and six-foot piston strokes and could carry 1,800 bales of cotton. Costing $22,000, the *Sharp* was regarded as a "plain neat and servicable boat." [14]

Still smaller riverboats navigated the upper reaches of the Yazoo and its tributaries during the four or five months of the year when the water levels were reasonably high. The *Duck River*, for example, was running regularly during 1847 between Vicksburg and Williams Landing, a point that the editor of the Yazoo *Whig* described as lying 300 miles as a steamboat traveled from the mouth of the Yazoo. These small steamers capable of carrying a thousand bales of cotton could reach the town of Grenada and during times of high water could penetrate the Tallahatchie as far as the village of Wyatt in Lafayette County. The "steam-keel" *Cotton Plant*, built for the Deer Creek trade, was typical of the smallest steamboats of the antebellum period. This steam-powered keelboat was making weekly trips from Rolling Fork and the plantations on Deer Creek to New Orleans during the winter of 1859–1860. Captain M. Porter charged $2.25 per bale for cotton from the upper Deer Creek plantations and $1.50 from the mouth of Rolling Fork. On an upward trip, he charged $0.75 per barrel for carrying salt pork, molasses, cement, and other "wet freight" and $0.50 per barrel for "dry freight." Keelboats were charging $0.75 a bale to carry cotton from the upper Deer Creek to the Yazoo River. [15]

Harry P. Owens, who has made an exhaustive study of navigation on the Yazoo River, determined that approximately 250 steamboats plied the river at various times between 1830 and the period of the Civil War. Most of them were small or medium-sized vessels of from 100 to 450 tons that

14. Vicksburg *Sentinel*, April 27, July 17, and October 2, 1834; Jackson *Mississippian*, November 2, 1859.

15. Vicksburg *Sentinel*, July 28, August 4, and November 24, 1847; Benjamin L. C. Wailes Journal, February 14, 1852 (Mississippi Department of Archives and History); Panola *Lynx*, January 11 and November 29, 1845; Jackson *Mississippian*, January 20, 1837; Vicksburg *Whig*, January 25, 1860.

usually made only one or two trips a year. No line or combination of boats was established on the Yazoo during the antebellum period, and all of the craft competed fiercely for cargoes and passengers.[16]

After 1822, steamboats operated on the Tombigbee River on a regular basis during the months of winter and spring when the water was high. In January 1845 the editor of the Jackson *Southern Reformer* announced that "steamers on the Tombigbee ascend freely as high as Columbus." In 1849, two light draft steamboats, the *Eighth of January* and the *Olive*, made scheduled ten-day round trips between Mobile and Cotton Gin Port, ninety miles north of Columbus. Somewhat larger steam packets, the *Aberdeen*, the *Clara*, and the *Wave*, were making the round trip between Aberdeen and Mobile in eight days. In January 1850 the Mobile *Alabama Planter and Weekly Herald and Tribune* reported that the *Olive* had gone up the north fork of the Tombigbee River to Fulton in Itawamba County, a point eight miles farther north than steamboats had hitherto reached. On its return trip, the *Olive* brought 624 bales of cotton to Mobile. The seasonal nature of water transportation in the valley of the Tombigbee was emphasized by the editor of the Columbus *Democrat*, who wrote in August 1849 that the steamboat *Motive* had arrived at the city from Mobile. "The arrival of a steamer in these waters, at this season of the year," the journalist commented, "is a matter that never before occurred within the memory of the 'oldest inhabitant.'" Most of the steamers plying the Tombigbee during the 1840s and 1850s were stern-wheelers carrying about a thousand bales of cotton. The *Emperor*, built in 1848 for the Mobile-Montgomery trade, was representative of the larger type of vessels used in the area. Her hull was 225 feet long, the beam was 32.5 feet, and the hold was 7.5 feet deep. She could carry 1,500 bales of cotton. According to the editor of the Mobile *Alabama Planter*, the *Emperor*'s "cabins are very spacious and fitted up in the richest style."[17]

16. Harry P. Owens, "The P. Line" (Paper presented to the Mississippi Historical Society, Cleveland, Miss., March 4, 1983); and *An Assessment of Historic Period Cultural Resources Along the Yazoo River Between Miles 75.6 and 273.0, Including Tchula Lake and Honey Island, Mississippi* (Oxford, Miss., 1979).

17. W A. Evans, "Steamboats on the Upper Tombigbee in the Early Days," *Journal of Mississippi History*, IV (1942), 217–19; James H. Stone, *Cotton Gin Port, Mississippi: The History of a Tombigbee River Town* (Oxford, Miss., 1969), 14–15; Jackson *Southern Reformer*, January 3, 1845; Mobile *Alabama Planter and Herald and Tribune*, December 4, 1848, January 15 and August 27, 1849, January 7, 1850; Columbus *Democrat*, August 15, 1849.

On the Pearl River, steamers were usually able to reach as high as Jackson and upon occasion to Neshoba County fifty miles above the capital. At times of high water, small steamers could reach Port Gibson on Bayou Pierre, and a small steamboat called the *Piney Woods* was built in 1844 to carry cotton to New Orleans from the Chickasawhay, a tributary of the Pascagoula River, which ran through Wayne and Greene counties in southern Mississippi. Indeed, enterprising steamboat captains of the 1840s and 1850s apparently went after cotton wherever there was water enough to float a good-sized log. Where they could not go, keelboat skippers did.[18]

Soon after steamboats assumed the task of transporting the cotton from the inland river towns to the seaports, railroads were constructed in Louisiana and Mississippi to facilitate the carrying of cotton bales from interior plantations to such river ports as Natchez, Grand Gulf, and Vicksburg. The Vicksburg and Jackson Railroad that went into limited operation in 1838 was the most economically significant line among the several begun during that prosperous decade.

Because the Vicksburg and Jackson Railroad linked the economic and political capitals of the state, its managers could always anticipate sizable revenues from passenger traffic. Even more important for its financial well-being, the route of the Vicksburg and Jackson traversed rich and comparatively densely populated plantation country throughout its entire length. Thus while construction was in progress, the laying of every mile of track produced additional business for the company. Trains began to run over five miles of line in May 1838, and by the ensuing November two round trips between Vicksburg and the Big Black River were being made on schedule daily. During that autumn the Vicksburg company charged passengers $1.25 for one-way trips between Vicksburg and the Big Black, and the freight on a bale of cotton from the end of the line was $0.74. From the beginning of its operations, the railroad earned almost enough to defray the expenses of operating trains over the portion of the line in active service. In December 1839, for example, trains were running regularly over twenty-eight miles of the Vicksburg line. In the middle of that month, the president of the company informed Governor A. G. McNutt that his cars had already transported 14,000 bales of the cotton crop of

18. Jackson *Southern Reformer*, November 11, 1844, January 3, 1845; Port Gibson *Herald*, December 28, 1843.

1839–1840 to Vicksburg. Since August, the railroad had grossed nearly $33,000 from the transportation of passengers and freight.[19]

The demonstrated earning capacity of the Vicksburg and Jackson ensured the survival of the railroad in the critical autumn of 1839 despite the onslaught of the great cotton depression of 1839–1849. In early 1840, all of the assets of the bankrupt Commercial and Railroad Bank of Vicksburg were placed in the hands of trustees who were charged with winding up the affairs of the suspended bank and operating the railroad on behalf of creditors of the institution. The directors of one of the larger of the northern creditors, the Bank of the United States, were so favorably impressed by the earning record of the Vicksburg railroad at this juncture that they advanced the quarter million dollars necessary for completing the line to Jackson. With these funds and the current earnings of the road, the Vicksburg and Jackson was able to open regular service between these towns in October 1840. Inasmuch as the whole cotton belt was in the grip of the most severe depression of the antebellum period, completion of the railroad was a remarkable achievement indeed.[20]

Still more remarkable, the Vicksburg railroad proceeded to produce substantial revenues throughout the 1839–1849 depression. Even in the depths of the depression, the company grossed $113,000 and netted $32,000 between August 1842 and July 1843. In 1846 when a slow economic recovery was in progress, the profits of the railroad were reported to be $73,000. In the second half of the decade of the 1840s, cotton production increased considerably in the region served by the railroad, and its freight business improved in proportion. During the cotton hauling season that lasted from September through February, the trains brought 32,000 bales to the Vicksburg depot in 1846–1847; the number of bales transported by the line rose to 44,000 during the ensuing season and to 49,000 in 1848–1849. Thus it is clear that the Vicksburg and Jackson was actually prospering during the 1839–1849 depression.[21]

Over a period of nearly twenty years, the Vicksburg and Jackson line was by far the most important railroad in Mississippi. During the 1840s

19. Vicksburg *Whig*, January 9, 1840; Eugene Alvarez, *Travel on Southern Antebellum Railrods, 1828–1860* (Tuscaloosa, 1974), 15–16.

20. Vicksburg *Whig*, February 20, 1840.

21. *Niles Register*, LXV (1844), 304; Caroline MacGill, *History of Transportation in the United States Before 1860* (Washington, D.C., 1917), 475; Vicksburg *Sentinel*, July 22, 1847, March 2, 1850; Raymond *Hinds County Gazette*, March 22, 1850.

the company operated two daily mixed trains of passenger and freight cars. For the sake of the passengers' safety and comfort, their cars were customarily situated as far as possible behind the smoke- and spark-belching, potentially explosive locomotive. In the late 1840s the company's rolling stock comprised seven locomotives, five passenger cars, forty-five boxcars, and twelve flatcars. Most of the members of the train crews were white mechanics, but the company also owned twenty black men, some of whom were employed on the locomotives as firemen.[22]

During the 1840s the Vicksburg and Jackson Railroad conferred concrete economic benefits upon the community that it served. Before the line went into service, stagecoach travelers spent more than twelve hours on the journey between Vicksburg and Jackson and paid fares of $10.00. When the railroad inaugurated service to Jackson in 1840, the railway fare from the city on the Walnut Hills was established at $4.00, and this rate was reduced to $2.00 before the close of the decade. The journey by rail took only two and a half hours to accomplish. Hauling cotton by wagon from Jackson to Vicksburg in the late 1830s cost at least $4.00 per bale. In 1850, the railroad was charging no more than $1.00 per bale. Hauling from the ports into the interior around Clinton in the 1830s cost from $1.50 to $2.00 per hundred pounds; this expense was reduced by the railroad in 1848 to $0.30 per hundredweight. Thus the railroad cut the cost of transporting cotton from Jackson to New Orleans to less than half of what it had been before the line was built.[23]

While the Vicksburg and Jackson was prospering during the early depression years, a rival Natchez and Jackson railroad was not as fortunate. Initially, the Natchez company appeared to flourish. Track laying began on December 8, 1836, and within a month a car was operating over a short distance, presumably pulled by horses. In May 1838 the people of the town "turned out *en masse* to witness the starting of the first locomotive that has been run in this State. . . . the locomotive is very appropriately styled the *Natchez*." The contractor, employing a large force of German laborers, pushed construction of the line during the remainder of the year, and the company began to haul cotton to the port on October 26, 1837, bringing in fifty-three bales from the Minor plantation on the road to Washington. During June 1838 the company realized between

22. Vicksburg *Sentinel*, October 20, 1847, March 28, 1848, September 15, 1849; Vicksburg *Whig*, February 3, 1848.
23. *De Bow's Review*, XI (1851), 594–95.

one and two hundred dollars per day carrying passengers and freight. At that time the roadbed had been completed and made ready for the rails for twenty miles beyond Washington. Track laying over this portion of the railroad was completed by the end of August 1839, and regular service over the whole twenty-five miles was inaugurated on the thirty-first. By October 1839 an additional thirteen miles of roadbed were nearing completion.[24]

Before the second section of the Natchez line could be placed in operation, worsening conditions of the Mississippi Railroad and Banking Company (formed in 1838 by merger of the railroad and the Planters Bank) forced its president, John A. Quitman, to order a halt to further construction on the railroad. In order to meet pressing obligations, Quitman sold all of the slaves belonging to the company, together with its sawmills, lands, and buildings. The company continued for a time to operate trains over the completed portion of the route but was not able to pay expenses out of the receipts from passengers and freight. During 1840, for example, the road carried no more than 4,800 bales of cotton and grossed less than $15,000. Having become hopelessly insolvent, the company suspended all services two years later and disposed of the rolling stock and railroad iron. With this failure the Natchez merchants surrendered the trade of the Pearl River valley to their competitors in Vicksburg.[25]

The short railroad from Grand Gulf to Port Gibson proved to be more viable than its much longer neighbor to the south. Construction was begun in December 1835, "two hours after the right-of-way had been secured for the Company." This work progressed steadily through 1836, and stockholders of the company became so enthusiastic toward the end of the year that they began to lay plans to extend the rails eastward to Jackson, a distance of sixty-five miles. Although work was interrupted by the panic of 1837, six miles of the roadway were graded and ready for the rails in December 1837, and one and a quarter miles remained to be constructed. In February 1840, cotton was being hauled over the railroad

24. Thomas D. Clark, *A Pioneer Southern Railroad from New Orleans to Cairo* (Chapel Hill, 1936), 29–37; James, *Antebellum Natchez*, 190–92; Jackson *Mississippian*, December 16, 1836; Natchez *Courier*, January 6, May 12, October 27, 1837, June 29, 1838, February 19, 1840; Vicksburg *Register*, May 10, 1837; *Niles Register*, LVII (1839), 64; Vicksburg *Whig*, October 1, 1839.

25. Vicksburg *Whig*, October 1, 1839, January 20, 1841; Natchez *Courier*, February 19, 1840.

from the Bayou Pierre to Grand Gulf, although service had not yet been extended to Port Gibson. Depression, collapse of the Grand Gulf banking company, and litigation over a portion of the right-of-way halted work on the road from 1840 to 1845. The company surrendered its banking privileges in 1843 and petitioned the legislature for permission to dispose of the railroad to another group with the resources required to finish the road. This transaction eventually took place, and in 1845 the line was finally placed in operation. Although the tracks were not laid beyond Port Gibson, the short line served a prosperous area around that village until the Civil War.[26]

The history of a railroad connecting Woodville, Mississippi, with St. Francisville, Louisiana, was quite similar to that of the Port Gibson and Grand Gulf line. Although the company was chartered by both state legislatures in 1831, it did not begin construction until 1836. Despite financial difficulties arising from the panic of 1837, the railroad bed was completed for half its length of twenty-seven miles by the beginning of 1838.[27]

Little more was accomplished toward placing the line in service until 1840, when the Louisiana legislature granted the company a new charter. During the next two years, the railroad was finally extended to Woodville with the assistance of planters along the route, who constructed portions of the roadway with their slaves. Because of faulty construction and inferior materials, the railroad was unable to operate efficiently during the first decade after it was finished. Partly in response to bitter complaints about unreliable service from its patrons, the railroad replaced the original iron straps in 1852 with modern iron rails of the T type and purchased a new locomotive, the *Eclipse*, which was capable of speeds approaching fifty miles an hour and of hauling 400 bales of cotton. Despite numerous accidents and interruptions of service caused by heavy rains and floods, the West Feliciana railroad continued to transport cotton

26. Jackson *Mississippian*, January 1, 1836; Natchez *Free Trader*, December 22, 1836, March 5, 1853; New Orleans *Bee*, September 3, 1836; Port Gibson *Correspondent*, November 29, 1839; Vicksburg *Sentinel*, January 9, 1838, February 27, 1840, February 17, 1845; Jackson *Southern Reformer*, December 26, 1843; Natchez *Courier*, October 19, 1854; Vicksburg *Whig*, November 7, 1860.

27. Merl E. Reed, *New Orleans and the Railroads: The Struggle for Commercial Empire, 1830–1860* (Baton Rouge, 1966), 45–51, 56.

from the plantations around Woodville to the river at St. Francisville until the end of the slavery era.[28]

While the great depression was lessening during the last half of the decade of the 1840s, proposals were advanced for building many railroads in various parts of Mississippi's Cotton Kingdom. For many reasons, however, no construction was undertaken on any new line before 1850 except for a ten-mile extension of the Vicksburg and Jackson Railroad to Brandon, in Rankin County.

Although the railroad from Vicksburg to Jackson was very profitable throughout the antebellum period, extension of the line eastward presented so many difficulties that the task was not completed until 1862. The Mississippi and Alabama Railroad Company had attempted to build a railroad from Jackson to Brandon during the late 1830s but had gone bankrupt in 1840. After two private reorganizations, the rechartered Mississippi and Alabama Railroad Company and the Southern Railroad Company failed in turn, the state of Mississippi undertook to extend the Vicksburg and Jackson line to Brandon, using public money to finance the construction project. Under the direction of three commissioners appointed by the governor, construction work on the line proceeded rapidly. By June 1850 thirteen miles of the road east of Jackson had been equipped with modern T-rails and a bridge erected over the Pearl River. Much of the work on the roadway was performed by sixty slaves belonging to the state. Trains began running regularly over the completed portion of the track during February 1850, and receipts from passengers and freight immediately began to defray operating expenses. By arrangement between the state commissioners and the directors of the Vicksburg and Jackson Railroad, the latter firm operated the trains for the state.[29]

During 1850 the legislature issued another charter of incorporation to the Southern Railroad Company. This act authorized the governor of the state to give the completed roadway to the company along with all property of the state connected with the operation as soon as twenty miles of rail had been laid east of Brandon. In this manner the state presented assets valued at more than $300,000 to the railroad company. The gifts

28. *Ibid.*, 50; Woodville *Republican*, June 15, 1852; Vicksburg *Whig*, May 10, 1856.
29. Vicksburg *Sentinel*, February 15 and March 7, 1845, June 1, 1850.

included sixty slaves, a locomotive, a passenger car, thirteen freight cars, and wagons, horses, mules, and grading equipment. In addition, the company was to receive future receipts into the 2 percent fund.[30]

Business was so brisk when the Southern Railroad Company took over ownership of the line east of Jackson that the facilities of the Vicksburg and Jackson company (which was operating the Southern's trains) were taxed beyond capacity. On July 9, 1851, President George S. Yerger of the Vicksburg and Jackson assured President A. M. Paxton of the Southern that the shortage of equipment would be remedied in time for the coming cotton season. Two powerful new locomotives had been delivered from the North; three older engines had been completely renovated in the railway workshops at Vicksburg; and three more were being overhauled. All of the old-fashioned four-wheel freight cars had been retired from service, and forty new eight-wheel cars were ready for use. With the added equipment the Vicksburg and Jackson was prepared to handle a thousand bales a day. The regular train running between Brandon and Jackson could haul an average of 200 bales, and the addition of another engine and cars could double the hauling capacity without straining the resources of the Vicksburg railroad.[31]

After the railroad reached Brandon, cotton production in the vicinity increased rapidly. Seventy-five hundred bales of the crop of 1851 were shipped from that station to Vicksburg. Two years later, more than 12,000 bales were loaded on the cars at Brandon. Similar increases in cotton shipments occurred during these years at other railroad stations in the interior counties lying between the Yazoo River and the Pearl. At Jackson, for example, cotton shipments rose from 21,600 bales in 1851 to 50,000 in 1853. From Clinton, 10,000 bales were sent to Vicksburg in 1851; the shipments rose to 16,000 two years later. The greatest proportional increase occurred at Raymond, where a spur of the Vicksburg and Jackson Railroad had just been placed in service. Shipments totaling 1,100 bales in 1851 were eclipsed by a crop of 7,000 bales in 1853. As a result of the economic development of the central province of the Cotton Kingdom made possible by the Vicksburg railroad, the number of bales received at Vicksburg by rail increased from 40,000 in 1847 to 98,000 in 1853.[32]

30. *Ibid.*, June 1, 1850.
31. Vicksburg *Whig*, July 23, 1851.
32. Jackson *Mississippian*, June 30, 1854; *De Bow's Review*, XVII (1854), 608.

Beyond Brandon the route of the Southern Railroad passed into an infertile region of pine forests containing comparatively few cotton farms and plantations. Not having many customers to serve, the line gained very little additional revenue as it moved toward Alabama. With rising costs and declining revenues in evidence, the directors found it increasingly difficult to raise fresh capital. As the company had little more than the company's share of the earnings of the Vicksburg-to-Brandon section of the line plus the receipts of the state 2 percent fund to draw on, relatively little progress was made. In September 1856, President William C. Smedes reported that the line was in operation only to Brandon, although an unfinished roadbed reached 82½ miles further east to the right-of-way of the as yet incomplete Mobile and Ohio Railroad, intersecting the latter in Lauderdale County.[33]

At that juncture, William C. Smedes found a remarkable solution for the financial difficulties of the Southern company. Soon after being elected president, he arranged for his financially embarrassed and economically unsound corporation to purchase the prosperous Vicksburg and Jackson Railroad from the stockholders and creditors of the old Commercial and Railroad Bank of Vicksburg. On a trip to Philadelphia, Pennsylvania, where the principal stockholders maintained their headquarters, Smedes arranged for the merger of the two lines, effective January 1, 1857. Shortly afterward the Mississippi legislature approved the consolidation of the two lines and made the required revisions in the charter of the Southern company. Thereafter, with the receipts of the Vicksburg and Jackson to draw upon, the Southern pushed construction more rapidly. In August 1858, trains were running eighty-three miles from Vicksburg to Morton. Sixty miles remained to be built to the Mobile and Ohio, and twenty-five of these had been placed under contract. With the aid of a half million dollars realized from bonds sold by Smedes in England and the northern states, and with another hundred thousand dollars from a state 3 percent internal improvement fund, the Southern was able to purchase the necessary rails and rolling stock to equip the line for operation between Vicksburg and Meridian, as the town at the intersection of the north-south and east-west railroads was named by Smedes. In preparation for putting the new track into service, the Southern ordered for September 1860 delivery 8 large locomotives, 4 first-class passenger cars, 3 mail and baggage

33. Vicksburg *Whig*, September 19, 1856.

cars, and 100 freight cars. With the exception of two miles between the Chunckey and Tallahatta creeks, the rails were laid to the line of the Mobile and Ohio at the end of 1860. A junction of the two railroads was achieved in 1861, and the extension of the line to Selma, Alabama, was finally completed in 1862. At that time the dream of linking the Atlantic with the Mississippi River via Montgomery finally became a reality, too late to be significant for the antebellum Cotton Kingdom.[34]

During the 1850s two north-south feeder railways connecting with the Vicksburg railroad operated in conjunction with the main east-west line. The first of these to be constructed was a road seven miles long, running from Bolton's Station on the Vicksburg and Jackson Railroad to the town of Raymond. In 1838 the Raymond Railroad Company was incorporated by the state legislature with a capital of $100,000. Construction of the Raymond road began in the autumn of that same year, and by November 1839 the rails had been laid to Ford's Creek, within one and a half miles of the Vicksburg and Jackson Railroad. Soon afterward the line was completed, and horse-drawn cars ran between Bolton's Station and Raymond beginning on January 28, 1840. At the start of service, passenger fare from Vicksburg to Raymond by way of Bolton's Station was set at four dollars and the freight on a bale of cotton from Raymond to Vicksburg was two dollars. During the 1840s, however, the line did not transport much cotton. In 1850 and 1851, the railroad was rebuilt and was equipped for the first time with a locomotive. As a result of these improvements, the Raymond line soon became a significant carrier of freight as well as passengers. In the first season of steam-powered operation, the train carried 1,100 bales to Bolton's Station. Business of the little railway increased steadily over the next several years and leveled off at approximately 6,000 bales, where it remained for the rest of the decade.[35]

The second of the branches of the Vicksburg and Jackson railroad to be placed in service was the Canton and Jackson Railroad. Track laying

34. *Ibid.*, December 24 and 25, 1856, August 14, November 24, December 8 and 29, 1858, December 7 and 24, 1859, July 4 and December 19, 1860; John F. Stover, *The Railroads of the South, 1865–1900: A Study in Control* (Chapel Hill, 1955), 17.

35. Charles R. Johnson, "Railroad Legislation and Building in Mississippi, 1830–1840," *Journal of Mississippi History*, IV (1942), 203; Natchez *Courier*, September 27, 1838; Vicksburg *Sentinel*, November 18, 1839, April 11, November 23, 1850, February 8, 1851; Vicksburg *Whig*, January 28, 1840, September 3, 1853; *De Bow's Review*, XI (1852), 594; Woodville *Republican*, July 9, 1850; Raymond *Hinds County Gazette*, September 23, 1857.

began at Canton on January 2, 1852, and proceeded gradually over the next few years. On July 1, 1856, the line between Jackson and Canton was formally opened, and the first locomotive to arrive received a tumultuous welcome at the northern terminus.[36]

While the Canton and Jackson line was still under construction, the company was taken over by the New Orleans, Jackson and Great Northern Railroad, which had been incorporated by the state of Mississippi in 1852. Subsequently the directors of the New Orleans company arranged with James Roach, president of the Vicksburg and Jackson Railroad, for the latter to operate the Canton and Jackson until the New Orleans line could link up with it at Jackson. Under the terms of the agreement, Roach's company supplied the rolling stock and ran the trains on the Canton road for several years, to the mutual benefit of the two railroad companies. Thus for a brief while the cotton trade of the region north of Jackson passed through Vicksburg and fattened the pockets of its merchants. When the New Orleans, Jackson and Great Northern reached the southern terminus of the Canton road in 1858, however, cargoes of cotton from the Canton trade area were routed over the line of the parent company, and the Vicksburg and Jackson Railroad and the merchants of Vicksburg accordingly ceased to enjoy the trade of north-central Mississippi. At the same time, the mercantile community of Vicksburg understandably lost some of its enthusiasm for railroads and railroad building.[37]

Two major north-south trunk-line railroads were built through Mississippi during the 1850s, one terminating at Mobile and the other at New Orleans. These trunk lines, unlike the older east-west lines, were designed to compete with steamboats rather than to complement them. For profits, these railroads depended upon the exchange of products between the states of the upper and lower Mississippi Valley. On their southward runs, the trains were to bring down corn, wheat, pork, beef, livestock, iron, coal, and manufactured goods while carrying northward cotton, tobacco, and sugar.[38]

The railroad linking Mobile with the mouth of the Ohio River was the first of the north-south lines to be placed under construction. In 1847 charters were granted to the Mobile and Ohio railroad by the legislatures

36. Clark, *Pioneer Southern Railroad*, 48–51.
37. Vicksburg *Whig*, December 3, 1858.
38. Robert S. Cotterill, "Southern Railroads, 1850–1860," *Mississippi Valley Historical Review*, X (1924), 396.

of Alabama, Mississippi, Tennessee, and Kentucky. Three years later the federal government awarded to the Mobile company a land grant consisting of alternate sections along the right-of-way through Alabama and Mississippi. Aid in the form of loans from Alabama and Mississippi and grants from Tennessee was also forthcoming from the states to be served by the M & O. In Mississippi many counties, towns, and individuals subscribed for stock in the company and helped to construct the road-bed. Moving northward from Mobile, beginning in 1852, the railroad reached Scooba Station in Clarke County, Mississippi, 170 miles from the port in May 1856. After the line had been continued to Macon, construction was halted for almost a year. Work was resumed in 1857, and 300 miles of track were in operation above Mobile by the end of 1859. On April 22, 1861, the line being built northward from Mobile joined with a section being constructed southward from Columbus, Kentucky, to complete the main line of the Mobile and Ohio.[39]

As the Mobile and Ohio moved northward through eastern Mississippi, it stimulated economic growth in that region much as the Vicksburg and Jackson had done in Warren and Hinds counties. This process was described in 1859 by a resident of Marion Station in Lauderdale County: "Since the completion of the Mobile and Ohio Railroad through our pine forests . . . society has been transformed, good schools are visible everywhere . . . and tall church spires are now prominently seen." "The lands," he continued, "that have been heretofore uncultivated . . . are being rapidly settled . . . and command high prices." Before the coming of the railroad, cotton growers in this area had been compelled to haul cotton fifty miles to the Tombigbee River, a situation that had held land values to almost nothing. After the rails reached eastern Mississippi, however, cotton cultivation increased wherever there was suitable soil. This extension of the Cotton Kingdom is reflected in the freight records of the M & O. In 1854, trains brought 6,000 bales of cotton to Mobile; in 1857 this number rose to nearly ninety thousand.[40]

Spurred on by progress being made by the Mobile and Ohio Railroad, advocates of a rival new Orleans line were able to secure charters from Louisiana and Mississippi in 1852 for the New Orleans, Jackson and Great Northern Railroad. The original plan was for the railroad to con-

39. *Ibid.*, 396–400; Vicksburg *Whig*, May 17, 1856.
40. Vicksburg *Whig*, February 24, 1858, October 5, 1859.

nect New Orleans with Nashville by way of Jackson, Mississippi, but lack of interest among investors along the route between Jackson and Nashville forced the directors to adopt a less ambitious program. Their new scheme provided for the purchase of two short connecting Mississippi lines that had already been chartered, the Canton and Jackson and the Mississippi Central. The latter road ran from Canton to a junction with the Memphis and Charleston at Lagrange, Tennessee. By incorporating these lines into its own system, the New Orleans, Jackson and Great Northern could connect with the rival Mobile and Ohio at Jackson, Tennessee, thereby gaining direct linkage with the northwestern railroad network.[41]

Aided by grants from the city of New Orleans and the state of Louisiana, by loans from the state of Mississippi, and by the sale of bonds in England and the northern states, the company was able to push the railroad slowly through the swampy terrain above New Orleans and then more rapidly through the piney woods of southern Mississippi. In April 1858, the New Orleans, Jackson and Great Northern reached Jackson, Mississippi, where it joined the already completed Canton and Jackson division. The subsidiary Mississippi Central Railroad was completed in January 1860, allowing continuous traffic to move between Columbus, Kentucky, and New Orleans. As in the case of the Mobile and Ohio, the New Orleans, Jackson and Great Northern was finished at too late a date to be of great economic significance to central and north Mississippi during the era of slavery but was to be of overwhelming military importance during the Civil War.[42]

Between 1857 and 1860 the cotton crops of Mississippi were exceptionally large. Thus upsurge in production was unquestionably due mainly to the construction of the two major north-south railroads through areas that had lacked adequate transportation facilities heretofore. Along the routes, new farms and plantations were quickly brought under cultivation, and existing agricultural establishments were enlarged. Although cotton statistics that would clearly define the changes brought about by the coming of the railroads are unfortunately lacking, information about the total value of farmlands is available for each county through

41. Cotterill, "Southern Railroads," 396–404; Reed, *New Orleans and the Railroads*, 88–107.

42. Reed, *New Orleans and the Railroads*, 88–107.

which the railroads ran for the years 1850, 1854, 1857, and 1860. In every county a very large increase in total value of farmlands occurred after rail transportation became available. After the Vicksburg and Jackson Railroad was extended to Rankin County in 1850, for example, the value of farmlands increased between that date and 1854 from $564,190 to $1,225,674; by 1860 the evaluation had risen to $3,346,169. Hence the value of farms and plantations in Rankin County increased almost sixfold in ten years because of the Southern Railroad. In similar fashion the total value of farmlands in Pike, Lawrence, and Copiah counties increased in six years by 85 percent when the New Orleans, Jackson and Great Northern Railroad reached Jackson. When that line reached Canton, land values in Madison County rose from $3,751,409 in 1854 to $8,181,595 in 1860. Along the line of the Mobile and Ohio, land values quadrupled in Clarke County between 1854 and 1860. These dramatic increases in land values strongly imply that the main-line railroads would have bestowed enormous benefits upon the agriculturists of Mississippi had there been no Civil War.[43]

43. *Seventh Census, 1850,* p. 456; *Eighth Census, 1860: Agriculture,* 84; and Appendix A.

8   Towns and Villages

In the Old World, rural areas generally existed to support urban centers, but in antebellum Mississippi and in the Old South generally, the relationship between town and country was reversed. There towns and villages were auxiliaries of the agricultural areas. The small urban centers of the state developed for the purpose of providing a variety of essential services for the peoples of farms and plantations. Both the state capital at Jackson and the county seats were founded to furnish such limited legal and administrative services as the slaveowning agricultural population required. The comparatively large river towns—Natchez, Vicksburg, and Columbus—and small villages in every county located on rivers or railroads provided facilities for moving the agricultural crops to market and for importing farm and plantation supplies. Both the administrative and the commercial urban centers also offered the rural population such important social services as medical treatment, religious instruction, education, and entertainment. Moreover, in many of the towns, mechanics provided building materials and manufactured and repaired farm equipment and machinery. Throughout the antebellum period, however, all of the towns in the state continued to be small because the population of the area they served was thin and scattered. Furthermore, the presence of the major cities of New Orleans and Mobile inhibited the growth of the river towns of Mississippi.[1]

Because of Mississippi's dispersed population and the competition of the two major seaports nearby, not a single town in the state came close to attaining a population of 10,000 persons during the era of slavery, and only Natchez passed 5,000. Vicksburg, the second largest town in the state and the foremost commercial center during the 1840s and 1850s, could produce no more than 4,591 residents when the federal census of 1850 was taken. The next three largest towns (Columbus, the principal market town of eastern Mississippi; Jackson, the state capital; and Holly Springs, the leading urban center of northern Mississippi) had populations at that time of about 3,000 each. Port Gibson ranked sixth with

1. Walter C. Hearn, "Towns in Antebellum Mississippi" (Ph.D. dissertation, University of Mississippi, 1969), is the most comprehensive treatment of urbanization in antebellum Mississippi.

slightly fewer than 1,500 permanent residents. Of the other urban centers of Mississippi on the eve of the Civil War, a mere handful exceeded a thousand in population, and most of the remainder were villages or hamlets numbering between 50 and 500 persons.[2]

Beyond a doubt, proximity to New Orleans stunted the growth of Natchez, Vicksburg, Columbus, and other lesser Mississippi market towns. In that era the Crescent City dominated the lower Mississippi Valley to an even greater degree than other cities of the Northeast were overshadowed by New York. New Orleans' extraordinarily favorable location on the first solid ground above the mouth of the Mississippi River conferred on its merchants a virtual monopoly of seaborne commerce for all regions that depended on the Mississippi River and its tributaries for transportation. In addition, volume of trade gave a competitive advantage over such ports as Mobile and Columbus, which were situated on smaller rivers emptying directly into the Gulf of Mexico.[3]

Mississippi's western river ports—Vicksburg, Natchez, Yazoo City, Grand Gulf, and Rodney—were merely economic satellites of the Old South's greatest city, with their functions limited to loading cargoes of cotton aboard New Orleans–bound steamboats and to receiving shipments of goods that came mostly from New Orleans wholesale houses. In the late 1830s, Vicksburg, Natchez, Rodney and Grand Gulf briefly attempted to challenge the Crescent City's monopoly of transoceanic commerce by employing steam towboats to pull seagoing merchantmen upriver to their own wharves, where the sailing vessels were loaded with cotton for shipment to Liverpool. While these experiments were technically successful, they ultimately failed to pass the iron test of economics. In the early 1840s, depression put an end to these efforts to establish direct trade with Europe, and powerful steam-powered presses constructed for the purpose of recompressing plantation cotton bales were closed down permanently. Thus the dominance of the large New Orleans commission merchants over the cotton trade of Mississippi was confirmed.[4]

2. *Seventh Census, 1850*, p. 448; *Eighth Census, 1860: Population*, 271.
3. Louis E. Atherton, *The Southern Country Store, 1800–1860* (Baton Rouge, 1949), 34–35; Gray, *Agriculture*, II, 714; Sydnor, *Southern Sectionalism*, 21–24; Harold D. Woodman, *King Cotton and His Retainers: Financing and Marketing of the Crop of the South, 1800–1825* (Lexington, Ky., 1968), 112, 189–95, 326.
4. Grand Gulf *Advertiser*, February 8, 1839; [Ingraham], *South-West*, II, 160, 169; James, *Antebellum Natchez*, 195–96; *Mississippi Free Trader and Natchez Ga-*

As a result, most mercantile houses in Mississippi River towns had to be content with retail trade, whereas the far more lucrative business of large planters generally went to New Orleans merchants. With the major source of profits from the southwestern Cotton Kingdom thus reserved for the Louisiana metropolis, capital accumulated comparatively slowly in river towns of Mississippi. Under these circumstances, urban centers along the lower Mississippi River could not develop into cities on the basis of commerce alone. When some of their particularly enterprising residents experimented with small-scale manufacturing, they encountered similarly formidable competition from New Orleans merchants, who could extend more favorable credit terms on northern products than the local manufacturers could match.[5]

Although the port towns of Mississippi were growing slowly, towns founded for administrative purposes grew even more slowly, a trait that reflected the relative insignificance of state and local government in that era. For this rule, Jackson provided an outstanding example. Established in 1821 by the legislature to serve as the seat of state government, Jackson until the 1850s trailed far behind Vicksburg, which had been founded as a cotton port at about the same time. At the close of the 1840s, federal census takers counted 3,678 Vicksburgers, for example, but only 1,881 Jacksonians.[6]

In the last half of the 1850s, however, Jackson began to overtake Vicksburg rapidly. When the New Orleans, Jackson and Great Northern Railroad intersected the Vicksburg and Jackson line, Jackson became a cotton shipping center as well as the state capital, and its merchants began to take over some of the business formerly enjoyed by Vicksburg houses. Furthermore, manufacturing on a scale of some significance came to Jackson in the closing years of the decade. Numerous county seats that were not as fortunate as Jackson in acquiring transportation and manufacturing facilities tended to stagnate. Lacking economic importance, ill-situated seats of county government such as Gallatin in Copiah County, Williamsburg in Covington County, Greensboro in Choctaw

---

zette, August 3, 1837, November 5, 1839; Moore, *Agriculture*, 55–56, 161–62; Natchez *Courier*, September 11, 1835; Raymond *Times*, October 19, 1838; Vicksburg *Register*, January 9, 1838.

5. Moore, *Agriculture*, 55–56; Vicksburg *Whig*, January 18, 1860.

6. *Seventh Census, 1850*, p. 448.

County, and Charleston in Tallahatchie County never became more than hamlets.[7]

Before railroads began to spawn new towns along their routes in the 1850s, the government of Mississippi was responsible for founding many, if not most, of the towns within the borders of the state. Conforming to the peculiar American system for populating the public domain, the legislature began this town-building activity during the territorial period. Under federal land laws surveyors moved first into a region that Congress had decided to open to settlement. After they had laid out township and section lines by which tracts of land could be located accurately, federal land offices were set up at convenient points to sell public lands to speculators and prospective settlers. In order to provide local government for purchasers of these lands, the territorial legislature and its successor, the state legislature, periodically enacted statutes creating counties, defining their boundaries, and either designating specific locations for their seats of government or empowering boards of police to choose the places where the courthouses would be erected. Usually these sites were placed close to geographic centers of the counties so that all inhabitants would have as nearly equal access to the machinery of local government as possible. As a rule, economic considerations were ignored while county seats were being located, an omission that blighted the prospects of many political towns from the outset.[8]

Early histories of original county seat towns usually followed a common pattern. Soon after a location for a county seat had been determined, a frame or log courthouse and a jail were constructed at state expense. Next a few simple buildings of similar construction were thrown up around the courthouse square to provide space for lawyers' offices, mercantile establishments, craftsmen's shops, taverns, a hotel, and perhaps a bank. Somewhat later, married residents of the new community erected homes on dirt streets paralleling the sides of the courthouse square. Finally the addition of a church or two, a Masonic hall, and sometimes a one-room schoolhouse completed a typical county seat hamlet. During

7. Martha Bowman, "A City of the Old South: Jackson, Mississippi, 1850–1860," *Journal of Mississippi History*, XV (1953), 1–32; William D. McCain, *The Story of Jackson: A History of the Capital of Mississippi, 1821–1935* (Jackson, Miss., 1953); Reed, *New Orleans and the Railroads*, 100; *Eighth Census, 1860: Manufacturing*, 287.

8. [Ingraham], *South-West*, II, 205; McLemore (ed.), *History of Mississippi*, I, 284–85; Hutchinson (comp.), *Code of Mississippi*, 70–96, 712.

the land rush into northern Mississippi in the mid-1830s, villages like these emerged with startling rapidity. In the case of Paulding in Jasper County, for example, five stores, a cotton gin, a gristmill and a tanyard, as well as establishments operated by a blacksmith, a shoemaker, and a chairmaker, were functioning within twelve months after the arrival of the first inhabitant in 1834. Having popped out of the ground like mushrooms, most of these courthouse hamlets soon attained their maximum size. Paulding, as late as 1850, still had fewer than 50 persons in its population.[9]

After journeying across central Mississippi in the 1850s, Frederick L. Olmsted described the towns along his route with the exception of Jackson as "forlorn, poverty-stricken collections of shops, groggeries, and lawyers' offices, mingled with unsightly and usually dilapidated dwelling houses." One of the towns he passed through consisted of nothing but a deserted blacksmith shop and a cabin occupied by the local postmaster; another town marked on his map was merely a crossroad grocery store.[10]

Southern travelers, lacking Olmsted's sophistication, tended to view the villages of Mississippi less critically. Micajah Adolphus Clark, for example, described Canton in 1857 as "a beautiful town situated on the Railroad from N.O., [the] Jackson and Central Road." "Canton," he wrote, "is surrounded by a level and rich farming country, having in it and around it a great deal of wealth." Clark noted that a new courthouse had just been completed and that a large two-story brick building 150 feet in length was under construction. He was informed that large quantities of cotton were brought there for shipment over the railroad. One mercantile firm owned by W. R. Luckett was selling goods locally at the rate of $150,000 each year. Clark, who had been a partner in a similar firm in Kosciusko, made arrangements to become a junior partner in Luckett's company. Returning to Kosciusko to settle his affairs, he passed through Grenada on the stage. "It is," he wrote, "a beautiful place with every appearance of wealth around. Magnificent buildings."[11]

The manner in which towns rose in Lafayette County was typical of the process of urbanization taking place in the Choctaw and Chickasaw Indian

9. [Ingraham], *South-West*, II, 166; Natchez *Free Trader*, August 25, 1835; *Seventh Census, 1850*, p. 448.
10. Olmsted, *Journey in the Back Country*, 159–60.
11. Micajah Adolphus Clark Journal, 1857 (Typescript in the South Caroliniana Collection, University of South Carolina), 3–4, 93.

cessions during the decade in which northern Mississippi became the more populous half of the state. In 1833, a land rush into northern Mississippi commenced when federal land offices were opened in Columbus and Chocchuma. That year immigrants seeking cotton lands purchased more than a million acres, and sales for the ensuing year were almost three times as large. Thousands of cotton farms and plantations went into cultivation in the former Indian reservations before the state legislature provided local government for the newcomers. Between 1833 and 1839 a host of little villages sprang up beside tributaries of the Yazoo and Tombigbee rivers, many of which were founded by land speculators.[12]

One of these villages grew up on the north bank of the Tallahatchie River in what was later to be Lafayette County. Originally called Mitchell's Bluff in honor of a pioneer land speculator, the village was renamed Wyatt when it was incorporated in 1838. Because small stern-wheeled steamboats having cargo capacities of about 750 bales of cotton were able to ascend the Yazoo and Tallahatchie rivers during periods of high water as far as Wyatt, the port became the market for a cotton-producing region of some consequence. Although the village was a little more than a year old, Wyatt's dirt streets were crowded with wagons laden with cotton and merchandise during the autumn of 1835. Steamboat freight rates between Wyatt and New Orleans were very high throughout the 1830s and 1840s yet much less than rates charged for hauling overland to Memphis, the nearest Mississippi River port. As a result, Wyatt flourished for nearly two decades. By 1842 the crop of cotton passing over Wyatt's wharves had increased to 10,000 bales annually, and in 1845 the total reached 25,000 bales. In this period marking Wyatt's zenith, five steamboats plied regularly between that port and New Orleans when the condition of the river permitted. At the height of its prosperity the Tallahatchie River port boasted sixteen stores, one of the largest hotels in northern Mississippi, and a small factory for manufacturing cotton gins.[13]

In February 1836, the state legislature divided the Chickasaw cession covering northeastern Mississippi into thirteen counties, of which Lafayette County was one. The act of February 9 authorized boards of police of these new counties to select sites for their respective county

12. [Ingraham], *South-West*, II, 95; Miles, *Jacksonian Democracy in Mississippi*, 118–19; Young, *Redskins, Ruffleshirts, and Rednecks*, 155–56.

13. James H. Stone, "The Economic Development of Holly Springs during the 1840's," *Journal of Mississippi History*, XXXII (1970), 351–52.

seats. Following the usual custom, the members of the board of police decided to place their courthouse in the center of Lafayette County. They accordingly accepted a donation of fifty acres of land tendered by a trio of land speculators, who doubtless expected to profit from the location of the seat of government in the midst of their landholdings. As a result of this choice, the county seat was pleasantly situated on relatively high ground in an area suitable for cotton growing, but the site was more than ten miles distant from the Tallahatchie River and about five miles from the Yocanapatafa River, the only other tributary of the Yazoo reaching into Lafayette County. Presumably the county officials chose to ignore prior claims of the then flourishing town of Wyatt because of its situation in the extreme northwestern corner of the county.[14]

In 1836 the fifty acres of land belonging to the municipality of Oxford were surveyed and offered for sale, and the town was granted a charter by the legislature in May of the following year. In July 1837, a resident of the new county seat reported to the editor of the Natchez *Free Trader* that more than 300 persons had already established their homes there. At that date Oxford consisted of six stores, two hotels, a church, and the houses of the inhabitants. Because no steam sawmill had as yet been erected in the vicinity, both houses and stores were constructed of logs. Instead of building the usual log courthouse, however, the board of police contracted for a building made of stone. The blocks of stone to be used in the walls were brought by water from Cincinnati to Memphis and from there were hauled to Oxford in wagons. In the town's second year, two schools and a second church were constructed.[15]

Lacking access to water transportation facilities and suffering from competition with Wyatt, Oxford made little progress until the late 1840s. Log houses were boarded over or were replaced with frame houses built of sawn lumber, but not much else transpired during the depression-ridden years between 1839 and 1845. In 1846, however, the economic climate changed for the better. After years of controversy the legislature decided to locate the state university at Oxford. In arriving at this decision the legislators were motivated by desire to place the important educational institution at a central location in northern Mississippi because the population was growing rapidly in the northern half of the state. They

14. J. Allen Cabaniss, *A History of the University of Mississippi* (Oxford, Miss., 1949), 7–8.
15. Natchez *Free Trader*, August 8, 1837.

also believed that Oxford's isolated situation off the travel routes would be beneficial for the students' health and morality, if not stimulating to the morale of the teenaged boys, who would surely have preferred to risk the epidemics and temptations of Natchez or Vicksburg.[16]

As soon as construction of the university's buildings began, the sleepy village of Oxford came to life. Although the town was still too small to be listed among the towns of Mississippi in the census of 1850, the ensuing decade brought many changes. Numerous comfortable frame residences of one or two stories were constructed within the municipal limits and on surrounding plantations, and at least two brick houses worthy of Natchez were erected by successful merchants during the late 1850s. In the middle of the decade the Mississippi Central Railroad was routed through Oxford, and by the close of 1857, trains linking the town with Memphis by way of Jackson, Tennessee, were running within a few miles of Oxford. In January 1860, the last gap in the north-south railroad was filled in, giving Oxford direct connections with New Orleans to the south and Chicago to the north.[17]

Soon after its completion, the Mississippi Central Railroad virtually destroyed Wyatt, which had been declining slowly in recent years. During the Civil War, Federal troops following the railway southward detoured far enough from their route to overrun Wyatt. Before leaving, they destroyed the village so thoroughly that its inhabitants never returned. Today, nothing but a graveyard and numerous brick-lined cisterns marks the place where Wyatt once stood.

Life spans of many original county seat towns were quite short. In many instances, the legislature subdivided large counties into two or three smaller ones when the population became too numerous by contemporary standards. On such occasions, the newly created counties were granted county seats of their own, whereas the courthouse of the abbreviated parent was usually shifted to a location more appropriate to its reduced dimensions. In other cases, poorly situated county seat villages lost their courthouses as a result of referendums to rival commercial villages that had grown up at river landings. When the seat of government was moved from one town to another, most of the inhabitants usually followed the courthouse to its new location. Sometimes former county seats

16. Oxford *Observer*, September 16, 1843; Cabaniss, *University of Mississippi*, 4–5.
17. Vicksburg *Whig*, February 8, 1860.

survived as stagnant hamlets; Warrenton was an example after the county seat of Warren County was transferred to Vicksburg in 1836. Because buildings were constructed cheaply of logs or lumber during a town's early years, property owners could move to new locations without serious inconvenience or financial loss. In fact, they occasionally took their houses and stores with them, dragging the buildings along on sleds pulled by oxen.[18]

Except for county seats, most incorporated towns were established as shipping points on rivers or railroads by real estate speculators who hoped to profit from selling some of their holdings as town lots. In almost every such case before 1850, promoters of a prospective town selected an elevated site beside a navigable stream in an area where the soil was suitable for cotton. Of course, in the prerailroad era the basic requirements of commerce dictated that market towns must be accessible to river vessels. Several factors influenced the choice of high ground when a town was being located. One of these was a universal conviction that swampy situations were unhealthy. Another factor was that people preferred to erect their houses on hills, where the cooler breezes were found in summer and where the plague of mosquitoes was less severe than in lower elevations. Furthermore, the natural drainage provided by a hilly site was vital to the well-being of city folk, for undrained streets could quickly become impassable under the pounding downpours of Mississippi. To be sure, a swampy disease-racked location did not prevent New Orleans from becoming the Old South's most populous city, but this was an exception to the rule. Here the advantage of proximity to the Gulf of Mexico outweighed the prevalence of disease and difficult drainage problems.

In Mississippi such successful market towns as Vicksburg, Natchez, and Columbus attracted permanent residents as much by their "salubrious" high elevations as by their superior transportation facilities. In the extraordinarily fertile Yazoo-Mississippi river valley, where plantations lined the banks of all navigable streams in 1860 but where no elevation rose more than a foot above high-water mark, no town of any consequence emerged during the antebellum period. Instead, Yazoo City, which like Vicksburg was located on a hillside at a point where a river mean-

18. Robert Lowry and William H. McCardle, *A History of Mississippi, from the Discovery of the Great River . . . to the Death of Jefferson Davis* (Jackson, Miss., 1891), 597–601, 611–16; Franklin L. Riley, "Extinct Towns and Villages of Mississippi," Mississippi Historical Society *Publications*, V (1902), 311–83.

dered close to the plateau at the edge of the alluvial plain, became the commercial and residential center for planters, merchants, and tradesmen of the southern portion of the valley. In the northern half of the Yazoo river system, Grenada at the head of year-round steam navigation on the Yalobusha River attracted residents and trade because of its favorable situation on hills bordering this tributary of the Yazoo River.

In many counties of the state, county seats and commercial towns came in pairs. In Jefferson County, to cite a few examples, Fayette was the county seat and Rodney the river port; in Yalobusha County, Coffeeville was the seat of government in 1840 and Grenada the center of commerce; in Tishomingo County, Jacinto was the county seat and East Port on the Tennessee River was the market town. In most such instances, the commercial centers tended to outstrip county seats, not infrequently taking over the governmental role from the older political towns. As was characteristic of society in the Old South, however, exceptions abounded for every generalization. Port Gibson, the old county seat of Claiborne County, at the close of the antebellum period had outgrown its port, Grand Gulf, by more than 100 percent. Holly Springs also deviated from the normal pattern of urban development. Although the town lacked water transportation facilities altogether, and its commerce had to be hauled overland by wagon for long distances until the late 1850s, Holly Springs nevertheless emerged as the principal trading town of the Chickasaw cession of north Mississippi.[19]

With the exception of Natchez, Vicksburg, and Columbus, where there were paved streets and sidewalks, brick buildings, and handsome residences surrounded by attractive gardens, the rural villages of antebellum Mississippi would appear primitive indeed to modern eyes. Although most of them were laid out on a familiar rectangular plan, their streets were usually slightly improved dirt roads, muddy in winter, dusty in summer, and always full of ruts and potholes. In the smaller towns, most of the buildings were wooden constructions one or two stories high. After larger towns had experienced devastation by fire once or twice, wooden structures were replaced by brick buildings. In residential areas of hamlets and towns, houses of the inhabitants clustered surprisingly closely together, as if the townspeople were afraid of solitude. The common houses of one or two stories were usually constructed of sawn lumber built on a very simple plan. Very few towns in Mississippi pos-

19. *Eighth Census, 1860: Population,* 271; Stone, "Holly Springs," 341–61.

sessed water or sewage systems, and the collection of garbage was customarily left to herds of pigs roaming at large. For drinking water most homeowners relied upon rainwater stored in brick-lined cisterns, for they believed with some justification that rainwater was more healthful than water drawn from shallow wells or creeks. Privies in the backyard near the cisterns, however, tended to invalidate this popular theory and helped perpetuate periodic epidemics of typhoid fever that afflicted the urban population. In all but the largest towns, buildings were heated by iron stoves or brick fireplaces in which wood was the universal fuel. Gas lights were to be found only in the larger towns and on some of the plantations; in the villages and hamlets, homes and stores were lighted at night by candles and lanterns burning oil or turpentine.

Despite their obvious deficiencies, the rural hamlets and villages of antebellum Mississippi were important to people who dwelt in their vicinity. A perceptive contemporary observer wrote in 1835: "Each town is the center of a circle which extends many miles around it into the country, and daily attracts all within its influence. The ladies come in their carriages 'to shop,' and the gentlemen, on horseback, to do business with their commission merchants, visit the banks, hear the news, dine together at the hotels, and ride back in the evening." Farmers came in their wagons to sell their crops and purchase their supplies from retail merchants. When court was in session at a county seat, everyone who could leave his farm or plantation assembled in town to enjoy the spectacles presented by the trials.[20]

Especially in the early decades of settlement, social life of the rural people revolved around villages and hamlets. In the period when planters had not yet built elaborate facilities for entertaining their friends, and when farmers had not yet organized their churches, whites of all classes depended heavily for social intercourse upon public balls held in the villages by bachelors. Families of farmers and planters were accustomed to traveling as much as thirty miles to take part in bachelor balls, which often were costume parties. In so doing, "families who reside several leagues apart . . . met together like the inhabitants of one city." Not least among the benefits of the village balls was the bringing together of young men and women from isolated homes who might otherwise have had difficulty in finding matrimonial partners.[21]

20. [Ingraham], *South-West*, II, 205–206.
21. *Ibid.*

As the oldest, largest, wealthiest, and most beautiful of Mississippi towns, Natchez was clearly unique. To be sure, the little city on the bluff was deprived of its political supremacy early in the nineteenth century, and its importance as a commercial center was reduced in the 1820s and 1830s by the extension of the Cotton Kingdom into central and northern Mississippi. Nevertheless, no rival challenged the preeminence of Natchez in social matters during the slavery era.[22]

Natchez's peculiar social distinction was derived from a small group of enormously wealthy planters who resided on the outskirts of the town. These extremely wealthy planters in the suburbs of Natchez made the little community into the social capital of the planter class of Mississippi. Elsewhere in the state, slaveowning cotton growers tried to imitate Natchez fashions in architecture, carriages, dress, manners, and customs.

The town of Natchez is somewhat younger than the agricultural settlements of the old Natchez District. It was founded in 1776 upon a shelf of land in front of the bluff upon which the modern city stands. In that year made famous by the Declaration of Independence, town lots were laid off and offered for sale in Natchez by order of Governor Peter Chester of British West Florida, who intended the new town to be an administrative center for the Mississippi River settlements. At the end of the year, the new village at the landing included four stores and a dozen houses. Anthony Hutchins, the largest landowner in the region, ruled over the settlement as justice of the peace while dominating its economic life as the Mississippi agent of a London commission house. When the town fell to the Spanish toward the end of the American Revolution, the population still numbered no more than a hundred souls. Under benign Spanish rule, the town grew slowly as its trade with Spanish New Orleans increased. In the early 1790s, when the region was shifting from a tobacco economy to a cotton economy, the Natchez landing boasted no fewer than a dozen taverns catering to river boatmen, who liked to break their journeys to and from New Orleans in order to sample entertainments for which Natchez-under-the-Hill was already notorious. Because warehouses, stores, and taverns had preempted most of the available space beneath the bluff, a second Natchez began to take shape around 1790 upon the top of the hill overlooking the original village and the river. A roadway cutting

22. James, *Antebellum Natchez*; Kane, *Natchez*, 1–21.

diagonally across the face of the bluff connected the two parts of the town.[23]

The second Natchez was laid out on the rectangular town plan that the northern city of Philadelphia had made fashionable, an example that was followed by all subsequent Mississippi towns. In 1795, the inhabitants of Natchez and the farmers and planters of the District began to prosper as a result of the introduction of Eli Whitney's cotton gin and the accompanying rapid spread of cotton growing throughout the vicinity. As the new century dawned two years after Natchez became part of the United States, some of the merchants handling the shipment of the new staple crop were reputed to be earning as much as $50,000 a year.[24]

When the territorial legislature of Mississippi incorporated Natchez in 1809, the town contained about 300 houses, many of which had been erected since 1800. These houses were generally small, built of sawn lumber, and usually equipped with balconies and porches. By 1812 the commercial community had expanded to include one commission house, two wholesale stores, four groceries, twenty-four dry goods shops, and the Bank of Mississippi. The professions were represented by eight physicians and seven lawyers. The social institutions included three elementary schools, two churches, a Masonic lodge, and a Mechanics' society. Six inns and a coffeehouse provided entertainment for travelers and permanent residents. The inhabitants received no garbage service, but water was delivered to stores and houses by twelve water carts.[25]

Because the growth of population in Mississippi followed the advancing frontier from the southwestern settlements toward the north and east, the old counties served by Natchez experienced no large increase in number of inhabitants during the remainder of the antebellum period. Consequently, the growth of Natchez was similarly slow. In 1818, the population was 2,034. At the height of prosperity in 1837, a census taken by the state reported that Natchez then had 3,737 white inhabitants, a figure that was not to be reached again before the Civil War. At that time, according to the editor of the Natchez *Free Trader*, the total number of buildings, including residences and stores, was about 600, or twice the number of structures that had stood in the town thirty years before. In

23. James, *Antebellum Natchez*, 18–19, 30, 34; Charles S. Sydnor, *A Gentleman of the Old Natchez Region: Benjamin L. C. Wailes* (Durham, N.C., 1938), 3–4.
24. James, *Antebellum Mississippi*, 44.
25. Sydnor, *Wailes*, 22–23.

the late 1830s, Natchez was shipping about 50,000 bales of cotton annually. With the advent of the depression of 1839–1849, people began to
move away from the increasingly impoverished town. In 1840, the federal
census listed 2,995 whites, 205 free blacks, and 1,625 slaves, revealing
that a quarter of the whites had moved out since 1837. The decline continued during the decade of the 1840s, with the white population shrink-
ing in 1850 to 2,710, and the number of slaves to 1,511. Free blacks, however, held their own in Natchez, totaling 213.[26]

With the return of prosperity to the southwestern Cotton Kingdom in
the 1850s, the downward trend in the population was reversed. The
Natchez city government conducted a census in 1856 and determined
that the population had increased to 6,098. Of this number, 3,607 were
whites, 2,089 were slaves, and 302 were free blacks. When Adams County
assessor A. D. Pickens took the federal census of Natchez in August
1860, he found that the population had been remarkably stable over the
past four years. In his original report, published in the Natchez *Free
Trader*, Pickens listed 3,753 whites, 2,103 slaves, and 176 free blacks. In
his published statement, however, Pickens noted that many residents
were absent from the city, as was usual for the time of year and that the
real total population was considerably larger than his total of 6,032. In
his final report Pickens apparently amended his returns to include absent
residents, for the published U.S. census for 1860 credited Natchez with
6,612 inhabitants. During the 1840s and 1850s, fluctuations in business
activity in the port resembled the population trends. Annual cotton shipments rose above 75,000 bales during the early 1850s but fell below
50,000 bales during the last half of the decade. According to the editor of
the Natchez *Free Trader,* the decline in the volume of exports resulted
from loss of business to the railroad connecting Jackson, Mississippi,
with New Orleans.[27]

From these statistics it is obvious that Natchez reached its zenith in the
1830s. At its peak just before the beginning of the 1839–1849 depression, Natchez was a bustling little city. Its more prominent buildings in-

26. William R. Hogan and Edwin A. Davis (eds.), *William Johnson's Natchez:
The Antebellum Diary of a Free Negro* (Baton Rouge, 1951), 3; Natchez *Free
Trader*, May 18, 1837; Natchez *Courier*, June 8, September 14, 1838, January 27,
1842; *Seventh Census, 1850*, p. 448.
27. Natchez *Free Trader*, November 7, 1859, August 6, 1860; *Eighth Census,
1860: Population*, 271.

cluded the Adams County courthouse; the city hall; the county jail; three
churches belonging to the Presbyterians, Methodists, and Episcopalians,
respectively; a Masonic hall; a theater; a hospital; a Mechanics' hall; an
orphan asylum; eleven hotels; a coffeehouse; and the Planters Bank, the
Agricultural Bank, and the Commercial Bank. Its industrial establishments included two cotton compresses, two steam sawmills, and a steam-
powered turning lathe as well as three printing offices. The city boasted
two daily newspapers, the *Courier* and the *Free Trader,* and a semi-
monthly publication, the *Southwestern Journal.*[28]

The city's list of social institutions was fairly lengthy. There were five
religious congregations—the Presbyterians, Methodists, Episcopalians,
Catholics, and Baptists—of which the last two had not yet constructed
their buildings. The Natchez Academy and several small schools for boys
or girls provided such education as was available. Volunteer military
companies were popular social organizations. The most prestigious of
these was the Natchez Fencibles, which had been active for many years.
Three others, the Natchez Guards, the Natchez Hussars, and the Natchez
Riflemen, had been organized since 1835. On a par with the military
companies was the volunteer firefighting organization, the Phoenix Independent Fire Company. Its three divisions manned the fire engines
Achilles and *Neptune* and the hose carriage *Water Witch.* Among numerous fraternal organizations were two Masonic lodges, two fraternities of
the Odd Fellows, and a Mechanics' society as well as organizations of the
Scots, Irish, and Germans. The town and surrounding country were supporting twenty-six practicing physicians and twenty-four lawyers.[29]

An English visitor, Charles A. Murray, was favorably impressed in
1835 by the part of Natchez that was located on top of the bluff. He saw
"many handsome, well-supplied shops" and was pleased that "the inhabitants have had the good taste to leave many rows of trees standing." He
observed that many of the prosperous merchants had constructed "villas,
prettily situated on the undulating slopes by which the town is surrounded." While he found the buildings handsome and the streets well
laid out, Murray described the condition of the streets as deplorable. Un-
paved and unlighted, they were muddy and abounded with holes deep
enough to sprain the ankle of an unwary pedestrian. The road leading

28. Natchez *Courier,* June 8, 1838.
29. *Ibid.,* and January 12, 1838.

from lower to upper Natchez was especially unpleasant to Murray. Wagons and carts using the road mired axle deep in the wet clay with which it was surfaced, and travelers on foot found the going slippery indeed.[30]

The depression that plagued the entire Cotton Kingdom from 1837 to the late 1840s was a time of particular misfortune for Natchez. Disaster after disaster befell the residents of the town during these years. In 1839, abruptly falling cotton prices coupled with the aftereffects of the panic of 1837 bankrupted the Mississippi Railroad Company and the Mississippi Shipping Company. Collapse of the projected railroad between Natchez and Jackson wrote finis to the efforts of the mercantile community to tap the trade of central Mississippi. Without the railroad, Natchez could no longer aspire to become more than a local marketing center. Similarly, failure to establish a large direct trade with England ended the dreams of the merchants of cutting into the profits of the New Orleans commission houses. Then in 1838 and 1839 a series of devastating fires swept the business section, destroying hundreds of thousands of dollars worth of property. As if these misfortunes were not enough, a line of tornadoes spawned by a hurricane swept across Natchez in 1840, sinking steamboats and flatboats at the landing and smashing stores and houses on top of the bluff. With the depression deepening year by year until 1845, the residents of the town were able to do little to repair the ravages of fire and wind. The depression also prevented the town from developing an economy based on textile manufacturing. Several successive attempts to operate the Natchez cotton factory successfully all failed during the mid-1840s, not to be revived. Unfortunately these experiments in textile manufacturing were premature. Had the mill been erected a half dozen years later, it would probably have been as profitable as the Wesson mill in Choctaw County or the McGehee mill at Woodville. Nothing, however, seemed to prosper in ill-starred Natchez until after the war with Mexico.[31]

In the 1850s a modest degree of prosperity returned to Natchez as a result of improved cotton prices. As the farms and plantations within Natchez's commercial orbit began to turn a profit once again, the retail

30. Hogan and Davis (eds.), *William Johnson's Natchez*, 4–5.
31. *De Bow's Review*, V (1848), 379–80; Hogan and Davis (eds.), *William Johnson's Natchez*, 265n; Jackson *Mississippian*, December 23, 1848; Jackson *Southern Reformer*, April 27, 1844; Moore, *Andrew Brown*, 37–38; Natchez *Courier and Journal*, June 23, 1847, June 28 and July 5, 1848; Port Gibson *Herald*, April 25, 1844; Ripley *Advertiser*, January 18, 1845; Vicksburg *Sentinel*, November 11, 1844, July 7, 1847.

storekeepers, tradesmen, and mechanics also experienced a gratifying improvement in business. The upsurge in demand was particularly noticeable in all facets of the building industry, for in both town and country long-delayed repairs of old buildings and construction of new houses and stores finally got under way.[32]

In the middle of the decade of the 1850s, many merchants in downtown Natchez enlarged their establishments to accommodate their growing volume of trade, and several new commercial buildings of some size were erected. Yet when Olmsted visited Natchez, he described the stores and residences that he saw in the city proper as "generally small and always inelegant." Another traveler who visited the town at about the same time as Olmsted, however, viewed the scene differently. He described wide, clean streets lined with shade trees and bordered with brick houses. "Many of the private residences within the city and its suburbs," he wrote, "are magnificent beyond description." A third visitor commented in 1859 that many of the residences were three stories tall and built of brick. The wide, clean streets, he reported, were sprinkled every day by water carts and were "brilliantly lighted every night with gas à la St. Charles Street, New Orleans." Obviously, Olmsted was comparing the houses and stores of Natchez with those in great northern cities, whereas the two southern observers had the buildings of Mobile and New Orleans in mind. It was certainly true, however, that the business district of Natchez during the final decade of the slavery era was that of a small town rather than a city.[33]

Between 1830 and 1860, Vicksburg was the chief rival of Natchez for first place among the towns of Mississippi. In many respects the towns were as alike as two peas in a pod. Both were river ports situated on tall hills bordering the Mississippi River. Both served as combined commercial centers and seats of government for their respective counties, and in both Warren and Adams counties large plantations rather than farms dominated the agricultural economy. Because of the prevalence of large plantations, the rural populations of both Warren and Adams counties were composed of more slaves than whites. Even the views presented to steamboat passengers were similar. From the river, observers saw wharves,

32. Natchez *Courier*, September 6 and 13, October 11, 1854; Natchez *Free Trader*, March 19 and April 9, 1860; Andrew Brown Ledgers, 1850–60 (Rufus F. Learned Collection, University of Mississippi Library).

33. Natchez *Courier*, May 3, September 6, 1854; Natchez *Free Trader*, July 1, 1859, March 19 and April 8, 1860; Olmsted, *Journey in the Back Country*, 36.

stores, and warehouses at the landings. Beyond these structures, located just above the high-water line, were streets lined with brick buildings ranging in height from one to three stories. The commercial districts of Natchez and Vicksburg were roughly the same size during the 1840s and 1850s, and the white populations were almost equal in number. In outward appearance their public buildings were very much alike. In the 1850s, for example, the citizens of both towns took pride in their large brick three-story public school buildings housing about 500 pupils each. Both towns had courthouses, hospitals, and churches of similar architecture and size.

Despite these many points of similarity, there were significant differences between Natchez and Vicksburg during the late antebellum period. Visitors to Vicksburg discovered no suburbs outside the city limits remotely resembling the succession of imposing mansions that made Natchez a byword for architectural elegance. Although large plantations dominated most of the countryside around Vicksburg, very few of their proprietors counted their slaves in hundreds like the cotton lords of Natchez. Only a relatively small number of Warren County planters could afford to erect elaborate residences of the Natchez variety, and most of these were still investing their profits in additional land and slaves with the ultimate object of becoming as rich as the Natchez elite.

The terminal and workshops of the Southern Railroad also served to differentiate Vicksburg from Natchez, symbolizing as they did the victory of the former over the latter in the contest for the commerce of the Pearl River Valley. But the additional cotton trade brought to Vicksburg was not the only benefit that the town derived from the railroad. The railway workshops provided employment for more than a hundred mechanics and laborers, many of whom were apparently slaves, and also furnished priceless technical training for young men who aspired to become skilled workmen. That two large foundries were able to operate successfully in Vicksburg during the 1850s was due in large part to the presence of the railroad.[34]

Founded in 1822, Vicksburg was two generations younger than Natchez. Although the strategic location of the Walnut Hills just downriver from

34. Vicksburg *Whig,* April 25, 1850, February 3 and March 8, 1853, July 19, September 6 and 27, November 22, 1854, March 28, 1855, November 29, 1856, January 1, 1858, September 7, 1859, May 26, 1860; Natchez *Courier,* September 28, 1858, May 26, 1860.

the confluence of the Yazoo and Mississippi rivers had been recognized in turn by the French, English, and Spanish, no town arose on the site for many years after the first farms had been established in the general vicinity. Meanwhile, Warrenton on the Big Black River, which empties into the Mississippi just south of the Walnut Hills, served for about two decades as the only port for interior cotton farms and plantations. In contrast to the geographical situation at Natchez, the terrain adjacent to the site of Vicksburg was too broken to attract pioneer settlers. Consequently, this land was occupied fairly late in the history of Warren County.

Newitt Vick, a planter and Methodist minister, was the first person to perceive that the Walnut Hills had commercial possibilities despite the difficult approach to the river's edge. Vick obtained title to the lands in about 1811 with the intention of founding a town there eventually but died in 1819 before he had implemented his plan. The administrator of Vick's estate, however, had the tract surveyed and began to offer lots for sale in 1822. For the first few years in the history of Vicksburg the rate of growth was fairly rapid. When the town was incorporated in 1825, the number of inhabitants was approximately 500. At that point in time about 4,000 bales of cotton were being shipped over the Vicksburg wharfboats each year.[35]

The village on the Walnut Hills experienced its most rapid growth during the "flush times" between 1830 and 1837 when the Choctaw and Chickasaw Indian cessions were being populated by white settlers and their slaves. By 1835 the population of Vicksburg had increased to about 2,000 people, and 30,000 to 45,000 bales of cotton were passing through the port annually. At that time Vicksburg ranked third among Mississippi port towns on the great river, following Natchez and Grand Gulf. In 1840, the total population was 3,104. Five years later a state census revealed that the white population of Vicksburg exceeded that of Natchez by about five hundred: the respective totals were Vicksburg, 2,865; Natchez, 2,327.[36]

35. Claiborne, *Mississippi*, 534–36; H. C. Clarke (ed.), *A General Directory for the City of Vicksburg* (Vicksburg, 1860).

36. Lorenzo A. Besançon, *Besançon's Annual Register for the State of Mississippi for the Year 1838* (Natchez, 1838), 207–208; Jackson *Mississippian*, January 10, 1834; [Ingraham], *South-West*, II, 169; *Niles Register*, XXXIX (1835–36), 41; *Sixth Census, 1840*, p. 58; Natchez *Courier*, February 11, 1846.

Despite the blighting effects of the panic of 1837 and the ensuing depression, the commerce of Vicksburg expanded steadily. Construction of a railroad connecting the river port with the state capital at Jackson speeded settlement of lands in the hinterland between the Big Black and Pearl rivers, and cotton produced in this region found its way to Vicksburg on the railway cars in ever-growing quantities. By the close of the 1850s, the yearly cotton trade of Vicksburg totaled 250,000 bales, roughly five times that of Natchez.[37]

In retrospect it is apparent that Vicksburg reached a peak of prosperity about the time of the panic of 1857. In 1858, merchants of the city as well as proprietors of Mississippi River packets began to feel the impact of new competition as soon as the railway between New Orleans and Jackson went into operation. Although shipping companies immediately reduced steamboat freight rates in order to hold their customers, increasing quantities of cotton made the journey to New Orleans by rail. Passenger traffic on the river also was affected adversely. In Vicksburg, retail trade began to diminish as Rankin, Madison, and Hinds county customers began to make their purchases in Jackson stores. With its basic economic position imperiled by competition from the railroads, the commercial leaders of the city with dubious logic attempted to restore their trade by investing heavily in a projected railroad running from a point on the Mississippi River opposite Vicksburg to Shreveport, Louisiana, and beyond to Texas.[38]

A description of Vicksburg as it appeared at the close of the era of slavery was published in *Harper's Weekly*:

> The city of Vicksburg is situated on the Walnut Hills, a range of wooded summits about four hundred feet high, and presents a fine appearance when viewed from below. From the tops of these elevations the flat alluvial country around can be seen for a long distance in every direction, and with its forests of oak and cotton-wood, interspersed with extensive plantations, forms a picture of great panoramic beauty. The main portion of the city lies near the water, and above it the hills are crowned with elegant private residences, or made conspicuous by the high walls of the public buildings. The Court-house, a huge structure of light gray limestone, crowns the summit of one of the hills, and is visible for a long distance up and down the river. The streets rise from the river with an abrupt and difficult ascent, and are cut with a regular grade through the bluffs and hills, directly to the edge of the levee. The town, when

37. *De Bow's Review*, XXVI (1859), 597–600.
38. Reed, *New Orleans and the Railroads*, 120–28.

viewed from the opposite bank, appears as if the houses were built on terraces, one above another, and the lower doors of one habitation are often times visible over the roof of the building in its immediate front.[39]

A. de Puy Van Buren, a young northern schoolteacher, noted in his journal that "the principal business streets have many fine commodious blocks of brick and stone. They are not crowded, but have the quiet composed air of the city mart. The levee is not paved, but covered today with goods, swarms of carts and drays, and moving things." Within the city limits there were about a hundred business establishments, including foundries, flour mills and gristmills, tanneries, sawmills, wholesale and retail stores, and shops of craftsmen and tradesmen. The principal public buildings at the beginning of the decade of the 1860s were the Warren County courthouse, completed in 1859 by the Weldon brothers at a cost of $100,000 and universally acknowledged to be the finest in the state; the municipal public schoolhouse having a capacity of about 600 pupils; the U.S. Marine Hospital; and the Vicksburg city hospital.[40]

By this date the inhabitants of Vicksburg had developed almost all of the religious, social, and civic institutions common to the older towns of the Southeast. Indeed, religion occupied a larger place in the lives of Vicksburgers than in the lives of the citizens of Natchez. In the commercial metropolis of the state, the Methodists, Baptists, Presbyterians, Episcopalians, Catholics and Jews were strongly entrenched. The fraternal orders were also very prominent in Vicksburg affairs. The Masons had erected a large brick building to house "three 'Blue Lodges,' a 'Chapter' or 'Council,' and an 'Encampment.'" There were two lodges of the Independent Order of Odd Fellows, a unit of the Sons of Malta, and an influential Mechanics Mutual Benefit Society. The city boasted three newspapers, the *Whig*, the *Sun*, and the *True Southron*. Demonstrating their civic spirit, the men of Vicksburg maintained two military companies, the Vicksburg Volunteers and the Vicksburg Sharp-Shooters, and four companies of the volunteer fire department.[41]

With regard to cultural resources, the town fared less well. Edward R.

---

39. *Harper's Weekly*, VI (1862), 482.

40. Van Buren, *Sojourn in the South*, 33; Peter F. Walker, *Vicksburg: A People at War, 1860–1865* (Chapel Hill, 1960), 8–9; Clarke (ed.), *Director of the City of Vicksburg*; *De Bow's Review*, XXVI (1859), 597–600; Natchez *Free Trader*, March 26, 1859.

41. *De Bow's Review*, XXVI (1859), 597–600.

Wells, another northern teacher, was dismayed to learn that "there is not a reading room or a public library or Literary Association of any kind in town. No public Lectures upon Literary or Scientific Subjects are delivered here, nor does there seem to be the least disposition to encourage any thing of the kind." Although Vicksburgers were guilty of neglecting science and literature, they patronized the theater with enthusiasm. From the 1830s to the close of the decade of the 1850s, several theaters and music halls connected with saloons provided a wide variety of entertainment, ranging from concerts and Shakespearean plays to performances that bordered on the burlesque. Despite their preoccupation with commerce and industry, the inhabitants of Vicksburg succeeded in making their little city a center of education, religion, and culture with much to offer the farmers and planters of northwestern Mississippi.[42]

Columbus on the Tombigbee River was the third largest river port in Mississippi and the principal commercial center of the eastern part of the state. Lowndes County, of which Columbus was the county seat, has a longer history of white occupancy than any other county in the Choctaw and Chickasaw cessions. In 1816 the Indian title to a small region in the Tombigbee River valley, including the area that was organized as Lowndes County in 1830, was extinguished. As early as 1817, settlers found their way into this triangle thrusting into the valley of the Tombigbee River, drawn there irresistibly by the lure of exceptionally fertile soils. In 1819 some of the necomers founded a town at a river landing that they called Columbus. In 1821, about the same time that Jackson and Vicksburg received their charters, Columbus was incorporated by the state legislature. The site chosen for Columbus happened to be located upon a sixteenth section, which meant that lots in the town could be leased but not purchased outright. Revenues derived from the leases were reserved by law for the support of education, and these funds were used to endow Franklin Academy from the early 1820s until the present day. Consequently, Columbus was distinguished from other southern towns by having a tuition-free public school for its white children, a school that lays claim to being the oldest of its kind in the Cotton Kingdom. Like other Mississippi cotton ports, Columbus flourished during the 1830s, languished during the depressed 1840s, and prospered as never before in the 1850s.[43]

42. Edward R. Wells Diary, 1854–55 (Mississippi Department of Archives and History); Hearn, "Towns in Antebellum Mississippi," 150–51.

43. *Besançon's Annual Register (1838)*, 161–63; Columbus *Democrat*, January 14, June 24, November 25, and December 23, 1837, December 4, 1839,

In 1834, Elisha Battle, an unusually well educated Baptist minister who traveled widely in Mississippi and who published descriptions of towns in various newspapers, paid a visit to Columbus. According to Battle's informants, Columbus had been growing rapidly since the late 1820s, for it had become possible for residents to obtain long-term leases on their lots that were tantamount to ownership of the property. The advantages Battle listed as contributing to Columbus's remarkable progress included the military road between Nashville and Jackson, Mississippi, which passed through the town, and steamboat service on the Tombigbee that gave planters access to the seaport of Mobile. Battle reported that Columbus already was regarded as the social as well as the economic headquarters for the northeastern part of the state. The population, which Battle estimated at close to 1,500 persons, included eleven lawyers, eight physicians, and a Methodist and a Presbyterian minister. In addition to Franklin Academy there were two private schools serving both boys and girls. One of these schools was operated by the Presbyterian minister. The business section of the town included twelve dry goods stores, four groceries, and a bookstore. As a minister, Battle was especially gratified by the moral atmosphere of Columbus, which contrasted vividly with the gaiety of Natchez. So many of the young unmarried women of Columbus, he was informed, were members of denominations that frowned upon dancing that the city bachelors had to invite young ladies from surrounding counties to their balls.[44]

During the 1830s, Columbus experienced the same kind of prosperity as Vicksburg. In 1837 the white population was 1,448, or half that of the city on the Walnut Hills. The business district at that time included twenty dry goods stores, three clothing stores, three drugstores, three chartered banks, two jewelers' establishments, two large warehouses, several bakeries and groceries, two hotels, a bathhouse, a bookstore, and two printing offices issuing weekly newspapers. Industry was represented by a factory for manufacturing cotton gins, a large steam sawmill, and the shops of numerous craftsmen. Franklin Academy, the tuition-free public school, was educating about 100 girls and 150 boys, with new buildings for pupils of each sex. In addition, a private school for girls had

---

January 23, February 20, and December 18, 1841; W. L. Lipscomb, *A History of Columbus, Mississippi, during the Nineteenth Century* (Birmingham, Ala., 1909), 13–121; McLemore (ed.), *History of Mississippi*, I, 356, 369.

44. Jackson *Mississippian*, August 15, 1834.

a student body of more than 50. The Methodists, Presbyterians, and Episcopalians had erected church buildings in Columbus, and the Baptists and Cumberland Presbyterians were planning to do likewise. The feminine religious community maintained three Sunday schools, three ladies' sewing societies, a Bible society, a foreign mission society, and a temperance society. For the menfolk there were a Masonic lodge and two well-supported volunteer military companies. Oddly enough, the city maintained four public wells but no engines for fighting fires. In one major respect, Columbus was less favorably situated than Natchez or Vicksburg. Unlike the Mississippi, which had enough water for steamboating the year around, the Tombigbee was open to navigation only about six months in the year. Fortunately, however, high water in the winter and spring permitted the cotton crop to move to Mobile after the harvest, the Columbus merchants by planning ahead could bring in their stocks of goods without serious inconvenience.[45]

In July 1852, Smith Kitchen of South Carolina visited Columbus and recorded in his journal: "This is a beautiful little town of considerable pretentions, with wide level streets, large and costly buildings." Smith was amazed by Columbus's water system. "Here we [saw] some of the first that we have seen yet of the artesian wells," he wrote, "the water running out three or four feet above the level of the streets of pure good water from the depth of six, seven and eight hundred feet below the surface of the earth."[46]

Toward the close of the era of slavery Columbus was described in *De Bow's Review* as "one of the largest and most beautiful interior towns in the South . . . , long . . . celebrated for the wealth of its inhabitants, the elegance of its society, and the general intelligence of its people." At that time the residential area of the town featured many handsome houses "adorned with the choicest gardens." As in the cases of Natchez and Vicksburg, the buildings that had been erected during the 1840s and 1850s were built of brick. Today numerous public and private buildings constructed during those decades still provide silent but eloquent testimony that Columbus was an important and prosperous social and commercial center of the old Cotton Kingdom.[47]

45. Natchez *Courier*, May 19, 1837; *Besançon's Annual Register (1838)*, 161–63.
46. Smith Kitchen Journal, 1852, 1862–65 (South Caroliniana Collection, University of South Carolina Library).
47. *De Bow's Review*, XXVII (1859), 113–14.

In keeping with the small urban populations, the governments of villages and towns of Mississippi were not very complicated during the antebellum period. The forms of these governments and the authority of the municipal officials were determined by special acts of incorporation passed by the state legislature, and these acts contained numerous minor variations. As a rule, however, villages were governed by boards, of selectmen, commonly seven in number. Selectmen were elected at large by voters who were qualified to vote in county and state elections and who had been residents of the municipality for a year. Selectmen served terms of one year, and they chose one of their number to serve as president of the board of selectmen for that year. The president of the board was also a justice of the peace and a magistrate. The police officer of the town was a constable or town marshal appointed by the board. A city clerk, a treasurer, an assessor and tax collector, and when appropriate a harbor master completed the list of city officials.[48]

Boards of selectmen were authorized by the state legislature to enact town ordinances and to levy taxes. The president of the board acting as city magistrate punished infractions of town ordinances with fines and short jail sentences. The board of selectmen also possessed the authority to issue licenses to such business establishments as groceries, dry goods stores, taverns, and boardinghouses and could tax business transactions conducted within the corporate limits.[49]

As towns like Natchez, Vicksburg, and Columbus grew larger, the responsibilities of the municipal authorities became more numerous and significant. In order to cope with changing conditions, the growing towns requested changes in their charters from time to time and almost always received the cooperation of the legislature. Amended town charters usually provided for division of the town into wards, each of which was represented on the board of aldermen by a representative elected by the voters of the ward. The old president of the board of selectmen was replaced by a salaried mayor who enjoyed greater authority than the president and who served terms of two years. The mayors were elected directly by the voters of the town rather than by the members of the board

48. Hearn, "Towns in Antebellum Mississippi," 32–46; John H. Moore, "Local and State Governments of Antebellum Mississippi," *Journal of Mississippi History*, XLIV (1982), 118.

49. Moore, "Local and State Governments," 117; *Revised Code of the Laws of Mississippi* (Natchez, 1824), 624–30.

as formerly. Often the amended town charter described a mayor as the "executive officer of the town." As such he was responsible for supervising the work of other municipal officials. Like his predecessor, the mayor was a justice of the peace, and he was generally required by law to preside weekly or even daily over a "Mayor's Court." Breaches of the peace and violations of city ordinances came under the mayor's jurisdiction, and he could levy fines and hand down jail sentences not to exceed ten days. As formerly, the aldermen making up the board or city council served one-year terms.[50]

Municipal authorities of villages had relatively few responsibilities. They preserved the peace in their communities, maintained the streets and boat landings, and dealt with problems of fire and sanitation. In such larger towns as Natchez, Vicksburg, and Yazoo City, however, a mayor and his council had many obligations. They erected and maintained city jails, city halls, hospitals, and school buildings; constructed and repaired streets, sidewalks, wharves, and drainage systems; provided for streetlights and water; supported police systems and volunteer fire departments; supervised the public health; regulated construction of buildings; and maintained a public market. City councils also controlled many aspects of commerce, writing ordinances ranging from fixing the price of bread to establishing a system of weights and measures. The city fathers wrote traffic laws, licensed drivers of coaches, wagons, and carts, and even established maximum speed limits as well as limiting the price of drayage. Furthermore, the council prohibited or regulated slave trading within the city limits, passed laws regarding the conduct and employment of slaves, and prohibited violations of the Sabbath. In order to perform these manifold duties, city councils employed growing numbers of full- or part-time public officials who were paid salaries from the city treasury.[51]

The agricultural economy of the state dramatically expanded during the last decade of the antebellum period as the railroads opened new regions to settlement and as a strong demand for cotton emerged. The larger commercial towns experienced comparable growth despite the blighting effect of competition from New Orleans and Mobile. The build-

50. *Revised Ordinances of the City of Vicksburg* (Vicksburg, 1855); Moore, "Local and State Governments," 117–18.
51. James, *Antebellum Natchez*, 77–100; Moore, "Local and State Governments," 118.

ing of tax-free public schools in particular gave them a new importance that promised to make them the intellectual centers of Mississippi in the near future. The Civil War and the destruction of the slave-plantation system wrecked the agricultural economy, however, and slowed the development of Natchez, Vicksburg, Jackson, and Columbus for the better part of a century.

9 Manufacturing

Although manufacturing never challenged the supremacy of agriculture in Mississippi before the Civil War, several complementary industries developed in the towns to provide essential services for farmers, planters, and townsmen as well as for steamboats and railroads. Lumber manufacturing, carried on from the earliest period of settlement by whites, was by far the largest and most economically significant of these pioneer industries. Manufacturing of iron and brass products, although a second industry of much smaller dimensions than lumbering, was nevertheless important as an adjunct to lumbering and agriculture. A third industry associated with metalworking, lumbering, and agriculture was the manufacture of wood products ranging from building materials such as tongue-and-grooved lumber, window sashes, and doors to plows, cotton gin stands, and other farm machinery and implements in which wood was the principal material. Finally, textile manufacturing, introduced into Mississippi during the 1840s, attained substantial dimensions in the ensuing decade. To be sure, only a small portion of the population of Mississippi was employed in these industrial enterprises. Yet Mississippi in 1860 unquestionably possessed the essential elements for developing a balanced agricultural and industrial economy.

While a few water-powered sawmills were operating in the old Natchez District during the first decade of the nineteenth century, the antebellum lumber manufacturing industry of Mississippi really began in earnest with the introduction of steam-powered sawmills. During 1808, five years after the first steam sawmill in the lower Mississippi Valley was set near New Orleans by James McKeever and Louis Valcourt, William Herrins erected in the vicinity of Natchez a sawmill powered by an eight-horsepower steam engine manufactured by Oliver Evans of Philadelphia. The Herrins mill was apparently the first one of its kind within the boundaries of the present state of Mississippi, and it continued in service until 1814. In that same year, Evans stated that two of his twenty-horsepower steam engines were driving sawmills at Natchez. One of these enterprises was located in Louisiana across the Mississippi River from Natchez. Owned by Reuben Nichols, the mill was erected in 1812. The other mill, employing an Evans twenty-horsepower engine, belonged to Peter Little, and it was situated at Natchez-under-the-Hill. During

1818, Samuel Clements constructed a second steam-powered sawmill on the ledge of earth below the Natchez bluffs. Thus by 1820 Natchez had become a center for the manufacture of lumber, mainly for local consumption.[1]

The brief period of prosperity in the Old Southwest following the War of 1812, which had stimulated the growth of a domestic lumber industry in Mississippi, came to an abrupt halt with the panic of 1819. For the next decade relatively little building was done on plantations or in towns, and very few new steam sawmills were erected. The return of prosperity during the 1830s, however, brought about a boom in the construction industry and resulted in the construction of numerous steam sawmills along the rivers of the state. Between 1830 and 1833, new mills were built at points that included Jackson, Vicksburg, Fort Adams, and Grand Gulf and in the Mississippi delta across the Mississippi River from Point Chicot, Arkansas.[2]

The land rush into the Indian cessions of North Mississippi in the mid-1830s generated an enormous demand for lumber, and many steam sawmills were erected along the rivers of the state. An advertisement typical of the times appeared in the Mobile *Register* during September 1836. In it the Aberdeen and Pontotoc Railroad and Banking Company offered lots for sale in Aberdeen, Mississippi, "emphatically the head of steam-boat navigation on the Tombigbee River." According to the real estate developers, the town already had a population of 500 persons, and "a Steam Saw Mill and Grist Mill are now in successful operation." A similar advertisement in the Columbus *Democrat* during April 1837 announced that sales of lots in Panola had begun in the previous December and that a steam-powered sawmill and gristmill were under construction. In the Yazoo-Mississippi valley, logging of cypress timber to feed the

1. Thomas Ashe, *Travels in America, Performed in 1806, for the Purpose of Exploring the Rivers . . . and Vicinity* (London, 1808), 339; Carter and Bloom (eds.), *Territorial Papers*, VI, 205; Claiborne, *Mississippi*, 143; Natchez *Mississippi Republican*, November 24, 1813, March 5, 1818; Wailes, *Report*, 169; Moore, *Andrew Brown*, 16–18; Natchez *Chronicle*, April 12, 1809; *Niles Register*, III (1812), 111.

2. Fort Adams *Mississippi Democrat*, December 22, 1831; [Ingraham], *South-West*, II, 174; Jackson *Mississippian*, January 10, September 26, 1834; Vicksburg *Advocate and Register*, October 7, 1831, May 10 and June 14, 1832, February 27, 1833, November 13, 1834, March 13, 1835; Vicksburg *Sentinel*, September 30, 1831, March 5, 1835.

206 The Emergence of the Cotton Kingdom

mills beside the Yazoo and Mississippi rivers had become a large and complex enterprise, and Yazoo City had recently become an important center for manufacturing rough cypress lumber. In April 1837, for example, the Jackson *Mississippian* reported that there were "four sawmills in operation within sight of Manchester," soon to be renamed Yazoo City. One new mill was equipped with a gang of thirteen saws and another with sixteen saws. These were exceptionally large sawmills in an era when a mill that could cut four boards from a log at a time was above average in size.[3]

Because the southwestern building boom was a corollary of good times among cotton growers and commission merchants, the collapse of cotton prices in the autumn of 1839 injured builders and lumbermen almost as quickly as farmers, planters, and commission merchants. Commercial and residential building promptly came to a standstill, and railroad construction was soon reduced to a fraction of its former dimensions. During the deep depression years from 1840 through 1844, lumbermen and members of the building trades endured particularly lean times. Many sawmills were sold by sheriffs at the doors of county courthouses, and many others ceased to operate. In a few cases, owners of large sawmills who had heavy investments in machinery, timber, and slaves were compelled by their fixed costs of continue to manufacture lumber. As their local markets were not absorbing their output, the mill owners had to seek new customers at river towns and plantations above New Orleans, and in the Crescent City itself. In particular, large lumber manufacturers at Yazoo City, Vicksburg, Natchez, and Baton Rouge began to compete vigorously with one another and with local sawmills for sales in New Orleans.[4]

With the beginning of general economic recovery throughout the Lower South in 1845, the lumber industry of Mississippi entered a fifteen-year period of expansion, technological progress, and increasing prosperity. Sawmills using circular saws rather than conventional reciprocating sash saws were introduced into the lower Mississippi Valley in

3. Mobile *Register*, September 2, 1836; Columbus *Democrat*, April 8, 1837; Jackson *Mississippian*, April 28, 1837; New Orleans *Picayune*, August 1, 1838; Vicksburg *Register*, November 8, 1837; Vicksburg *Sentinel*, March 23, 1838; Yazoo City *Whig*, September 27, 1839, May 28, 1841.
4. Yazoo City *Whig*, September 27, 1839, October 8, 1841; Moore, *Andrew Brown*, 36, 40–46.

the late 1830s, and by the middle of the following decade had proven to be very effective for cutting yellow pine, cypress, and hardwood planking. Although small steel circular saws had been used in cotton gins and woodworking since the beginning of the nineteenth century, saws large enough to cut through logs were not manufactured until the 1830s. Rotating at high speeds, these circular saws cut through sawlogs much more rapidly than sash or gang saws and required less power to drive them. Furthermore, circular saws were particularly useful for trimming and butting boards, as well as cutting paneling and laths. They were so useful in this regard that circular saws were often installed in establishments already equipped with gang sawmills to perform specialized tasks. more important for the lumber industry, however, the circular sawmills were constructed simply of light materials and were easily erected and disassembled. A portable steam-powered circular sawmill manufactured in Baltimore by George Page and Company became very popular in the Old Southwest during the 1840s and 1850s because Page and similar machinery could be moved close to sources of timber supplies and then relocated when the logs were exhausted. Circular sawmills had as their cardinal advantage the fact that they were inexpensive. As a result of these numerous merits, rotary sawmills driven by small steam engines were erected in large numbers along the watercourses in the Yazoo-Mississippi delta. Enormous quantities of their rough cypress lumber were shipped by flatboat to Vicksburg, Baton Rouge, and New Orleans during the 1850s. At their destinations these cargoes of plank were converted by planing mills into finished molding, tongue-and-grooved ceiling boards, wallboards, weatherboards, and other items of building material suitable for use by the carpenters.[5]

During the late 1840s and 1850s, steam sawmills in a wide variety of sizes could be found in most of the towns of Mississippi, and many more were at work on cotton plantations and in the forests from which they were drawing their raw material. The U.S. census of 1860 enumerated 227 lumber-manufacturing establishments in the state that were powered by steam engines or water wheels. Inasmuch as no sawmills were listed for Adams County, and only two for Warren County, the number reported by the marshals was obviously far below the correct total. Despite

5. Natchez *Courier*, September 30, 1856; Hickman, *Mississippi Harvest*, 24, 33; Moore, *Andrew Brown*, 54–56, 120–23.

the absence of accurate statistics, it is clear that the manufacturing of lumber was a major enterprise during the 1850s.[6]

During the 1840s and 1850s, a separate large lumber industry developed in the thinly settled longleaf pine forests of southern Mississippi to supply overseas markets with yellow pine lumber and timber. Although there were no steam sawmills in the region before 1835, within five years ten had been built in Hancock County and two in Jackson County; and ten more were constructed in Lawrence County in the interior during that same period. In 1849–1850, mills in Hancock and Jackson counties manufactured 12 million feet of lumber and consumed more than 50,000 logs. One of these mills, owned by the firm of Walker and Toulme, produced 1,200,000 feet of pine lumber. During the 1850s, seven mills on the shores of the Bay of St. Louis shipped a million feet annually. During this period most of the timber used by these mills was cut on government lands by professional loggers and was brought down to the coastal mills by water. By the end of the decade of the 1850s, much of the timber accessible to streams large enough for rafting had been cut away. The large expansion of the postwar lumber industry in this era was made possible by the construction of railroads through the stands of timber between the rivers and creeks.[7]

By far the largest of the lumber enterprises in Mississippi during the 1850s was Andrew Brown and Company of Natchez. The headquarters of the firm and the principal sawmill were located under the hill at Natchez; the main outlet for its products was a lumberyard in New Orleans. The firm obtained logs from cypress forests in the swamps of the Yazoo River Valley and rafted them down the Yazoo and Mississippi rivers to Natchez. Most of the firm's lumber was transported to New Orleans in flatboats manned by slaves and employees of the company. During the fifties, Brown contracted with many small sawmill operators for their entire supplies of lumber, which he used to supplement the production of the Natchez sawmill. He similarly purchased logs from logmen in the Yazoo delta as well as maintaining logging crews of his own who were cutting on lands belonging to the company. Brown also operated one of the largest of the nation's woodworking factories in New Orleans, where he supplied shutters, doors, windows, and mantels and parts for staircases made of

6. *Eighth Census, 1860: Manufactures,* 285–294.
7. Hickman, *Mississippi Harvest,* 15–42.

cypress, white pine, yellow pine, cherry, walnut, cedar, or mahogany, as the customers preferred. Thus, Brown's firm operated from the northern Yazoo-Mississippi River delta to New Orleans.[8]

Andrew Brown, founder and principal partner in Andrew Brown and Company, twice remodeled and enlarged the sawmill that Peter Little had originally constructed and operated. After emigrating from Scotland to Natchez during the early 1820s, Brown joined Little's construction business as an architect. In 1828, however, the Scot purchased the mill from Little and went into business for himself. Prospering during the early 1830s, Brown increased the capacity of his sawmill in 1835 from 3,000 to 10,000 feet of lumber per day, or 2 million feet per year, by replacing the old sash sawmill that worked only a single saw blade with a four-bladed gang sawmill. At the same time he installed a hundred-horsepower steam engine in place of the original twenty-horsepower steam engine. Needing a larger crew for the new mill, Brown purchased five slaves to add to his force of twelve slaves then working in the mill and lumberyard. Then and later, Brown relied primarily upon slave workmen, permanently employing only white clerks and sawyers in addition to the owners of the company. When shorthanded the lumberman hired white workmen to supplement his regular crew of slaves, and these whites worked alongside the slaves in the mill and yard and on flatboats transporting lumber to points south of Natchez on the Mississippi. Some of the slaves working for the company belonged to Brown personally, others belonged to the company, and some were hired from local slaveowners.[9]

During 1858–1859, Brown completely remodeled the Natchez sawmill a second time. He purchased new machinery of the latest design from the Ottawa Iron Works of Ferrysburg, Michigan, and installed the machines with the assistance of an expert sent to Natchez by the manufacturer. One of Brown's new mills was a circular sawmill equipped with an automatic log feed; the other was a conventional mill using a single muley saw instead of gang saws. The muley saw, mounted in iron frames instead of the wooden frames of the gang saws, cut much more rapidly than the old-fashioned arrangement. Once the renovation was complete, the Natchez mill boasted a daily capacity of 40,000 feet of lumber. The Brown sawmill at Natchez then became one of the largest in the South, exceeding in size

8. Moore, *Andrew Brown.*
9. *Ibid.*, 22–23, 27, 30, 134.

all of the mills at Mobile and almost equaling the huge Vale Royal mill at Savannah, Georgia, and the Wappo mill at Charleston, South Carolina. In the first twelve months of operation after the new machinery was installed, Brown's sawmill manufactured 3 million feet of lumber. Even this production, however, was far below the mill's theoretical capacity. In 1859 and 1860 the Brown sawmill grossed more than $60,000 each year.[10]

With the development of a sizable steam-powered lumber-manufacturing industry in the states bordering the lower Mississippi River and with increasing mechanization of cotton and sugar plantations, several machine shops and foundries were established at strategic locations in Mississippi to supply replacement parts and maintenance services for steam engines and machinery. In this prewar era very little steel was utilized in the manufacture of engines, boilers, and machinery because it was prohibitively expesive. Instead, cheaper but less durable iron and brass were the principal materials from which engines, boilers, and the moving parts of sawmills, cotton gins, cotton presses, gristmills, flour mills, and corn fodder mills were made as well as plowshares and points for harrows. Because moving parts of brittle cast iron were easily broken and parts of soft wrought iron quickly became worn, a convenient source of supply for repalcement parts for engines and machinery was indispensable to owners of machinery. Even large northern factories did not manufacture engines or machinery having interchangeable parts, and few of them maintained stocks of spare parts from which to supply their customers. To be sure, the factories could fabricate these items on special order for their southern customers, but because of the distance involved the factories could not deliver them promptly. As a rule, therefore, southern owners of machinery resorted to the closest foundry and machine shop for parts and maintenance services.

In machine shops such as these, workmen had to be capable of machining every part of steam engines, just as they had to be able to make all parts of sawmills, cotton gins, and other machinery. Thus in even the smallest shops, mechanics were prepared to cast a simple cog wheel or to make a complicated steam valve. In larger shops, machinists could turn cylinders and pistons of many sizes to close tolerances, and a few of the shops were equipped to manufacture high-pressure steam boilers, the most demanding metalwork of all. Although machinists purchased iron

10. *Ibid.*, 114–16, 119–20.

pipe and plates, copper tubing, gauges, and valves from northern manufacturers, they could make everything else required.

In the period from 1830 to 1860 the principal foundries and machine
shops of Mississippi were located in Natchez and Vicksburg on the Mississippi River and at Biloxi and Handsboro on the Gulf coast. In addition, a large foundry was situated in northern Mississippi at Holly
Springs, whereas smaller shops operated in Jackson and Canton. All of
the railroads in Mississippi maintained repair shops that were equipped
to work in both metal and wood, but none offered its services to the general public. During the 1840s and 1850s an unusually large railroad
workshop in Vicksburg repaired and rebuilt locomotives and constructed
passenger and freight cars. Unlike similar shops in the Southeast, however, the Vicksburg railroad machine shops never manufactured complete
locomotives.[11]

In 1832, William W. Gaines established on the Vicksburg commons the
first foundry and machine shop of consequence in Mississippi. This
Vicksburg selectman, machinist, and ginwright specialized in the manufacture of cotton gins and various kinds of plantation mills that employed
metal running gear imported from northern foundries. He also did a
brisk business in converting older model gins to more efficient types by
replacing obsolete wooden parts with cast iron gear. In 1832, Gaines installed a small furnace in his workshop and began to manufacture his
own iron castings. With this furnace in operation, Gaines began to make
everything that went into his cotton gins except for the circular cotton
saws of English cast steel. Gaines also manufactured and stocked grate
bars for the furnaces of plantation and sawmill steam engines. He obtained his supplies of pig iron and coal from northern flatboatmen and
maintained a coal yard as a sideline.[12]

In 1834, Abram B. Reading purchased the busy little Vicksburg
foundry from Gaines. Reading was a prosperous lawyer of Vicksburg
who invested widely in commercial and industrial enterprises. His practice was to take succeessful merchants or mechanics as minor partners,
placing them in charge of the daily workings of a firm while he handled

11. Vicksburg *Whig*, April 25, 1850, Feburary 3 and March 8, 1853, July 19,
1854, November 29, 1856, September 7, 1859.

12. Jackson *Mississippian*, January 10, 1834; Vicksburg *Advocate and Register*,
March 22 and May 10, 1832, January 8 and March 19, 1834; Vicksburg *Whig*,
May 26, 1860.

the business affairs. Reading ran the Vicksburg Foundry in this manner until 1854, when he bought out Solomon Zimmerman and employed a superintendent to manage the establishment for him. In September of that year the editor of the Vicksburg *Whig* wrote that the Vicksburg Foundry was "supplying planters in all this region with every variety of machinery for steam saw mills, gin presses . . . and *repairing* and *mending* at shorter notice than it takes . . . to get a letter to the proprietors of Foundries in Cincinnati or Louisville, and for less price than is charged above, inclusive of freight." [13]

Throughout the 1850s the machine shop was continually employed in turning out sawmill and plantation steam engines of from eight to fifty-five horsepower. Orders poured in during the last few years of the decade, and the shop produced engines at the rate of one per week. Reading added a boilermaking shop that could manufacture boilers of any size or type needed for sawmill or plantation steam engines. Besides steam engines and boilers, Reading made both circular sawmills and sash sawmills as well as screw and lever types of cotton presses. Although still fabricating metal parts for cotton gins, the Vicksburg Foundry had discontinued the manufacture of complete ginstands by 1857, and the foundry was working only in metal. During the last few years of the antebellum period, Reading regularly employed about a hundred workmen in his ironworks. Twenty-eight of these workers were slaves belonging to the firm of A. B. Reading and Brother, the name of the company operating the foundry in 1860. In addition Reading and Brother owned two women, who presumably cooked for the slave mechanics, and ten boys twelve years old or younger. A. B. Reading also personally owned ten slaves on the plantation where he resided and another fifty on a second plantation. As a result of wise management and favorable location, Reading was able to compete with northern foundries on equal terms despite the disadvantage of having to import both iron and coal. Reading was able to deliver and install his engines and machinery for a sum no greater than the price of a similar northern item when the cost of transportation was added to the bill. In 1860, Reading's Vicksburg Foundry was by far the largest and most successful ironworks in Mississippi, and more extensive establish-

13, Deed Book G (Office of the Warren County Chancery Clerk, Vicksburg), 81–82; Vicksburg *Whig*, January 1, 1840, January 25, 1845, January 8, 1846, September 2 and 27, 1854; Vicksburg *Register*, March 5 and 19, 1834, January 31, March 4 and 14, 1838; Vicksburg *Sentinel*, March 15, 1838.

ments of this kind were to be found in the lower Mississippi Valley only in New Orleans.[14]

With cotton plantation owners and lumbermen of the region experiencing prosperity during the early 1850s, there was such a strong demand for engines, machinery, and repair services that a second large foundry and machine shop was set up in Vicksburg. Three men who had been associated for many years with the Vicksburg and Jackson Railroad erected this ironworks "on the levee." A. M. Paxton, the senior partner, like Reading, was a successful lawyer who invested heavily in railroad stock and who was a director of the railway company. A junior partner, James Roach, was a railroad official in charge of the general operation of the line. The third member of the new firm, S. T. VanLoon, resigned his post as superintendent of the railroad workshop in order to take charge of the new foundry and machine shop. This firm planned to manufacture passenger and freight cars for the Vicksburg railroad as well as steam engines and machinery for plantation and sawmill use. After operating successfully for three years, the Paxton foundry burned to the ground, with complete loss of patterns, tools, and machinery. Paxton, however, was not deterred by this loss of $20,000 and rebuilt the establishment on an enlarged scale. In 1858 the foundry resumed the manufacture of steam engines, cotton presses, corn mills, and parts for plantation machinery. At the end of the decade this ironworks employed about fifty men and was manufacturing engines at the rate of two a month. Paxton's establishment survived the Civil War, and it operated throughout the remainder of the nineteenth century. With the Vicksburg foundry and the railroad workshops, Paxton's ironworks made Vicksburg the major center of metalworking in Mississippi during the late antebellum period.[15]

Although economic conditions were less favorable in Natchez than in Vicksburg for foundries and machine shops, the older of these river towns did support small foundries during the last three decades of the antebellum period. The first of these foundries was opened by John Spitler and Richard Wilds as the Natchez Foundry and Gin Factory during 1836,

14. Manuscript Census Returns, 1860, Warren County, Schedule 1; New Orleans *Times Picayune*, January 19 and May 8, 1861; Vicksburg *Whig*, September 6 and November 22, 1854, January 1, March 2, and May 26, 1858, January 4 and May 22, 1860, May 8, 1861, July 1, 1862.

15. Natchez *Courier*, September 28, 1858, Vicksburg *Herald*, January 11 and February 18, 1866; Vicksburg *Register*, March 15, 1838; Vicksburg *Whig*, February 3, March 8 and 15, 1853, March 28, 1855, May 26 and September 25, 1860.

employing facilities owned by the Bellevue Steam Cotton Press. This ironworking establishment came into the possession of Maurice Lisle, a young machinist from Delaware, during 1845. He moved the machinery into the large brick building formerly used as a depot by the defunct Natchez and Jackson Railroad. Operating with a force of twenty to twenty-five workmen, Lisle on order manufactured steam engines, sawmills, draining machines, iron screws for Newell cotton presses, and gearing for cotton gins, gristmills, and sawmills. He also performed considerable repair work on steamboats during the slack steamboating season. In the early 1850s, the Natchez Foundry operated three forges and eleven lathes. It annually consumed 250 tons of pig iron from Pittsburgh and 3,000 barrels of coal. In 1855 the machine shop, steam engine, and all metalworking machinery were destroyed by fire. Only the casting shop, pattern warehouse, and office were saved. The loss, estimated at $10,000 represented approximately half of Lisle's capital. Nevertheless, he erected a fireproof brick building the following year and equipped it with machinery of the latest model, including a new steam engine and boiler, iron planing machine, "self-acting" lathes, a drill press, and a bolt cutter. Unfortunately the panic of 1857 brought his creditors down upon Lisle before the rebuilt ironworks could become profitable. In 1858, C. B. Churchill bought the foundry and lot upon which it stood at auction for approximately $10,000. The purchaser continued the operation of the ironworks, producing $50,000 worth of engines and machinery in 1859.[16]

A second foundry was established in Natchez during the early 1840s by Wilkins, Humason & Company. In 1848, this firm employed thirty workmen and manufactured steam engines, sawmills, and plantation machinery. At the close of the decade Swann and Abbott bought the foundry from the original proprietors. Disaster quickly overtook the new owners, however, as the City Foundry burned to the ground in 1851. Having no fire insurance, Swann and Abbott were ruined financially, and they did not attempt to rebuild the City Foundry.[17]

16. James, *Antebellum Natchez*, 206; Natchez *Courier*, February 24, April 7, and November 25, 1837, June 8, 1838, August 6, 1840, June 14, 1843, October 23, 1852, November 2, 1854, May 19, 1855, March 25, 1857, December 21, 1858; Natchez *Free Trader*, October 4, 1845, March 9, 1848, November 29, 1854, March 26 and August 23, 1859; *Eighth Census, 1860: Manufactures*, 285.
17. *De Bow's Review*, V (1848), 379; James, *Antebellum Natchez*, 205–206; Natchez *Courier*, June 14, 1843; Natchez *Free Trader*, March 9, 1848, October 29,

During the 1850s a small ironworking industry flourished on the Mississippi Gulf coast to service the numerous steam-powered sawmills in the region. Two of the combined foundry and machine shops were large enough to manufacture steam engines as well as spare parts for mills and engines. At Handsboro, J. N. Bradford and Company manufactured $80,000 worth of engines and sawmill machinery in 1850, whereas a similar establishment at Biloxi belonging to S. B. Hand turned out twenty-five steam engines valued at $62,500. During the late 1850s Bradford marketed his engines at New Orleans and Vicksburg as well as on the Gulf coast. In 1860, the combined capital investment of the two shops was estimated at $29,500. Between them they employed seventy workmen and produced $165,000 worth of sawmills and steam engines.[18]

At the opposite end of the state from the Gulf coast, the town of Holly Springs emerged as a center of ironworking during the 1840s and 1850s. As the cotton-growing area of northeastern Mississippi was not well served by the Mississippi-Yazoo river system, planters and sawmill owners needed the services of a foundry. This need was met by the erection of such a shop in Holly Springs during the mid-1830s. At first the foundry produced nothing but cast iron plows, but in 1839 the proprietors added steam-powered lathes and facilities for casting parts for sawmill and plantation machinery. The foundry maintained a precarious existence during the depression of the 1840s but grew rapidly with the revival of the cotton economy in the 1850s. After Wiley P. Jones and W. S. McIllwaine became the owners, the foundry began to specialize in the manufacture of cast and wrought iron building supplies. Its work soon became famous, and it filled contracts for iron shutters, gutters, columns, fences, and other prefabricated iron items for builders as far distant as Vicksburg and New Orleans. In 1860, the foundry of Jones, McElwain and Company employed 100 workers and provided 1,350 tons of castings valued at $120,000 and eight tons of brass worth $8,000. In 1987 specimens of its work could still be seen in the Warren County courthouse built in 1860 by William, George, and Thomas Weldon and preserved as a museum. In

1851; New Orleans *Times Picayune*, October 28, 1851; Vicksburg *Sentinel*, January 6, 1844.
18. Hickman, *Mississippi Harvest*, 34; Hilgard, *Geology and Agriculture of Mississippi*, 366–67; Jackson *Mississippian*, May 18, 1849; New Orleans *True Delta*, May 16, 1858; *Eighth Census, 1860: Manufactures*, 287; Vicksburg *Sentinel*, May 4, 1850; Vicksburg *Whig*, May 22, 1860; Wailes, *Report*, 200–205.

addition to this extensive ironworks, the workshops of the Mississippi Central Railroad were located in Holly Springs during the late 1850s.[19]

Besides the workshops employing twenty or more workmen that I have already described, there were several others of smaller size. In Jackson, for example, James O. Stevens operated a foundry and machine shop during the 1850s. His workshop manufactured sawmills, a portable horsepower machine, and a very few small steam engines. Another workshop of similar nature in Madison County employed two workmen in repairing steam engines and other machinery. Still another foundry in Tishomingo County employed four workmen. In all likelihood numerous other shops operated by individual ginwrights, millwrights, and engine wrights, like the Jackson Foundry, escaped the notice of census takers at the close of the antebellum period.[20]

Just as competition from northern iron manufacturers inhabited the growth of Mississippi foundries and machine shops, so did large northern farm implement and wagon factories dominate the market in the Old Southwest. As a result, only two cotton gin manufacturers and one implement factory distributed their products outside their immediate vicinity during the antebellum era.

By far the most successful cotton gin factory in Mississippi before the Civil War was located in east Mississippi at Aberdeen. Benjamin D. Gullett, inventor of an improved cotton gin, during 1852 erected the shop from which the factory ultimately developed. Not having the capital necessary for constructing and equipping a factory for manufacturing his gin on a large scale himself, Gullett formed a partnership with Richard S. Gladney. The firm's enlarged workshop went into operation in 1856, manufacturing Gullett's wire brush cotton gin, corn mills, winnowing fans, cotton threshers, and a patented mechanical cottonseed planter.

19. Les Crocker, "An Early Iron Foundry in Northern Mississippi," *Journal of Mississippi History*, XXXV (1973), 113–15; *Eighth Census, 1860: Manufactures*, 289; William B. Hamilton, "Holly Springs, Mississippi, to the Year 1878" (M.A. thesis, University of Mississippi, 1931), 27, 49–50; Holly Springs *Gazette*, March 30, 1839, February 3, 1843, May 4, 1844, June 8 and 28, 1845; New Orleans *Times Picayune*, November 4, 1860; Stone, "Holly Springs," 359; Vicksburg *Whig*, March 28, 1860.
20. Brandon *Republican*, May 18, 1863; Columbus (Ga.) *Daily Sun*, May 23, 1863; Jackson *Daily News*, March 7, 1860; Jackson *Mississippian*, June 29, 1858; Raymond *Hinds County Gazette*, January 8, 1862; *Eighth Census, 1860: Manufactures*, 289, 292.

Gullett and Gladney also manufactured such building supplies as doors, window sashes, and blinds; ran a planing machine, turned in wood and iron; and repaired plantation machinery. The favorable response given the Gullett gin by planters inspired the partnership to invade the lower Mississippi Valley. Gullett opened a factory in Amite City, Louisiana, to manufacture the gins for sale in the New Orleans market. In 1860, Gunnison, Chapman & Company of New Orleans bought Gladney's interest and employed the inventor to superintend the manufacture of his gins in their New Orleans factory in addition to their regular line of portable circular sawmills and Chapman's Patent Cotton Press.[21]

In Aberdeen, R. C. Beckett, Sr., purchased Gladney's interest in the Aberdeen Gin Factory and formed a partnership with Dr. John L. Tindall. Beckett and Tindall then constructed a large factory on Maple Street, consisting of two long brick buildings. In one building was a blast furnace and facilities for casting the metal parts for the gins. In the other building, which was two stories high, were the wood and metal machine shops. The steam engine that supplied the power for these machine tools was enclosed in a brick room built onto the main building. Among the machine tools in the factory were lathes for cutting iron and steel, grinders, cutters for making the steel cotton saws, and such woodworking tools as bandsaws, circular saws, planers, and tongue-and-groove machines. The cotton gins were assembled on the second floor and were carried from the building by means of a ramp. A lumber-drying kiln was housed in another small brick building fifty feet distant from the main structure. In 1860 the gin department, under the direction of J. M. Matheny, was fabricating gin stands at the rate of one per day. These gin stands featured steel saws ranging in number from forty-five to eighty and sold for prices ranging from $225 to $400. The large seventy- or eighty-saw gin stands were designed to be driven by steam; the smaller gin stands could be propelled by mechanical horsepower. The owners of the Aberdeen Gin Factory purchased scrap iron locally and imported pig iron from the upper Mississippi Valley. This pig iron was brought in by water before the Mobile and Ohio railroad became operative; afterward it came down from Tennessee by rail. In 1859 the Aberdeen

21. *American Cotton Planter and Soil of the South,* I (1857), 40, 103; Jackson *Mississippian,* February 3, 1854; *Southern Cultivator,* XVII (1859), 238, and XVIII (1860), 342, 366–67.

Gin Factory employed twenty-five workmen and produced gins worth $50,000.[22]

A gin factory similar to the one at Aberdeen was active in Kosciusko during the 1850s. At the beginning of the decade T. G. Atwood was manufacturing a cotton gin stand of his own invention in a small workshop. The editor of the Vicksburg *Sentinel* called these machines "the best gin stands now in use in this section of the county." These gins were not mass-produced or "finished and furnished in showy style, flimsily put together, like many of those from Yankee firms," but were "carefully and strongly made." Within a few years, however, Atwood's business increased to such a degree that he had to resort to the very sort of manufacturing condemned by the Vicksburg journalist. In 1858, he was employing forty mechanics in his Kosciusko factory. One of his latest gins was displayed at the state fair in Jackson. According to the Vicksburg *Whig*, this machine was a "beautiful piece of workmanship, with all of the latest improvements." At that time many of Atwood's gins were being sold through a Vicksburg agency. In 1860, the Kosciusko gin factory, capitalized at $100,000, produced $75,000 worth of cotton gins.[23]

Although Vicksburg and Natchez were trading centers for plantation regions, neither town developed a significant manufacturing establishment for cotton gins, plows, or wagons that was larger than a workshop. Obviously such items could be manufactured in the North and transported to the Mississippi River ports by water more cheaply than local workshops could make them. In the case of cotton gins, local mechanics at Natchez and Vicksburg were unable to compete successfully with the products of Daniel Pratt's factory at Prattville, Alabama, or with Samuel Griswold's gins, manufactured at Griswoldville, Georgia. As the proprietors of these industrial establishments in the Lower South possessed no other intrinsic advantages than skill and good business judgment, it is likely that absence of enterprise was a determining factor in the failure of Mississippi cotton gin manufactories to progress beyond the workshop stage of industrial development.

22. R. C. Beckett, "Antebellum Times in Monroe County," Mississippi Historical Society *Publications*, XI (1910), 89–92, 100–101; *Eighth Census, 1860: Manufactures*, 290.

23. Vicksburg *Sentinel*, April 16, 1850; Vicksburg *Whig*, November 6, 1858, October 19, 1859; *Eighth Census, 1860: Manufactures*, 285.

During the 1850s, wagons and agricultural implements were manufactured in Mississippi on a factory basis in only one establishment. This was the Southern Implement Manufacturing Company, located at Jackson and owned by Martin W. Phillips, Z. A. Phillips, and Robert Kells, which began operations in 1859. Four buildings, the largest of which was a three-story brick structure measuring 40 feet by 100 feet, made up the factory complex. This steam-powered factory, employing about forty skilled workmen, was equipped with modern woodworking machinery, including a planing machine, several shapers, circular saws, lathes, and morticing machines. Lacking a foundry, however, the company purchased all of its iron and steel castings from the ironworks in Vicksburg. The owners planned to install a foundry and forges, but the outbreak of the Civil War upset their design.[24]

Martin W. Phillips had organized the Southern Implement Manufacturing Company to make a cast steel plow designed by Thomas E. C. Brinley of Kentucky. Having purchased the rights from the inventor, Phillips hired the Kentuckian to supervise production in the Jackson factory. Brinley planned and directed the construction of the factory buildings and took charge of the subsequent operations of the industrial establishment. Brinley's plow, which had previously gained a favorable reputation in the upper Mississippi Valley, was equally well received by farmers and planters in Mississippi, who purchased them as fast as they were manufactured. In addition to the Brinley plow, the Jackson factory produced cotton gins, cotton threshers, scrapers, sweeps, harrows, wheelbarrows, carts, and wagons. The wagons ranged in size from one- to six-horse units and were designed to be drawn by either horses or oxen. Most of the wagons were equipped with wooden axles, but cutomers could obtain iron axles upon special order. Coming into the market at a favorable time, the products of the Jackson factory sold briskly at the plant and at agencies in Vicksburg and Natchez. In 1861, the factory began to make carriages and caissons for cannon on contract with the state of Mississippi. As a result of its production of war materials for the state and Confederate governments, the Southern Implement Company was burned by

24. *American Cotton Planter and Soil of the South*, III (1859), 270; Jackson *Mississippian*, July 27, 1858; Moore, *Agriculture*, 189–91; *Southern Cultivator*, XVII (1859), 39, XVIII (1860), 259; Vicksburg *Whig*, April 23, 1861.

Federal troops in 1863 together with Joshua and Thomas Green's textile mill and the state penitentiary.[25]

During the last two decades of the antebellum period, several small textile mills were established in Mississippi, with the first two built in Natchez. John Robinson, a Scottish mechanic, erected the earliest of these industrial establishments during 1842 at Torrey's store on the defunct Natchez and Jackson Railroad. There he constructed a two-story building and installed a twelve-horsepower steam engine, 60 wool spindles, and 260 cotton spindles. Soon afterward, John Robertson of Robertson, Osgood and Wells, a firm from Boston, purchased a vacant three-story brick building that had formerly housed the bankrupt Natchez Cotton Press and converted the building into a second textile factory. When it was completed, the factory contained 2,000 spindles and ten looms, powered by a twenty-eight-horsepower steam engine. The daily capacity of the new Robertson factory was 300 yards of linsey-woolsey made of a mixture of wool and cotton and 500 yards of coarse cotton lowells. Both enterprises encountered great difficulty in selling their manufactured goods during these depression years, and both were compelled to resort to manufacturing cotton and woolen goods for planters on toll, in the way that gristmills operated. When this expedient did not solve their financial problems, Robinson and Robertson both failed. In November 1844, Samuel T. McAlister, senior partner in the commission house of Watson and McAlister of New Orleans and Natchez, purchased the larger textile factory from the Boston firm. During 1845, McAlister produced cloth for slave clothing and cotton bagging for baling cotton and for cotton-picking sacks with a work force of one white manager, twenty adult male slaves, six adult female slaves, and four children. McAlister, like his predecessors, however, was unable to show a profit, and he committed suicide on January 3, 1846. Two Natchez mechanics, Henry Wood and Alexander Clarkson, subsequently tried to operate the factory with financial assistance from Dr. Stephen Duncan, but they also failed. The factory was then closed permanently.[26]

Soon after the Natchez textile mills failed, a Georgia company estab-

25. Brandon *Republican*, May 18, 1863; Moore, *Agriculture*, 189–91; *Southern Cultivator*, XVII (1859), 39; Vicksburg *Whig*, April 23, 1861.

26. John H. Moore, "Mississippi's Antebellum Textile Industry," *Journal of Mississippi History*, XVI (1954), 83–85; James, *Antebellum Natchez*, 204–205; Natchez *Free Trader*, May 5, 1842, February 27, 1845, January 6 and March 17,

lished a textile mill in Choctaw County, Mississippi, that was soon to become famous throughout the Old Southwest as a model of industrial efficiency and profitability. In 1847, James M. Wesson, Daniel L. Booker, Richard Ector, John P. Nance, and Thomas J. Stanford of Columbus, Georgia, who had all been associated with textile mills in that city, organized a company in 1847 and obtained a charter in January 1848 from the Mississippi legislature for the Mississippi Manufacturing Company. Anticipating that the charter would be granted, Wesson during 1847 purchased a site for a factory on McCurtain's Creek, a tributary of Big Black River, where James G. Drane had formerly operated a water mill. The following year Wesson led a party of about thirty workmen and their families from Columbus, Georgia, to Drane's Mills, later to be renamed Bankston. There, under his direction, the Georgia mechanics first erected a water-powered sawmill and a machine shop. Then, using lumber from the sawmill, they constructed a three-story wooden building 108 feet long and 48 feet wide to house the textile mill and associated machinery. Meanwhile, mechanics fabricated spinning machinery in the machine shop, which they installed in the main building of the factory. In December 1848 the textile mill, powered by an eighty-horsepower steam engine, began operating with 500 spindles and a crew of twelve workers. In May 1850 the mill was producing daily 280 pounds of spun cotton thread that sold for twenty cents per pound. All of the workers in the textile mill were white, but the engineer in charge of the steam engine was black. At that time workmen were installing a gristmill, a wheat flour mill, and a wool-carding machine in the factory.[27]

At about this time twelve heavy looms designed for weaving heavy cotton osnaburgs and linseys (which were woven from cotton and wool) arrived from Patterson, New Jersey, and were installed in the factory. In June 1850, Wesson reported in *De Bow's Review* that "we are now running about 800 spindles, 10 cards, 12 looms and all the accompanying necessary machinery for spinning and weaving. We have 500 spindles and five cards more, not [yet] finished." In addition, Wesson was operating a

---

1846, June 23 and 30, 1847, March 9, 1848, January 3 and March 17, 1849, July 10, 1852; John Robertson to Andrew Brown, February 18, 1846, in Andrew Brown Papers.

27. Moore, "Textile Industry," 86–87; Columbus (Ga.) *Enquirer*, July 29, 1840, August 7, 1844, March 4, 1846; Jackson *Mississippian*, December 22, 1848, June 8, 1849; New Orleans *Delta*, December 4, 1848.

"double cylinder wool card that cards the wool twice as well as most of the country cards that have only one, and will turn off two hundred pounds of rolls a day, for which we charge 8 c[ents]. a pound" to card wool for a customer. Wesson also announced that his machine shop was prepared to manufacture machinery for sale. According to James G. Drane, who represented Choctaw County in the Mississippi senate and who lived near the textile mill, the profits of the Mississippi Manufacturing Company were more than 20 percent.[28]

Despite periodic reports of large profits earned by the Mississippi Manufacturing Company, the firm was barely able to meet expenses for several years. Wesson experienced great difficulty in disposing of cloth woven by his mill during the early 1850s, and demand for thread and yarn was not large. Most of the company's earnings at that time apparently came from the grist and flour mills, from the sawmill, and from the wool-carding machines. In 1854, however, Wesson began to emphasize the manufacture of woolen cloth that did not meet as much competition from plantation loom houses as did the all-cotton and mixed cotton and woolen fabrics, and he made arrangements with an experienced commission house to distribute his fabrics in the principal market towns. As a result of these changes, the company in 1855 realized a net profit of $22,000 on a capital investment of $60,000. According to the editor of the Raymond *Hinds County Gazette*, "the goods have obtained an excellent reputation, and the [woolen] Kerseys, in particular, are acknowledged to be superior to anything of the kind ever sold in the South."[29]

Business was brisk for the Choctaw County textile mill during the last five years of the decade. In 1858 the editor of the Grenada *Locomotive* reported that the capitalization of the Mississippi Manufacturing Company had risen to $80,000 and that the profits of the mill had not fallen below 30 percent for four years. Wesson was using more wool than could be obtained locally, and he was having to import large quantities from New Orleans. In February 1858, for example, a steamboat unloaded at Grenada a shipment of 30,000 pounds of wool that Wesson had purchased in the Crescent City at twelve cents a pound. Nevertheless, cotton yarns, cotton osnaburgs, jeans, and linsey-woolseys continued to be the prin-

28. *De Bow's Review*, IX (1850), 433; Natchez *Courier*, January 29, 1850.
29. Raymond *Hinds County Gazette*, November 19, 1856; Vicksburg *Whig*, September 13, 1855, January 22 and 25, September 19, October 7, 1856, November 20, 1857, March 17, 1858.

cipal products of the textile mill. In 1858, Wesson planned to expand production of cloth by adding twenty more looms. The company was also making considerable money from its flour-milling operation. In 1857 the mill ground 60,000 bushels of wheat raised by neighboring farmers and planters. By then Wesson was reaping the reward of a program that he had carried on for several years to encourage agriculturists in the region to raise wheat. As part of his program Wesson imported seed wheat and sold it to farmers and planters. Wesson also was raising foodstuffs for his employees at that time. He killed and cured 25,000 pounds of salt pork during 1857. In August 1858, Wesson wrote that his original plan had been to dispose of his manufactures locally, but "since we have increased our operations and established a character for our goods we defy competition and place our goods in New Orleans, Vicksburg & Jackson and other large towns and cities of the State." In that year the factory contained 1,000 cotton spindles, 500 wool spindles, 20 looms, and 1 wool carding machine, and the work force numbered 80 men and women.[30]

Although Wesson used a few slaves to operate his steam engine and "in some of the preparatory departments which are very dusty," most of his factory workers were white. He believed that hired whites were less expensive than either bought or hired slaves and that they were more efficient than blacks. He nevertheless admitted that slaves "were equal to the task." Like many other southern industrialists of the 1850s, Wesson maintained a paternalistic and authoritarian attitude toward his employees. The little village of Bankston was in every regard a company town. Originally located away from towns and travel routes in order to provide few distractions for the employees and their families, Bankston was Wesson's plantation. He would not permit whiskey to be sold in the vicinity, and he saw to it that the inhabitants of Bankston received religious instruction proper to factory hands. He said that "178 Souls are fed by labour for us in and about the Mills. All of whom have the benefit of weekly preaching, as well as sabboth [sic] school instruction, so that while the children are brought up to industrious sobriety, and taught the doctrine of economy of time, as well as money, they are instructed in letters and elevated in morals." Of the adults, he added in obvious satis-

30. Vicksburg *Whig*, March 10 and September 29, 1858; John H. Moore (ed.), "The Textile Industry of the Old South as Described in a Letter by J. M. Wesson," *Journal of Economic History*, XVI (1956), 201–202.

faction, "The improvement in the Character and standing of the men and their families who have been for any length of time in our employment is such as hardly to be believed."[31]

When he visited Bankston in September 1858, John J. Williams, editor of the *Planter and Mechanic* and secretary of the Mississippi Agricultural Bureau, was "particularly struck with the quietness, good order, and sound morality of the little town. The operatives, male and female, all looked cheerful and contented, which of course, bespoke liberal and punctual compensation for their labor"—or perhaps fear of their stern employer![32]

In 1859 a correspondent of the Mobile *Mercury*, who was probably J. M. Wesson, described the company town of Bankston. "When the factory was established," he wrote, "Bankston was but a rough place, situated in a muddy creek bottom, and surrounded by a rough population. . . . We were living almost in the woods, and our operatives in rough board shanties." "Now, he continued, "we are living on the hills round about, with lawns and flower gardens, and orchards, and they in neat comfortable houses, well arranged in nice streets and shady groves." "We have," he wrote in a spirit that Wesson would certainly have shared, "moreover, the best of municipal regulations, which are generally observed, or if violated, strickly enforced." In the town was "a flourishing Sunday School, kept up all winter; a Baptist and a Methodist church; and . . . a lodge of the Independent Order of Good Templars, a temperance order, numbering about sixty members, all good men and true."[33]

In 1860 the census taker reported that the Mississippi Manufacturing Company was capitalized at $80,000. Forty-five males and forty females were employed in the mill, with thirty of the women in the cotton mill and ten in the woolen mill. The value of wool consumed by the factory was more than double that of cotton, $28,750 and $11,805, respectively. The value of the finished cotton goods, however, almost equaled that of the woolen products at $34,200 and $37,800. The labor cost in the cotton mill was $6,600 and in the woolen mill $6,000. Thus in that year the textile mill cleared 23.5 percent on its capital investment. When the investment of approximately $15,000 in the buildings and residences of the workers in the company town is included, the percentage of earnings

31. Moore (ed.), "Letter by J. M. Wesson," 201–205.
32. Jackson *Mississippian*, September 15, 1858.
33. *Ibid.*, January 3, 1860.

drops to 19.8, a figure that is still impressive in agricultural antbellum Mississippi. Wesson, the moving spirit of this little industrial enterprise, was described by the editor of the Kosciusko *Chronicle* as an "enterprising manufacturer, . . . a thorough going railroad man, . . . the warmest advocate of Temperance in all Choctaw, the most untiring friend of agriculture, and one of the best Whigs in the whole country."[34]

Secession of the state of Mississippi from the Union and the outbreak of the Civil War greatly enhanced the economic importance of the textile factory at Bankston. When the state government undertook to equip troops for home and Confederate service in 1861, the Mississippi Manufacturing Company and the textile mill operated by the state penitentiary in Jackson produced all of the uniforms. The textile mill was expanded during the war years, and the Confederate government established additional manufacturing facilities at Bankston, including a shoe manufactory. On May 1, 1864, Colonel George W. Brent reported to General Braxton Bragg from Columbus, Mississippi, that "the Quartermaster's Department receives here from a neighboring factory from ten to twelve bales of jeans and linseys per week which are at once converted into clothing. The number of garments manufactured weekly varies from 1,000 to 1,500. The material is excellent." The factory continued to operate until January 5, 1865, when a detachment of the Fourth Iowa cavalry "destroyed large quantities of quartermaster's and subsistence stores, together with a large cloth mill, tannery, shoe-making establishment, and their contents." According to the report of Colonel Edward F. Winslow, 500 men were employed in the Bankston factories at that time.[35]

J. M. Wesson in 1871 built a second textile mill, which operated successfully at Wesson in southern Mississippi for the remainder of the century. He was the only one of the prewar textile manufacturers of Mississippi to continue industrial activities in the postwar era.[36]

During the 1850s a textile mill in Jackson belonging to the state peni-

34. *Eighth Census, 1860: Manufactures*, 286; Vicksburg *Whig*, March 21, 1860.

35. John K. Bettersworth, *Confederate Mississippi: The People and Policies of a Cotton State in Wartime* (Baton Rouge, 1943), 23, 145, 219; *The War of the Rebellion: A Compilation of the Official Records of the Union and Confederate Armies* (Washington, D.C., 1880–1901), Ser. I, Vol. XXXIX, Pt. 2, pp. 565–66, and Vol. XLV, Pt. 1, p. 852.

36. John K. Bettersworth, *Mississippi: A History* (Austin, Tex., 1959), 247–49; A. M. Muckenfuss, "The Development of Manufacturing in Mississippi," *Mississippi Historical Society Publications*, X (1909), 172.

tentiary was almost as successful as the Mississippi Manufacturing Company. This state-owned industrial enterprise originated in an operation like many found on cotton plantations intended to supply the inmates of the penitentiary with clothing. Convicts spun thread and yarn with a hand-cranked device that removed seed from seed cotton, carded the fiber, and spun it in one continuous operation. Other convicts then wove the thread and yarn into coarse cloth on a hand loom. In a prison tailor shop the cloth was worked into clothing.[37]

By 1847 the number of convicts confined in the penitentiary had increased to such an extent that the prison clothing shop was unable to provide them with uniforms. Joseph Moseley, the prison superintendent, therefore obtained permission from the state legislature to install a steam-powered textile mill. By 1849 the prison mill was manufacturing 1,700 yards of osnaburgs, 300 yards of linseys, and 400 pounds of yarn weekly. The following year Moseley increased the capacity of the mill to 6,000 yards of cotton cloth per week.[38]

Moseley at first disposed of the surplus products of the penitentiary textile mill through auctions held in Jackson. As production increased, the superintendent expanded his market by opening agencies in such large cities as Mobile, New Orleans, and St. Louis. In the late 1850s, however, local customers were buying such large quantities of cloth directly from the mill that A. M. Hardin, Moseley's successor as superintendent, decided to close the outlets in the cities.[39]

In 1857 the penitentiary textile mill was rebuilt and enlarged after a fire destroyed the original factory. The new mill was designed for a work force of 150, and its equipment included 2,304 cotton spindles, 24 cotton-carding machines, 76 looms for weaving osnaburgs, and 4 looms for cotton twills as well as a full complement of machinery for making linseys and cotton batting. A sixty-horsepower steam engine manufactured in Jackson provided power for the textile mill and other machinery in the penitentiary complex. Between November 1, 1860, and October 31,

37. Moore, "Textile Industry," 90–94; Jackson *Southern Reformer*, September 6, 1845; Jackson *Southron*, December 16, 1841; *Mississippi Senate Journal*, 1841, pp. 193–253.

38. *Mississippi House Journal*, 1850, pp. 246–68; Natchez *Courier*, December 4, 1849.

39. *Mississippi House Journal*, 1850, pp. 404–408, 1854, pp. 59–80, 1856–57, pp. 15–17, 1861–62, appendix, pp. 1–104. Also see Vicksburg *Sentinel*, February 7, 1852.

1861, the new textile factory manufactured $88,743 worth of goods. During the years of the Civil War the penitentiary produced military supplies ranging from gun carriages to tents, and in its last year of operation delivered goods valued at $172,608. On May 17, 1863, Federal troops commanded by General Ulysses S. Grant destroyed the penitentiary mills.[40]

Judge Edward McGehee, a large planter of Wilkinson County and a founder of the Woodville and St. Francisville Railroad, was largely responsible for the construction of a fifth textile mill in the town of Woodville. In 1849 McGehee organized a company and traveled to Lowell, Massachusetts, to obtain information about textile manufacturing. Returning to Mississippi he engaged Thomas Weldon to construct a factory upon plans probably obtained in Lowell and employed Colonel James Woodworth, an experienced manufacturer, to be superintendent of the mill. McGehee also hired several skilled workmen from the Dog River factory in Alabama. On February 7, 1851, the company advertised that it wished to hire fifty operatives. According to the advertisement, women could earn from three to eight dollars per week. The company was willing to hire whole families and furnish them with comfortable homes and "liberal wages."[41]

On April 8, 1851, the Woodville Manufacturing Company began manufacturing cloth, with a bolt of lowell being the first to come from the looms. The factory was then equipped with 4,000 spindles and eighty looms, and fifty workers were employed. An eighty-horsepower engine manufactured in Cincinnati provided power for the machinery. In October 1851 the editor of the Clinton (Louisiana) *Floridian* reported that the establishment was turning out 38,000 yards of lowells per week in addition to an unspecified quantity of linseys. According to the journalist, the textile machinery consisted of "two lappers and willows for preparing the cotton, thirty-six cotton cards, two drawing frames, four railway heads, five spindles, one batting card, two wool cards, one jack, four thousand spindles, two spoolers, two warpers, four dressers, eighty looms, and all corresponding machinery." The mill was then employing

40. Jackson *Mississippian*, December 9, 1857, January 6 and August 11, 1858, March 13, 1860; *Mississippi House Journal*, 1861–62, appendix, pp. 49–104, 1862–63, pp. 95, 89–101. Also see Brandon *Republican*, May 18, 1863.

41. Moore, "Textile Industry," 94–96; *Biographical and Historical Memoirs of Mississippi* (Chicago, 1891), I, 1193; Woodville *Republican*, July 9, 1850, April 8, 1851; Vicksburg *Whig*, February 12, 1851.

125 workers at wages of $4.25 per week. The workers were housed in three two-story brick buildings, with each building containing four apartments.[42]

Soon after the Woodville factory went into operation, McGehee discharged Superintendent Woodworth and assumed control of the mill himself. In 1852, McGehee replaced the white men and women who had been employed in the factory with slaves, most of whom belonged to him, and subsequently worked the factory with slave labor until it was destroyed in 1863. During the mid-1850s McGehee bought out the other shareholders and operated the factory as a family enterprise.[43]

After McGehee took over the Woodville textile factory, shirting, lowells, linseys, and kerseys of his manufacture became staples of the mercantile trade of the larger towns of the state. An advertisement run by James Gorton and Company of Natchez in the Natchez *Courier* was typical of many during the 1850s. Under the heading "Home Manufacture," the company announced that it had just received delivery of "ten bales 7–8 and 4–4 Woodville Cottons for negro clothing and cotton sacking," which they were selling at the same price as "Lowell goods." R. D. Howe and Company of Vicksburg similarly advertised in June 1856: "Just received from the Manufactory a few bales 7–8 and 4–4 of this justly celebrated brand [Woodville lowells]."[44]

According to the 1860 census the Woodville Manufacturing Company was capitalized at $110,000. Fifty men and fifty women were employed in the woolen and cotton mills, with eighty-seven being assigned to manufacturing cotton goods. In that year the mills produced woolen goods valued at $10,707 and cotton goods valued at $81,928. During that period the factory consumed $39,995 worth of cotton and $6,919 worth of wool. McGehee reported that his labor had cost $17,880, although it is not clear how he arrived at this figure inasmuch as the workers were slaves who belonged to him. Assuming that his labor costs were as reported, McGehee earned a net profit of $29,034 for the year, a return upon the capital in-

42. Woodville *Republican*, April 8, 1851; Vicksburg *Whig*, October 8, 1851.
43. Woodville *Republican*, September 9, 1851; Robert S. Starobin, *Industrial Slavery in the Old South* (New York, 1970), 13, 120; *Biographical and Historical Memoirs of Mississippi*, I, 1193.
44. Natchez *Courier*, January 27, 1852, September 4, 1857; Vicksburg *Whig*, May 19, 1852, November 22, 1853, June 27 and September 19, 1856.

vested of 26 percent. He was thus making as much from his investment as Wesson.[45]

The Woodville factory continued to operate successfully during the first two years of the war, although under increasing difficulties. In October 1862, for example, J. Burruss McGehee was forced to inform Andrew Brown that he was unable to supply the goods that the lumberman had ordered and that the company would pay money owed Brown "by check on Britton & Co., Bankers, at Natchez." In April of the following year Scott McGehee wrote to Brown that they were exchanging lowells for wool, "paying 15¢ pr lbs for best article of clean washd Wool, & charging 45¢ pr yd for the 4/8 and 50¢ pr yd for the 4/4 Lowell." The factory was able to continue operation for only a few more months.[46]

During July 1863, Brigadier General Thomas E. G. Ransom reported from Natchez, Mississippi, that a detachment of 350 cavalry had raided Kingston, Liberty, and Woodville. "At Woodville," he wrote, "he [Major Worden] burned a large cotton factory, containing forty looms engaged in manufacturing cloth for the rebel army."[47]

During 1856 the banking and mercantile firm of Joshua and Thomas Green constructed a sixth Mississippi textile mill in the city of Jackson, the Pearl River Mills. Located on the west bank of Pearl River within the city limits, the factory went into full production on June 9, 1858, with Samuel Poole as superintendent. At that time the factory was producing 7–8 lowells, cotton thread and yarns, and cotton rope for baling and for plow lines. By August 1858, Poole had brought the woolen mill into production and was selling 7–8 lowells at eleven cents per yard, linseys at twenty-eight cents per yard, jeans at forty cents per yard, cotton yarns at twenty cents per pound, and cotton sewing thread at forty cents per pound. The editor of the Vicksburg *Whig* commented that "cotton goods are manufactured in our own State of better quality than any brought to our markets from abroad. . . . The Pearl River Mills at Jackson are making Lowells, Linseys, Jeans, etc., at extremely low prices."[48]

45. *Eighth Census, 1860: Manufactures*, 292.
46. J. Burruss McGehee to Andrew Brown, October 9, 1862, and Scott McGehee to Andrew Brown, April 16, 1863, in Andrew Brown Papers.
47. *Official Records*, Ser. I, Vol. XXIV, Pt. 2, p. 685.
48. Moore, "Textile Industry," 96–97; *Biographical and Historical Memoirs of Mississippi*, I, 815–16; Marcellus Green, "Biography of Joshua Green for the

The Green textile mill had been in business for only two years when the federal census of 1860 was taken. The capitalization then was $100,000, and the company manufactured $42,200 worth of cotton goods and $109,500 worth of woolen goods during the previous year. Thus the new textile enterprise was specializing in woolen rather than cotton goods and was the state's largest manufacturer of woolens. The Greens employed 186 workers in the woolen mill and only fifty-four in the cotton mill. Unlike other textile mills in the state, the Jackson factory employed many more men than women, 200 men to 40 women. Like Wesson, the Greens utilized white labor almost exclusively. The company showed a net profit of $25,500 for the previous year, a 25.5 percent return on the capital investment.[49]

On May 15, 1863, Federal troops commanded by General Grant seized the city of Jackson and occupied it for two days. On May 18 the Brandon *Republican* reported that "Green's Cotton Factory, together with all the machinery, 300 bales of cotton, and all the buildings connected with the factory" were burned, as were J. A. Stevens' foundry and Phillips' implement factory and the state penitentiary. Grant later wrote in his *Memoirs* that he and General William T. Sherman found the textile factory in full operation the day after his army had taken the city and that they were astonished to observe that their entrance into the factory attracted no notice either from the management or from the workers. "We looked on for a while," he recalled, "to see the cloth which they were making roll out of the looms, with 'C.S.A.' woven in each bolt." The Union generals told the operatives to leave the building with what cloth they could carry, and then ordered the establishment to be burned.[50]

During the latter half of the 1850s, only two other textile plants were erected in Mississippi, neither of which was large enough to be of particular significance. Of the two lesser establishments, one was a small cotton mill with a capitalization of $15,000, employing twenty-four people in Tishomingo County. The other was the Columbus Manufactur-

---

Historical Society of Mississippi" (Typescript in the Mississippi Department of Archives and History); Jackson *Mississippian*, June 9 and July 21, 1858; Vicksburg *Whig*, June 16 and August 11, 1858.

49. *Eighth Census, 1860: Manufactures*, 287.

50. Brandon *Republican*, May 18, 1863; Ulysses S. Grant, *Personal Memoirs of U. S. Grant* (New York, 1892), I, 507.

ing Company, Columbus, Mississippi, a manufacturer of woolen hats for slaves. This concern produced woolen cloth for sale only as a sideline and on such a small scale that only eight workers were employed in that business. In 1858, James M. Wesson wrote: "The Columbus Manufacturing Co. at Columbus, in this state, have a small engine and only using one slow working machine capable of turning out five doz. hats per day. These are made of *wool*, not cotton, or mixed, equal in value to two or three such as we get from the north." According to Wesson, the Columbus firm was adding machinery to make a felt saddle blanket.[51]

Mississippi's various industries fared differently during the Civil War. Most of the sawmills survived the war years unscathed except for the loss of domestic markets for their products. Some of the larger enterprises like Andrew Brown and Company of Natchez also lost money they had invested in slaves, but this was not as severe a loss as planters experienced from the same cause. Surprisingly, the large foundries and machine shops did not become casualties, although Stevens' shop in Jackson was put to the torch. The Federal army did not destroy the machine shops of Natchez and Vicksburg or the large shop of the Southern Railroad in the latter town, although Reading's foundry had been fabricating cannon for the Confederates. Presumably, the northern troops needed the services of the ironworking establishments. After the fall of Vicksburg, however, the Union forces targeted the textile mills of the state for destruction, and by the conclusion of the conflict had burned every mill worthy of being called a factory. After the war, the textile industry, unlike the lumber and ironworking industries, had to make a completely new beginning.

51. *Eighth Census, 1860: Manufactures*, 289, 292; Paulding *Eastern Clarion*, May 4, 1859; Moore (ed.), "Letter by J. M. Wesson," 204.

10 White Inhabitants of the Towns

Just as the commercial towns of antebellum Mississippi existed primarily to move the cotton crops to market, so did a class of commission merchants exist in those towns to handle the details of transporting cotton crops from the river ports of the state to the seaports of New Orleans and Mobile. As fast as they harvested and ginned their crops of cotton, farmers and planters hauled their cotton bales to the nearest interior river port in large wagons carrying from five to eight bales pulled by several teams of oxen. There the wagoners delivered the bales into the care of commission merchants, who placed the bales in warehouses until they could be loaded on board southbound steamboats. Upon accepting a load of cotton, a commission merchant gave the wagoner a receipt listing each individual bale of cotton by the serial number that the owner had stenciled upon it. Acting as the cotton grower's agent, the merchant arranged insurance for a shipment, often of fifteen bales or less, and transported the cotton by steamboat to the seaport, where it was delivered into the custody of another commission merchant.[1]

Usually, the commission merchants of Columbus, Aberdeen, Vicksburg, Rodney, Yazoo City, and Natchez were partners or agents of larger commission houses in Mobile or New Orleans, or they had standing arrangements with such businesses in those cities. In Natchez during the 1850s, for example, Mason and Metcalf advertised that they were "prepared to make advances on consignments of *Cotton* and Produce to their friends in New Orleans," the firm of Watts and De Saulles. William K. Henry, who maintained a plantation supply house in Natchez, announced that he would "advance cash on cotton to be shipped to my friends in New Orleans, and goods to cotton stowed with me, making no charge except drayage." Cartwright and Doniphan, grocery and commission merchants, were agents for Oakley and Hawkins of New Orleans. They "made liberal *advances* on *cotton* consigned to their correspondents in New Orleans."[2]

The commission houses in New Orleans and Mobile received and

1. Gates, *Farmer's Age*, 152–53; Gray, *Agriculture*, II, 711–20; Moore, *Agriculture*, 54–55.
2. Natchez *Courier*, June 5 and July 10, 1850, May 17, 1854.

stored cotton sent to them, maintaining records for each individual bale. In preparation for offering cotton for sale, the merchants had each bale of cotton graded, placing a sample of cotton with the records pertaining to it. As a rule, the seaport commission merchants determined whether a client's cotton would be sold immediately to buyers in the city, held in the warehouse against an anticipated price rise, or shipped to markets in New York or overseas to Liverpool. Commission merchants made these crucial decisions rather than the cotton grower because they had better sources of information about movements of the market than their customers did. After a planter's cotton had been sold, the commission merchant credited his acount with the amount of the sale, less the costs of transportation, storage and handling of the cotton, insurance, any other expenses incurred in the complicated transaction, and the commission charged by the merchant. Customarily, the commission merchants charged 2.5 percent for each transaction, such as selling the cotton or paying for transportation or insurance.[3]

Commission merchants acted as purchasing agents for their customers as well as selling agents. Generally, a planter submitted a single large order for routine supplies needed for the next year's operations of the plantation. The commission merchant then purchased the items requested by his customer and dispatched the goods by steamboat as soon as they became available. Cost of the goods and their transportation plus the commission of the merchant was debited to the customer's account. Moreover, during the course of a year, planters frequently sent small orders for goods or services to their commission merchants, who handled the requests as they did the large annual purchases.[4]

Because planters usually placed their annual orders for plantation supplies during the summer or fall before their crops had been sold, it was customary for their commission merchants to advance them credit against their cotton crop. The usual charge for such advances was from 8 to 10 percent per annum. Not infrequently proceeds from sale of a planter's crop were insufficient to cover his indebtedness to his commission merchant. In such cases, the commission merchant merely carried

3. Atherton, *Southern Country Store*, 28–29; Eaton, *Southern Civilization*, 200–201; Gray, *Agriculture*, II, 711–14; Woodman, *King Cotton and His Retainers*, 22–25, 35–36.

4. Atherton, *Southern Country Store*, 29–30; Woodman, *King Cotton and His Retainers*, 30–33, 43.

the debt forward until the following year, in hopes that a larger crop or better prices would balance his customer's account. In situations where a planter wished to make unusually large purchases of such items as slaves or land, his commission merchant often helped him to obtain loans from other lenders, charging him a finder's fee for the service. In other respects, commission merchants served their customers as banks would today. Planters, for example, drew upon their accounts with their commission merchants as people today do upon checking accounts in banks. In order to pay for local purchases, planters often wrote drafts upon their accounts that the commission merchant honored when these documents were presented to him.[5]

Because their customers's annual orders for plantation supplies did not vary much from year to year, commission merchants were able to anticipate what they would want and could take steps to obtain supplies of plantation goods in advance of the season. Many of them built warehouses and stocked them with common staples of the plantation trade that they had purchased for resale. Thus such a commission merchant could sell goods to his clients, making both a commission and a profit on the transaction. These commission merchants became, in fact, wholesale distributors of such items needed in quantity by plantations as blankets, clothing and shoes for slaves, bagging and rope for cotton gins, salt pork called mess pork, hoes, axes, tools, plows and other farm tools and implements, and iron for blacksmith shops. Accordingly, commission merchants tended to become merchandisers of manufactured goods as well as financiers and providers of services.[6]

Commission merchants located in the trading centers of Mississippi dealt not only with planters but also with lesser cotton growers. They received cotton bales from many small farmers and consolidated their numerous small crops into shipments large enough to be of interest to buyers in the seaports. Sometimes they sold on behalf of these small customers as they did for planters, but more often they purchased these small lots of cotton outright. In the latter case, they then resold the cotton in the seaports on their own account. Both in the interior river towns and in the large seaports, some commission merchants thus be-

5. Atherton, *Southern Country Store*, 30; Gray, *Agriculture*, II, 713; Woodman, *King Cotton and His Retainers*, 34–42.
6. Woodman, *King Cotton and His Retainers*, 30.

came cotton buyers themselves, a situation that sometimes created a conflict of interest between themselves and their planter customers.[7]

Planters usually relied upon the services of a single commission house over a period of years, but it was not at all unusual for a planter to send cotton to several commission merchants in a single year. Unless a cotton producer were heavily indebted to him, or he had a written contract, a commission merchant was not able to compel a customer to deal solely with him. Competition was too vigorous among the many merchants of all sizes in the business for them to deal very arbitrarily with cotton growers.[8]

The relationship between Daniel O. Williams of Hinds and Issaquena counties and his commission merchants was typical of the associations of planters and commission merchants generally. During the 1850s, Williams' Danover Plantation on Deer Creek in Issaquena County was managed by his elder son, Sampson, who received one-quarter of the profits earned on the plantation as his salary. Sampson Williams transported their cotton bales down Deer Creek by steam keelboat to Cammack's Landing on the Yazoo River and there placed them in charge of the mercantile firm of Christmas and North. These merchants stored the cotton until they could load it aboard a steamboat bound for New Orleans, charging Williams for their services. Bypassing Yazoo City and Vicksburg merchants, Williams' cotton went directly from Cammack's Landing to Cleveland Brothers and Company of New Orleans, who disposed of the cotton for Williams. After they had completed a sale, Cleveland Brothers mailed Williams a report listing the serial numbers and weights of each bale and the price for which it was sold. The report also included the amounts paid out on Williams' behalf for freight, river and fire insurance, drayage, storage and weighing, and the commission charged Williams by the commission house.[9]

In a typical report dated August 4, 1855, Cleveland Brothers reported on shipments totaling fifty bales of cotton sent to them from Cammack's Landing on three steamboats, *Hill, Southern Belle,* and *Orion,* which

7. Ralph W. Haskins, "Planter and Cotton Factor in the Old South: Some Areas of Friction," *Agricultural History,* XXIX (1955), 2; Woodman, *King Cotton and His Retainers,* 68–71.
8. Eaton, *Southern Civilization,* 204; Haskins, "Planter and Cotton Factor," 10; Woodman, *King Cotton and His Retainers,* 32, 64–68.
9. Williams Papers.

they had sold to Gwathney and Company on July 31. The cotton, weighing 22,622 pounds, had brought eight and one-eighth cents per pound. From the total of $1,838.04 received for Williams's cotton, the commission merchants had deducted $134.35. On twenty-six bales the freight from Cammack's Landing to New Orleans had been $1.00 per bale, and on the other twenty-four bales, $1.25 per bale. Drayage, storage, and weighing charges came to $0.30 per bale. In addition, Williams was charged $2.00 for "Picking 2 Bales," which presumably were too full of trash to sell as Cleveland Brothers received them. Cleveland Brothers charged Williams 2.5 percent for a total of $45.95. Unlike many planters, Williams did not take out "river and fire" insurance on his shipments of cotton.[10]

As usual, Cleveland Brothers sent Williams an annual statement of his account for the year 1855 on June 30, 1856. The merchants had sold 284 bales of cotton for him and had credited Williams with the amount of $9,627.61. In addition, they had collected $1,299.03 owed Williams by G. M. Pinchard and Company, probably from other sales of cotton. Cleveland Brothers paid Williams 8 percent interest on his money in their keeping calculated upon the number of days a sum remained on their books. That year this interest amounted to $241.63. Advances they made to Williams against the next year's crop were calculated at the same rate of interest in the same manner. For goods and services rendered Williams, Cleveland Brothers paid out $3,251.81, leaving the Issaquena planter and his son with a credit of $7,873.09, which they considered to be profit on the 1855 crop.[11]

Like Daniel O. Williams, almost all of the large cotton planters preferred to transact most of their business with established commission houses in Mobile or New Orleans rather than with merchants in nearby river ports. Unable to participate in the most lucrative part of the marketing of the state's cotton crop, commission merchants of Vicksburg, Natchez, and Columbus had to content themselves with the lesser role of carrying on the commerce of small planters and farmers. In order to be able to market the cotton that came into their hands to advantage, the commission merchants of Mississippi found it desirable to establish a link with a seaport mercantile house that would provide them with the same assistance that was given the big planters. Also, like the planters,

10. Cleveland Brothers to D. O. Williams, August 4, 1855, *ibid.*
11. Cleveland Brothers to D. O. and S. Williams, June 30, 1856, *ibid.*

they relied upon the commission merchants of Mobile and New Orleans for financing. A local commission merchant had to be able to extend advances to his clients exactly as the big seaport houses had to give credit to large planters. Furthermore, local commission merchants tended to become merchants of plantation and farm supplies as often as the seaport merchants, although the scope of their operations made them retailers rather than wholesalers. They obtained their stock of goods from seaport wholesalers on credit and distributed supplies to their farmer and small planter customers on credit. Thus whether they were junior partners in New Orleans or Mobile firms or merely customers of those houses, the commission merchants of Mississippi towns were subordinate to the merchants of the cities.[12]

Mississippi commission merchants made many attempts to lure the planters away from the larger commission houses of the seaports but usually without success. In 1852, for example, the merchants of Columbus conducted a campaign against their competitors in Mobile. As at Vicksburg and Natchez, the larger planters of the Tombigbee Valley were accustomed to purchasing "their yearly supplies of dry goods, grocery and Negro materials of all kinds of descriptions" in the seaport. Trying to break this long-standing association, the merchants of Columbus agreed among themselves that they would cut prices to the Mobile level. According to the editor of the Columbus *Southern Standard*, the merchants offered to "duplicate any bill purchased in Mobile, adding only the expenses incident to transportation, and upon the same terms, freight and charges only added." They also announced that they would make advances for twelve months to planters on exactly the same terms as the Mobile commission houses. Although this battle in the continuing war between the local and Mobile commission merchants was won as usual by the seaport merchants, merchants in Columbus nevertheless prospered in an impressive manner. By 1860, William M. Crozart had accumulated real and personal property valued at $320,000; A. S. Humphries, $250,000; H. Johnston, $136,000; Charles Baskerville, $120,000; William B. Weaver, $108,000; and J. R. Otley, $100,000. Six others, William D. Humphries, Atrum Murdock, E. J. Munger, Thomas Cannon, A. Simpson, and Gray Chandler, were worth between $50,000 and $100,000.[13]

12. Vicksburg *Register*, November 10, 1836.
13. Columbus *Southern Standard*, April 3, 1852; *Biographical and Historical Memoirs of Mississippi*, I, 506–507, 1043; Manuscript Census Returns, 1860, Lowndes County, Schedule 1.

Some idea of the business of a moderately successful Vicksburg commission merchant who dealt in plantation supplies can be obtained from an unusually detailed advertisement that appeared in the Vicksburg *Whig* during January 1861. Duff Green, of Duff Green and Company, who published the advertisement, while by no means one of the wealthier members of the Vicksburg mercantile community, was nevertheless a businessman to be respected. In 1850 he owned fifteen slaves in Vicksburg, thirty-five on a plantation, and an imposing four-story brick residence, valued at approximately $45,000. He was a junior partner in the firm of J. J. Green and Benjamin Crump of New Orleans, shipping cotton from Vicksburg to New Orleans on their behalf. He also maintained a large stock of plantation supplies that he sold to planters and farmers on credit; however, unsettled economic conditions prevailing in the lower Mississippi Valley in the secession winter of 1860–1861 forced Green, in company with other Vicksburg merchants, to discontinue the practice of making advances.[14]

Not anticipating that business would fall off as a result of the political crisis, Green had purchased a large stock of goods. In the hardware line he had stocked 50 dozen Ames shovels, 10 dozen Ames spades, 50 dozen hoes of various kinds and makes, 200 pairs of trace chains, 2 dozen ox chairs, 100 kegs of nails, and 10 dozen each of horse and mule hames. His supply of dry goods included 75 pairs of blankets, 30 bales of lowell cloth, 5 bales of jeans, and 5 bales of linsey cloth, 25 cases of shoes, and 10 cases of rubber boots. For his customers's cotton gins he had on hand 50 coils of rope, 300 pieces of Kentucky hemp bagging, and 10 bales of hemp bagging from India. For feeding plantation slaves, Green had 100 barrels of mess pork and 25 tierces each of Stagg and Duffield hams for the whites. For those planters and farmers who cured some of their own meat, he had 200 sacks of coarse salt in addition to 100 sacks of fine salt for human consumption. For sweetening the food of slaves, Green offered 50 barrels and 50 half barrels of molasses. For the use of whites, he had on hand 57 hogsheads of various grades of sugar. Also for white tables he had stocked 100 barrels of several grades of wheat flour and 150 bags of coffee beans from Rio. For improving the digestion of his cus-

14. Walker, *Vicksburg*, 8–9; Jonathan Beasley, "Blacks—Slave and Free—Vicksburg, 1850–1860," *Journal of Mississippi History*, XXXVIII (1976), 11; Manuscript Census Returns, 1860, Warren County, Schedule 1; Vicksburg *Whig*, January 2, 1861.

tomers and for protecting them no doubt against the bite of snakes, he was able to furnish 150 half barrels of Magnolia whiskey as well as 50 barrels of superior and costly "fine old whiskey." He also carried large quantities of lard, rice, dried white beans, and tobacco. In addition his staples included soap, starch, and candles. Green did not carry corn, a bulky item that he left to produce merchants to handle, or such heavy plantation hardware as steam engines, cotton gins, or farm implements.[15]

Frederick Stanton of Natchez was perhaps the most successful commission merchant of antebellum Mississippi. Born in Belfast, Ireland, in 1798, Stanton emigrated to the United States in 1817. After a brief stay in New York City, he settled in Natchez and found employment in a mercantile house as a clerk. Like many other bright, industrious but impecunious young men who could read, write, and cipher, Stanton learned the commission business as an employee of an established firm and then went into business for himself. Good fortune had placed him in the right place at the right time. When prosperity returned to the Old Southwest in the early 1830s, Stanton was a successful commission merchant in Natchez with extensive contacts in New Orleans. In 1832, on the eve of the boom of the mid-1830s, Stanton formed a partnership with H. S. Buckner and H. B. Hamer to operate commission houses in New Orleans, Natchez, and Yazoo City. The New Orleans branch was known as Buckner, Stanton and Company; that in Natchez as Stanton, Buckner and Company; and the one in Yazoo City as H. B. Hamer and Company. Each of the partners held equal shares in the business. The firm prospered enormously during the 1830s but fell victim to the severe depression that began in 1839. Hamer died in the spring of 1842, dissolving the partnership, and Buckner, Stanton and Company of New Orleans went into bankruptcy during July of that same depression year. Shortly afterward Stanton filed for bankruptcy in Mississippi, and assignees appointed by the courts in Louisiana and Mississippi took over the assets of the partnership. Lawsuits over the disposition of the assets of the partners finally resulted in nullification of the bankruptcies in Louisiana and Mississippi and produced a judgment against them for more than $700,000.[16]

15. Vicksburg *Whig*, January 2, 1861.
16. *Biographical and Historical Memoirs of Mississippi*, II, 818; Yazoo City *Whig*, August 11, 1854: New Orleans *Delta*, July 20, 1854; Gates, *Farmer's Age*, 148; James, *Antebellum Natchez*, 156–57; Kane, *Natchez*, 284–87; Woodman, *King Cotton and His Retainers*, 21–26, 66, 187.

With that remarkable resilience displayed by many businessmen of the Old Southwest, Stanton reentered the commission business and proceeded to make a second great fortune during the 1850s. Like Richard Abbey of Natchez and many other men who had prospered as merchants, the Irishman invested in plantations and slaves. In 1857 he erected a splendid mansion, Stanton Hall, at the cost of $130,000 and spent $40,000 on its furnishings, which included carved marble mantels imported from Italy. When he died in 1859, Stanton owned six plantations in Louisiana and Mississippi, totaling 15,000 acres and 444 slaves, producing annually more than 3,000 bales of cotton.[17]

Surprisingly, retail merchants enjoyed about as much prosperity as local commission merchants in the commercial towns of Mississippi during the 1850s. In Vicksburg, for example, among the corps of commission merchants, Harvey Jenkins possessed real and personal property worth $155,000; William McCutchen, $105,000; Charles Smedes, $78,000; and C. A. Manlove, $62,000. A. Genella, a china merchant, was worth $140,000; T. J. Finney, who manufactured and sold carriages, $100,000; N. G. Wilson, importer of ice, $84,000; Morris Emmanuel, druggist and former mayor, $80,000; F. R. Finley, dry goods merchant, $78,000; Daniel Swett, hardware merchant, $65,000; William H. Stevens, who sold clothing for men and boys, $62,000; and J. A. Coulson, dispenser of fine clothing, $48,000. Most of these merchants owned their stores, warehouses, and residences, and almost all of them possessed families of household slaves.[18]

Although historians have generally paid little heed to the Old South's merchant class despite its obviously significant role in society, a few generalizations about members of this class can be made with safety. Intelligent, energetic, and reasonably well educated young men found attractive op-

17. Natchez *Courier*, April 26, 1854; *Biographical and Historical Memoirs of Mississippi*, II, 818; Gates, *Farmer's Age*, 148; James, *Antebellum Natchez*, 156–57; Kane, *Natchez*, 285; Frederick Stanton Estate Records (Office of the Adams County Chancery Clerk, Natchez, Box 173); Will of Frederick Stanton in Will Book III, 125–29 (Office of the Adams County Chancery Clerk, Natchez); Natchez *Free Trader*, March 30, 1858.

18. An inventory of a Natchez mercantile establishment is given in Estate of Benjamin Wade (Office of the Adams County Chancery Clerk, Natchez); Beasley, "Blacks," 11; Vicksburg *Sentinel and Expositer*, February 28, 1837; David Riggs, "Charles Conway Flowers (1842–1929): Vicksburg Colonel and Entrepreneur," *Journal of Mississippi History*, XLVI (1984), 171; Manuscript Census Returns, 1860, Warren County, Schedule 1; Walker, *Vicksburg*, 20.

portunities for advancement in southern commerce. In Mississippi, openings for clerks were usually available in mercantile houses, and advancement was rapid for employees who proved themselves to be able, industrious, and dependable. After learning the business, capable clerks either became junior partners or established competing firms of their own. During periods of prosperity, well-managed mercantile firms realized large profits, and numerous merchants became wealthy in a remarkably short while. In periods of depression, however, fortunes could be lost in the business community even more quickly than they had been acquired. The panics of 1837 and 1857 and the depression of the early 1840s took especially heavy tolls among the merchants of Mississippi. Frederick Stanton, the commission merchant of Natchez, as already mentioned, was wiped out in the panic of 1837 but gained an even larger fortune in the 1850s. For merchants, high risks and large profits went hand in hand.[19]

Practically nothing has been written by historians about the social lives of merchants in antebellum Mississippi. It may be assumed, however, that virtually all of their waking hours were devoted to their vocations during the business season, lasting through the months of fall and winter, except for Sundays and holidays. When the weather turned warm in the spring, ushering in the seasons for malaria, cholera, and yellow fever, those members of the mercantile community who could afford to travel left for the North to purchase stocks of goods for the coming year. Among those who remained behind, all who had the means to do so removed their families to country retreats to wait for the first frost, which was believed to dispel the danger from infection. Because most of the year's business was transacted during and immediately after the harvest season, members of the mercantile community worked long hard hours for half a year and took their leisure during the other half.[20]

In this era merchants were as concerned with civic affairs as are men of business today. They typically served without compensation as members of the city government, were active members of volunteer firefighting companies or military organizations, and played vigorous roles in local fraternal and political organizations. Most of the merchants of Mississippi were affiliated with the Whig party, and a high percentage of them

19. Kane, *Natchez*, 284–87.
20. For the memoirs of a Mississippi merchant, see Fulkerson, *Early Days in Mississippi*.

were members of the Methodist church. Because commerce required elaborate records, merchants as a class were more interested in elementary education than were other white Mississippians, and due mainly to their efforts, large tax-supported tuition-free schools were established during the 1840s and 1850s in all of the major trading centers. Furthermore, merchants were enthusiastic advocates of railroads, taking the lead in promoting municipal subsidies for railroads and plank roads. Successful merchants were usually small slaveholders, owning house servants themselves and hiring or buying slaves to work as porters in their stores and warehouses.

According to Joseph H. Ingraham, even on crowded streets merchants by their appearance were easily distinguished from planters. In Ingraham's opinion the diligent pursuit of commerce left characteristic imprints on the countenances of merchants, just as following the sea made sailors unmistakable. In his eyes the faces of Natchez businessmen were so like those he had seen in Boston or New York that he sometimes fancied that he was encountering old acquaintances. Although Ingraham may have been guilty of exaggeration, many merchants of the larger Mississippi towns had indeed migrated there from the Northeast and thus may well have resembled northern city dwellers of the middle class.[21]

In Mississippi the importance of bankers declined drastically during the panic of 1837 and the ensuing depression of the 1840s. The state revoked all bank charters during the early 1840s and did not incorporate any more before the Civil War. A few unchartered financial partnerships that called themselves banks did operate during the 1850s, but they were no more significant than individual commission houses. Joshua Green, a druggist of Jackson, for example, opened such a banking house in the state capital during 1854 in partnership with his brother Thomas. Wirt Adams and Company carried on a similar financial business in Vicksburg and Jackson. In Natchez, Britton and Koontz acted as local bankers as well as cotton brokers. In the absence of incorporated banking institutions, however, most Mississippians obtained credit from commission houses or private lenders. Nevertheless, in the larger towns of the state a few bankers were wealthy during the last decade of the antebellum period. In Natchez during 1860, to cite a few examples, C. A. Britton, banker and cotton broker, was the largest slaveowner in the city, with

21. [Ingraham], *South-West*, II, 34–35.

thirty-seven slaves, and George W. Koontz, banker, was worth $103,000. In Vicksburg, J. H. Johnson, banker, was the wealthiest man in the city, with property valued at $600,000. James Roach, a partner in the banking firm of Wirt Adams and Company, was worth $100,000. Before joining that company, Roach was a cashier for the Vicksburg Commercial and Railroad Bank and later was cashier for the Southern Railroad Company.[22]

White Mississippians, like other subjects of King Cotton during the era of slavery, were both susceptible to disease and notoriously prone to engage in litigation. Consequently a great many members of the medical and legal professions flourished like the proverbial green bay tree in this part of the Old Southwest. Most of these physicians and lawyers elected to set up their offices and residences in villages or towns so as to be centrally located for both rural and urban clients. Although there were about twice as many physicians as lawyers in the state of Mississippi, both professions were represented about equally in the larger towns. After reporting in the August 17, 1838, issue of the Natchez *Courier* that fifty lawyers and thirty doctors were practicing in Vicksburg, the editor commented sourly that "they will soon form a community large enough to live, all of them, by practicing on members of their own profession."[23]

At the close of the antebellum period, fourteen physicians, four dentists, and nineteen lawyers maintained offices in Natchez. At that same time, Vicksburg contained the offices of fourteen physicians, four dentists, and fifteen lawyers. Kosciusko, a small town in Attala County, had four physicians, three dentists, and nine lawyers.[24]

The richest lawyers in the state made their homes in Columbus during the 1850s rather than in Natchez or Vicksburg, thereby attesting to the exceptional affluence of Lowndes County in that era. Among the wealthiest in that Tombigbee River cotton port were James T. Harrison, who was

22. McLemore (ed.), *History of Mississippi*, I, 294; Hutchinson (comp.), *Code of Mississippi*, 324–35; *Biographical and Historical Memoirs of Mississippi*, I, 815–16; Haskell M. Monroe, Jr., James T. McIntosh, Lynda L. Crist, Mary S. Dix, and Richard E. Beringer (eds.), *The Papers of Jefferson Davis* (Baton Rouge, 1971–), II, 241n5; James, *Antebellum Natchez*, 163, 166, 203; Manuscript Census Returns, 1860, Warren County, Schedule 1.

23. The census of 1860 listed 1,708 physicians, 620 lawyers, 2 surgeons, 103 dentists, and 1,714 merchants in Mississippi (*Eighth Census, 1860: Population*, 273).

24. Manuscript Census Returns, 1860, Attala and Warren Counties, Schedule 1.

worth $250,000 in 1860, and Beverly Mathews, the owner of property valued at $168,000. Three others, William S. Barry, a U.S. congressman, E. B. Fort, and Isham Harrison, were each worth in excess of $100,000. In wealth the bar of Natchez ranked close behind Columbus. The most prosperous lawyer there, Joseph D. Shields, was worth $180,000. George M. Davis, George H. Sellers, and Douglas Wallworth were each owners of property valued in excess of $100,000.[25]

Because its peak of prosperity had occurred in recent years, Vicksburg had not given its attorneys such opportunities to amass large fortunes as had Natchez and Columbus. After Abram B. Reading, a lawyer who had acquired property valued at $435,000 largely through his mercantile and manufacturing interests, William C. Smedes was Vicksburg's wealthiest attorney, with property worth $140,000. He owned a 1,000-acre cotton plantation located on the Mississippi River three miles below Vicksburg and another 360-acre plantation thirteen miles from the city. A former law partner of Seargent S. Prentiss, Smedes had acquired Belmont, the handsome residence that Prentiss had constructed in 1842. In 1860, he gave his occupation as "farmer" to the census taker. Walker Brooke, who was worth $85,000, came next, followed by Alexander M. Paxton. The latter attorney, as already mentioned, was the proprietor of a large iron foundry and owner of a cotton plantation worked by thirty-five slaves. Armistead Burrell, who brought the famous turreted and moated brick "castle" in 1859, was worth $50,000, and Thomas A. Marshall, $33,500. Ten other attorneys were worth less than $20,000 each.[26]

Attorneys practicing in small towns of the state were generally less prosperous than their counterparts in Columbus, Natchez, and Vicksburg. In Port Gibson, for example, the most successful lawyers were L. N. Baldwin, $165,000; Henry T. Ellett, $70,000; J. B. Thrasher, $35,000; and G. V. Moody, $23,000. Josiah A. P. Campbell, who later became chief justice of the state supreme court, with $38,000 was the wealthiest lawyer in Kosciusko.[27]

25. Manuscript Census Returns, 1860, Adams and Lowndes Counties, Schedule 1.

26. Warren County Personal Assessment Book, 1860, and Warren County Real Estate Assessment Book, 1857 (Vicksburg Old Courthouse Museum); Manuscript Census Returns, 1860, Warren County, Schedule 1; Dallas C. Dickey, *Seargent S. Prentiss: Whig Orator of the Old South* (Baton Rouge, 1946), 49, 231, 280, 285, 346.

27. Harris G. Warren, "People and Occupations in Port Gibson, 1860," *Journal of Mississippi History*, X (1948), 108–109.

In large towns or small, skillful lawyers profited from the disputes of planters and men of business. Even in times of depression when planters and merchants were suffering financially, the legal profession encountered no slackening in its trade. When lawyers did encounter financial difficulties during panics or depressions, their troubles usually stemmed from unwise investments in commerce or real estate, not from the absence of clients.

Perhaps more than other members of the urban middle class, lawyers were able to develop collateral careers in other fields of endeavor. Besides entering into politics, they often took advantage of opportunities to invest in business enterprises that came their way as a result of their handling of the legal affairs of factors, merchants, and manufacturers. Some, like Abram B. Reading of Vicksburg, eventually became so immersed in manifold business enterprises that their legal practices were virtually abandoned. Others, like Robert J. Walker of Natchez, became land speculators on a vast scale. Still others, like Joseph E. Davis of Warren County, bought cotton lands and slaves until they were able to retire from the courtroom to spend the rest of their remaining days as planters.[28]

Most of the political heroes of Mississippi first came to public notice as colorful courtroom lawyers. War heroes such as Jefferson Davis and John A. Quitman were exceptions, but even they had found it necessary to become lawyers in order to launch successful political careers. In a world where sources of public entertainment were distinctly limited, lawyers enjoyed some of the advantages of modern stars of stage, screen, and television. While court was in session, spectators from town and country flocked into the courtrooms to savor the legal arguments along with their plugs of tobacco and an occasional pull at a little clay jug. Spectators wagered on the outcome of cases with the same enthusiasm that they displayed at horse races, fires, and cockfights, and cheered their favorite attorneys as modern sports fans applaud their winning athletic teams. Inasmuch as this public admiration gained from declaiming to juries was easily translated into votes, lawyers were more tempted than most people to campaign for public office or for posts of honor in the state militia. Consequently, most of the full-time public officials—such as U.S. congressmen and senators and members of the elected state judiciary—were, of course, members of the legal profession.

28. James P. Shenton, *Robert John Walker: A Politician from Jackson to Lincoln* (New York, 1961); Hermann, *Pursuit of a Dream*, 4–34.

The economic and social status of practicing physicians was somewhat less clearly apparent than the position of lawyers in antebellum Mississippi. Ingraham commented in 1835 that "physicians make money much more rapidly than lawyers, and sooner retire from practice and assume [the role of] the planter. They, however, retain their titles, so that medico-planters are now numerous, far out-weighing the regular practioners." Augmenting the total of nonpracticing physicians was a common custom among planters of providing medical educations for their sons even though these young men were destined for careers as cotton growers. Planters regarded medical training as the most practical education for members of their class because their heaviest investments were in disease-prone slaves. Consequently, a great many large cotton planters employed the title of doctor of medicine while practicing their profession only upon their slaves. Dr. Stephen Duncan, for example, bore this title proudly, although he actually dispensed medicines to the public only during his early manhood. Planters who claimed the title of M.D. can usually be detected in the census schedules from their residence on plantations. By the same token, physicians living in towns may be assumed to have been working members of the medical profession.[29]

An absence of state regulations with regard to medical qualifications also tended to obscure the role of physicians in Mississippi society. Reputable physicians had usually received formal training in medical schools—mainly in the North—and were entitled to the degree of doctor of medicine. As in the case of lawyers, however, would-be physicians could obtain admission into the profession by way of a version of the apprentice system in which candidates worked and studied under the direction of practicing physicians. Still others practiced legal though faintly disreputable medicine as herb or steam doctors. Although the takers of federal censuses listed all kinds of physicians alike, respectable physicians were always enrolled in the state medical society.

Despite Ingraham's opinion as to the relative earning powers of physicians and lawyers, the censuses of 1850 and 1860 suggest that medical practice was not as lucrative an avenue to wealth as the law. Nevertheless, established physicians unquestionably earned respectable middle-class incomes. In Columbus, for example, nine lawyers and six physicians were worth more than fifty thousand dollars in 1860. The wealthier phy-

29. [Ingraham], *South-West*, II, 85–86; Kane, *Natchez*, 205.

sicians in Columbus were S. B. Malone, $157,000; Robert F. Mathews, $141,000; R. M. Talerfer, $120,000; G. W. Vaughan, $98,000; B. C. Hairston, $90,000; and R. E. Lanier, $69,000. In the village of Craw-fordville in Lowndes County, the retired physician J. T. Edmonds, aged seventy, owned property valued at $155,000. Also in Crawfordville were E. H. Gregory, who was worth $98,000; N. F. Scules, $83,000; and James M. Baird, $70,000. E. H. Strong, worth $93,000, lived in West Point, and C. A. Oliver, $93,000, in the hamlet of Tibbee.[30]

If we judge by the 1860 census, the medical profession was not nearly as profitable in Vicksburg as in Columbus. None of the fourteen physi-cians practicing in the city at the close of the 1850s owned property val-ued at as much as $40,000. A. L. C. Magruder was worth $30,000; R. B. Scott, $30,000; G. K. Birchett, $24,000; and William Balfour, $23,000. J. Lightfoot, the most prosperous of four dentists, was worth $11,000. In Warrenton, a Dr. McElrath was worth $80,000, the highest valuation of property held by a physician in Warren County.[31]

The physicians of Natchez at the close of the antebellum period were faring like those of Vicksburg. With the notable exception of William Harper, a fifty-five-year-old physician from Maine who was worth $110,000, the fourteen medical doctors of the state's oldest city were worth less than $35,000. The retired seventy-two-year-old physician H. Lyle possessed property worth only $28,000. Of the practicing doc-tors, Spencer Wood, aged fifty, was the wealthiest, with $32,000. The dental surgeon C. H. Dubbs, aged fifty, was perhaps the most financially successful dentist in the state, with property valued at $33,500. Most of the physicians could hardly be classed with the rich. Walter Stewart, thirty-five, owned only $15,000 worth of property; James L. Meng, $13,000; H. H. Leggett, aged fifty, $11,000. The remainder were worth less than $5,000 each.[32]

In Port Gibson, there were seven physicians and one dentist in 1860. Of this number A. E. Thomas, aged forty, who owned seven slaves and who was worth $20,000, was the wealthiest. A. H. Peck, aged fifty-one, owned two slaves and personal and real estate valued at $19,000. R. G. Wharton, aged forty-five years, was third, with eight slaves and property

30. Manuscript Census Returns, 1860, Lowndes County, Schedule 1.
31. Manuscript Census Returns, 1860, Warren County.
32. Manuscript Census Returns, 1860, Adams County.

248 The Emergence of the Cotton Kingdom

worth $12,000. S. F. Abbey, aged fifty-six, came fourth with two slaves and $11,000. The remaining three physicians, the three youngest, had each accumulated less than $600. George W. Sevier, the only dentist, at age forty-eight, owned eight slaves and property valued at $7,500. The slaves belonging to these medical men were household servants and their children.[33]

Ministers of the Episcopal, Presbyterian, and Methodist churches were generally members of the urban middle class, although they rarely enjoyed the financial success of merchants, lawyers, or physicians. Prosperous Baptist ministers were more often found among the ranks of large farmers or small planters. Because of their social positions, some ministers were able to marry daughters of wealthy planters or urban businessmen and might thus join the financial upper class. The outstanding success story of such a clergyman was Charles K. Marshall, a Methodist minister of Vicksburg. Marshall early gained fame throughout Mississippi as a pulpit orator and throughout his life was in great demand as a speaker. He married a daughter of Newitt Vick, founder of the city of Vicksburg, and through her eventually acquired ownership of a strategically located portion of the Vicksburg riverfront. As a result, Marshall was worth $102,000 in 1860. He was thus the wealthiest as well as the most popular clergyman in Mississippi at that time. Lyell Smedes, an Episcopal minister of Vicksburg, duplicated Marshall's achievement when he married Susan Dabney, daughter of Thomas S. G. Dabney, who owned a 4,000-acre plantation. Smedes, however, did not live to enjoy his triumph, for he died a few weeks after his marriage. W. W. Lord, the Episcopal minister in Vicksburg during the 1850s, was socially prominent, although his property was valued at a mere $10,000. George Clinton, a Methodist minister in that same city, at age twenty-five was worth $7,000. In Columbus, William Halbert, fifty, was by far the most financially successful of the ministers of that city. He owned property worth $90,000. William B. Owings, forty-four, of the Methodist church, was worth $10,000, and Elzy Williams, forty-eight, of the village of Caledonia was worth a respectable $15,000.[34]

33. Warren, "Port Gibson," 108–109.
34. *Biographical and Historical Memoirs of Mississippi*, II, 364; Claiborne, *Mississippi*, 536; Mobile *Register*, February 25, 1845; Montgomery (Ala.) *Mail*, December 24, 1858; Natchez *Courier*, May 20, 1857; Vicksburg *Whig*, January 29, 1852, February 26, March 8, 22 and 24, 1853, July 26, 1856, June 16, 1858;

Another large segment of the urban middle class of Mississippi was made up of prosperous "mechanics," as contractors in the construction industry, manufacturers, mill owners, and other persons making their livings from mechanical pursuits were known to antebellum Americans. As a class, mechanics lacked some of the status enjoyed by merchants, lawyers, and physicians, possibly because as skilled craftsmen they had worked with their hands during early stages of their careers. According to the standards of the Old South, it was more honorable to expand a career as an architect into a profitable construction business than it was to reach the status of a prosperous contractor by way of success as a master carpenter or mason. Yet affluent mechanics were not entirely excluded from the charmed social circles of the urban middle class because, in the final analysis, wealth was the overriding factor in determining social position.[35]

That mechanics sometime became very affluent indeed in the Cotton Kingdom of antebellum Mississippi can be demonstrated in Columbus, Natchez, and Vicksburg. The highly successful owners of Columbus industrial establishments in 1860 included Q. A. Harvey, a blacksmith worth $138,000; Hezekiah Kirkpatrick, another blacksmith, worth $34,000; John B. Miller, a machinist, worth $30,000; James S. Lull, architect, worth $90,000; Jerome Womelsdorff, cabinetmaker, $37,000; G. W. Hargness, brickmason, $30,500; J. S. Shaw, brickmason, $30,000; Lewis Green, carpenter, $71,000; Thomas W. Brown, foundryman, $69,000; John M. Symons, sawmill proprietor, $50,000; and W. C. Nickles, wagon manufacturer, $20,000.[36]

In Natchez, Thomas Rose, a master carpenter who owned twenty-two slaves, was worth $82,500; Andrew Brown, architect, sawmill owner, and the largest slaveholder in the town with fifty-six slaves, owned property in Adams County alone that was valued at $80,000. James Brown, a master mason with eighteen slaves, was worth $21,000; Steven Odell, a gunsmith with twenty-seven slaves, and John Rountree, a saddler, with twenty-two slaves, were worth $21,000 each. In Vicksburg, John Adams, a master car-

Yazoo City *Democrat*, February 18, 1846; Susan Dabney Smedes, *Memorials of a Southern Planter*, xiii; Manuscript Census Returns, 1860, Lowndes and Warren Counties, Schedule 1.

35. For a biography of a successful Mississippi mechanic, see Moore, *Andrew Brown*.

36. Manuscript Census Returns, 1860, Lowndes County, Schedule 1.

penter, was worth the amazing sum of $220,000. George Wyman, a butcher, was worth $26,000; William Beaty, saddler, $20,000; and H. Metcalf, brickmaker, $29,000; and John A. Klein, sawmill owner, $60,000. Reading Brothers and Company's foundry was valued at $100,000.[37]

According to the census of 1860, surprisingly few whites were employed in the building trades, although the construction industry was experiencing unprecedented prosperity during the last half of the 1850s. In Vicksburg, no more than forty white carpenters were listed, of whom six were apparently master craftsmen. In addition to the carpenters, there were only twenty house painters, five brickmasons, and three plasterers in the town. Larger numbers of white construction workers made Natchez their headquarters. Eighteen in the little city on the bluff were master carpenters, and 111 were journeymen carpenters. Eleven of the master carpenters were slaveowners, the largest being Thomas Rose. The house painting trade was represented by three master painters and twenty-six journeymen; all three of the master painters were slaveowners. In the category of brick and stone masons, there were seven slaveholding master craftsmen and twenty-five journeymen. Two of the former, Charles Reynolds and James Brown, owned twenty-two and eighteen slaves, respectively. There were seventeen plasterers, including two master plasterers who owned two slaves each. There were also eleven cabinetmakers and ten sheetmetal workers. Four of the latter were slaveowners, and one, Robert Walker, owned property including eight slaves worth $24,000. In Vicksburg, the census listed only four tinners. All of the master craftsmen in the building trades employed hired slave journeymen more or less regularly, and the total number of black construction workers in antebellum Mississippi probably exceeded the whites by a large margin.[38]

White journeymen in the construction and woodworking industries resented competition from unfree blacks, especially in times of depression, and frequently sought to have blacks excluded from the trades by city ordinance and state legislation. Master craftsmen, however, found it to their advantage to use black skilled workmen and always managed to do so. Apparently they preferred slave craftsmen as employees to white journeymen, because the blacks were more easily managed than the whites. That blacks could be obtained more cheaply than whites is uncertain.[39]

37. Manuscript Census Returns, 1860, Adams and Warren Counties.
38. Natchez *Courier*, June 5, 1850; Manuscript Census Returns, 1860, Adams and Warren Counties.
39. Sydnor, *Slavery in Mississippi*, 8.

As a rule, mechanics owned more slaves than other members of the urban middle class. Merchants occasionally employed slaves as porters and drivers of drays, but like physicians and lawyers, most of them owned no slaves other than house servants and their progeny. Master craftsmen and proprietors of manufacturing establishments, however, employed as many black skilled workmen as they could afford to purchase or hire. Indeed, the number of slaves they owned was as accurate an index of the financial and social status of mechanics as it was of cotton planters.

Throughout the antebellum period, members of the urban middle classes, as well as some planters, invested their surplus capital in enterprises outside their main field of activity. These pragmatic businessmen took advantage of economic opportunities wherever they appeared. Successful commission merchants, retail merchants, bankers, lawyers, physicians, or manufacturers almost always bought cotton plantations at some stage in their careers. They also invested in commercial and industrial enterprises of many varieties. Many examples of this spirit of enterprise can be cited. Seargent S. Prentiss, a lawyer, erected Vicksburg's largest hotel during the 1830s and was one of the town's most active real estate developers. Abram B. Reading, also a lawyer, invested in such diverse Vicksburg enterprises as a sawmill, a blacksmith shop, a foundry, and several mercantile houses as well as a plantation. John A. Klein, by profession a jeweler, purchased a sawmill and became Vicksburg's largest manufacturer of lumber. Consequently, it is impossible for a modern historian to determine which subdivision of the urban middle class was the most financially successful. The commission merchants, however, supplied the most important service to agriculture and were accordingly the most economically significant of the several urban classes.

The urban lower middle class was made up largely of petty shopkeepers, tradesmen, and wage-earning employees of merchants, mechanics, and lawyers. In this category, clerks were an important element. In 1860, for example, 168 clerks were employed in the city of Vicksburg, with only 16 of them being older than forty years of age and 30 being between thirty and forty years old. Of these clerks, 30 were married, and 11 apparently owned their own homes. Ten clerks were slaveowners, and 8 owned property worth more than $5,000. Charles Gaskins, an exceptionally wealthy forty-five-year-old clerk in Daniel Swett's hardware store, was worth $70,000. Hugh Markham owned property valued at $14,200, and Gordon Robinson, a broker's clerk, $14,000, including nine slaves. Alexander Legrande, a sawmill clerk, owned $6,000 worth of real estate and two skilled slaves worth $2,500. By far the greater number of the clerks of Vicksburg were unmarried young men in their twenties who lived in boardinghouses. Except during depression years, the services of clerical workers were in strong demand in the commercial centers of Mississippi, and they accordingly received wages ranging from $50 to $100 per month. As room and board cost them considerably less than $25 per month, clerks of frugal habits were able to save money, buy slaves, and invest in business ventures.[40]

During the 1840s and 1850s, Andrew Brown employed many clerks in his Natchez sawmill and lumber company. These young men came from a wide range of backgrounds. In addition to Brown's only son, Andrew Brown, Jr., A. J. Postlethwaite and William I. Key kept the company records and acted as salesmen during the 1840s. Postlethwaite was a member of a family long prominent in the history of Natchez, and Key, a nephew of Brown's wife, was an immigrant from Scotland like his employer. Among others, Henry S. Solomon and John C. Brown worked for Brown during the 1850s. Brown, no relation to the lumberman, was a local working man, and Solomon came to Natchez from New Jersey as a carpenter seeking employment in his trade. Most of the young men who worked for Brown in a clerical capacity rose rather rapidly in the business world. Postlethwaite became a successful retail clothing merchant; Key became a junior partner in Brown's firm, handling its interests in New Orleans; and John C. Brown left the lumber company to become the Natchez representative of the New Orleans commission house of Mandeville and McIlhenny. Solomon remained in Brown's employ until his death from consumption in 1859, virtually managing the Natchez sawmill for him after 1853. Brown relied very heavily on the one-time carpenter after his son's death in 1849 and in many ways seems to have looked upon him as a foster son. During the many months of illness preceding his death, Solomon lived in Brown's house and was nursed by Brown's wife and daughter.[41]

Brown's clerks received the usual wages paid for clerical services in the towns of Mississippi. During the depression years of the 1840s, Andrew Brown, Jr., Key, and Postlethwaite received from $75 to $80 monthly. After he became the sawmill clerk in the early 1850s, Solomon drew a

40. Manuscript Census Returns, 1860, Warren County, Schedule 1.
41. Moore, *Andrew Brown*, 124–27.

salary of $100 a month. John C. Brown, who worked for Brown from 1850 to 1852, was compensated at the rate of $1,000 a year. When John Shanks took Solomon's place in 1859, Brown paid him $80 per month. John Paul, who served as clerk of the New Orleans lumberyard and the woodworking factory, received the highest salary of any of Brown's clerks. Because the salary scale was higher in New Orleans than in Natchez or Vicksburg, Paul drew $150 per month, three times the salary of an overseer on a large plantation.[42]

Skilled workmen who received daily wages were almost as large a segment of lower-middle-class society in Mississippi as clerks. This category included a very wide variety of specialists. In larger towns were to be found journeyman carpenters, cabinetmakers, brickmasons, stonemasons, wheelwrights, carriage makers, machinists, foundrymen, blacksmiths, tinsmiths, coppersmiths, silversmiths, gunsmiths, house painters, carriage painters, ginwrights, millwrights, steam engine engineers, bakers, butchers, shoemakers, plasterers, barbers, watchmakers, harness makers, sawyers, tailors, gas pipe fitters, confectioners, piano tuners, stonecutters, milliners, dressmakers, and many other artisans. Artisans like these apparently received wages of approximately $2.50 per day and board. In 1829, Brown paid carpenters at that rate, as well as machinists hired to repair sawmill machinery. He either paid their board bills at the rate of $15 per month or allowed them $0.50 per day if they preferred to provide their own meals. In 1849, the lumbermen was still paying skilled workmen $2.50 per day. Throughout the period between 1820 and 1860 sawyers were employed at Brown's Natchez sawmill at salaries ranging from $75 to $100 per month. As a result of the economic boom in the 1850s, the wages of construction workers rose along with the wages that Brown paid for hired slaves. In fact, journeymen bricklayers struck successfully for higher wages in Vicksburg in 1854, raising their rate from $3.00 to $3.50 per day.[43]

By far the largest concentration of unskilled white workers in antebellum Mississippi was located in Natchez. At the close of the decade of the 1850s, 214 unskilled white workmen were residing in that city, whereas 73 were to be found in Vicksburg and 17 in Columbus. In the

42. *Ibid.*, 125
43. *Ibid.*, 130; Andrew Brown Ledger, 1829–36, and Andrew Brown Day Book, 1848–51, in Andrew Brown Papers; Natchez *Courier*, August 2, 1854.

case of Vicksburg, the number of unskilled white workmen had declined noticeably since the middle of the 1840s. In 1844 a census of the town taken by the county assessor and tax collector had enumerated 144 laborers, twice as many as in 1860. As might be expected, nearly three-fourths of the Natchez laborers were immigrants from Ireland; American-born workmen accounted for about a fourth of the total. Only nine laborers had come from foreign countries other than Ireland; five were from England, one from Canada, two from Germany, and one from Italy. Although a fourth of the Natchez laborers were married, only eleven of them had accumulated any property of their own. Of these, eight owned personal property or real estate valued between $200 and $500. One was worth $1,400; another, $1,500; and the third, $11,000. Contrary to expectations, the white manual laborers of Natchez were not young men, as two-thirds of them were over thirty years of age. Throughout the antebellum period, unskilled white workmen in Mississippi received relatively generous wages. Except in periods of severe depression they were paid a minimum of a dollar a day and board. On such wages single men were able to afford lodgings in roominghouses, and most married laborers rented houses for their families. Only in very rare instances, however, did manual workmen acquire ownership of their residences.[44]

Larger towns like Natchez and Vicksburg provided numerous types of employment for white laborers. Contractors used them for constructing levees, railroad roadbeds, and for digging drainage ditches and foundations for buildings. In sawmills and lumberyards they were used for stacking and loading lumber and for handling logs. Many laborers found jobs on rafts and flatboats and with logging crews serving the mills of the towns. Many other white workmen and hired slaves were employed by brickyards. Still others in large numbers worked as stevedores on steamboats and at boat landings. A few found work in machine shops, small factories, and in railroad repair shops. In all of these various types of employment, white manual workers labored alongside hired slaves, usually without outward signs of racial friction.

One of the manual workmen listed by the federal census of 1860 as residing in Natchez was Manual Sparling, a thirty-five-year-old native of Maine. Sparling came to Natchez in 1858 as part of a crew sent south to install new machinery in Andrew Brown's sawmill that had been manu-

44. Manuscript Census Returns, 1860, Adams, Lowndes, and Warren Counties.

factured by the Ottawa Iron Works, of Ferrysburg, Michigan. Favorably impressed by Sparling's pleasant personality and industriousness, Brown offered the workman a permanent job in his organization at twice the usual wage. Sparling accepted Brown's offer and continued in his employ until 1867. In 1860, Sparling was promoted to the position of head sawyer in the Natchez mill with the impressive salary of $115 a month and board. From this isolated case it appears that the category of laborer as used in compiling the census of 1860 covered an unexpectedly wide range of incomes and types of employment.[45]

Such limited employment as existed in antebellum Mississippi for women was to be found in the towns. Women of the middle class made up a majority of teachers in both private and public schools, and they operated most of the business establishments that catered to members of their sex, such as dressmaking and millinery shops. Women of the lower middle classes supported themselves mainly by operating roominghouses and boardinghouses or by working in women's shops. Women of the lower classes were employed as domestics, midwives, laundrywomen, and prostitutes. A few women who operated businesses inherited from their deceased husbands were interesting exceptions to the general rule. To cite two examples, a widow ran a slaughterhouse in Vicksburg, and another, Harriet N. Prewitt, edited the Yazoo City *Whig* during the 1850s.[46]

Although the white inhabitants of urban centers provided some goods and services for their fellow town dwellers, in almost all cases they conducted most of their business affairs with farmers and planters in the vicinity. From commission merchants to seamstresses, shopkeepers relied largely upon rural customers. Lawyers found planters to be their most profitable clients, and even the physicians carried on most of their practice with patients outside the limits of the town. Among the professional classes, ministers may have been exceptions to the rule, but even they served congregations containing many farmers and planters who lived within riding distance of urban churches. Sawmills, foundries and machine shops, blacksmith shops, and shops operated by such craftsmen as ginwrights, carriage makers, saddlers, harness makers and shoemakers,

---

45. Moore, *Andrew Brown*, 130.
46. Manuscript Census Returns, 1860, Warren and Yazoo Counties, Schedule 1; Yazoo City *Whig*, 1854.

all depended upon the agricultural population. Only in New Orleans, the Lower South's only city, could urban workers and professionals make a living by trading with other townsmen. In Mississippi, towns were merely convenient points where the rural folk could obtain nonagricultural services.

11 Urban Blacks

Although most of the white residents of the urban centers of antebellum Mississippi supported themselves by providing the rural population with goods and services, the blacks of those towns were much less involved with the agricultural economy than the whites. Most of the free blacks earned their livelihoods by serving or trading with the urban whites. Slaves, who composed the larger part of the urban black community, generally worked as domestics or were employed in business establishments where they had little association with rural whites. Hired slaves who belonged to planters, however, were somewhat different. Working in the towns as craftsmen, draymen, or industrial workers, they made significant contributions to the incomes of their rural owners through the wages they earned in town.

Before the Civil War, urban black society in Mississippi was composed of a host of slaves topped by a small body of free blacks who were envied by the slaves and distrusted by the whites. Compared with the total number of slaves in the state, the combined free black populations in town and country were negligible in size. From a total of 182 in 1800, the number of free blacks in Mississippi increased to a peak of 1,366 in 1840, declining thereafter to 773 in 1860.[1]

At all times the great majority of free blacks in Mississippi were town dwellers. Although a great many of them had white ancestors and in fact owed their freedom to this inheritance, very few, if any, had been bequeathed land and slaves by their planter parents. Society in Mississippi, unlike Louisiana, where a Latin tradition permitted planters openly to acknowledge that they had fathered children born of slave women, found its base in English custom and was so hostile to miscegenation that white men hardly dared do more than free their mulatto offspring. Fathers of mulattoes never publicly admitted kinship with these children or named them in their wills as heirs. The right to inherit plantations and slaves was reserved in Mississippi solely for legitimate children of white property owners. Consequently, no mulatto planter class of the kind to be found in Louisiana or Latin America developed in Mississippi. Although

---

1. *Fifth Census, 1830*, p. 36; *Sixth Census, 1840*, pp. 58–59; *Seventh Census, 1850*, p. 449; *Eighth Census, 1860: Population*, 266–67.

a few free blacks such as William Johnson of Natchez did become owners of plantation and slaves, virtually all purchased such property themselves. When preparing their mulatto sons for emancipation, white fathers in Mississippi often had them taught a craft or trade and sometimes set them up in business when they were freed.[2]

In 1840, Wilford Hoggatt provided a glaring exception to the rule that land and slaves were not to be passed on to mulatto children. Hoggatt was a member of a wealthy planter family of Adams County and resided on a 4,000-acre plantation in St. Helena Parish, Louisiana. When writing his will, Hoggatt directed that eight mulatto children of his former slave Febe who were living in Natchez be freed and that they receive equal shares of his land and slaves upon coming of age. In deference to the racial views of Mississippians, however, Hoggatt maintained that Febe had purchased her own freedom, and he did not acknowledge that her children were his offspring.[3]

Because whites believed that the mere sight of a free black was unsettling to slaves, planters were loath to employ free blacks—even skilled free blacks—on plantations. Although some free blacks became small farmers, usually in the vicinity of towns, most of the members of this class were forced to earn their livelihoods in the urban centers rather than in agricultural regions of the state.[4]

Because opportunities for employment of free blacks were available in proportion to the size of towns, most of them in the Old Southwest settled in river ports. In 1840, more than half of the free black population of Mississippi was located in the old Natchez District, with 572 living in the four river counties: Adams, Claiborne, Jefferson, and Warren. In Adams County, which contained the largest group of free blacks in the state, 207 of a total of 283 resided within the city limits of Natchez. In Warren County, 71 of 104 free blacks lived in Vicksburg.[5]

Twenty years later, at the close of the antebellum decade, the free black population of Natchez was composed of 108 adults eighteen years of age

2. Charles S. Sydnor, "The Free Negro in Mississippi Before the Civil War," *American Historical Review*, XXXII (1927), 782; Ira Berlin, *Slaves Without Masters: The Free Negro in the Antebellum South* (New York, 1974), 222.

3. Hogan and Davis (eds.), *William Johnson's Natchez*, 333n.

4. Sydnor, *Slavery in Mississippi*, 203.

5. Berlin, *Slaves Without Masters*, 219–22; Sydnor, "Free Negro in Mississippi," 782.

or older and 100 children under eighteen, a distribution by ages that shows the Natchez free black community to have been maintaining its numbers by natural increase. By contrast, the free black population of Vicksburg declined drastically during the depression decade of the 1840s, falling from 71 in 1840 to 24 in 1850. From that low point the number of free blacks rose slightly to 27 in 1860. Inasmuch as the census of 1850 enumerated 7 male and 8 female adults and the census of 1860 reported 7 adults of each sex, the addition of 3 children to the community was less than would be expected. In Warrenton, the oldest village in Warren County, there was not a single free black in 1860.[6]

In Vicksburg the small colony of free blacks was composed largely of mechanics and tradesmen. Four barbers, two blacksmiths, and a drayman made up the adult male contingent in 1850. As in Natchez, the barbers appear to have been the most prosperous. Henry Lee, for example, owned one slave in 1851 and seven in 1856. In 1861, Lee and William Newman, another free black, each purchased a $250 Confederate bond. Kitty Foote was the wealthiest of the free black women. She owned eleven slaves in 1856 and was worth $2,100, according to the census of 1860. Jordan Chavis, who lived outside the city, owned twenty slaves in 1853, which made him the wealthiest free black in Warren County. As in Natchez, the free blacks were almost all of mixed African and European ancestry, and they apparently held themselves aloof from the society of slaves.[7]

Unlike Vicksburg, Port Gibson, the county seat of Claiborne County, increased its free black population from three in 1850 to twenty-three in 1860. At the later date, ten free blacks also resided in Grand Gulf, the other urban center of Claiborne County. In 1850 there were twenty-four free blacks in Columbus and twenty-six in Pass Christian on the Gulf coast. According to Glover Moore, during the 1850s there also was a small community of free blacks in Aberdeen, a port town on the Tombigbee River. Although most of them were manual laborers, one of them, Scott Keyes, was a businessman of some consequence. A barber by trade, Keyes was the proprietor of a bathhouse and a combined bakery and con-

6. Manuscript Census Returns, 1860, Adams County, Schedule 1; Beasley, "Blacks," 15; Sydnor, "Free Negro in Mississippi," 782.
7. Walker, *Vicksburg*, 50; Beasley, "Blacks," 15–16.

fectionary shop as well as a barbershop. Clearly, however, the free black community in Natchez was the most significant one of its kind in the state.[8]

By 1860 the body of free blacks in Natchez had existed for a sufficiently long time and in large enough numbers to become stratified much like white small-town society. On the topmost level a small middle class dominated the free black community both socially and economically. Members of this class were successful tradesmen who had accumulated some money, real estate, and slaves. Members of these families moved largely within their own social circles, shunning the "darkey balls," or other entertainments patronized by slaves and lower-class blacks. They patterned their behavior on their white middle-class neighbors, who transacted business with them on a basis of equality but who excluded them from their homes and social organizations. Such middle-class free blacks as these were observers but not participants in the civic life of the town. They were not permitted to vote or hold political office, to sit on juries, or to belong to militia companies. Yet, like the slaves, they could serve in firefighting organizations, and they were called upon by whites to contribute money to worthy causes. In short, they were part of the economic structure of Natchez but not of its political or social order.[9]

Probably the most successful member of this class and certainly the most well known to modern historians was William Johnson, a prosperous Natchez barber. In 1820, eleven-year-old William was emancipated by act of the state legislature at the request of his owner, William Johnson of Adams County, who was probably his father, and subsequently assumed his benefactor's surname, according to the custom of the time. Young William's mother, Amy Johnson, and his older sister, Delia, had received their freedom several years earlier. Soon after he gained his freedom, William was apprenticed to James Miller, a free black barber who had married Delia Johnson. While William was learning the trade, Miller's establishment became the most prosperous barbershop in Natchez, patronized by the leading white citizens of the city. Completing his apprenticeship in 1828, Johnson went into business on his own. He bought a barbershop in Port Gibson and operated it with

8. Harris G. Warren, "Population Elements of Claiborne County, 1820–1860," *Journal of Mississippi History*, IX (1947), 77, 81, 83; *Seventh Census, 1850*, p. 448; McLemore (ed.), *History of Mississippi*, I, 439.

9. Hogan and Davis (eds.), *William Johnson's Natchez*, 11–12.

good results for two years. In 1830, Johnson purchased his brother-in-law's barbershop on Main Street in Natchez, as Miller wished to leave the city to try his luck in New Orleans. Having earned the respect of the whites, Johnson was issued a license in 1832 by the Adams County Court and Police Board that authorized him to continue to reside in the state of Mississippi. A year later, the young barber purchased the old brick building in which his shop was situated.[10]

During the booming mid-1830s, Johnson engaged in widely varied business activities. He lent small sums of money to white businessmen, erected and rented out two commercial buildings, built a residence for his family, and began to buy small parcels of farmland situated about seven miles from Natchez. In 1838, he contracted with George Weldon, one of the state's leading builders, to construct a three-story brick building at a cost of $3,400. Within a year after the edifice was completed, Johnson paid Weldon the last of the money owed him. Johnson also expanded his principal business enterprise during the 1830s by opening two additional barbershops in Natchez. One of the new shops was located in a small hotel not far from his Main Street shop; the other was in Natchez-under-the-Hill. Johnson staffed his three shops with free black barbers and with slaves whom he hired or purchased. He also bought a few slaves to work his growing farm acreage, which he cultivated with the aid of a succession of white overseers. Although his farm, which eventually included about 700 acres, was never very profitable, Johnson enjoyed his status as a small slaveowning cotton planter too much to shift his capital to more financially rewarding commercial investments.[11]

In the 1840s, Johnson was the unchallenged leader of the Natchez free blacks by virtue of his wealth. He had earned the good will of the white business community by shrewd business sense and fair dealing, and he counted some of the most socially prominent members of the plantation aristocracy among his friends. Adam Bingaman, for example, took an interest in Johnson's welfare, and on at least one occasion dined with the barber after a hunt in the vicinity of Johnson's land. Nevertheless, in his associations with upper- and middle-class whites, Johnson scrupulously observed the limits that whites set upon their relationships with blacks. When Johnson's career was cut short by murder at the hands of another free black landowner in a dispute over land boundaries, Natchez whites

10. *Ibid.*, 19–21.
11. *Ibid.*, 21–40.

generally regretted the loss of the black businessman. Unfortunately, Johnson's assassin escaped punishment on a legal technicality. The only witness to the crime was a black, who was ineligible to testify in court against anyone other than another black. Because the prosecutor was unable to prove that the killer was not a white, the murderer was allowed to go free.[12]

Her inheritance from William Johnson made Ann Johnson, his widow, the wealthiest member of the free black community of Natchez in 1860. At that time she owned land, houses, and eight slaves valued at $16,000. Other members of the free black middle class in that period included Nelson Fitzgerald, a servant worth $12,000, and Robert McCary, a barber, friend, schoolteacher, and former competitor of William Johnson, worth $3,000. During the period of Reconstruction, the barber's son, William McCary, was prominent in local Republican politics, serving as sheriff of Adams County in 1874. For three decades the Johnsons, the McCarys, and the Fitzgeralds were regarded as the cream of free black society, together with the Barlands, who lived on farms outside the city limits. All of these families were owners of real estate and slaves.[13]

Below the small relatively affluent free black middle class in Natchez was a much larger group of tradesmen and craftsmen who made up a lower middle class. This element in 1860 included fourteen carpenters, six barbers, two blacksmiths, a steward on a steamboat, a baker, a daguerreotype artist, a gardener, and a hostler in a livery stable. Lower-middle-class black women were dressmakers or seamstresses by trade, nineteen in number in 1860. A free black lower class was made up of drivers of drays, manual laborers, and domestic servants. At various periods of time, some poor free blacks earned livings as peddlers, woodchoppers, fishermen, small farmers, and prostitutes.[14]

Unlike a vast majority of slaves engaged in agriculture, the free blacks of Natchez were overwhelmingly of mixed African and European ancestry, with mulattoes outnumbering true blacks by a ratio of six to one. Furthermore, the latter were relegated to the lowest stratum of free black society. Elite families belonging to this society were considered to be blacks apparently only by virtue of the harsh racial distinctions drawn by

12. *Ibid.*, 52–64.
13. *Ibid.*, 11, 43; Manuscript Census Returns, 1860, Adams County, Schedule 1.
14. Manuscript Census Returns, 1860, Adams County, Schedule 1.

Anglo-Saxon jurisprudence. William Johnson, for example, was the son of a mulatto mother by a white father and was therefore at least three-fourths white. In Latin American or French colonial societies, Johnson would have fallen naturally into the ruling class. In similar fashion, the family of Hoggatts, who were freed according to the will of the wealthy planter Wilford Hoggatt by his nephew and heir, Nathaniel Hoggatt, were three-fourths to seven-eighths white. In all probability, black slaves perceived no physical dissimilarity between most of the Natchez free blacks and their white neighbors.[15]

Even though slaves may have regarded Natchez free blacks as more white than black, the whites of Mississippi certainly considered them to be more black than white. In Natchez, to be sure, free blacks were treated with exceptional tolerance by the dominant whites. Elsewhere, however—and even in Natchez to a lesser degree—free blacks were objects of suspicion, fear, and sometimes hatred. Whites generally believed that the mere presence of free blacks in the community was detrimental to the institution of slavery, for slaves could observe in them that blacks could exist in a condition other than bondage. Furthermore, whites knew that free blacks possessed inherent capabilities to assist slaves in escaping or in organizing servile insurrections because they could move about more freely than slaves.

Until 1822 conditions in Mississippi were relatively favorable for free blacks. In that year news reached the Old Southwest that a revolt involving thousands of slaves in the low country of South Carolina had been narrowly averted as a result of a faithful house servant's warning to his mistress. Prolonged questioning of slaves and free blacks by the authorities of Charleston produced testimony that slaves on plantations within a radius of seventy miles had been organized under the leadership of Denmark Vesey, a free black who was a successful and highly respected Charleston carpenter. Although no revolt actually occurred, ninety-three blacks were tried for conspiracy, and of this number thirty-five were eventually executed and thirty-one transported out of the state. Although Richard C. Wade has suggested that the Vesey plot was lacking in substance, whites throughout the Lower South were alarmed by these grim events.[16]

15. Natchez *Courier*, August 16, 1855; Berlin, *Slaves Without Masters*, 273.
16. Eaton, *History of the Old South*, 258–59; John Hope Franklin, *From Slavery to Freedom: A History of American Negroes* (2nd ed.; New York, 1956), 187,

In Mississippi, where blacks almost outnumbered the whites, the state legislature moved swiftly to reduce the danger of similar servile insurrections. During the 1823 legislative session, the black code was extensively revised, with free blacks receiving special attention. Intending eventually to reduce the number of free blacks residing in Mississippi, the legislators decreed that no free black would in future be permitted to move into the state. Any free black who should attempt to do so would become liable to sale at public auction for terms of involuntary servitude as long as twelve months. Furthermore, those free blacks who were already residents of the state when the act became law and those who were subsequently born to free black parents residing legally in the state were required to register with a county court at three-year intervals. After the black code was revised in 1823, free blacks could not move freely about the state or obtain employment legally unless they could produce certificates of freedom obtained from a register of a county court. Furthermore, even free blacks who complied with this provision of the law still faced legal impediments if they sought employment outside the county where they were registered. Unless they could prove that they were already employed when questioned by officers of the law, they could be arrested and jailed as vagrants. The act of 1823 also deprived free blacks of the right to own firearms and ammunition or to buy and sell goods on the Sabbath.[17]

The 1823 law severely restricted relationships that free blacks could maintain with slaves other than those belonging to them. They were forbidden to sell whiskey to slaves on penalty of a flogging, and they were prohibited from selling any kind of merchandise outside the limits of incorporated towns. The latter restriction prevented them from becoming itinerant peddlers who would have opportunity to contact plantation slaves. In the same spirit, free blacks were denied the right to attend any gathering after dark at which slaves were present, or to be present at any time of day when slaves were receiving instruction in reading or writing. Under the new law, free blacks became liable to severe floggings if they provided slaves with forged certificates of freedom or harbored runaways.[18]

The act of 1823 left no doubt as to the subordinate status of all free

---

210, 225, 257, 351; Richard C. Wade, "The Vesey Plot: A Reconsideration," *Journal of Southern History*, XXX (1964), 143–61.

17. Hutchinson (comp.), *Code of Mississippi*, 512–25; Sydnor, "Free Negro in Mississippi," 780.

18. Hutchinson (comp.), *Code of Mississippi*, 520, 526, 534.

blacks with respect to whites. If a free black subjected a white to verbal abuse or to physical violence, however slight, the black became liable to punishment not to exceed thirty-nine lashes on the bare back. Furthermore, the act deprived free blacks of the right to testify in court in cases involving whites.[19]

As an aftermath of the slave revolt in Southampton, Virginia, led by Nat Turner in August 1831, the Mississippi legislature further circumscribed the legal rights of free blacks. An act that became law on December 20, 1831, prohibited free blacks from preaching the gospel, specifying a penalty of thirty-nine lashes for each violation. This act also expelled all free blacks between the ages of sixteen and fifty years from the state, excepting only those persons in this age bracket who were licensed to remain in the county of their residence by the county court. In issuing or denying such residence licenses to free blacks, the county courts enjoyed full discretion under the terms of the act of 1831 to determine whether an applicant was "of good character and honest deportment" and whether it was "expedient and proper" for him to remain in Mississippi. Moreover the act gave county courts complete authority to revoke residence permits of free blacks at any time. After passage of this act, free blacks were able to reside in Mississippi only as long as they remained in the good graces of the white ruling class. If a free black made himself obnoxious to the whites in any manner, he could be compelled legally to depart from the state never to return.[20]

In 1841, free blacks of the lower Mississippi Valley were imperiled by one of the panics caused by reports of planned slave insurrections that frequently swept through the region. During July an overseer on a plantation near Bayou Sara reported that he had overheard some slaves discussing a projected revolt that was to involve slaves on both sides of the Mississippi River from Bayou Sara to Natchez. In the vicinities of Bayou Sara and Woodville, the authorities made many arrests, and under questioning some slaves implicated whites and free blacks in the alleged conspiracy. The whites in the towns became extremely alarmed and took steps to strengthen their security. In an inland town far removed from the scene of the abortive uprising, the white inhabitants of Holly Springs, for example, held a meeting to devise means of preventing large numbers of

19. *Ibid.*, 515, 517.
20. *Ibid.*, 533–34.

blacks from coming into the town. On August 13, 1841, the editor of the Holly Springs *Southern Banner and Conservative* announced that "the authorities of New Orleans, Vicksburg, &c., are taking the most vigorous steps to rid the county of free negroes." A vigilance committee in Natchez, led by municipal officers, was organized to rid the city of free blacks who had not obtained licenses as the state law of 1831 required. They also examined all the free blacks living in Natchez, and in many instances revoked their permits to reside in the county. Similar action in Vicksburg severely reduced the free black population of that town. Why the alarmed whites focused upon the free blacks was explained by the editor of the Holly Springs *Southern Banner*. "There is no doubt," he wrote, "about the absolute necessity of making every one of them leave the county, and when we get entirely free of them, the main source of communication between the slaves of the South and the Abolitionists will be cut off." As a result of the fear-inspired persecution, many of Mississippi's free blacks were driven from the state and the remainder intimidated.[21]

Soon after the insurrection scare of 1841, the Mississippi legislature in 1842 took action to prevent the number of free blacks in the state from increasing in the future by eliminating the principal means by which slaves became freedmen. In that year the legislature deprived slaveowners of their long-established privilege of emancipating their slaves by will and also made unlawful the common practice of taking slaves into free states for the purpose of emancipating them. After passage of this legislation, slaves could be freed legally in Mississippi only by special act of the state legislature. As this was an expensive and time-consuming process, few owners of slaves bothered to avail themselves of the privilege during the remainder of the antebellum period.[22]

Thus by 1842 free blacks were forbidden to immigrate into Mississippi from other states, and very few slaves could join the ranks of resident blacks by the process of emancipation. Free blacks lived with the constant threat of expulsion from their homes hanging over them, and apparently a good many unfortunates did suffer the penalty of exile. As a result of these adverse forces activated by the whites, the free black population of the

21. Yazoo City *Whig*, August 6, 1841; Holly Springs *Southern Banner and Conservative*, July 9 and August 13, 1841; Hogan and Davis (eds.), *William Johnson's Natchez*, 12–13; James, *Antebellum Natchez*, 179–80; Natchez *Courier*, August 4 and 28, 1841; Natchez *Free Trader*, August 7, 10, 12, and 14, 1841.
22. Hutchinson (comp.), *Code of Mississippi*, 539–40.

state decreased sharply during the 1840s and 1850s. Indeed, the plight of free blacks became so precarious during the last decade of the slavery era that a few even petitioned the state legislature for permission to sell themselves into slavery.[23]

If unskilled whites and free black manual laborers composed the lowest tier of the Mississippi urban social pyramid, town slaves were the stones of its foundation. Although by no means as numerous in proportion to whites as rural slaves, town slaves nevertheless made up a substantial portion of the urban population. In 1860, slaves represented from 32 to 36 percent of the populations of Natchez, Vicksburg, Jackson, and Holly Springs and slightly less than half of the inhabitants of Columbus. Although Richard Wade has ascertained that slavery was declining in the seaboard cities of the South during the later decades of the antebellum period, that trend was not apparent in the census statistics of 1850 and 1860 with respect to the inland towns of Mississippi. Instead the urban slave population there was growing, though not as rapidly as the white population. In the last ten years of the slavery era, to cite a few examples, the number of slaves residing in Natchez rose from 1,511 to 2,132; in Vicksburg, from 1,176 to 1,402; and in Columbus, from 1,222 to 1,590. Despite the prosperity prevailing at that time throughout the Black Belt of Mississippi, slaveowners were definitely not withdrawing slaves in significant numbers from the towns to work in the cotton fields.[24]

In villages and towns of Mississippi, male and female house servants owned or hired by members of the middle and lower middle classes composed a very large portion of the urban blacks. The living conditions of these house servants were unquestionably more favorable than those of tens of thousands of slaves engaged in agriculture and in some respects were preferable to the lot of town slaves employed in other occupations. House servants ordinarily lived together as families in separate quarters on the premises of their owners or employers. Because of their proximity to the whites, urban house servants were furnished housing superior to the facilities that were usually provided for slaves on farms and plantations and to the housing of other town slaves. Because their food was prepared in the same kitchens as their owners' meals and was usually taken

23. Sydnor, "Free Negro in Mississippi," 781.
24. Richard C. Wade, *Slavery in the Cities: The South, 1820–1860* (New York, 1964), 243–46; Beasley, "Blacks," 4–9; Hearn, "Towns in Antebellum Mississippi," 27; *Seventh Census, 1850*, p. 448; *Eighth Census, 1860: Population*, 271.

from the same pots, urban house servants enjoyed diets of higher quality and wider variety than did any other slaves except plantation house servants. Furthermore, they probably received better medical care than did most slaves, being attended by the physicians who treated their employers. Finally, house servants could learn to read and write if they wished to do so. Without doubt, however, the greatest advantage that urban house servants enjoyed over other town slaves was the closest approximation to a normal family life that the institution of slavery permitted. As the censuses of 1850 and 1860 attested, families of urban house servants more often than not included both fathers and mothers. Indeed, these families were seldom matriarchal. On the debit side of the ledger, urban house servants spent more of their waking hours under close supervision by their masters and mistresses and were therefore not able to sample nocturnal black social activities as freely as slaves who lived away from their owners or employers.[25]

In the final analysis, urban house servants as a class were better educated and more steeped in white middle-class culture and religion than were any other town slaves and to that degree were better prepared to take their place in society after 1865 than were most of their fellows. Unfortunately, however, the skills they learned in the households of their owners did not fit them for economic independence as well as the vocational training received by slaves employed by white mechanics.

Male slaves belonging to members of the white urban middle class and to resident planters were often employed outside the households of their owners while their wives worked as domestics. Some worked in the stores or offices of their owners; others were hired out to various kinds of employers in the town. Still others were allowed to hire their own time and to seek employment for themselves. Apparently most of the wagons, carts, and drays used in the larger towns, for example, were operated by slaves who were furnished with teams and vehicles by their owners. These slaves paid their owners a stipulated monthly wage and maintained themselves on the remainder of their earnings.[26]

John Hunter, who belonged to Ayres P. Merrill II, a planter of Adams County, was the best-known and respected slave in Natchez who hired his

25. Manuscript Census Returns, 1860, Adams, Hinds, Lowndes, Madison, Warren, and Yazoo Counties, Schedule 1; Wade, *Slavery in the Cities*, 28–33, 57, 111, 132–35; Beasley, "Blacks," 9–10.
26. Beasley, "Blacks," 11.

own time. For about twenty years, Hunter worked for merchants and professional men in Natchez as a porter, janitor, and handyman, earning an exceptional reputation for industry and trustworthiness. He was employed as a porter by the Agricultural Bank for nearly a decade. Highly trusted by the bank officials, Hunter was often assigned the task of counting gold and silver coins, and in his stay with the bank handled hundreds of thousands of dollars. His planter owner allowed Hunter to find his own employment and required only that the slave pay him a monthly sum. Merrill exercised virtually no authority over Hunter, who conducted his business affairs virtually as a free man. Hunter was very religious, and he assumed the responsibility of providing religious instruction for Merrill's young slaves. Unlike most black preachers of the era, Hunter insisted that his services be conducted with dignity and decorum. Although Merrill repeatedly urged Hunter to withhold part of the wages due his owner to purchase garments appropriate to his respectable position, the black modestly insisted upon wearing plain and inexpensive clothing. Merrill related that Hunter took great pride in never failing to pay his hire in full on the first of each month. When Hunter was an old man, he moved to Memphis with Merrill. He carried with him many glowing recommendations from former employers, and he experienced no difficulty in obtaining jobs in Memphis of the sort to which he was accustomed. When Hunter died in 1859, Merrill wrote a lengthy and detailed biography for the Natchez *Courier*, because the slave known widely as "Uncle John" in his later years had so many white friends in that city.[27]

Skilled black craftsmen and tradesmen made up another numerous and comparatively fortunate category of urban slaves. According to the testimony of W. B. Tebo, editor of the Natchez *Free Trader*, "slaves of the South . . . are our mechanics, carpenters, smiths, wagon and plough makers, sawyers, millers, ginners, etc." On another occasion, Tebo complained that "a man can scarcely get any mechanical job done that is not executed in whole or in part by a 'sable arm.'" In like vein Ingraham commented that the black population of the Mississippi towns included "mechanics, draymen, hostlers, laborers, hucksters, and washwomen, and the heterogeneous multitude of every other occupation, who fill the

27. Natchez *Courier*, February 25, 1859; Kane, *Natchez*, 312–33; Hogan and Davis (eds.), *William Johnson's Natchez*, 777.

streets of a busy city—for slaves are trained to every kind of manual labor." [28]

Such skilled black workmen as blacksmiths, carpenters, brickmasons, house painters, and wheelwrights and ginwrights were usually trained as apprentices by white master craftsmen. Frequently plantation owners selected intelligent young slaves to be bound out for several years to master workmen in order to increase the value of the slaves beyond the level of agricultural workers. For his part of the bargain, the white master craftsman benefited from the slave's labor during the period of indenture at no cost to himself apart from that of the slave's food, clothing, and shelter. At the close of a slave's period of apprenticeship, his owner had several options open to him. He could utilize the slave's newly acquired skills on the plantation, he could hire out the slave artisan at high wages, or he could sell the slave to a master craftsman at a much higher price than a first-class field hand would command. During both the 1830s and the 1850s, slave carpenters and blacksmiths commonly sold for prices ranging from $2,300 to $2,500, whereas field hands were worth between $1,000 and $1,500. According to the editor of the Charleston (South Carolina) *Courier,* an unofficial record was established in 1856 when a carpenter was sold in Adams County, Mississippi, for the sum of $3,700. [29]

In a typical advertisement an Adams County slaveowner offered for sale at auction a journeyman carpenter who had completed an apprenticeship with a white master craftsman. J. R. Stockman, the auctioneer, advertised "a very likely and valuable Negro man, 25 years old, a carpenter by trade, . . . [who] has a chest of tools." [30]

White mechanics were always desirous of acquiring the services of well-trained slaves, preferably by purchase but often by hire. In Ingraham's words, "the Negro is the third arm to every working man who can possibly save money enough to purchase one." The following are two typical examples. In 1858 the executor of the estate of William Purnell, a Natchez carpenter, offered some of his property for sale, including "a negro man named Tom Robinson, a carpenter by trade; a mulatto man slave named William Parker, a carpenter by trade; a negro woman slave

28. Natchez *Free Trader,* January 3 and May 12, 1849; [Ingraham], *South-West,* II, 249.
29. Natchez *Courier,* February 21 and September 28, 1855; Natchez *Free Trader,* October 2, 1855, February 15, 1858; Hogan and Davis (eds.), *William Johnson's Natchez,* 218; Charleston (S.C.) *Courier,* April 12, 1856.
30. Natchez *Free Trader,* April 4, 1849.

named Caroline, a house servant, cook." The slave carpenter, William Parker, was purchased by James S. Johnson during 1858 but ran away from his new owner in 1859. An English master mason, James Brown of Natchez, owned nine male slaves, one female, and eight children.[31]

Master workmen also stood ready to employ plantation carpenters and other skilled black artisans when their services were not needed on the plantation. Indeed, demand for skilled slaves was so consistently strong that George J. Dicks, a saddlemaker and one-time mayor of Natchez, recommended buying slave mechanics for the wages they could earn as an especially lucrative form of investment for surplus capital.[32]

Horace, a slave mechanic who belonged to Robert Jemison, Jr., an Alabama builder who was active in the construction industry in western Alabama and eastern Mississippi, was a notable example of a slave who rose to a responsible position. In Jemison's employ the slave architect designed and constructed bridges, the most important of which was that over the Tombigbee River at Columbus, which he completed in 1845. An earlier project was described by a correspondent of the Columbus (Georgia) *Enquirer* who reported that "the superior Bridge across the Chattahoochee River at Florence, built by 'honest' John Godwin and Horace is now ready for crossing." John Jackson, who belonged to the Weldon brothers, had an equally distinguished career. A draftsman and artist, Jackson drew the plans for many of the public buildings erected by William, George, and Thomas Weldon, including the courthouses still standing at Raymond and Vicksburg, and he painted the drop curtain at the Odd Fellows Hall in Port Gibson. Still another successful slave carpenter was David Rolfe, who belonged to William H. Moss of Corinth. Rolfe gained a reputation among the whites as an exceptionally skilled craftsman and, according to the editor of the *Corinthian Pillar*, "frequently amused himself by criticizing the order of architecture in Corinth." At the extremely advanced age of 114 years, Rolfe constructed a large frame residence for his owner. His death at age 117 was noticed both in the Corinth newspaper and in the Memphis *Eagle*.[33]

Among Mississippi's slave craftsmen, Simon Gray of Natchez had by

31. [Ingraham], *South-West*, II, 249; Natchez *Courier*, November 25 and December 9, 1856, January 5, 1858, September 13 and 28, 1859; Manuscript Census Returns, 1860, Adams County, Schedule 1.

32. Natchez *Courier*, February 13, 1858.

33. Starobin, *Industrial Slavery in the Old South*, 171–72; Vicksburg *Whig*, December 12, 1843; Columbus (Ga.) *Enquirer*, July 15, 1840; Fulkerson, *Early Days in Mississippi*, 130–31; Natchez *Courier*, October 8, 1856.

far the most outstanding career. Trained as a carpenter during his youth, Gray was hired in 1835 by his owner, Andrew Donnan, a blacksmith and merchant, to Andrew Brown, architect, building contractor, and owner of a sawmill. At that time Brown was contracting to build bridges and culverts for towns and counties in the old Natchez District, and he employed Gray on these projects for three years, giving the black workman increasing responsibility as he demonstrated exceptional talents. In the late 1830s, Brown expanded his market by shipping lumber in flatboats from his Natchez sawmill to plantations and towns along the Mississippi River. Instead of hiring a white flatboat captain, Brown placed Gray in charge of a flatboat crew, which took one or two flatboats at a time on what Brown called coasting trips. Soon Gray was not only filling lumber orders but making sales himself, for which he collected large sums of money. He was taught to read and write and cipher by two nephews of Andrew Brown who accompanied him on a downriver trip. Subsequently, Gray kept records and maintained a correspondence with Brown's clerk while away from Natchez. As he proved to be skillful at working mixed crews of whites and blacks, and reliable in his business dealings, Gray became widely respected along the river. When writing Brown, his customers invariably referred to the riverman as Captain Gray.[34]

During the 1850s, Brown gave Gray much broader authority. Gray assumed full charge of transportation of lumber, directing traffic from mills on the Yazoo River with which Brown was doing business as well as carrying the output of the Natchez mill to New Orleans. Brown, in addition, often sent Gray into the Yazoo swamps to buy timber from loggers working along the river and its many tributaries. On these purchasing expeditions, Gray carried very large amounts of cash. For many years he had carried a pass that authorized him to travel anywhere on the Mississippi River or its tributaries, and nothing prevented him from making his way to the North with ample funds in his pocket. Nevertheless, he served Brown to that lumberman's complete satisfaction until 1863. During the confusion generated by Grant's campaign against Vicksburg, which completely disrupted the logging operations in the Yazoo basin that Gray was directing for Brown, the elderly riverman evidently decided to retire. Brown lost contact with him at this time and never

34. Moore, *Andrew Brown*, 83–86; John H. Moore, "Simon Gray, Riverman: A Slave Who Was Almost Free," *Mississippi Valley Historical Review*, XLIX (1962), 472–74.
35. Moore, *Andrew Brown*, 87–92; Moore, "Simon Gray," 476–84.

learned what had happened to him. Thus passed from the scene one of the very few slave business executives of the Old South.[35]

In town, skilled slave craftsmen lived much like white journeymen, although they themselves received far less money for their services than did their white counterparts. Black artisans customarily worked with whites in the same crews, performing the same duties and being required to labor neither more nor less hard than the white wage earners. When a day's work was done, their time became their own until they were due back on the job the following day. As a rule, slave mechanics were fed and lodged in boardinghouses much like those patronized by lower-middle-class whites, the costs of room and board being defrayed by their employers. Of course, these boardinghouses served blacks only; white journeymen lodged in similar establishments that catered to their own race. Unlike most slaves, black artisans usually received a small weekly sum as spending money, and they had many opportunities to earn money in their spare time that they could keep for their own use. It was not at all unusual for owners of responsible skilled black workmen to permit them to hire their own time, although state law and city ordinances forbade this practice. In such cases a slave would pay his owner the monthly wage that his services would command if he were hired to a white employer. The slave craftsman could use for his own purposes such moneys as he could earn by taking on jobs himself above the sum due his owner. Trusted slaves of this kind came close to being free, although their incomes necessarily fell below those of white workmen with similar skills by the amount of the wage paid to the owner.[36]

Slave carpenters apparently often made some spending money for themselves by taking on small jobs for whites in their free time. Incensed by this practice, the editor of the Vicksburg *Whig* reminded the city authorities in 1855 that a city ordinance stated: "It shall not be lawful for any slave, without the written authority of the master or employer, bearing date of the day of such hiring, to go at large and hire himself or herself out, or to make contract for work to be done." The ordinance specified a penalty of five to fifty dollars for the master or employer of a slave violating the provisions of the city law, and a flogging of from five to thirty-nine lashes for the erring slave. Passage of ordinances of this kind always indicated that the forbidden action was an everyday occurrence, and these prohibitions usually had little effect.[37]

36. Sydnor, *Slavery in Mississippi*, 178–80.
37. Vicksburg *Whig*, August 25, 1855.

The similarities between skilled slaves and white journeymen may have extended farther than historians suspect. In imitation of the local white mechanics' society, black craftsmen of Natchez organized a mechanics' association of their own in 1859. When information that blacks had held a formal meeting complete with banquet and speeches reached Tebo, the editor who often spoke out on behalf of white journeymen, he became extremely agitated. Fulminating against "secret gatherings and communings of free blacks and negroes," and their utilizing "signs, grips, tokens, and pass words," Tebo demanded that a state law against assemblages of blacks in greater numbers than five be enforced against the black organization. This mechanics' society may well have been the first black labor organization in the southern United States.[38]

Slaves employed in such industrial enterprises as sawmills, brickyards, carriage, wagon or implement factories, foundries, machine shops, and railroad workshops made up still another important share of the slave populations in such towns as Natchez, Vicksburg, Columbus, and Holly Springs. Some of these industrial slaves belonged to the firms for which they worked, others were owned by individual proprietors, and still others were hired from planters or urban owners. Although some of the industrial slaves may have acquired special skills, most appear from surviving evidence to have been used as manual laborers. Like the skilled artisans of the building trades, industrial slaves were fed and housed in black boardinghouses, and they were seldom bothered by white supervisors when off the job. Having fewer chances to earn money in their free time than the black craftsmen, industrial slaves were probably considered poor customers by proprietors of stores and grogshops who sold to blacks. Furthermore, as women were not used in industrial operations other than textile mills except occasionally as cooks, industrial slaves would not generally have been able to have a family, and they probably found female companionship hard to obtain. Most of the industrial slaves were called upon to perform strenuous labor, although white laborers on the same jobs worked just as hard as the slaves. Although we know little about their views of industrial employment, they apparently did not often ask their owners to return them to the plantation. Their relatively free nightly social life in the towns seems to have more than compensated the slaves for the heavy labor required of them in the mills and workshops.[39]

38. Natchez *Free Trader*, April 14, 1859.
39. Moore, *Andrew Brown*, 133–48.

Other unskilled slaves employed as stevedores on the wharves, manual laborers in the lumberyards and warehouses, and those in other pursuits requiring only physical strength, lived much as did the industrial slaves. Although they enjoyed few comforts and had almost no chance of bettering their lot, they nevertheless preferred town to country life.

Outside the towns, white society in Mississippi was content to leave the responsibility for regulating the conduct of slaves to slaveowners and their employees. Minor violations of state laws, breaches of plantation discipline, and failures to observe the established rules of etiquette with respect to members of the white ruling class were generally dealt with by plantation owners and their overseers rather than by officials of local or state government. By and large this neofeudal arrangement worked well enough to satisfy the whites. Consequently, county and state governments did not become unduly involved in the disciplining of rural blacks. To be sure, the state maintained the militia to suppress slave uprisings, and the counties sent out patrols at night to apprehend blacks who had left the farms or plantations of their owners without permission. But neither state nor county took much interest in slaves who remained on the property of their owners. Although state law prescribed flogging and branding for slave felons, in practice punishment of rural lawbreakers was left to the owners, unless the crimes in question were capital offenses. By the same token, slaves convicted of even serious crimes were not confined in the state penitentiary, which was reserved exclusively for white malefactors. In all probability, most slave criminals were carried by their owners to distant points and sold to unwary buyers instead of being punished like white lawbreakers. White victims of slave crimes obtained compensation by suing the slaveowners for damages in the civil courts. A situation this curious to modern observers could exist without essential change for many decades only because the plantation system effectively separated most of the rural whites from the agricultural black population.[40]

In town such insulation of the whites from frequent contact with blacks was impossible. Wherever they went, whites encountered blacks—on the streets and wharves, in the stores, cafes, hotels, and saloons—for white urban society was thoroughly permeated by slaves. Furthermore, the slaves whom white visitors and residents saw in large numbers, not being under anyone's direct supervision, were less deferential to strange whites

40. Sydnor, *Slavery in Mississippi*, 83–85.

than were plantation blacks. Indeed, newspapers of the last three decades of the antebellum era were filled with complaints about the impoliteness of slaves in the towns. From time to time even bitterer remarks appeared in the press referring to the unrestrained nocturnal activities of slaves and free blacks. According to editors and their correspondents, free blacks and slaves habitually congregated in groggeries and cheap groceries where whiskey was sold to them illegally. There they caroused noisily far into the night, disturbing the slumber of white citizens. Drunken blacks staggering through the streets annoyed whites and sometimes caused them to fear for their lives. All too often slaves seeking to obtain something of value to trade for whiskey committed thefts, burglaries, and many other petty crimes. In 1854, for instance, the editor of the Natchez *Courier* inveighed against "prowling negroes whose principal interest is the hen roost, but who manage to pick up and carry off every thing else that they can easily lay their hands on." Possibly even more criminal in the eyes of this editor were blacks who stole copies of the *Courier* for sale to "persons in this city generally considered respectable." His temper really reached a boiling point a few months later when the city marshal raided a "nest of crime and beastiality," arresting several male slaves and two white females. The blacks were severely flogged, but the white women were merely jailed as vagrants by frustrated city officials who scarcely knew how to deal with miscegenation of this type.[41]

Fairly early in the nineteenth century it became apparent that a system for disciplining slaves that worked very well on farms and plantations was not effective in towns of even moderate size. To a degree, urban slaveowners were able to control the conduct of house servants who lived and worked on their property. Proprietors of sawmills, woodworking shops, brickyards, cotton compresses, and other establishments using large slave labor forces that worked under the direct supervision of white employees were also able to enforce discipline among their black workers but only during working hours. After dark the slave laborers in these establishments scattered throughout the poorer parts of town where they resided, not to be seen by their employers or their white assistants until the next working day. Meanwhile the conduct of the slaves was left to their own discretion. Similarly, many other employers of slaves in towns were unable to supervise them very closely even during working hours because of the nature of their employment. Adding to the problem, many

41. Natchez *Courier*, June 14 and September 20, 1854.

blacks from surrounding farms and plantations came into town every day on errands for their owners, and still more slipped into town at night without asking anyone's permission. After nightfall, almost all of the town blacks—with the possible exception of some house servants—were virtually able to come and go as they pleased.

As concern over lack of discipline among urban blacks infected white residents of the towns and rural whites who transacted business in towns, both the state government and many town governments began to intervene. In large part, the resulting state laws and municipal ordinances were intended to compel slaveowners and employers to fulfill their responsibilities to white society with regard to slaves in their charge. Often, however, slaveowners refused to observe either the spirit or the letter of those portions of the black code that pertained to slavery in the towns. After the law of 1842 made emancipation of slaves all but impossible, for example, some slaveholders who would have liked to free certain slaves did the next best thing—they allowed favored slaves to live and work in town as though they were free. Many others permitted trustworthy blacks to reside in town and find employment for themselves, privileges for which the blacks paid their owners part of their earnings. Still others allowed slaves with mercantile talents to purchase fish, game, fowl, meat, eggs, and vegetables that they peddled to white townsfolk, sharing their profits in some cases with the owners and in other cases keeping all the proceeds for themselves.

Because all of these practices by rural slaveowners resulted in swelling urban black populations with slaves for whom no one was immediately answerable, the state legislature passed laws prohibiting slaveholders from extending such privileges to their slaves. Fines ranging from twenty to fifty dollars were decreed for each instance in which an owner allowed a slave to live as a free man, or to hire himself out, or to engage in trade. Believing that the most serious threat to public safety in the towns arose from slaves' being permitted to roam about at night, the legislators passed an act requiring that all slaves residing in towns be housed on the lot containing the house of the owner or employer or else on a lot adjacent to the owner's residence. Persons failing to obey this law were subject to exceptionally severe fines ranging from two hundred to a thousand dollars for each offense.[42]

42. Natchez *Free Trader*, October 18, 1858; *Revised Code of the Statute Laws of Mississippi*.

As was true for almost all legislation connected with the institution of slavery, slaveowners ignored these state laws with impunity. In Natchez, for example, Andrew Donnan permitted his slave, Simon Gray, to live as a free man without hindrance from the authorities. While employed in Andrew Brown's lumber company, Gray traveled wherever he wished, purchased timber and sold lumber for his employer, carried on business ventures of his own, learned to read with one of Brown's nephews as a tutor, and owned and used firearms. In short, Gray's owner and his employer both daily violated each of the state's restrictions without once being called to account for their actions. To be sure, Brown was a very influential citizen, being the largest manufacturer and slaveowner in Natchez, as well as being one of the town's wealthiest residents and a sometime member of the city council. Yet there is no evidence to suggest that his immunity from prosecution was in any way exceptional. Juries of slaveowners simply could not be expected to convict one of their own. Consequently, state laws reducing the rights of slaveowners to deal with their blacks as they saw fit were unenforceable. Similarly, the state found it easier to regulate free blacks than slaves who had the protection of powerful slaveowners behind them.[43]

Because state law was ineffective in dealing with the root cause of black misconduct in the towns, a refusal by many slaveowners to restrict their slaves to their premises, municipalities enacted ordinances intended to supply discipline that slaveowners were neglecting or refusing to enforce. Towns, for example, commonly imposed nine o'clock curfews on all blacks who did not have written permission to be abroad after that hour and required nonresident slaves to leave the city limits before nightfall. Slaves without passes who fell into the hands of watchmen patrolling the streets at night were arrested, jailed, and brought before the city magistrate. Usually a curfew violator received the customary thirty-nine lashes on his bare back unless his owner or employer chose to pay a fine for him instead. Brown, for one, always paid fines without protest whenever any of his slaves were arrested for curfew violations, and he never tried to prevent his black workers from going about at night. Consequently, Brown's blacks were hardly inconvenienced by curfew ordinances of the river towns. Although, to be sure, Brown was an unusually indulgent owner and employer of slaves, there is no reason to believe that other em-

43. Moore, *Andrew Brown*, 83–92; Moore, "Simon Gray," 472–84.

ployers of hired blacks were significantly stricter with their employees during off-duty hours.[44]

According to the editor of the Natchez *Courier*, Brown was by no means the only slaveowner or employer in the city who refused to restrict the movements of his slaves after working hours. He complained about a "practice now becoming very common of giving permission to slaves (particularly females) to hire their own time; a means by which they contrive to appropriate three-fourths of their time to idle prowling about the city." He reminded the city authorities that permitting slaves to violate the curfew was illegal. "There is a law on this subject," the journalist fulminated, "and it is the duty of somebody to enforce it."[45]

In addition to complaining about the nocturnal social activities of slaves, some white townspeople objected to slaves being allowed by their owners or employers to buy and sell foodstuffs within the city limits. In all of the urban centers of Mississippi, slaves from neighboring farms and plantations supplied the municipal markets with most of the fish, game, fowl, eggs, butter, fruit, and vegetables sold there. In some cases, planters and farmers sent slaves to town to sell products of their poultry yards, dairies, and vegetable gardens for them. In others, the slaves disposed of fish they had caught or chickens, eggs, and vegetables they had raised themselves with their owners' consent. In both instances, the rural slaves who brought fresh foodstuffs to market provided townsmen with a useful service to which no one objected. Other town slaves, however, were shrewd enough to become middlemen in the local commerce in fresh foodstuffs. Slave entrepreneurs waylaid slaves from the plantations on the way to market in order to purchase their goods from them at relatively low prices. Then the enterprising town slaves hawked their wares in the streets, selling to house servants or white housewives at prices somewhat higher than those charged in the municipal market. Busy housewives preferred to pay slightly more at their door rather than waste time on daily visits to the market. Consequently the trade of the slaves cut deeply into the business of the markets.

In 1858 the editor of the Natchez *Free Trader* charged that slave ped-

---

44. Beasley, "Blacks," 17–25; Hearn, "Towns of Mississippi," 29; [Ingraham], *South-West*, II, 72; McCain, *Story of Jackson*, I, 176–78; Moore, *Andrew Brown*, 141.

45. Natchez *Courier*, September 7, 1838.

dlers were actually controlling prices of fresh food in his city. Fresh fish originally sold by fishermen at twenty-five cents per string were vended by slave peddlers at prices ranging from thirty to forty-five cents. "One Negro woman's 'say so' controls the butter market," he noted angrily. "To her black majesty's nod all bow or go without buttered bread." The commerce in chickens, ducks, and geese was similarly dominated by only four or five slaves. According to the newspaperman, the price of meat alone was free from slave control.[46]

The situation in Natchez described by the editor of the *Free Trader* had continued to exist for many years despite efforts of the city councilmen to outlaw buying and selling by town slaves. The city code held that "it is not lawful to . . . purchase any article of provisions on the way to market and within the city limits, or to persuade any one to desist from attending market with provisions, or to enhance the price thereof." The code also forbade the resale within ten days of articles purchased in the municipal market. Slaves violating the ordinances were upon conviction to be whipped, and free blacks were to be fined. As these ordinances were not enforced, they may be taken merely as evidence of common activities on the part of city blacks about which some whites complained.[47]

Similarly, city ordinances prohibiting free blacks and whites from selling to slaves testify that a great many whites were willing to do business with those slaves who had money or valuables to sell. State laws and city ordinances were powerless to suppress the purchase of whiskey by slaves, for example. According to a correspondent of the Natchez *Courier*, "hundreds of Negroes are nightly drunk in consequence of the attention paid to them by the grogshops on the roads leading out of Natchez." If the practice continued, he warned, keepers of shops selling whiskey or brandy to slaves would be dealt with unpleasantly by a vigilance committee.[48]

In similar spirit, a flatboatman selling liquor to slaves near Vicksburg was given ten hours to leave the vicinity by a "delegation of gentlemen." In Macon, whites organized a vigilance committee to prevent "all loose and improper traffic both amongst the Negroes themselves and between them and white persons." In another instance the editor of the Jackson *Mississippian* in 1841 attacked "several Negro doggeries" where "Negroes of this city and neighborhood congregate by the hundreds . . . to

46. Natchez *Free Trader*, October 18, 1858.
47. *Ibid.*, October 18, 1858.
48. Natchez *Courier*, August 13, 1840.

carouse . . . and where they are fast being corrupted and made worthless to their owners." As usual in such cases, the editor suggested that a vigilance committee rid the town of the erring tavern keepers, having no faith in the official agencies of law enforcement.[49]

Free blacks and slaves in the towns were fond of gambling in their spare time and usually combined their games of chance with drinking bouts on nights of the weekend. Apprehending slaves engaged in these pastimes was the principal duty and pleasure of city night watchmen, but the task of the policemen was made difficult by assistance given to the slaves by some lower-class whites. Quite often pretty shopkeepers who surreptitiously vended whiskey to slaves also provided quarters for their black customers in which they could gamble, drink, and dance. In a case of this kind, a keeper of a Vicksburg beer parlor was brought before the mayor's court charged with allowing ten blacks to gamble in his establishment. The slaves were flogged, and the white punished with a fine.[50]

Occasionally the ire of the white community fell upon a lower-class white who was consorting openly with blacks of the opposite sex. In such a case, a Vicksburg vigilance committee warned William Dollins (also known as Bill Dollar) that if he did not cease to live with a black woman he would "fare roughly" at their hands. Yet similar conduct by a middle-class slaveowner would not have been brought to public attention, although it would have met with silent disapproval.[51]

In Jackson, white distaste for slaves congregating together in the town at night took an extreme form in 1860. On April 6 of that year the city board of aldermen enacted an ordinance designed to prevent slaves who had obtained passes from their masters to go to church from going somewhere else instead. This ordinance was aimed primarily at some blacks who belonged to members of the Methodist church. For reasons that are not clear, the white Methodist congregation had erected a separate building on their lot for their slaves. Thereafter, the black Methodists conducted their own religious services apart from the whites. This "African Methodist Church" was the forerunner of many black churches that split off from parent white churches after Emancipation. Maintaining that the new city ordinance would break up the African Methodist church and

49. Vicksburg *Whig*, January 2, 1861; Natchez *Courier*, September 7, 1838; Jackson *Mississippian*, September 23, 1846.
50. Vicksburg *Whig*, October 31 and November 27, 1860.
51. *Ibid.*, January 2, 1861.

would greatly inconvenience the membership of the white Methodist church, a delegation of white Methodists successfully protested the action of the board of aldermen. On the understanding that a white who was designated officially by the white Methodist church would attend every meeting of the black Methodist congregation, the aldermen repealed their ordinance on April 20, 1860. After the city ordinance was revoked, the black Methodists had only to abide by a state law that required slaves attending meetings at night to have passes from their masters. In this case, as in so many others, slaveowners were able to assert their rights with regard to their slaves against the general white public interest.[52]

Protected in this fashion from enforcement of restrictive city and state laws by jealousy of slaveowners for their prerogatives, town slaves largely escaped regulation of their conduct by public officials. Generally speaking, what an owner or employer permitted a slave to do he could do in defiance of elected officials. Inasmuch as owners of town slaves allowed their blacks considerable latitude when their services were not required, these slaves were able to enjoy themselves in a fashion unknown to plantation slaves. They were able to congregate in gatherings ranging from "darkey balls," described by William Johnson in his diary, to gambling parties in vacant warehouses, homes of free blacks, or saloons operated by friendly whites.

Even as town slaves enjoyed more forms of recreation than did their rural fellows, so could they turn to crime more profitably than could blacks on the farms and plantations. On plantations slaves seldom had an opportunity to steal anything of value other than cotton or foodstuffs. In town, however, there were many houses, stores, and warehouses to be burglarized, many pockets to be picked, and drays hauling goods between wharves and warehouses to be looted. In larger urban centers such as Natchez, Vicksburg, and Columbus, petty crimes against property were commonplace, and the culprits were seldom caught. Crimes committed by blacks against the persons of whites, on the other hand, were quite rare, for punishment was certain to be extremely severe. Black thieves, however, obviously received ready cooperation from a lawless element among the whites because such whites purchased stolen articles from them and sold them whiskey and other things that the blacks desired.

52. McCain, *Story of Jackson*, I, 191–92.

Many town slaves probably committed crimes because of their resentment against their condition of bondage as much as because they felt the urge to slake their thirst or fill their pockets. Arson, a very common crime that brought no direct profit to the criminal, was apparently committed in many cases by slaves seeking revenge for real or fancied wrongs. Hardly a town or village went for as much as a decade without experiencing major conflagrations in its business district. Although many of these fires undoubtedly were started accidentally, a common suspicion among the whites that slaves had deliberately set the fires was often justified. On numerous occasions the city authorities or volunteer firemen found evidence of igniting devices and inflammables in burned buildings, or in buildings that had somehow failed to catch fire. This occurrence was so common, in fact, that newspapers customarily closed their accounts of fires with a stock phrase "The fire is believed to have been started by incendiaries," as arsonists were then called. Of course, some cases of arson may have involved burglars who fired the building to cover their crimes, but others were apparently pointless, unless revenge was the motive. To be sure, some mentally unbalanced whites may have set fires for the excitement, but a large proportion of the incidents were the work of disgruntled and frustrated slaves.

Although rural slaves were able to express their resentment against the institution of slavery by running away, most of their absences were of short duration. Lacking money, credentials, and knowledge of geography, and usually being illiterate, field hands had almost no chance of making their way to the free states of the upper Mississippi Valley without outside assistance. Urban slaves, however, were far better equipped to make a serious break for freedom. Many of them had learned to read and write and consequently could manufacture passes or even forge free papers. Quite a few possessed skills in demand, which permitted them to support themselves while making the long journey to the North. Furthermore, skilled urban blacks were not closely supervised as a rule, so they could be away for several days before being missed. Perhaps even more important when planning an escape, town slaves had detailed knowledge of the river transportation system that allowed them to stow away on vessels bound upriver. In all probability most of the slaves who managed to escape from Mississippi to a northern state made the journey on one or more riverboats. Whites suspected with apparent justification that crewmen on steamboats would hide a runaway slave on board if they were offered a sufficiently large bribe. They even suspected that some steamboat captains were guilty of taking fugitive slaves aboard in order to work them without wages. In any event, some town slaves did succeed in making their way to freedom.[53]

Richard Wade's theory that slavery was breaking down in large southern cities during the late antebellum period appears to have been valid also for the larger towns of Mississippi. Although the number of slaves employed in these towns were obviously increasing as the need for black labor continued to grow, employers of these slaves found it less and less expedient to impose on them the controls that were the essence of the system of slavery. In order to obtain the cooperation from a slave that was necessary if a job was to be accomplished profitably, urban employers had to reward the worker with relaxed discipline, privileges unknown to plantation slaves, and even payment of a nominal wage. These forces working to render urban slavery obsolete were too great to be overcome by the opposition of municipal authorities or even by the power of the state. As a result, urban slaves were existing in a condition midway between slavery and freedom when the Civil War put an end to the institution. Furthermore, employment in the towns had prepared urban blacks for freedom in a fashion unknown to the agricultural world. They knew how to earn a living for themselves in a wage economy and were also ready to enter political life when the chance afforded. From this group many successful black politicians emerged during the period of Reconstruction. Just as European towns in the Middle Ages had been alien to medieval society and subversive of its institutions, so were the towns of Mississippi inimical to the perpetuation of the restraints of slavery.[54]

53. For an example of a skilled, literate town slave who made good his escape to Canada, see John H. Moore (ed.), "A Letter from a Fugitive Slave," *Journal of Mississippi History*, XXIV (1962), 99–101; Moore, *Andrew Brown*, 147–48; Sydnor, *Slavery in Mississippi*, 109–110.
54. Beasley, "Blacks," 18–24; Wade, *Slavery in the Cities*, 242–81.

12 Secession from the Union

Between 1795 and 1860 the inhabitants of the Old Southwest developed a mature agricultural economy based upon production of a single commercial crop—cotton—using slave-worked plantations that remarkably resembled contemporary factories. During the final two decades of the antebellum period, southwesterners sought prosperity by concentrating their efforts upon improving the efficiency of their one-crop system, whereas the people of the older southeastern province of the Cotton Kingdom were traveling a different path by diversifying their agriculture with grains and fruits and by erecting factories. While trying to produce ever cheaper and more abundant cotton, the people of the Old Southwest developed superior prolific varieties of their staple, improved their methods of cultivation, and devised more effective methods of organizing and directing slave labor. At the same time, they significantly reduced the cost of their product by rendering their plantations almost self-sufficient in foodstuffs and clothing. Moreover, during the 1840s and 1850s, cotton growers materially increased the acreage under cultivation by invading Arkansas and Missouri, by constructing railroads through regions in the already settled states that were not adequately served by water transportation, and by clearing more land on existing farms and plantations. During the last decade of the prewar era, Arkansas added 1,151,506 cultivated acres; Louisiana, 1,144,876 acres; Mississippi, 1,705,650 acres; Tennessee, 1,722,744 acres; and Alabama, 2,027,873 acres. Missouri brought 3,308,446 acres under cultivation during this period, but only a small portion of these lands located in the southeastern part of the state were planted in cotton.[1]

Because of the new lands brought under the plow and because of improvements in farming methods, the crops of cotton shipped to market through New Orleans increased to immense size during the last half of the decade of the 1850s. Between the crop years 1844–1845 and 1859–1860, exports from New Orleans rose from 900,000 bales of 400 pounds to 2.2 million bales. Mobile, drawing upon Alabama and eastern Mississippi, also shipped 500,000 to 600,000 bales each year during the 1850s. According to the *Annual Report* of the New Orleans *Price Current, Com-*

---

1. *Preliminary Report on the Eighth Census, 1860* (Washington, D.C., 1860), 196.

mercial Intelligencer, and Merchants' Transcript, the total amount of cotton shipped from all American ports during the crop year running from September 1, 1860, to September 1, 1861, was 3.5 million bales. In this period exports from the port of New Orleans amounted to 1,915,852 bales, or 55 percent of the whole crop. Figures for the preceding 1859–1860 crop year provided by the U.S. census were both more detailed and more accurate than those published by the New Orleans *Price Current.* According to the census of 1860, the total American crop for the 1859–1860 crop year was 5,387,052 bales, the largest crop of the entire era of slavery. The states of the lower Mississippi Valley—Missouri, Arkansas, Louisiana, Tennessee, and Mississippi—between them produced 2,685,290 bales, and Alabama, the other state of the Old Southwest, contributed an additional 989,955 bales. The southeastern portion of the Cotton Kingdom—Virginia, North Carolina, South Carolina, Georgia, and Florida—had fallen far behind the Old Southwest. The combined crops of these states were a mere 1,278,646 bales, barely more than the 1,202,507-bale crop of Mississippi. Texas, with 431,463 bales, furnished most of the remainder of that year's giant crop.[2]

During the last two decades of the antebellum period, Mississippi was the South's foremost cotton-producing state, having pulled ahead of Georgia at least as early as the crop year of 1839–1840. Georgia temporarily surpassed Mississippi in 1849–1850, a year in which adverse weather in the lower Mississippi Valley reduced the exports of cotton from New Orleans to less than 850,000 bales. By the last year of the decade of the 1850s, however, Georgia, which had increased the acreage under cultivation by 1,684,279 acres, had nevertheless dropped back to fourth place in cotton production, behind Mississippi, Alabama, and Louisiana. On the credit side of the ledger, Georgia had emerged in that period as the Lower South's leader both in industrialization and in diversification of crops and was already known by its present title, the Peach State, because of its extensive commercial fruit orchards.[3]

In the Old Southwest the slave-plantation system pioneered by plant-

2. New Orleans *Price Current, Commercial Intelligencer, and Merchants' Transcript,* May 20, 1854, August 25, 1855, August 7, 1858, and September 1, 1866; *Eighth Census, 1860: Agriculture,* xciv.

3. *Sixth Census, 1840,* p. 359; *Seventh Census, 1850,* p. lxxxii; *Eighth Census, 1860: Agriculture,* xciv, 185; New Orleans *Price Current,* August 25, 1855; *Preliminary Report on the Eighth Census,* 196; Bonner, *Georgia Agriculture.*

ers of the old Natchez District was phenomenally successful from the late 1790s through the 1820s, and the wealth amassed by some of the early river planters was in large part responsible for touching off a land rush of epic proportions into Alabama and Mississippi during the 1830s when the federal government offered former lands of the Creek, Cherokee, Choctaw, and Chickasaw Indians for sale. During the boom, which lasted from 1833 to 1837, the flood of immigrants seeking cotton lands greatly enlarged the domain of the Cotton Kingdom in the Old Southwest, and most of the newcomers purchased land and slaves on credit. As a class, the new immigrants, being encumbered by debts, were precariously situated financially when the avalanche of cotton from the freshly opened lands flooded the cotton markets at a time when Great Britain was already experiencing overproduction in its textile industry. The soaring cotton prices of the 1830s turned sharply downward during the 1839–1840 crop year and continued to plummet until much of the crop of the Old Southwest was sold for less than four cents per pound in 1843–1844. During these years hosts of indebted owners of land and slaves were ruined, and the continued existence of the slave-plantation system of growing cotton was itself placed in doubt. Slaves were not paying for themselves, and cotton could not be raised profitably at that low level under the existing system of farming. Anyone who advanced the theory so popular during the late 1850s that cotton was king of the economic world would have been hooted down or perhaps even been physically assaulted. The very institution of slavery tottered during the early 1840s as its economic foundations appeared to collapse. Miraculously, however, the slave-worked cotton plantation as a basic economic unit revived almost overnight, and with its recovery slavery regained its former economic value. The social value of slavery as the only means of preserving white supremacy, it should be noted, was never questioned in this crisis as it had been in Virginia in 1831. Desperate planters facing financial ruin introduced changes in their basic farming methods during the depths of the depression that were so far-reaching as to constitute an agricultural revolution, and against heavy odds they succeeded in saving their system. By the late 1840s, planters were making money once again at levels of cotton prices that they had formerly regarded as ruinous. By 1852, their agricultural innovations had so improved the efficiency of cotton plantations that the remainder of the decade became the most productive and profitable years for the producers of cotton in the history of the Cotton Kingdom. In the words of Congressman Reuben Davis of Mississippi, "the wealth of the people was increasing rapidly, and the land seemed to be basking in God's benediction."[4]

Ironically, the very success of the agricultural revolution in coping with the decade-long depression was to prove ultimately disastrous for the southern people. In fact, the prosperity generated by innovations introduced into agriculture paved the way for not one but two catastrophes that were to afflict the South almost simultaneously.

The first of these disasters was that eternal foe of American agriculture—overproduction. Huge cotton crops produced in the American South between 1855 and 1861 outpaced the international demand and filled the warehouses of the South's principal customer, Great Britain, to overflowing, although this momentous development was overlooked at the time by economists on both sides of the Atlantic. The size of the carryover of cotton was so large that it would inevitably have seriously reduced cotton prices over the next few years even if the output of the cotton states had not continued to grow. Even more ominous for the future of southern cotton growers, other countries, such as Egypt, India, China, Brazil, and Russia, were beginning to export cotton in competition with the United States. The combination of very large crops in the American South with the emergence of foreign suppliers had already begun to reduce cotton prices even before the Civil War. Cotton prices reached their peak for the decade on the New York market at 13.5 cents per pound during 1857 and then declined to 12.25 cents in 1858, to 12.0 cents in 1859, and then dropped to 11.0 cents in 1860. Secession of the cotton states in the winter of 1860–1861 followed by the outbreak of hostilities soon afterward checked the continued decline in cotton prices by disrupting the normal flow of southern cotton to overseas customers. By creating artificial shortages the Civil War temporarily reversed the downward trend of international cotton prices and held them at very high levels until 1868, when the new fundamentals of the international cotton market asserted themselves. The postwar depression, which began in the Cotton South at that time and lasted until the turn of the twentieth century, was the result much less of changes wrought by military defeat than

4. Moore, *Agriculture*; McLemore (ed.), *History of Mississippi*, I, 310–50; Reuben Davis, *Recollections of Mississippi and Mississippians* (Boston, 1891), 374.

of worldwide overproduction of the staple that had been the South's monopoly for the first half of the nineteenth century.[5]

The other catastrophe afflicting the South during the second half of the nineteenth century was, of course, the Civil War. Although the breakup of the United States was the result of convergence of many forces, southerners in the cotton states themselves made the crucial decision to take their states out of the Union, and it was from that choice that subsequent military, social, political, and economic disasters resulted.

The leaders of the white ruling class in the Lower South made that fateful decision mainly because they had regained confidence in the slave-worked cotton plantation that was the basic unit in their socioeconomic system. Although the cotton growers of the Lower South were only just beginning to emerge from a decade of depression that had shaken their society to the core, they demonstrated in the political crisis of 1850–1851 that a majority in every southern state lacked sufficient confidence in themselves and in their institutions to undertake a revolution. During the controversy over the admission of California into the Union as a free state, the whites in every state rejected the leadership of secessionists who proclaimed that southerners could preserve their prosperity and the institution of slavery only by forming a new slaveowning nation of their own. Even though secessionist spokesmen warned convincingly that slavery could be abolished by constitutional amendment in their lifetime with votes of new free states to be created from the territory seized from Mexico, the majority of whites in the Lower South voted to accept that risk when they cast their ballots for political candidates who supported the Compromise of 1850.[6]

Even in Mississippi, where the secessionists enjoyed almost as much popular support as in South Carolina, the day was carried by a combination of Whigs and Democrats who wished to preserve the Union. In the crucial race the two U.S. senators, Henry S. Foote and Jefferson Davis, were pitted against each other in a race for the governorship, with secession of the state as the basic issue. Foote, who supported the Compro-

5. Gray, *Agriculture*, II, 1026–27; Phillips, *American Negro Slavery*, 370.
6. John H. Moore, "Economic Conditions in Mississippi on the Eve of the Civil War," *Journal of Mississippi History*, XXII (1960), 167–78; Holman Hamilton, *Prologue to Conflict: The Crisis and Compromise* (Lexington, Ky., 1964), 184–86.

mise of 1850 and based his campaign on preservation of the Union, won over Davis, the hero of the battle of Buena Vista and a moderate secessionist. Foote's triumph first over the ultrasecessionist governor and war hero John A. Quitman, who abandoned the race for reelection when he saw that the cause of secession was failing, and then over an even more popular war hero, Davis, who had taken Quitman's place as the Democratic candidate, was an extraordinary anomaly in a state that revered military valor and usually rewarded it with political office.[7]

Ten years later, the electorates of Mississippi and six other cotton-producing states reversed that antisecession decision, although the issues were essentially the same as in 1850. What had changed was the economic climate in the Cotton Kingdom. Farmers, planters, lumbermen, merchants, construction workers, and manufacturers were all enjoying an unprecedented prosperity, and as is usual in booms they all expected these good times to continue indefinitely. In Mississippi, farmers as well as planters were enjoying prosperity, and they fully shared in the planters' overconfidence in the cotton economy. Filled with defiance toward northern critics of slavery and of southern patriotism, for example, a Mississippi small farmer trumpeted in the *Southern Cultivator*: "I am a full-blooded Southern Rights man, and anything reflecting injuriously on the South fires my blood." "We have resources within ourselves," he proclaimed, "to study and practice not only agriculture but arts and sciences without the aid of any other part of the world. Our soil will grow every article which we really need. . . . Let us live within ourselves and knuckle to no power on earth." Senator Albert G. Brown, of that same state, was a spokesman for the upward-mobile farmers and small planters. During the 1850s his message to his constituents was that "neither Old England nor New England will make war on us—our cotton bags are our bonds of peace." Reuben Davis, the U.S. congressman from Mississippi, warned that an interruption of the flow of cotton fiber from the southern states "would produce a shock from which the monetary affairs of the world would not recover in the five hundred years, . . . [and] the operatives of the free states would be left without employment, and

7. McLemore (ed.), *History of Mississippi*, I, 302–306; Cleo Hearon, "Mississippi and the Compromise of 1850," Mississippi Historical Society *Publications*, XIV (1914), 200–215; Robert E. May, *John A. Quitman: Old South Crusader* (Baton Rouge, 1985), 253–64.

would see their country reduced to a state of ruin which no imagination can portray." [8]

In those exhilarating days of large crops and favorable prices for cotton during the later 1850s, no one warned of the dangers of overproduction of the staple, although many had done so during the 1837–1845 period. Instead, political, intellectual, and economic leaders focused their attention upon those evils that the federal government might perpetrate upon the people of the South if it were to fall under the domination of northern antislavery forces. Furthermore, many articles published in the English press during the 1850s led southerners to believe that a new proslavery republic would have powerful allies in the nations that purchased southern cotton. The following comment appearing in the London *Cotton Supply Reporter* during 1860 represented informed English public opinion: "If war should at any time break out between England and America, or . . . the cotton crop fall short . . . our mills would be stopped for want of cotton, employers would be ruined, and famine would stalk abroad among the hundreds and thousands of work people." So common was this thesis that it became the cliché: "Grass will grow in the streets, if . . ." [9]

Senator Jefferson Davis of Mississippi, who had inherited the mantle of John C. Calhoun and who was soon to head the government of the ill-starred Confederate States of America, was a devout believer in the theory "Cotton is King." During the late 1850s he wrote on one occasion: "Cotton wraps the commercial world and binds it . . . in bonds to keep the peace with us which no Government dare break." His conviction, which ultimately proved fatal for the Confederacy, was that the cotton-growing states "united . . . will have ample power for their own protection, and their exports will make them allies of all the commercial and manufacturing powers." In Davis' case, the extraordinary financial success of his elder brother, Joseph E. Davis, as a cotton planter on Davis Bend in Warren County, had undoubtedly given him an exaggerated respect for the slave-worked cotton plantation as an economic unit and for

8. *Southern Cultivator*, XVIII (1860), 154; M. W. Clusky (ed.), *Speeches, Messages and Other Writings of the Hon. Albert G. Brown* (Philadelphia, 1859), 597; Reuben Davis, *Speech of the Hon. Reuben Davis, of Mississippi, on the State of the Union, in the House of Representatives, December 22, 1858* (Washington, D.C., 1858), 4–5.

9. London *Cotton Supply Reporter*, February 3, 1860.

the cotton-based economy of the South. In any event, Davis was to stake the success of the Confederacy upon a belief that England and France would be forced to come to the aid of the southerners in order to obtain cotton. Davis' gamble might well have succeeded had not English stocks of cotton been built to an all-time high by the enormous crops of 1857–1858 through 1860–1861. Because of the overproduction of those years, the mills of Great Britain had ample time to locate other sources of raw material before they were forced to suspend operations. Consequently Britain was not compelled to use its navy to break the Union blockade of the Confederate ports, and the Confederacy was unable to defeat the United States without outside assistance.[10]

In retrospect we can see that the river planters of Mississippi played a starring role in the history of the Old Southwest. They first provided the agricultural leadership that made an astonishing economic success of the southwestern Cotton Kingdom. Then, as a consequence of that success, they became largely responsible for preparing the way for the secession of the states of the lower Mississippi Valley. Although most of the established large planters of the state opposed secession, a coterie of large planters appealing to the fears and ambitions of farmers and small planters succeeded in leading their state out of the Union. Representatives of the newly rich planter class, notably John A. Quitman and Jefferson Davis, were able to override the opposition of such members of the older great planter class as Stephen Duncan, and under their influence the state legislature and a constitutional convention determined to take Mississippi out of the Union even before John Brown's raid into Virginia strengthened the secessionist cause. Finally, in the person of President Jefferson Davis, the Mississippi river planters led the Confederacy to final defeat and destruction of southern society. Thus because of the river planters of Mississippi the history of the antebellum Southwest became a modern version of a classic Greek tragedy. The gods, made jealous by the success of the great planters, filled these mortals' minds with delusion and pride so that they destroyed themselves and their society by their own misguided efforts.[11]

10. Clement Eaton, *Jefferson Davis* (New York, 1977), 167; Dunbar Rowland (ed.), *Jefferson Davis, Constitutionalist: His Papers, Letters, and Speeches* (Jackson, Miss., 1923), IV, 257, 542; Henry Blumenthal, "Confederate Diplomacy: Popular Notions and International Realities," *Journal of Southern History*, XXXII (1966), 152–56; Emory M. Thomas, *The Confederate Nation, 1861–1865* (New York, 1979), 174–75.

11. I. A. Newby, *The South: A History* (New York, 1978), 229–30.

Appendix A

Taxable Land and Slaves in Mississippi in 1854
and 1857

Counties	Valuation of lands, 1854	Valuation of lands, 1857	Increased value	Taxable slaves, 1854	Taxable slaves, 1857	Increase
Adams	$4,440,019.00	$4,680,811.00	$240,792.00	14,005	13,586	—
Amite	1,056,624.31	1,293,848.83	237,224.52	6,604	7,000	396
Attala	945,924.00	1,521,102.70	575,178.70	3,007	3,914	907
Bolivar	1,973,599.84	6,465,838.91	4,492,239.07	3,069	5,847	2,778
Calhoun	790,574.00	1,081,525.60	290,951.60	1,184	1,314	130
Carroll	2,204,719.00	3,449,741.00	1,245,022.00	10,431	11,590	1,150
Chickasaw	2,070,151.00	2,738,866.08	668,715.08	6,131	7,546	1,415
Choctaw	849,076.50	1,545,560.25	696,483.75	3,067	3,600	533
Claiborne	2,593,385.75	2,788,831.25	195,445.50	11,244	11,162	—
Clarke	593,748.75	734,812.50	141,063.75	2,292	2,964	672
Coahoma	785,055.04	3,344,455.28	2,559,400.24	1,926	3,653	1,727
Copiah	1,369,694.34	2,082,647.88	712,953.54	5,945	7,419	1,474
Covington	139,612.50	321,630.89	182,018.39	1,111	1,307	196
De Soto	3,169,918.00	4,710,083.00	1,540,165.00	10,267	11,725	1,458
Franklin	479,816.25	776,525.80	296,709.55	3,636	4,031	395
Greene	54,204.50	64,780.75	10,576.25	601	600	−1
Hancock	421,575.00	513,490.85	91,919.85	1,299	1,046	—
Harrison	1,184,920.00	1,101,410.50	—	946	974	28
Hinds	4,343,126.00	6,350,550.00	2,007,424.00	17,430	18,888	1,458
Holmes	2,073,213.00	3,723,713.00	1,650,500.00	8,555	9,722	1,167

Jackson	396,917.00	426,630.00	29,713.00	809	841	32
Jasper	321,316.00	1,165,219.00	843,903.00	2,291	3,182	891
Jefferson	1,702,014.00	2,274,741.50	572,727.50	10,547	11,003	456
Jones	27,545.35	159,156.00	131,610.65	302	361	59
Kemper	1,133,111.44	1,194,112.00	71,000.56	4,190	4,900	710
Lafayette	1,472,993.50	2,145,641.00	672,647.50	5,374	6,281	907
Lauderdale	815,757.30	1,099,572.25	283,814.95	3,021	3,675	654
Lawrence	364,918.17	1,012,084.00	647,165.83	2,993	3,508	515
Leake	588,136.00	1,127,365.00	539,229.00	2,081	2,492	474
Lowndes	2,546,081.75	5,133,460.25	2,587,378.50	13,189	14,672	1,483
Madison	3,751,409.00	4,687,418.00	936,009.00	15,300	16,157	857
Marion	120,003.00	183,864.00	63,861.00	2,024	1,976	—
Marshall	3,812,781.00	4,926,624.75	1,113,843.75	14,460	15,510	1,050
Monroe	3,691,029.50	4,892,502.00	1,201,472.50	11,732	12,155	423
Neshoba	388,129.00	894,853.00	506,724.00	1,521	1,836	315
Newton	443,295.00	925,661.66	482,366.66	1,376	1,889	513
Noxubee	2,560,264.12	4,382,509.67	1,821,885.55	11,645	12.973	1,328
Oktibbeha	941,424.00	1,887,263.50	945,839.50	5,140	5,961	821
Panola	2,338,442.73	3,473,303.00	1,134,860.27	7,780	8,783	1,003
Perry	56,863.10	75,230.70	18,367.60	723	684	—
Pike	627,298.50	1,223,327.00	596,028.50	3,625	3,859	234
Pontotoc	2,221,729.00	2,845,196.52	623,467.52	5,670	6,561	891
Rankin	1,225,673.60	1,750,106.00	524,432.40	4,662	5,327	665

continued on next page

Counties	Valuation of lands, 1854	Valuation of lands, 1857	Increased value	Taxable slaves, 1854	Taxable slaves, 1857	Increase
Scott	284,102.00	1,022,179.00	738,077.00	1,323	2,042	719
Simpson	328,565.00	449,580.00	121,015.00	1,778	1,954	176
Smith	203,785.00	705,455.00	501,670.00	1,203	1,634	431
Sunflower	813,775.00	2,406,962.50	1,593,187.50	1,513	1,993	480
Tallahatchie	1,036,123.10	2,872,265.58	1,836,142.48	2,953	3,957	1,004
Tippah	2,105,943.75	2,586,314.68	480,370.93	4,993	5,633	640
Tishomingo	2,005,684.00	2,660,777.50	655,093.50	2,989	3,368	379
Tunica	934,876.00	1,987,101.25	1,052,225.25	1,301	1,946	645
Warren	3,718,924.80	4,743,981.25	1,025,056.45	12,163	12,556	393
Washington	5,083,194.00	7,416,162.00	2,332,968.00	9,357	11,185	1,828
Wayne	106,492.80	155,690.50	49,197.70	1,406	1,519	113
Wilkinson	2,223,366.50	2,553,465.50	330,099.00	13,164	13,327	163
Winston	755,606.00	1,089,475.00	333,869.00	2,699	3,394	695
Yallobusha	1,646,911.00	2,366,371.15	719,460.15	7,810	8,489	688
Yazoo	3,255,474.75	5,571,555.93	2,316,081.18	11,438	13,574	2,136
Total	90,950,585.17	141,747,536.37	50,880,460.70	326,861	368,182	42,163

Note: The corrected total for column 3 is 50,796,951.20; that for column 6 is 41,321.

SOURCE: Statement of Madison McAfee, auditor, public accounts, published in Jackson *Mississippian*, August 10, 1858.

Appendix B

Some Cotton Crops of Mississippi

1837

Vicksburg *Register,* February 20, 1838, quoting from the Woodville *Republican*:

Mississippi Statistics
Calculated from the [state] Census of 1837

There are in the State 1,048,530 acres of land in cultivation. Deduct ⅓ for corn, and it leaves 699,020 acres cultivated in cotton, nearly.

The crop of the state is 317,783 bales. This amount produced from 699,020 gives one bale for every 2 ½ acres.

There are in the State 163,941 slaves, estimating ⅔ of these, or 109,294 as hands, it gives an average of 2 ²⁹⁄₃₀ bales per hand.

The crop of 317,783 bales, at 10 cents, or $40 per bale, yields an income of $12,711,320.

1839

Benjamin L. C. Wailes, *Address Delivered in the College Chapel before the Agricultural, Horticultural, and Botanical Society of Jefferson College on the 24th of April, 1841* (Natchez, 1841), 17–18:

To return to the statistics of our own State there was raised in 1839, according to the returns of the Marshall, in round numbers,

428,800	Bales of Cotton
13,161,300	Bushels of Corn
196,200	Bushels of Wheat

By the same returns we have in 1840,

109,200	Horses and Mules
623,150	Neat Cattle
1,001,600	Swine

In the quantity of cotton raised, Adams county ranks first; having produced in 1839–50, 730 Bales, 10,000 more than any other county and about one nineth of the whole crop of the State. Warren, Wilkinson, Madison, Jefferson, Washington, Yazoo rank next in importance; none of the counties, not enumerated, produce over 12,000 bales.

1848

Jackson *Mississippian,* July 20, 1849:

> Crop of Mississippi.—The crop of last season amounted to 2,665,000 bales—
> that of Mississippi alone being 612,500. We do not believe from present ap-
> pearances that we shall raise this season in Mississippi 300,000 bales. . . . We
> have never witnessed a season of rain so continuous as to the present.

1852

American Cotton Planter, II (1854), 31:

> *Nita-Yuma, Deer Creek, Miss.*
> *Nov 22nd, 1853*

> Mr. Editor:—The State of Mississippi owes $12,000,000; which a portion of
> her citizens says she is unable, and her creditors say she is unwilling to pay.
>   Her cotton crop of 1852 is put down at 492,000 bales. As these averages an
> average of 400 lbs. and this weight rules in our courts and private adjustments,
> we will make it amount to 500,000 bales. . . .
>   H[enry]. W. Vick

Bibliography

Primary Sources

Manuscripts

Allen, Charles. Plantation Book. Mississippi Department of Archives and History, Jackson.

Blackwell, Edmund B. Papers. William R. Perkins Library, Duke University, Durham.

Broadside Collection. Mississippi Department of Archives and History, Jackson.

Broadside Collection. In possession of John Hebron Moore, Tallahassee, Florida.

Brookdale Farm Journal. Mississippi Department of Archives and History, Jackson.

Clark, Micajah Adolphus. Journal. Typescript in the South Caroliniana Collection, University of South Carolina, Columbia.

Elly, William R. Plantation Book. Mississippi Department of Archives and History, Jackson.

Erwin, William Ethelbert. Plantation Book. Southern Historical Collection, University of North Carolina, Chapel Hill.

Fraser, John Baxter. Papers. MS in possession of Margaret DesChamps Moore, Tallahassee, Florida.

Hunt, Abijah, and David Hunt. Papers. Mississippi Department of Archives and History, Jackson.

Jayne, Joseph M. Plantation Account Book. William R. Perkins Library, Duke University, Durham.

Killona Plantation Journal. Mississippi Department of Archives and History, Jackson.

Kitchen, Smith. Journal. South Caroliniana Library, University of South Carolina, Columbia.

Leak, Frances Terry. Diary. Typescript in Southern Historical Collection, University of North Carolina, Chapel Hill.

Learned, Rufus F. Collection. University of Mississippi Library, Oxford.

McCall, Dugal. Plantation Journal. Southern Historical Collection, University of North Carolina, Chapel Hill.

Newstead Plantation Records. Southern Historical Collection, University of North Carolina, Chapel Hill.

Quitman, John A. Papers. Mississippi Department of Archives and History, Jackson.

Steel, Ferdinand L. Diary. MS in possession of Edward M. Steel, Jr., Morgantown, West Virginia.

Wade, Walter. Plantation Diary. Typescript in Mississippi Department of Archives and History, Jackson.

Wailes, Benjamin L. C. Papers. Mississippi Department of Archives and History, Jackson.

Wells, Edward R. Diary. Mississippi Department of Archives and History, Jackson.

Williams, Daniel O., and Sampson Williams. Papers. MS in possession of John Hebron Moore, Tallahassee, Florida.

Government Documents

United States

Bureau of the Census. *Fifth Census of the United States: 1830.*

———. *Sixth Census of the United States: 1840.*

———. *Seventh Census of the United States: 1850.*

———. *Eighth Census of the United States: 1860.* 4 vols.

———. Manuscript Census Returns, 1860: Mississippi. Schedules 1 and 2.

———. *Preliminary Report on the Eighth Census, 1860.* Washington, D.C., 1862.

Carter, Clarence E., and John Bloom, eds. *The Territorial Papers of the United States.* Vol. VI of 27 vols. to date. Washington, D.C., 1934–.

Davis, Reuben. *Speech of the Hon. Reuben Davis, of Mississippi, on the State of the Union, in the House of Representatives, December 22, 1858.* Washington, D.C., 1858.

Patent Office. *Annual Reports of the Commissioner of Patents, Agriculture, 1849–1862.* Washington, D.C., 1850–62.

The War of the Rebellion: A Compilation of the Official Records of the Union and Confederate Armies. 130 vols. Washington, D.C., 1880–1901.

Mississippi

Hilgard, Eugene W. *Report on the Geology and Agriculture of the State of Mississippi*. Jackson, Miss., 1860.

Hutchinson, Anderson, comp. *Code of Mississippi, 1798–1848*. Jackson, Miss., 1848.

Mississippi House Journal. 1850–62.

Mississippi Senate Journal. 1841.

Revised Code of the Laws of Mississippi. Natchez, 1824.

Rowland, Dunbar, and Albert G. Sanders, eds. *Mississippi Provincial Archives, 1704–1743: French Dominion*. 3 vols. Jackson, Miss., 1932.

Wailes, Benjamin L. C. *Report on the Agriculture and Geology of Mississippi, Embracing a Sketch of the Social and Natural History of the State*. Philadelphia, 1854.

County

Adams County. Chancery Court Records: Will Book III. Natchez.

———. Estates. Vol. X. Natchez.

Warren County. Chancery Court Records: Deed Book G. Vicksburg.

———. Personal Assessment Book, 1860. Old Courthouse Museum, Vicksburg.

———. Real Estate Assessment Book, 1857. Old Courthouse Museum, Vicksburg.

City

Revised Ordinances of the City of Vicksburg. Vicksburg, 1855.

Newspapers

Mississippi

Aberdeen *Independent*. January 15, 1853.

Brandon *Republican*. May 18, 1863.

Canton *Herald*. December 1, 1837.

Canton *Independent Democrat*. December 2, 1843.

Carrollton *Mississippi Democrat*. August 27, 1845.

Columbus *Democrat*. 1837–49.

Columbus *Southern Standard*. April 3, 1852.

Fort Adams *Mississippi Democrat*. December 22, 1831.

Grand Gulf *Advertiser*. July 28, 1836, and February 8, 1839.

Holly Springs *Gazette*. 1839–45.

Holly Springs *Southern Banner and Conservative*. July 9 and August 13, 1841.

Jackson *Daily News*. March 7, 1860.

Jackson *Mississippian*. 1834–60.

Jackson *Southern Reformer*. 1843–45.

Jackson *Southron*. 1841–43.

Mississippi Free Trader and Natchez Gazette. August 3, 1837, and November 5, 1839.

Natchez. February 20, 1830, and January 22, 1831.

Natchez *Chronicle*. April 12, 1809.

Natchez *Courier*. 1835–60.

Natchez *Courier and Journal*. 1847–48.

Natchez *Free Trader*. 1835–60.

Natchez *Mississippi Free Trader and Natchez Gazette*. 1836–52.

Natchez *Mississippi State Gazette*. 1818–19.

Natchez *Mississippi Republican*. November 24, 1813, and March 5, 1818.

Natchez *Southern Galaxy*. 1828.

Oxford *Observer*. September 16, 1843.

Panola *Lynx*. 1845.

Panola *Picayune*. May 2, 1853.

Paulding *Eastern Clarion*. May 4, 1859.

Port Gibson *Correspondent*. November 29, 1839.

Port Gibson *Herald*. 1843–45.

Raymond *Hinds County Gazette*. 1850–62.

Raymond *Times*. 1838–41.

Ripley *Advertiser*. January 18, 1845.

Vicksburg *Advocate and Register*. 1831–40.

Vicksburg *Herald*. January 11 and February 18, 1866.

Vicksburg *Register*. 1834–38.

Vicksburg *Sentinel*. 1831–52.

Vicksburg *Whig*. 1839–62.

Woodville *Republican*. 1850–52.

Yazoo City *Whig*. 1839–54.

Other

Charleston (S.C.) *Courier*. April 12, 1856.
Columbus (Ga.) *Daily Sun*. May 23, 1863.
Columbus (Ga.) *Enquirer*. 1838–56.
Columbus (Ga.) *Southern Sentinel*. April 11, 1850.
London *Cotton Supply Reporter*. February 3, 1860.
Macon (Ga.) *Messenger*. December 17, 1846.
Mobile *Alabama Planter and Herald and Tribune*. 1848–50.
Mobile *Mail*. December 24, 1858.
Mobile *Register*. September 2, 1836, and February 25, 1845.
Montgomery (Ala.) *Advertiser*. December 22, 1858.
Montgomery (Ala.) *Journal*. December 20, 1849, and December 23, 1854.
New Orleans *Bee*. September 3, 1836.
New Orleans *Commercial Times*. June 20, 1846.
New Orleans *Delta*. 1848–60.
New Orleans *Picayune*. August 1, 1838.
New Orleans *Price Current, Commercial Intelligencer, and Merchants' Transcript*. 1854–66.
New Orleans *Times Picayune*. 1851–61.
New Orleans *True Delta*. May 16, 1858.
Prattville (Ala.) *Southern Statesman*. August 27, 1859.

Contemporary Periodicals
Mississippi

Jackson *Planter and Mechanic*. 1857.
Natchez and Washington *Southern Planter*. 1842.
Raymond *Southwestern Farmer*. 1842–43.

Other

Albany (N.Y.) *Cultivator*. 1843.
Augusta (Ga.) *Southern Cultivator*. 1843–61.
Baltimore (Md.) *American Farmer*. 1820.
De Bow's Review. 1812–60.
Harper's Weekly. 1862.

Montgomery (Ala.) *American Cotton Planter.* 1853–56.
Montgomery (Ala.) *American Cotton Planter and Soil of the South.* 1857–61.
Niles Register. 1812–49.
Petersburg (Va.) *Farmers' Register.* 1833–42.
Scientific American. 1859.

Published Letters, Journals, Travel Accounts, and Reminiscences

Ashe, Thomas. *Travels in America, Performed in 1806, for the Purpose of Exploring the Rivers . . . and Vicinity.* London, 1808.
Bailey, Francis. *Journal of a Tour in the Unsettled Parts of North America in 1796 and 1797.* London, 1856.
Baldwin, Joseph G. *The Flush Times of Alabama and Mississippi: A Series of Sketches.* New York, 1854.
Bassett, John S., ed. *The Southern Plantation Overseer as Revealed in His Letters.* Northampton, Mass., 1925.
Beckett, R. C. "Antebellum Times in Monroe County." Mississippi Historical Society *Publications,* XI (1910), 87–102.
Besançon, Lorenzo A. *Besançon's Annual Register for the State of Mississippi for the Year 1838.* Natchez, 1838.
Cauthen, Charles E., ed. *Family Letters of the Three Wade Hamptons, 1782–1901.* Columbia, S.C., 1953.
Claiborne, John F. H. "A Trip Through the Piney Woods." Mississippi Historical Society *Publications,* IX (1906), 487–538.
Clusky, M. W., ed. *Speeches, Messages and Other Writings of the Hon. Albert G. Brown.* Philadelphia, 1859.
Creecy, James R. *Scenes in the South and Other Miscellaneous Pieces.* Washington, D.C., 1860.
Cumings, F. *Sketches of a Tour to the Western Country . . . Commenced at Philadelphia in the Winter of 1807, and Concluded in 1809.* Pittsburgh, 1810.
Dalrymple, Margaret F., ed. *The Merchant of Manchac: The Letterbooks of John Fitzpatric, 1768–1790.* Baton Rouge, 1978.
Davis, Reuben. *Recollections of Mississippi and Mississippians.* Boston, 1891.
DesChamps, Margaret B., ed. "Some Mississippi Letters to Robert Fraser, 1841–1844." *Journal of Mississippi History,* XV (1953), 181–89.

Fulkerson, Horace S. *Random Recollections of Early Days in Mississippi.* Edited by Percy L. Rainwater. Baton Rouge, 1937.

Grant, Ulysses S. *Personal Memoirs of U.S. Grant.* Vol. I of 2 vols. New York, 1892.

Griffin, Lucille, ed. "The Plantation Record Book of Brookdale Farm, Amite County, 1856–1857." *Journal of Mississippi History,* VII (1945), 23–31.

Hall, James. *A Brief History of the Mississippi Territory, to Which is Prefixed a Summary View of the Country Between the Settlements on the Cumberland River and the Territory.* Salisbury, N.C., 1801. (Reprinted in Mississippi Historical Society *Publications,* IX [1906], 539–76.)

Hogan, William R., and Edwin A. Davis, eds. *William Johnson's Natchez: The Antebellum Diary of a Free Negro.* Baton Rouge, 1951.

Hundley, Daniel R. *Social Relations in Our Southern States.* Edited by William J. Cooper. Baton Rouge, 1979.

Hutchins, Thomas. *An Historical Narrative and Topographical Description of Louisiana and West Florida.* Philadelphia, 1794.

[Ingraham, Joseph H.]. *The South-West, by a Yankee.* 2 vols. 1835; rpr. New York, 1968.

Kellar, Herbert A., ed. *Solon Robinson: Pioneer and Agriculturist.* 2 vols. Indianapolis, 1936.

McCain, William D., and Charlotte Capers, eds. *Memoirs of Henry Tillinghast Ireys: Papers of the Washington County Historical Society, 1910–1915.* Jackson, Miss., 1955.

McKenzie, E. *An Historical, Topographical, and Descriptive View of the United States of America and Lower Canada.* 2nd ed. New Castle upon Tyne, 1819.

Monette, John W. "Progress of Navigation and Commerce on the Waters of the Mississippi River and the Great Lakes, A.D. 1700 to 1846." Mississippi Historical Society *Publications,* VII (1903), 479–523.

Monroe, Haskell M., Jr., James T. McIntosh, Lynda L. Crist, Mary S. Dix, and Richard E. Beringer, eds. *The Papers of Jefferson Davis.* Vol. II of 4 vols. to date. Baton Rouge, 1971–.

Moore, John H., ed. "A Letter from a Fugitive Slave." *Journal of Mississippi History,* XXIV (1962), 99–101.

———, ed. "The Textile Industry of the Old South as Described in a Letter by J. M. Wesson." *Journal of Economic History,* XVI (1956), 200–205.

————, ed. "A Visit to South Mississippi in 1852: Some Selections from the Journal of Benjamin L. C. Wailes." *Journal of Mississippi History*, XVIII (1956), 18–32.

Olmsted, Frederick L. *A Journey in the Back Country*. New York, 1860.

Orr, James A. "A Trip from Houston to Jackson, Miss., in 1845." Mississippi Historical Society *Publications*, IX (1906), 173–78.

Rawick, George P., ed. *The American Slave: A Composite Biography*. Ser. 1, 2, and Supp. 31 vols. Westport, Conn., 1977.

Riley, Franklin L., ed. "Diary of a Mississippi Planter, January 1, 1840, to April, 1863." Mississippi Historical Society *Publications*, X (1909), 305–481.

Rose, Willie Lee, ed. *A Documentary History of Slavery in North America*. New York, 1976.

Rowland, Dunbar, ed. *Jefferson Davis, Constitutionalist: His Papers, Letters, and Speeches*. Vol. IV of 10 vols. Jackson, Miss., 1923.

Rowland, Eron, ed. *Life, Letters, and Papers of William Dunbar of Elgin, Morayshire, Scotland, and Natchez, Mississippi: Pioneer Scientist of the Southern United States*. Jackson, Miss., 1930.

Russell, Robert. *North America, Its Agriculture and Climate: Containing Observations on . . . Cuba*. Edinburgh, 1857.

Schultz, Christian. *Travels on an Inland Voyage Through the . . . Territories of Indiana, Louisiana, Mississippi and New Orleans; Performed in the Years 1807 and 1808*. Vol. II of 2 vols. New York, 1810.

Singleton, Arthur. *Letters from the South and West*. Boston, 1824.

Smedes, Susan Dabney. *Memorials of a Southern Planter*. 4th ed. Edited by Fletcher M. Green. New York, 1965.

Sparks, William H. *The Memories of Fifty Years: Containing Biographical Notices . . . in the Southwest*. Philadelphia, 1870.

Steel, Edward M. "A Pioneer Farmer in the Choctaw Purchase." *Journal of Mississippi History*, XVI (1954), 229–41.

Van Buren, A. de Puy. *Jottings of a Year's Sojourn in the South; or Impressions of the Country and Its People; with a Glimpse of School-teaching in That Southern Land, and Reminiscences of Distinguished Men. . . .* Battle Creek, Mich., 1859.

White, George. *Historical Collections of Georgia*. New York, 1854.

Secondary Sources

Books

Alvarez, Eugene. *Travel on Southern Antebellum Railroads, 1828–1860.* Tuscaloosa, 1974.

Atherton, Louis E. *The Southern Country Store, 1800–1860.* Baton Rouge, 1949.

Baldwin, Leland D. *The Keelboat Age on Western Waters.* Pittsburgh, 1941.

Berlin, Ira. *Slaves Without Masters: The Free Negro in the Antebellum South.* New York, 1974.

Bettersworth, John K. *Confederate Mississippi: The People and Policies of a Cotton State in Wartime.* Baton Rouge, 1943.

———. *Mississippi: A History.* Austin, Tex., 1959.

Bidwell, Percy W., and John I. Falconer. *History of Agriculture in the Northern United States, 1620–1860.* 1925; rpr. New York, 1941.

Biographical and Historical Memoirs of Mississippi. 2 vols. Chicago, 1891.

Blassingame, John W. *The Slave Community: Plantation Life in the Antebellum South.* New York, 1972.

Boles, John B. *Black Southerners, 1619–1869.* Lexington, Ky., 1983.

Bonner, James C. *A History of Georgia Agriculture, 1732–1860.* Athens, Ga., 1964.

Brandfon, Robert L. *Cotton Kingdom of the New South: A History of the Yazoo-Mississippi Delta from Reconstruction to the Twentieth Century.* Cambridge, Mass., 1967.

Cabaniss, J. Allen. *A History of the University of Mississippi.* Oxford, Miss., 1949.

Cathey, Cornelius O. *Agricultural Development in North Carolina, 1783–1860.* Chapel Hill, 1956.

Claiborne, John F. H. *Life and Correspondence of John A. Quitman, Major General, U.S.A., and Governor of Mississippi.* 2 vols. New York, 1860.

———. *Life and Times of Gen. Sam Dale, the Mississippi Partisan.* New York, 1860.

———. *Mississippi, as a Province, Territory and State, with Biographical Notices of Eminent Citizens.* Jackson, Miss., 1880.

Clark, John G. *New Orleans, 1718–1812: An Economic History.* Baton Rouge, 1970.

Clark, Thomas D. *A Pioneer Southern Railroad from New Orleans to Cairo.* Chapel Hill, 1936.

Clarke, Erskine. *Wrestlin' Jacob: A Portrait of Religion in the Old South.* Atlanta, 1979.

Collins, Bruce. *White Society in the Antebellum South.* New York, 1985.

Cotterill, Robert S. *The Southern Indians: The Story of the Civilized Tribes Before Removal.* Norman, 1954.

Davis, Charles C. *Cotton Kingdom in Alabama.* Montgomery, 1939.

Davis, Edwin A. *Louisiana: A Narrative History.* 3rd ed. Baton Rouge, 1971.

Degler, Carl. *Neither Black nor White: Slavery and Race Relations in Brazil and the United States.* New York, 1971.

DeRosier, Arthur H., Jr. *The Removal of the Choctaw Indians.* Knoxville, Tenn., 1970.

Dickey, Dallas C. *Seargent S. Prentiss: Whig Orator of the Old South.* Baton Rouge, 1946.

Donnell, E. J. *Chronological and Statistical History of Cotton.* New York, 1872.

Dunbar, Seymour. *History of Travel in America.* 2nd ed. New York, 1937.

Eaton, Clement. *The Growth of Southern Civilization, 1790–1860.* New York, 1961.

———. *A History of the Old South: The Emergence of a Reluctant Nation.* 3rd ed. New York, 1975.

———. *Jefferson Davis.* New York, 1977.

Flynt, J. Wayne. *Dixie's Forgotten People: The South's Poor Whites.* Bloomington, Ind., 1979.

Franklin, John Hope. *From Slavery to Freedom: A History of American Negroes.* 2nd ed. New York, 1956.

Gates, Paul W. *The Farmer's Age: Agriculture, 1815–1860.* New York, 1960.

Genovese, Eugene D. *Roll, Jordan, Roll: The World the Slaves Made.* 1974; rpr. New York, 1976.

Gray, Lewis C. *History of Agriculture in the Southern United States to 1860.* 2 vols. 1933; rpr. Gloucester, Mass., 1958.

Gutman, Herbert C. *The Black Family in Slavery and Freedom.* New York, 1976.

Hamilton, Holman. *Prologue to Conflict: The Crisis and Compromise.* Lexington, Ky., 1964.

Harrison, Robert W. *Alluvial Empire: A Study of State and Local Efforts Toward Land Development in the Alluvial Valley of the Lower Mississippi River.* Little Rock, 1961.

Haynes, Robert V. *The Natchez District and the American Revolution.* Jackson, Miss., 1976.

Hermann, Janet S. *The Pursuit of a Dream.* New York, 1983.

Hickman, Nollie. *Mississippi Harvest: Lumbering in the Longleaf Pine Belt, 1840–1915.* Oxford, Miss., 1962.

Hilliard, Sam B. *Hog Meat and Hoecake: Food Supply in the Old South.* Carbondale, Ill., 1972.

Holmes, Jack D. L. *Gayoso: The Life of a Spanish Governor in the Mississippi Valley, 1789–1799.* 1965; rpr. Gloucester, Mass., 1968.

Hunter, Louis C. *Steamboats on the Western Rivers: An Economic and Technological History.* Cambridge, Mass., 1949.

James, D. Clayton. *Antebellum Natchez.* Baton Rouge, 1968.

Jordan, Weymouth T. *Hugh Davis and His Alabama Plantation.* Tuscaloosa, 1948.

Kane, Harnett T. *Natchez on the Mississippi.* New York, 1947.

Lipscomb, W. L. *A History of Columbus, Mississippi, During the Nineteenth Century.* Birmingham, Ala., 1909.

Lowry, Robert, and William H. McCardle. *A History of Mississippi, from the Discovery of the Great River . . . to the Death of Jefferson Davis.* Jackson, Miss., 1891.

McCain, William D. *The Story of Jackson: A History of the Capital of Mississippi, 1821–1935.* 2 vols. Jackson, Miss., 1953.

MacGill, Caroline. *History of Transportation in the United States Before 1860.* Washington, D.C., 1917.

McLemore, Richard A., ed. *A History of Mississippi.* Vol. I of 2 vols. Hattiesburg, Miss., 1973.

Mathews, Donald. G. *Religion in the Old South.* Chicago, 1977.

May, Robert E. *John A. Quitman: Old South Crusader.* Baton Rouge, 1985.

Miles, Edwin A. *Jacksonian Democracy in Mississippi.* Chapel Hill, 1960.

Moore, John H. *Agriculture in Antebellum Mississippi.* New York, 1958.

———. *Andrew Brown and Cypress Lumbering in the Old Southwest.* Baton Rouge, 1967.

Newby, I. A. *The South: A History.* New York, 1978.

North, Douglas C. *The Economic Growth of the United States, 1790–1860.* 1961; rpr. New York, 1966.

Oakes, James. *The Ruling Race: A History of American Slaveholders.* New York, 1983.

Ott, Thomas O. *The Haitian Revolution, 1789–1804.* Knoxville, Tenn., 1973.

Owens, Harry P. *An Assessment of Historical Period Cultural Resources Along the Yazoo River . . . Mississippi.* Oxford, Miss., 1979.

———, ed. *Perspectives in American Slavery.* Jackson, Miss., 1976.

Owens, Leslie H. *This Species of Property: Slave Life and Culture in the Old South.* 1976; rpr. New York, 1978.

Owsley, Frank L. *Plain Folk of the Old South.* Baton Rouge, 1949.

Phillips, Ulrich B. *American Negro Slavery: A Survey of the Supply, Employment, and Control of Negro Labor as Determined by the Plantation Regime.* 1918; rpr. Gloucester, Mass., 1959.

———. *Life and Labor in the Old South.* Boston, 1929.

Posey, Walter B. *Frontier Mission: A History of Religion West of the Southern Appalachians to 1861.* Lexington, Ky., 1966.

Quick, Edward, and Herbert Quick. *Mississippi Steamboating: A History of Steamboating on the Mississippi and Its Tributaries.* New York, 1926.

Reed, Merl E. *New Orleans and the Railroads: The Struggle for Commercial Empire, 1830–1860.* Baton Rouge, 1966.

Remini, Robert V. *Andrew Jackson and the Bank War: A Study in the Growth of Presidential Power.* New York, 1968.

Rowland, Dunbar. *History of Mississippi: The Heart of the South.* 2 vols. Chicago, 1925.

Scarborough, William K. *The Overseer: Plantation Management in the Old South.* Baton Rouge, 1966.

Schlesinger, Arthur M., Jr. *Age of Jackson.* Boston, 1950.

Shenton, James P. *Robert John Walker: A Politician from Jackson to Lincoln.* New York, 1961.

Sheridan, Richard B. *Sugar and Slavery: An Economic History of the British West Indies, 1623–1775.* Baltimore, 1973.

Skates, John R. *Mississippi: A Bicentennial History.* New York, 1979.

Smith, Alfred G., Jr. *Economic Readjustment of an Old Cotton State: South Carolina, 1820–1860.* Columbia, S.C., 1958.

Stampp, Kenneth M. *The Peculiar Institution: Slavery in the Ante-Bellum South.* New York, 1956.

Starobin, Robert S. *Industrial Slavery in the Old South.* New York, 1970.

Stone, James H. *Cotton Gin Port, Mississippi: The History of a Tombigbee River Town.* Oxford, Miss., 1969.

Stover, John F. *The Railroads of the South, 1865–1900: A Study in Control.* Chapel Hill, 1955.

Sydnor, Charles S. *The Development of Southern Sectionalism, 1819–1848.* Baton Rouge, 1948.

———. *A Gentleman of the Old Natchez Region: Benjamin L. Wailes.* Durham, N.C., 1938.

———. *Slavery in Mississippi.* 1933; rpr. Gloucester, Mass., 1965.

Taylor, George R. *The Transportation Revolution, 1815–1860.* New York, 1957.

Thomas, Emory M. *The Confederate Nation, 1861–1865.* New York, 1979.

Vaissière, Pierre de. *Saint-Domingue: La Société et la vie Créoles sous l'Ancien Régime, 1629–1789.* 2nd ed. Paris, 1909.

Van Deburg, William L. *The Slave Drivers: Black Agricultural Labor Supervisors in the Antebellum South.* Westport, Conn., 1979.

Wade, Richard C. *Slavery in the Cities: The South, 1820–1860.* New York, 1964.

Walker, Peter F. *Vicksburg: A People at War, 1860–1865.* Chapel Hill, 1960.

Watt, Sir George. *The Wild and Cultivated Cotton Plants of the World: A Revision of the Genus Gossypium . . . Improvement of the Staple.* London, 1907.

Weaver, Herbert. *Mississippi Farmers, 1850–1860.* Nashville, 1945.

Whitaker, Arthur P. *The Spanish American Frontier, 1783–1795: The Westward Movement and the Spanish Retreat in the Mississippi Valley.* New York, 1927.

Woodman, Harold D. *King Cotton and His Retainers: Financing and Marketing of the Crop of the South, 1800–1825.* Lexington, Ky., 1968.

Young, Mary E. *Redskins, Ruffleshirts, and Rednecks: Indian Allotments in Alabama and Mississippi, 1830–1860.* Norman, 1961.

Articles

Beasley, Jonathon. "Blacks—Slave and Free—Vicksburg, 1850–1860." *Journal of Mississippi History,* XXXVIII (1976), 1–32.

Blumenthal, Henry. "Confederate Diplomacy: Popular Notions and

International Realities." *Journal of Southern History*, XXXII (1966), 151–71.

Bowman, Martha. "A City of the Old South: Jackson, Mississippi, 1850–1860." *Journal of Mississippi History*, XV (1953), 1–32.

Cotterill, Robert S. "Southern Railroads, 1850–1860." *Mississippi Valley Historical Review*, X (1924), 396–405.

Crocker, Les. "An Early Iron Foundry in Northern Mississippi." *Journal of Mississippi History*, XXXV (1973), 113–26.

Evans, W. A. "Steamboats on the Upper Tombigbee in the Early Days." *Journal of Mississippi History*, IV (1942), 217–24.

Genovese, Eugene. "Yeoman Farmers in a Slaveholder's Democracy." *Agricultural History*, XLIX (1975), 331–42.

Haskins, Ralph W. "Planter and Cotton Factor in the Old South: Some Areas of Friction." *Agricultural History*, XXIX (1955), 1–14.

Hearon, Cleo. "Mississippi and the Compromise of 1850." Mississippi Historical Society *Publications*, XIV (1914), 183–227.

Johnson, Charles R. "Railroad Legislation and Building in Mississippi, 1830–1840." *Journal of Mississippi History*, IV (1942), 195–206.

McDonald, Forrest, and Grady McWhiney. "The Antebellum Southern Herdsman: A Reinterpretation." *Journal of Southern History*, XLI (1975), 147–66.

Moore, John H. "Cotton Breeding in the Old South." *Agricultural History*, XXX (1956), 94–104.

———. "Economic Conditions in Mississippi on the Eve of the Civil War." *Journal of Mississippi History*, XXII (1960), 167–78.

———. "Local and State Governments of Antebellum Mississippi." *Journal of Mississippi History*, XLIV (1982), 104–34.

———. "Mississippi's Antebellum Textile Industry." *Journal of Mississippi History*, XVI (1954), 81–98.

———. "Simon Gray, Riverman: A Slave Who Was Almost Free." *Mississippi Valley Historical Review*, XLIX (1962), 472–84.

Moore, Margaret DesChamps, "Religion in Mississippi in 1860." *Journal of Mississippi History*, XXII (1960), 223–38.

Muckenfuss, A. M. "The Development of Manufacturing in Mississippi." Mississippi Historical Society *Publications*, X (1909), 163–80.

Perry, Percival. "The Naval Stores Industry in the Old South, 1790–1860." *Journal of Southern History*, XXXIV (1968), 509–26.

Posey, Walter B. "The Advance of Methodism into the Lower South." *Journal of Southern History*, II (1936), 439–52.

Riggs, David. "Charles Conway Flowers (1842–1929): Vicksburg Colonel and Entrepreneur." *Journal of Mississippi History*, XLVI (1984), 163–78.

Riley, Franklin L. "Extinct Towns and Villages of Mississippi." Mississippi Historical Society *Publications*, V (1902), 311–83.

Rothstein, Morton. "The Agricultural South as a Dual Economy: A Tentative Hypothesis." *Agricultural History*, XLI (1967), 372–82.

Stone, James. H. "The Economic Development of Holly Springs During the 1840's." *Journal of Mississippi History*, XXXII (1970), 341–61.

Swearingen, Mack. "Thirty Years of a Mississippi Plantation: Charles Whitmore of 'Montpelier.'" *Journal of Southern History*, I (1935), 198–211.

Sydnor, Charles S. "The Free Negro in Mississippi Before the Civil War." *American Historical Review*, XXXII (1927), 769–88.

Wade, Richard C. "The Vesey Plot: A Reconsideration." *Journal of Southern History*, XXX (1964), 143–61.

Warren, Harris G. "People and Occupations in Port Gibson, 1860." *Journal of Mississippi History*, X (1948), 104–15.

———. "Population Elements of Claiborne County, 1820–1860." *Journal of Mississippi History*, IX (1947), 75–87.

Dissertations, Theses, and Unpublished Papers

Green, Marcellus. "Biography of Joshua Green for the Historical Society of Mississippi." Typescript in the Mississippi Department of Archives and History.

Hamilton, William B. "Holly Springs, Mississippi, to the Year 1878." M.A. thesis, University of Mississippi, 1931.

Hearn, Walter C. "Towns in Antebellum Mississippi." Ph.D. dissertation, University of Mississippi, 1969.

Owens, Harry P. "The 'P' Line." Paper presented to the Mississippi Historical Society, Cleveland, Miss., March 4, 1983.

Stone, James H. "Black Leadership in the Old South: The Slave Drivers of the Rice Kingdom." Ph.D. dissertation, Florida State University, 1976.

Index

188–93; founding of, 3, 188; free blacks of, 258–63; incorporated, 189; lawyers of, 243–45; manual laborers of, 253–54; mechanics of, 249–51; merchants of, 188, 232, 236, 239–40, 242; physicians of, 243, 247; population of, 177, 188–90; railroad of, 166–67; river traffic of, 158–59, 161; schools of, 191; slaves of, 267–80; under foreign rule, 2–5; volunteer military companies, 191

Natchez Foundry and Gin Factory, 213–14

Natchez Indians, 2, 5

Natchez Trace, 156

Naval stores, 116, 154–55

Nelson, Samuel, 66

Newell, Tom, 152

Newman, William, 259

New Orleans: commercial dominance of, 177–78; cotton exported from, 285–86; cotton prices at, 8; founding of, 1; growth of, 6; merchants of, 19, 50, 59, 61, 67, 220, 232, 236–38, 252; manufacturers of, 58, 67, 208–209, 212–13, 217; railroad of, 173–75, 184; river traffic of, 156–63, 182; unhealthy situation of, 185

—trade of: in cattle, 147–49; in cottonseed, 13–14; in lumber, 208–209, 272; in naval stores, 154–55; in steam engines, 215; in textiles, 223, 226; in wool, 222; with cotton planters, 25, 58, 123

Newsome, George, 111

New York and Mississippi Land Company, 19

Nichols, Reuben, 204

Nicholson, Henri Necaise, 148

Nutt, Dr. Rush: developed Petit Gulf cotton, 12; introduced steam power for ginhouses, 70

Oakland College, 139

Oakley, Hawkins and Company, 232

Oats, 55

Oliver, C. A., 247

Olmsted, Frederick Law, 110, 181, 193

Orr, James A., 21

Orr, W. K., 58, 62

Osyka, 91

Ottawa Iron Works (Ferrysburg, Mich.), 209

Owens, Harry P., 162–63

Oxford, 183–84

Page, George, and Company (Baltimore), 207

Panic of 1837, pp. 15, 17–20, 167, 192, 196, 241–42

Panola, 205

Parker, William, 270

Pass Christian, 147, 259

Paul, John, 253

Paulding, 181

Paxton, Alexander M., 70, 170, 213, 244

Pearlington, 150

Pearl River Mills, 229

Pensacola, 3, 146

Perkins, John, 118

Phillips, Martin W.: agricultural authority, 21; manufacturer of farm implements, 48, 219; on bindings for cotton bales, 66; on cotton gins, 60–63; on cotton presses, 65; on cotton scrapers, 41; on cowpeas, 35; on cultivators, 40–41; on destructive farming methods, 30; on ginhouses, 72; on gristmills, 67; on hoes, 50; on hogs, 26; on mules, horses and oxen, 51, 56; on plows, 38–39, 46; on seed planters, 42

Phillips, Z. A., 219

Physicians, 189, 199, 246–48, 251

Pickens, A. D., 190

Pinchard, G. M., and Company, 236

Planters, 116–39; adopted incentive system for managing slaves, 95–106; definition of, 116–17; developed system of soil conservation, 89–90; during British era, 73–76; during the 1830–38 boom, 15–17, 19–20, 25–26; during Spanish era, 4, 8, 73–74; education of, 137–39; houses of, 87–90; intellectual interests of, 137–38; landholdings of, 17, 108–109, 119, 121–23; mechanized cotton plantations of, 37–72, 91; number of, 118–21; political affiliations of, 138; religious affiliations of, 138–39; slaveholdings of, 17, 23–24, 74, 87, 108–109, 119, 121–23, 131, 135; social background of, 5–6, 15, 131; wives of, 84, 94–95, 137

—River: and improved cotton varieties, 11–13, 27–29, 133–34; and secession, 292–93; and soil conservation methods, 30–34, 133–34; and tobacco plantations, 4–5; develop plantation machinery, 10–11; during British era, 2–3; during Spanish era, 3–4; move of, into Mississippi Valley, 117; use steam engines to power ginhouses, 69–72; wealth of, 8, 16, 117–18, 122–28

by, 282–84; teamsters, 268; unskilled, 274–75
Smedes, Lyell, 248
Smedes, William C., 171, 244
Smith, Benjamin Whiting, 90
Soil: conservation of, 31–32, 86; erosion of, 7–8, 30–32, 44, 86–87; exhaustion of, 30–31, 89–90; types of, 6–8, 30
Solomon, Henry S., 252–53
Southern Implement Company, 219, 230
Spalding, Thomas, 37
Sparks, William H., 148
Sparling, Manual, 254–55
Specie Circular, 18
Speculators, land, 18–20
Spence, David W., 131
Spitler, John, 213
Stagecoaches, 166
Stanford, Thomas J., 221
Stanton, Buckner and Company, 239
Stanton, Frederick, 117–18, 238–41
Stapleton, Wright, 102
Steamboats, 156–64; on Deer Creek, 162; on the Mississippi River, 157–61; on the Pearl River, 164; on the Tombigbee River, 163; on the Yazoo River, 182, 261–63
Steel, Ferdinand L., 23, 32, 49
Stevens, James O., 216, 230–31
Stevens, William H., 240
Steward, James A., 42
Stockman, J. R., 270
Stuart, Oscar J. E., 43–44
Summit, 56
Surget, Francis, 117
Swann, Abbott and Company, 214
Sweet potatoes, 22, 75, 121, 127, 135–36, 148
Swett, Daniel, 240, 251

Tarpley, Colin S., 15–22
Taylor, Calvin, 151
Taylor, Dr. E. T., 61–62
Taylor, E. T., & Company, 58–59, 61–62, 68
Tebo, W. B., 269–70, 274
Tibbee, 247
Tindall, Dr. John L., 217–18
Tobacco, 2–5, 37, 73–74, 76–77
Torrey's store, 220
Townes, James M., 46
Towns: commercial, 177–79, 181–82, 185–200; county seat, 177, 179–81; dominated by New Orleans, 178–79;

government of, 201–202; purposes of, 177; sizes of, 177–78
Turner and Quitman, 118
Turner, Nat, 265
Turner, Polly, 102
Turner, William, 102

U.S. Land Office, 18
U.S. Marine Hospital, 197
U.S. Patent Office, 55
University of Alabama, 139
University of Mississippi, 139, 183–84

Valcourt, Louis, 204
Vale Royal sawmill (Savannah), 210
Van Allen, K., 67
Van Buren, A. de Puy, 67, 70, 87, 155, 197
VanLoon, S. T., 213
VanLoon, Paxton & Company, 65
Vick, Henry W., 27, 29
Vick, Newitt, 195, 248
Vicksburg: bankers of, 243; clerks of, 251–52; cotton trade of, 210–13; dentists of, 243; descriptions of, 193–98; free blacks of, 258–59; incorporation of, 195; lawyers of, 243–45, 251; manual laborers of, 253–55; manufacturers in, 210–13; mechanics of, 249–51, 253–54; merchants of, 46–47, 58–59, 233, 235, 238–40, 251; military organizations of, 197; population of, 195; railroads, 164–66, 169–73, 176; river traffic of, 159–62; slaves of, 267, 271, 274, 280–81
Vicksburg Foundry, 69–70, 211–13
Vigilance committees, 280–81

Wade, Dr. Walter, 68
Wade, Richard C., 263, 267, 284
Wagoning, 6, 15, 52–53, 144, 166, 192, 232, 268
Wagons, 170, 182
Wailes, Benjamin L. C., 12, 31, 33, 57, 65–66, 70–71, 150, 154
Walker, Robert, 250
Walker, Robert J., 245
Walker, Toulme and Company, 208
Wallworth, Douglas, 244
Walnut Hills, 166, 194–96
Wappo sawmill (Charleston), 210
Ward, Junius, 90, 111
Warrenton, 184–85, 195, 247, 259
Washburn, A. W., 30, 43, 123
Washington, 87, 166